APPS, TECHNOLOGY AND YOUNGER LEARNERS

This book provides an in-depth analysis of the challenges, potential and theoretical possibilities of apps and considers the processes of change for education and home learning environments. Drawing together a diverse team of international contributors, it addresses the specific features, context of use and content of apps to uncover the importance of these tools for young children's learning.

Apps, Technology and Younger Learners focuses on ways that apps support early years and primary school learning, connect various learning spaces and engage children in a range of edutainment and knowledge-building activities. The current state of knowledge and key research questions in the field for future study are identified and clear messages are provided at the end of each chapter.

Focusing on empirical studies and strong theoretical frameworks, this book covers four key parts:

- Understanding the learning potential of children's apps;
- Key app challenges;
- Empirical evidence; and
- Future avenues.

This book is an essential guide for educators, postgraduate students, researchers and all those interested in the advantages or challenges that may result from integrating apps into early education.

Natalia Kucirkova is Senior Lecturer in Childhood, Youth and Education Studies at Manchester Metropolitan University, UK.

Garry Falloon is Associate Professor in the School of Curriculum and Pedagogy at the University of Waikato, New Zealand.

'A must read for anyone concerned with the education of preschool and primary age children in today's always connected digital environment.'

—**Michael Levine**, Founder and Executive Director of the Joan Ganz Cooney Center at Sesame Workshop

'We should think differently about learning and how we support young learners because of the affordances of apps on mobile devices. Whether you agree with that statement or not, you should read this book.'

—**Peter Twining**, Professor of Education (Futures) at the Open University, UK, and Co-Editor in Chief of Computers & Education

'Working with notable scholars from Europe, USA, Canada, Australia to Hong Kong, the editors have embraced principles of cultural sensitivity and an understanding of the complex socio-cultural nature of technology deployment in schools. This is an admirable collection with impeccable credentials.'

—**Michael A. Peters**, Professor of Education at the University of Waikato, New Zealand

'What makes this book unique is the target group of young learners, as well as the international perspectives represented in the diverse contributions in the book. I strongly recommend this book to anyone interested in children's edutainment and knowledge building practices.'

—**Ola Erstad**, Professor and Head of Department, Department of Education, University of Oslo, Norway

'Brings together a fascinating and diverse collection of research and deep thinking and is essential reading for anyone attempting to understand the complexity and wonder of the app and the mobile device in the hands of younger learners.'

—**Dr John Potter**, Academic Head of Learning and Teaching, UCL Institute of Education, University College London, UK

APPS, TECHNOLOGY AND YOUNGER LEARNERS

International evidence for teaching

Edited by Natalia Kucirkova and Garry Falloon

Routledge
Taylor & Francis Group

LONDON AND NEW YORK

First published 2017
by Routledge
2 Park Square, Milton Park, Abingdon, Oxon OX14 4RN

and by Routledge
711 Third Avenue, New York, NY 10017

Routledge is an imprint of the Taylor & Francis Group, an informa business

British Library Cataloguing in Publication Data
A catalogue record for this book is available from the British Library

Library of Congress Cataloging in Publication Data
Names: Kucirkova, Natalia, editor. | Falloon, Garry, editor. Title: Apps, technology and younger learners : international evidence for teaching / edited by Natalia Kucirkova and Garry Falloon. Description: Abingdon, Oxon ; New York, NY : Routledge, 2017. Identifiers: LCCN 2016020503 | ISBN 9781138927872 (hardback) | ISBN 9781138927889 (pbk.) | ISBN 9781315682204 (ebook) Subjects: LCSH: Education, Elementary--Computer-assisted instruction. | Application software. | Computer-assisted instruction. | Educational technology. | Internet in education. Classification: LCC LB1028.5 .A66 2017 | DDC 372.0285--dc23LC record available at https://lccn.loc.gov/2016020503

ISBN: 978-1-138-92787-2 (hbk)
ISBN: 978-1-138-92788-9 (pbk)
ISBN: 978-1-315-68220-4 (ebk)

Typeset in Bembo
by Fish Books Ltd.

Visit the eResources website: www.routledge.com/9781138927889

MIX
Paper from
responsible sources
FSC
www.fsc.org   FSC® C013604

Printed and bound by CPI Group (UK) Ltd, Croydon, CR0 4YY

CONTENTS

List of illustrations   *x*
Foreword   *xiv*
Preface   *xvii*

PART I
Understanding the learning potential of children's apps   **1**

1   Apps and learning: A sociocultural perspective   3
    Roger Säljö

2   Learning from apps in the home: Parents and play   14
    Jenny Radesky and Barry Zuckerman

3   First principles of teaching reading with e-books
    in the primary grades   27
    Kathleen Roskos

PART II
Key app challenges   **39**

4   Reading between the lines: Market scan and analysis
    of language- and literacy-focused children's apps   42
    Sarah E. Vaala

5 Teaching and learning with tablets: A case study of
  twenty-first-century skills and new learning   57
  Nicola Yelland

6 App maps: Evaluating children's iPad software for twenty-first-
  century literacy learning   73
  Karen E. Wohlwend and Jennifer Rowsell

7 Touch design and narrative interpretation: A social semiotic
  approach to picture book apps   89
  Sumin Zhao and Len Unsworth

8 Put their learning in their hands: Apps supporting
  self-regulated learning   102
  *Julie Mueller, Karin Archer, Eileen Wood and
  Domenica De Pasquale*

PART III
Empirical evidence   **117**

9 The use of tablet technology to support development of
  early mathematical skills: A cross-cultural comparison   121
  Nicola J. Pitchford and Laura A. Outhwaite

10 'Makes learning easier – they're active': Using apps in early
   years mathematics   135
   Nigel Calder

11 Adults and children make meaning together with e-books   147
   Kathrin Rees, Susan Rvachew and Aparna Nadig

12 Literacy teaching with tablets in bilingual primary
   classrooms: The Malta TabLit Study   163
   Charles L. Mifsud and Louisa Grech

13 iPad-supported learning and development for a child with
   mild cerebral palsy   175
   Elaine Khoo

14 Enhancing science learning with BYOD (Bring Your Own
   Device) in a primary school in Hong Kong   192
   Yanjie Song and Wai Ying Ku

15 Bringing Pudsey to life: Young children's use of augmented
reality apps 207
Jackie Marsh and Dylan Yamada-Rice

PART IV
Future avenues **219**

16 Digital play: Conceptualising the relation between real,
augmented, and virtual realities 223
Marilyn Fleer

17 iPads, apps and student thinking skill development 235
Garry Falloon

18 Trans- and intra-apps: Innovating the app market and use 252
Natalia Kucirkova

19 A model of mobile knowledge building with apps for
pre-service teacher education 265
Kevin Burden

20 Young children in an education context: Apps, cultural
agency and expanding communicative repertoires 280
Karen Daniels

Index *293*

LIST OF ILLUSTRATIONS

Figures

3.1	The four-part instructional framework	30
4.1	Child age ranges mentioned in app descriptions	47
4.2	Language and literacy skills most commonly mentioned in app descriptions	49
4.3	Teaching strategies most commonly mentioned in app descriptions	49
4.4	Incidences of 'benchmarks of educational quality' mentioned in app descriptions	50
4.5	Nature of adult-directed information within app content	52
4.6	Differences in app descriptions and app content based on presence of benchmarks of educational quality in app description	53
5.1	Year 2 e-books on life cycles	63
5.2	Counting in threes	65
5.3	Mathematical arrays for counting in threes	66
5.4	An earthquake in Haiti	67
5.5	Things we can do to save our planet (Maisie)	68
5.6	Graph of the most frequent form of recycling items	68
6.1	Visualizing thinking with iPads	77
6.2	Alice creating a love story	79
6.3	*Toontastic* app map	80
6.4	Photos of parallel play in virtual and physical worlds	82
6.5	*Grandma's Kitchen* app map	83
6.6	*PuppetPals* app map	84
6.7	*JibJab Jr. Books* app map	85
7.1	Touch design: A social semiotic perspective	94
7.2	Examples of touch designs in *The Heart and the Bottle*	97
8.1	Periodic table of iPad apps (Junkins, n.d.)	105

8.2	The padagogy wheel (Carrington, 2015)	106
9.1	Illustrations of children using the tablet technology and interactive apps	125
10.1	The visual, numeric and symbolic engagement with the *Multiplier* app	137
10.2	Two students using the *Multiplier* app	139
10.3	Using *TouchCounts* to challenge children to group numbers to make fives	141
11.1	Example screens from interactive iRead With e-book app	153
12.1	Examples of different contexts for tablets' integration into the literacy lessons	168
12.2	An example of students (7- to 8-year-olds) working collaboratively when using tablets	170
13.1	The iPad's user-friendly touchscreen	180
13.2	iPad apps that reinforce the use of two hands are useful to Max. The left and right arrows act as visual and tactile signposts to guide both hands' movements	181
13.3	Apps with reward systems such as in Maths Bingo motivates Max's learning	183
13.4	Max drawing a picture from the cartoon characters 'Tom and Jerry' on *Paper 53*	185
14.1	Group's inquiry learning process	200
14.2	Group work on the structure of Faba bean	201
14.3	Group work on the structure of Lily	202
15.1	Child using the *QuivAR* app	213
15.2	Apps mapped against the play/creativity continuum	215
16.1	Digital play	229
17.1	The school's virtues *COGs* framework	238
17.2	Students worked in various locations	239
17.3	A typical Studiocode coding setup	242
17.4	Students' use of resources and thinking types	246
19.1	The Knowledge Building Continuum	270
20.1	Building a robot: Toca Robot Lab by Toca Boca©	283
20.2	Making a pop group	288

eResources

5.1	Year 2 e-books on life cycles	63
5.2	Counting in threes	65
5.3	Mathematical arrays for counting in threes	66
5.4	An earthquake in Haiti	67
5.5	Things we can do to save our planet (Maisie)	68
5.6	Graph of the most frequent form of recycling items	68
6.1	Visualizing thinking with iPads	77
6.2	Alice creating a love story	79

6.3	*Toontastic* app map	80
6.4	Photos of parallel play in virtual and physical worlds	82
6.5	*Grandma's Kitchen* app map	83
6.6	*PuppetPals* app map	84
6.7	*JibJab Jr. Books* app map	85
7.1	Touch design: A social semiotic perspective	94
7.2	Examples of touch designs in *The Heart and the Bottle*	97
8.1	Periodic table of iPad apps (Junkins, n.d.)	105
9.1	Illustrations of children using the tablet technology and interactive apps	125
10.1	The visual, numeric and symbolic engagement with the *Multiplier* app	137
10.2	Two students using the *Multiplier* app	139
10.3	Using *TouchCounts* to challenge children to group numbers to make fives	141
12.1	Examples of different contexts for tablets' integration into the literacy lessons	168
12.2	An example of students (7- to 8-year-olds) working collaboratively when using tablets	170
13.1	The iPad's user-friendly touchscreen	180
13.2	iPad apps that reinforce the use of two hands are useful to Max. The left and right arrows act as visual and tactile signposts to guide both hands' movements	181
13.3	Apps with reward systems such as in Maths Bingo motivates Max's learning	183
13.4	Max drawing a picture from the cartoon characters 'Tom and Jerry' on *Paper 53*	185
15.1	Child using the *QuivAR* app	213
16.1	Digital play	229
17.1	The school's virtues *COGs* framework	238
17.2	Students worked in various locations	239
17.3	A typical Studiocode coding setup	242

Tables

4.1	Language/literacy skills and teaching strategies rarely or never encountered in children's apps	48
6.1	Comparing print literacy and participatory literacies	74
6.2	Participatory literacies rubric and benchmarks	78
6.3	Comparing apps across five dimensions of participatory literacies	86
8.1	Means and standard deviations of student technology use	108
8.2	Means and standard deviations of students' preferred tools for learning	108
8.3	General thematic codes in responses to the question of how the mobile devices assist students in learning	109

8.4	General thematic codes in responses to the question of how the mobile devices made learning difficult for students	109
9.1	Summary of methodology adopted in Malawi and UK studies	127
9.2	Mean improvements in maths ability (% gain) over the intervention period for the Maths Tablet groups in Malawi and the UK	130
9.3	Between-group effect sizes (Cohen's *d*) across Standards 1–3 in Malawi case	131
11.1	Feature overview of three books (B1–B3) used in reading protocol B	149
11.2	Participant characteristics	150
14.1	Seamless inquiry-based learning activities on 'Flower and Seeds'	196
14.2	Percentage of each category mentioned by the students in pre-Q1	197
14.3	Percentage of each category mentioned by the students in post-Q1	198
14.4	Pre-Q2 percentage of related concepts in nodes, links and link labels in the map	199
14.5	Post-Q2 percentage of related concepts in nodes, links and link labels in the map	199
15.1	Augmented reality apps, play and creativity	212
17.1	The *Thinking Types* framework	241
17.2	Inter-rater agreement	242
17.3	Sample data coded by *Thinking Types*	244
20.1	Building a robot	285
20.2	Steering a robot	287
20.3	Josie makes a pop group	289

Text boxes

9.1	Core features of the onebillion maths apps	124
9.2	Examples of items from apps and how children interact with them	126

Appendices

11.1	D11107, protocol B, original language English	160
11.2	D33101, protocol B, original language French	161
15.1	The Analysing Children's Creative Thinking (ACCT) Framework (Robson, 2014)	217

FOREWORD

Educators are under increased pressure to improve students' achievement and engagement; as such, they are challenged to find appropriate ways to create meaningful, relevant, and appropriate lessons and units while simultaneously focusing on learning outcomes. Currently, schools throughout the world are moving toward exploration or implementation of one-to-one computing, most frequently in the form of mobile devices (tablets or smartphones), which may be school provided, or Bring Your Own Device (BYOD) programmes. Given the reality of these mobile devices, software has been developed in the form of apps (applications), which are small programs designed to accomplish specific goals and take advantage of global information access. Kucirkova and Falloon's new edited book, *Apps, Technology and Younger Learners: International evidence for teaching* offers an incredible array of papers that provide theoretical perspectives and empirical research, carefully grounded in the extant literature, to assist every educator in meeting this challenge.

We are all aware of the many challenges facing educators as they assist learners in reaching their potential. We must not assume that every teacher is savvy about appropriate educational uses of technology, even if they appear to be digitally connected or skilled users of Twitter, Facebook, or even text messaging. Overbay *et al.* (2011) suggested that our task is not about technology, but rather about people. We know that teacher beliefs about technology are predictors of technology usage and influence the decisions they make when planning for technology integration (Ertmer and Ottenbreit-Leftwich, 2010; Miranda and Russell, 2012; Zhao and Frank, 2003). Thus, educators who explore this book will have a greater understanding of why and how they can integrate mobile devices and apps into their classrooms and daily practice.

Right now, learners and educators are able to find and use authentic data, images, simulations, animations, and other ways to gain understanding about our complex world (Hutchison *et al.*, 2012; Yen *et al.*, 2012). It is an imperative to ensure that educators understand how to teach with new technologies, and in new ways. Through this book, educators will gain insight to assist them in engaging their learners and, in particular, learn that 'There is more to mobile learning than simply having portable wireless devices accessible to students' (Hodges and Prater, 2014, p. 76).

This international book recognizes the complexity and context of cultural differences. The authors state that two critical insights guided them. First, they recognized the 'cultural sensitivity and historical acumen necessary for a deeper understanding of the complex issues surrounding children's learning with apps (and technology-mediated learning more generally).' Second, they explained that every use of technology must be considered with the 'complex socio-cultural nature of technology deployment in schools.' These two guiding and overarching precepts make it possible for each educator to more fully use the information in a way that is appropriate to his/her location, students, and community.

The book is divided into four sections that encourage readers to delve deeper and deeper into the appropriate use of apps. The first section, Understanding the learning potential of children's apps, provides the background, context, and developmental aspects of mobile devices and apps, for young children. It sets the stage for asking questions about why and how one might bring these into a classroom.

The second section, Key app challenges, addresses the many concerns inherent in this enterprise, and makes progress in answering the questions that frequently arise as the notion of introducing apps to young children is contemplated. What are the fears? How do educators and parents evaluate apps? What are the specific ways that apps can be used to support personalized learning and student outcomes? These and others are addressed in this section.

While all the chapters in this book provide data from empirical studies, the third section, Empirical evidence, provides very specific studies that are designed to help understand the benefits, or lack thereof, which may result from integrating apps into the early education classroom. The authors of these chapters provide extremely even-handed approaches to the use of these tools, and offer practical recommendations for educators.

The final section, Future avenues, continues the balanced approach to the topic by challenging readers to consider the potential that may result from implementing apps into young children's learning. What are the opportunities not yet imagined? What future research is possible or essential given the expo-nential growth of these tools? For whom might these apps offer unimagined prospects?

The editors, authors, and reviewers are to be congratulated on their efforts to provide this exceptional addition to every library, professional development experi-ence, and learning community. I recommend this book highly to all who have an interest in finding appropriate ways to take advantage of the affordances of mobile devices and apps, but also who wish to recognize the challenges involved. I fervently hope that this book will be the first step in a global sharing of best practices and lessons learned among educators.

Lynne Schrum, Ph.D.
Dean and Professor
Abraham S. Fischler College of Education
Nova Southeastern University

References

Ertmer, P. A. and Ottenbreit-Leftwich, A. (2010). Teacher technology change: How knowledge, confidence, beliefs, and culture intersect. *Journal of Research on Technology in Education, 42*(3), 255–284.

Hodges, C. B. and Prater, A. H. (2014). Technologies on the horizon: Teachers respond to the Horizon Report. *TechTrends, 58*(3), 71–77.

Hutchison, A., Beschorner, B. and Schmidt-Crawford, D. (2012). Exploring the use of the iPad for literacy learning. *The Reading Teacher, 66*(1), 15–23.

Miranda, H. P. and Russell, M. (2012). Understanding factors associated with teacher-directed student use of technology in elementary classrooms: A structural equation modeling approach. *British Journal of Educational Technology, 43*(4), 652–666.

Overbay, A., Mollette, M. and Vasu, E. S. (2011). A technology plan that works: Administrators should keep five lessons in mind as they implement new technology initiatives. *Educational Leadership, 68*(5), 56–59.

Yen, J., Lee, C. and Chen, I. (2012). The effects of image-based concept mapping on the learning outcomes and cognitive processes of mobile learners. *British Journal of Educational Technology, 43*(2), 307–320.

Zhao, Y. and Frank, K. A. (2003). Factors affecting technology uses in schools: An ecological perspective. *American Educational Research Journal, 40,* 807–840.

PREFACE

Editing a volume with international contributors is always an enriching and challenging experience and, for Garry and me, has been a result of transatlantic collaboration over two years. Recognising synergies in our own work was helpful in understanding the connections between the empirical research and practices documented by our various contributors. The book's authors work in contexts ranging from Europe, USA, Canada, Australia to Hong Kong, reflecting the global nature of technology-mediated learning and education. As editors, we were keen to capture the diverse voices that make up contemporary research on children's apps. We therefore invited contributors working in a variety of paradigms and using different approaches and diverse methodological approaches. The result is a book containing a collection of wide-ranging chapters that, collectively, highlight the benefits, limitations, and potential of apps for young learners.

Before we go further, it is worth reminding the readers of two critical insights that guided our editorial process, and which we hope will guide the reading of the book. The first insight relates to the cultural sensitivity and historical acumen necessary for a deeper understanding of the complex issues surrounding children's learning with apps (and technology-mediated learning more generally). Lisa Guernsey fittingly summarised the complex nature of evaluating technology-mediated effects as '3Cs' in her book *Into the minds of babes: How screen time affects children from birth to age five* back in 2007: Context, Content, and the Individual Child. These 3Cs imply that understanding the effects of an iPad app on a child's learning requires gathering information about the context in which this app is used, and the content represented by and through the app. It also requires knowledge about the particular child's needs and learning priorities, and his or her cultural and socio-economic background. Without a more nuanced understanding of all three Cs, it would be very difficult to determine the efficacy of an app and the learning process it facilitates. The authors in this book recognise and reflect the importance of the 3Cs, as well as that of the fourth C: Connectedness, or the interlinked nature of all these Cs in practitioners' and researchers' work with children's apps (Kucirkova, 2015). We encourage the reader to keep in mind these 4Cs, as they engage with the diverse chapters in the volume.

The second insight concerns the complex socio-cultural nature of technology deployment in schools. The question of what works and doesn't work for apps and education cannot be answered without acknowledging what Lydia Plowman (2015) and Plowman and colleagues (2010) call 'ethnotheories' – the cultural beliefs that underlie the practices of people of a particular culture. In this case, ethnotheories influence the ways in which parents and teachers select and use, or don't use, apps in their homes or classrooms, and the ways in which researchers interpret their findings and draw up new theories. This volume is a deliberate attempt to bring together several distinct and unique accounts of children's apps, and in this way, to highlight the salience of parents' and teachers' ethnotheories in relation to the everyday use of children's apps.

All authors in the book touch in one way or another on some common features of apps, which have become central to lines of investigation for researchers working in this area. In particular, our authors cover the importance of touch manipulation for learning; customisation of the reading experience for various subjects – including literacy and mathematics; how apps can support the learning of students with special needs; considerations for selecting quality educational apps; and how theory can help us reconceptualise the role and place of apps for a range of learning purposes. Given the novelty of mobile technologies and their presence in young children's lives, it comes as no surprise that most studies in this volume are based on snapshot or cross-sectional data. They thus offer preliminary findings that will help in preparing future studies on these topics, and which reinforce the message that app research needs more comprehensive and longitudinal data to offer conclusive findings. We hasten to add that all stakeholders involved in the use of children's apps have a responsibility here, including teachers, app developers, and parents/caregivers.

As editors, we felt privileged to be able to include chapters that showcase both empirical and theoretical work. The authors connect innovation with a socio-cultural perspective, and revise current theories of reading, play, and learning to help us better understand the potential of apps to support learning in diverse settings. We contend that it is only through rigorously designed, theoretically based studies that we can gain a nuanced understanding to guide app publishers and producers to improve the quality of their offerings, and thereby help overturn the 'Digital Wild West' (Guernsey et al., 2012).

References

Guernsey, L. (2007). *Into the Minds of Babes: How Screen Time Affects Children from Birth to Age Five*. New York, New York: Basic Books.

Guernsey, L., Levine, M., Chiong, C. and Severns, M. (2012). *Pioneering Literacy in the Digital Wild West: Empowering Parents and Educators.* Washington, DC: Campaign for Grade-Level Reading.

Kucirkova, N. (2015). The Cs in Children's Screen Time: Some Food for Thought, *Huffington Post.* Available from: www.huffingtonpost.co.uk/dr-natalia-kucirkova/the-cs-in-childrens-screen-time_b_8034994.html (accessed 20 May 2016).

Plowman, L., McPake, J. and Stephen, C. (2010). The Technologisation of Childhood? Young Children and Technology in the Home. *Children & Society, 24*(1), 63–74.

Plowman, L. (2015). Researching Young Children's Everyday Uses of Technology in the Family Home. *Interacting with Computers, 27*(1), 36–46.

PART I

Understanding the learning potential of children's apps

In Chapter 1, Prof Roger Säljö opens the book with an illuminating historical account backgrounding the uniqueness of humankind's ability to develop symbolic technological tools and systems designed to enhance and extend thinking and learning processes. Insightfully, he laments on the apparent failure of successive rounds of technological innovation to trigger promised transformations to education systems worldwide, citing Larry Cuban's argument that computers in schools were often 'oversold and underused'. However, Roger's appraisal of mobile devices and their apps, the most recent round of technological innovation to hit our education institutions, reveals something of a different picture. Through well-crafted analysis and reference to empirical work, Roger outlines how these devices, which have become so seamlessly integrated into virtually every aspect of our lives, offer unrivalled potential to support learning across ages, cultures and places. However, as history has signalled in the past, Roger warns that mobile devices and apps face an uphill battle to make any real impact on education systems, which are increasingly being subjected to ideological whims that push them backwards towards compliant, standardised models of learning and assessment.

In Chapter 2, Jenny Radesky and Barry Zuckerman provide another larger conceptual orientation in apps research: they consider apps from a developmental perspective. Drawing on the main developmental theories and extant research, Radesky and Zuckerman evaluate the potential and impact of play-based learning with apps, with a specific focus on the key domains in children's development (including cognitive and social–emotional development) and how they relate to children's social, creative and digital play. Developmental perspectives are often overlooked in qualitatitve research and Chapter 2 provides the necessary explanation for supporting learning opportunities and avoiding stereotyped presentation of the educational potential of apps. Corresponding to the rationale of many traditional developmental theories, the chapter presents theoretical frameworks in a sequence, finishing with a suggestion for future research topics.

In Chapter 3, Kathleen Roskos extends Roger Säljö's argument in her analysis of the potentials and limitations of literacy apps. Roskos thus maps the process of learning to a specific domain: that of using ebooks in literacy learning, which, in the age of increasing accountability, face challenges gaining traction in classrooms, as teachers struggle to develop effective instructional methods that take full advantage of the new capabilities they offer. Roskos points out that teachers should not 'throw the baby out with the bathwater', but instead combine the best of traditional literacy teaching practices with the unique and powerful features and capability of ebooks. To assist the development of motivating and engaging literacy learning opportunities, Roskos offers a valuable framework of practical principles formulated to 'blend the best of both worlds', useful for guiding educators attempting to integrate ebooks into their literacy learning programmes.

Overall, Part I provides some key orientation regarding the potential of apps for the learning and play of pre- and primary-school aged children. This represents a solid foundation for considering the empirical work with apps represented in subsequent chapters of the book.

1

APPS AND LEARNING

A sociocultural perspective

Roger Säljö

DEPARTMENT OF EDUCATION, COMMUNICATION AND LEARNING, UNIVERSITY OF GOTHENBURG, GOTHENBURG, SWEDEN

In a short period, apps have become part of our lives in activities such as shopping, banking, gaming and social networking. Apps are essential elements of contemporary lifestyles relying on increasingly portable devices, especially smartphones, and constant online presence. Apps (and the touch screen) serve as sites where children at an early age learn to engage in symbol manipulation, and they provide entry points to digital literacy practices. In the chapter, the uses of apps in educational settings are discussed. The development of apps for instructional purposes is intense. Apps have affordances that are important for learning in many areas, and they are also significant in the sense that children come to school with media habits contingent on extensive use of such tools. But to play a productive role for teaching and learning, apps (and other digital tools) have to be integrated into well-designed instructional activities relevant to curricular goals.

Keywords: Apps, apps and learning, learning, digital tools and learning, digital literacy

Introduction

Humans have an impressive talent for learning. We are able to cumulate experiences and insights in ways that have no counterpart among other species. Through our ability to communicate by means of a symbolic language, we are also able to share knowledge and information with each other in ways that must be considered as unique. For instance, we can learn about nature and significant historical events through stories that other people tell us, and, even more remarkably, we can read about such events in books, newspapers and magazines. We do not have to be present at the site of an event to know a lot about it; we learn through virtual experiences.

An important ingredient of this talent for learning and sharing of knowledge is technology. Scientists may tell us that our DNA is very close to that of our closest relatives among the primates (chimpanzees), but our next of kin in a biological sense do not read and write, they have no printing press or libraries, nor do they make or watch television programs or surf the Internet to find out what is happening in the world. Only humans have such resources and engage in practices that involve collaboration, information sharing and community building between large numbers of individuals, many of whom do not know each other personally. And technology plays a vital role in all such activities.

In most theories of learning, and cognition more generally, of the past century, technology plays little or no role. Even though they are different in most respects, representatives of behaviorist, cognitivist and neuroscience perspectives study learning at the level of the individual as changes in behaviors, as the acquisition of new concepts or cognitive schemata or in terms of changes in synaptic connections and/or neurobiological processes in the brain. Knowledge, skill and human capacities are seen as residing within the individual, and the locus of learning, accordingly, must be sought there, in behaviors, minds or brains. An alternative perspective, and the one that will be pursued here, is to view humans as tool-makers and tool-users, and as capable of collaborating with – and through – technologies, artefacts designed for specific purposes. And these tools are significant for the manners in which we think, learn and communicate; we design the world we live in, and our ways of learning and thinking adapt to these designed environments.

Thus, learning and cognitive capacities more generally are not purely intra-cranial phenomena; rather what we construe as mental processes, when inspected more closely, rely on 'mergers and coalitions' (Clark, 2003, p. 3) with technologies, or what in the Vygotskian tradition is referred to as cultural tools (Vygotsky, 1978). For instance, and as an illustration, our capacity to remember is no longer limited by how good we are at memorizing. Paper and pencil and/or a digital device, such as a smartphone, dramatically extend how much information we are able to store and recall, and for how long we will remember. In the latter case, our remembering takes place in collaboration with a technology to which we have outsourced some of the cognitive burdens of storing information. In fact, by collaborating with such tools – External Memory Systems or EMS (Donald, 2010) – most of the limit-ations in capacity, accuracy and permanence that apply to the human memory no longer play any decisive role. Such examples of mergers between minds and technologies could be multiplied by looking at how we make calculations, keep time, navigate and engage in a range of other practices.

Learning, thinking and symbolic technologies

To understand human learning and thinking in a meaningful manner, we therefore have to include the capacity of people to use and master the cultural tools that are significant in their society. Also, before attending to the wonders of recent digital technologies, and what they do to the manners in which we learn, we must make a brief turn to history and consider how we got where we are in terms of our capacities to learn and think. My focus here will be on what Donald (2010, p. 70) refers to as 'symbolic technologies', i.e. non-biological tools created over millennia by people to 'represent, communicate and store knowledge' (op. cit.).

Evidence of intent symbol-making – stone carvings, rock paintings and engravings on egg shells – tells us that such practices have a very long history (Texier *et al.*, 2010). It is likely that some of these early forms of symbol-making – and media use – served cognitive functions, for instance, for storing information or keeping track of time (early forms of calendars, cf. Marshack, 1972). However, the ability to store information outside the human body took a giant leap when writing emerged some 5,000 years ago in Mesopotamia (in present-day Iraq). In the latter context, writing was the cultural solution to the problems of keeping track of information in the growing city-states with a complex economy, and where contracts, book-keeping, tax-registers and other forms of documentation were necessary to regulate social life. Here we see the emergence of 'document societies' (Thomas, 2001) relying on a new and advanced intellectual technology, cuneiform writing. Writing was done on clay tablets, the hard disks of their time, and in this sense the technology is both symbolic (use of a script, images and other symbols) and material (implemented on clay tablets that could be stored and inspected).

Symbolic technologies require socialization of people's minds. This is the other side of the coin; such forms of expression presuppose that people are part of inter-pretive communities where members know how to decipher and produce symbols. The cultural response to the technological inventions of this time was another invention: schooling and formal instruction (Kramer, 1963, p. 229ff). The scribal schools in Mesopotamia, with classrooms, pupils, teachers, lectures and many of the other elements we recognize from present-day schooling, is one of the very first examples in history of a systematic intellectual training of the mind, a shaping of the cognitive and communicative skills that took place through the activity we now refer to as studying.

Through history, many other inventions have transformed the way we communicate and participate in knowledge practices. Perhaps the most significant one, second only to the technology of writing, was the invention of the printing press in the mid-nineteenth century. The German smith and engraver Johannes Gutenberg (c. 1398–1468) designed a printing press with movable type that made it possible to print books in large numbers and at a fraction of the cost of hand-copied texts. This innovation transformed societies and paved the way for mass literacy and mass education, and its significance for the spread of knowledge and information can hardly be overestimated. Mentalities of people changed as they could access knowledge that was preserved over time and publicly available through books (Eisenstein, 1997).

Learning and digital technology

Computers, computing and digitization appeared shortly after the Second World War. Information (of any kind: pictures, music, texts) could now be converted into digital form as discrete units – bits – in binary code. Digitization makes it possible to access, process, store and share information in novel ways. Databases can be built and searched. Computing and digitization have come to play a significant role in almost all social activities, our personal lives, as well as in production systems, transport and health care. For one thing, our homes and cars are full of sensors and digital devices. The impact on society of digitization is profound, and many argue that we now live in post-industrial, globalized network societies that have emerged as a consequence of the affordances of new communication technologies (e.g., Castells, 1996).

Early on in the development of computers, questions were raised about how education and instruction could profit from these inventions. Already in the late 1950s, ambitious and fairly large-scale experiments were launched to test the potentials of the technology. During the following decades, large numbers of projects sought to implement computers in classrooms with moderate to low success (Cuban, 1986). There was a strong commitment from policy makers, but much less enthusiasm from teachers. With the introduction of personal computers in the 1970s and 1980s, the attempts to transform education by means of computers gained new momentum. The PC (or its equivalent) had its own operating system, memory and software and could be operated by a user as an independent unit or connected to a LAN (local area network) by means of a cable or, later, a wireless connection. During the middle of the 1990s, the World Wide Web and the Internet appeared on the scene, and this was to have dramatic effects on society and pose new challenges to educational institutions.

The personal computer as a tool for learning attracted a lot of interest among researchers and educators. Strong advocates – technophiles – saw PCs as 'children's machines' (Papert, 1993) where young people could learn and develop by exploring the world at their own pace and according to their own interests. Following this spirit of promoting independent learning through the use of 'powerful technologies', a favorite metaphor of this line of reasoning, some went as far as to predict that there 'won't be any schools in the future' (Papert, 1984, p. 38), but, in hindsight, this is not what happened (in fact, more children than ever are at school now, and they spend more time in classrooms than previous generations, and the demand for schooling is increasing indefinitely, it seems, cf. World Bank, 2012).

But there have always been sceptics who have strongly questioned such claims. Cuban (1986) analyzed how media innovations (motion picture, television, etc.) during the twentieth century had been predicted to revolutionize education, but, as we know, this did not happen. Cuban's conclusion was that the new technologies simply did not fit into the ways in which schooling is organized and teachers did not see the use of them. The same argument could be made for computers. In an analysis of computer use in US schools, Cuban (2001) later argued that computers were 'oversold and underused'. And there is much truth to this. For instance, in many schools computers were kept in special rooms, which were locked and had to be booked in advance. This made it very difficult to integrate the digital resources into curricular activities in a productive manner. Also, there were many other problems; the software did not suit teaching requirements and, as we approach the millennium shift, student access to the Internet was a problem. In many countries restrictions were imposed that limited the usability of computers for seeking information and knowledge.

But another dramatic transformation happened between the end of the twentieth century and the beginning of the twenty-first century when digital tools were getting smaller, increasingly portable and versatile. They were soon to be in our pockets, briefcases and school bags, and when wireless broadband connectivity improved, the situation – and the world – was about to change.

Learning and mobility

In the 1980s, PDAs – personal digital assistants – appeared. These were handheld computers in miniature format that were used as personal managers with key-boards, memory cards and, eventually, web browsers, and later they would have full mobile phone functionality. PDAs were multipurpose tools that were forerunners of what we now recognize as smartphones. Somewhat later, another device that was to be important for instruction – and for the development of apps – was invented: the tablet computer with a touch screen (with a pop-up virtual key-board), circuitry and battery all in one device. Tablets were marketed just after the turn of the millennium, but it was with the introduction of the iPad in 2010 that this user-friendly tool began to spread across the world.

When people carry smartphones, tablets and perhaps also a light-weight laptop with them everywhere, we live in a different world. For instance, students now bring such devices with them into the classroom, and the problem for education becomes how to respond to the development of constant access to the Internet. One response has been to avoid using them as they undoubtedly may disrupt traditional instructional formats. Another response has been to begin asking questions about how they could be integrated into instructional practices, and what it means to learn and know with constant online access to information. This challenge is very real. In many countries, the proportion of young people who have a smartphone is over 90 percent, and the tablet has spread very rapidly to families, preschools, schools and universities. In Sweden, for example, more than 50 percent of two-year-olds are active on the Internet (2014), and here the tablet and apps play an important role (Findahl, 2014). It is in this context of portable technologies with touch screens, constant access to the Internet and a wide acceptance by all generations, but especially by the young, of mobile devices, that we should see the significance of the phenomenon of apps.

Learning and apps

Apps – mobile applications – are specially designed software. The forerunners of present-day mobile apps were calculators, calendars and games. Through the need to be able to offer interesting content and activities, major players in the digital industry opened up for the production and sale of apps that could be incorporated into mobile phones, tablets and other devices. As technologies became smarter and cheaper and connectivity improved, people simply wanted more services. The space that was created for apps generated an immense creativity with thousands of companies, some quite small and some that have grown to become world-wide conglomerates. The distribution was efficient through online sites. Today there are, it seems, apps for everything, and the app industry is a multibillion-dollar industry. Your pizza restaurant will have one, the museum or festival you are about to visit will prepare you for what is to come through their own app, and you use one for handling your bank businesses (most of us hardly go to the bank anymore). And there are apps for predicting the weather, for music, chatting, quizzes, for monitoring your health and counting calories, geocaching, navigating and so on. And, of course, there are hundreds of apps for gaming.

A substantial proportion of apps are advertised as educational. Many educational apps concern such activities as literacy and numeracy (both early and more advanced forms), foreign language learning, science learning, learning to play and compose music, interactive geographical and anatomy atlases. There are popular apps that allegedly explain almost everything, and that allow you to simulate how an engine, a space craft or a camera works, how electricity is generated in various types of power plants and so on. There is also a large number of apps that have an edutainment element to them, i.e. they embed maths, science and literacy learning in a game.

It is an empirical question what resources of this kind will mean for education, and all over the world policy-makers, educational innovators and teachers struggle to adapt to these new circumstances (see Chapter 13 for an example). And this is not easy. But, if we learn from the past, it is obvious that the devices by themselves will not automatically improve instructional practices, nor facilitate student learning. How the possibilities and advantages of apps, as any technology, are made use of is very much a situated affair and will depend on how they are integrated into curricular activities (Beach and O'Brien, 2015). But there are some general trends that are well worth considering. Even if technologies do not determine instructional practices, they may still have interesting features and functionalities that are productive for pedagogical purposes.

Learning and literacy in out-of-school practices

A dramatic effect of digital technology, and specifically of mobile technology, is that schools no longer have control over the symbolic experiences that children make. Not too long ago, children would associate starting school with learning to read. Many had no extensive experiences of being involved in such symbolic activities before coming to school. This is now very different for a growing proportion of children in the world. Very early in their lives, many children learn how to use mobile technologies and they have access to the Internet. And here the tablet, the smartphone and apps play important roles by lowering the threshold at which children are able, and are invited to, engage in symbolic forms of activity. The technology of the touch screen and the apps that children learn to handle rather quickly, provide an interactive environment that has specific affordances (Gibson, 1979). When pressing the game or story app, children immediately encounter symbolic activities that they learn to engage in and that spark their interest. And to be able to engage with games, stories and other activities, they need to familiarize themselves with letters, numbers and other symbols, i.e. they are drawn into early forms of literacy. Thus, by interacting with apps, children not only encounter symbols, the apps also trigger activities. This is different from children's relationship with print-technology, such as picture books. Here, children are usually in the hands of parents to get on with the activity, and the nature of the interactivity is different.

In this sense, the threshold for engaging with symbols is lower, and learning of many important skills have moved outside school. Many apps require what can be referred to as proto-literate activities in terms of understanding symbols and realizing how you combine them to move on in a game or a story. Continued engagement will no doubt result in children becoming increasingly sophisticated in how to manipulate symbols to reach desired ends. To what extent such activities are compatible with curricular learning goals is an empirical question, but a reasonable guess is that mobile technologies and apps will lower the levels at which many children develop literacy and literacy-relevant skills (operational skills such as searching information, using software, finding shortcuts, etc.).

Instructional uses of apps

Mobile technologies and apps, and digital technologies more generally, have not been developed for educational purposes, as I have pointed out. However, they are now so much a feature of everyday life that education – willingly or unwillingly – has to consider how to adapt. Children come to school with established and fairly advanced communicative and cognitive habits that have emerged through engage-ment with such tools, and this has to be taken into account. Otherwise, many of the instructional activities in school will seem alien to students.

In the literature there are studies, though not too many, of how apps may be incorporated into school practices (cf., for instance, Castek and Beach, 2013; Hutchison *et al.*, 2012). But, as we may expect, the success of such initiatives will be contingent on the pedagogical ideas and how these are implemented. To argue that apps improve learning is as useful as saying that books do. Technological definitions of apps (or any other device) say little, if anything, about them as elements of pedagogical practices. Many of the obstacles that have been perceived by teachers to stand in the way of using educational software generally, most likely apply to apps as well (Hutchison and Reinking, 2011).

But still it is obvious that apps have potentials that may be beneficial and serve as interesting and complementary resources in instruction. They are easy to download and are of low cost. Designers put in a lot of effort to make them accessible for users in a technical sense. Given the high acceptance of tablets in preschools in many countries, apps, in the hands of preschool teachers, may support early literacy and numeracy learning, especially for children who are slow to develop such skills (MacClanahan and Stojke, 2013). In research, games of this kind encouraging children to discover how to pair sounds/audio segments with letters/text segments, have been shown to produce positive effects when it comes to developing phonemic awareness (Richarson and Lyytinen, 2014). In principle, and as a pedagogical idea, software that is dedicated to this type of exercise is far from new. But the accessibility of apps with different designs, the presence of the tablet and the smartphone, and the growing willingness of teachers to make use of such resources, are factors that in combination increase the likelihood that apps will play a significant role in instructional settings.

Another feature of the mobile technologies and apps that is interesting from an instructional point of view is that they seem to contribute to reorganizing the interactional patterns between instructors and students. In a study in Norwegian preschools, Sandvik et al. (2012) investigated how iPads and a story-telling app (Puppet Pals™, in which children could create stories/fairy tales) were used. The analysis of how the children collaborated around such an activity, and the role that the preschool teacher played, shows that there was a relatively egalitarian interactional structure when creating the story. Even if the teachers led the activity, the children were able to contribute to the development of the story-line by suggesting how to go on, and they did this both through verbal and non-verbal (pointing, dragging) initiatives. The teacher scaffolded the students in a kind of 'guided participation' framework (Rogoff, 1993), where they provided feedback on vocabulary and facilitated the understanding of how to introduce genre-specific elements in the unfolding story to make it interesting/coherent. The authors point out that 'the children's smooth turn-taking in controlling is strengthened by the device's portability and shared display', and this makes it 'easy for them to cooperate, easy to participate and easy to share' (p. 216). Thus, the technology contributes to creating a collaborative context in which children, who often possess operational skills in how to handle the tools, are allowed to play an active role in the progression of the activity as an educational experience. Again, the technology does not automatically produce such situations of collaboration and knowledge-sharing between children, nor between children and adults (cf. Plowman et al., 2010), but it undoubtedly has potential for creating situations of joint activity.

An educationally interesting feature of apps is that they provide 'access points' (Giddens, 2002) to complex forms of knowledge and conceptual worlds, i.e. they support our understanding and mastering of problems and principles that we otherwise could not handle. At the time of writing this chapter, Apple's App Store has eight different carbon emission (or footprint) calculators for download. These apps allow the user to estimate their carbon footprints, to relate them to their consumption habits and lifestyle and to make all kinds of comparisons. Very few, if any, of the users understand the science and the calculations behind an app of this kind (i.e. the chemistry, physics, environmental science, etc. it builds on). But in spite of this, people with some familiarity with digital technology need only a short introduction in order to understand how to estimate their carbon footprints and to realize how footprints relate to how they live and what could be changed (see Fauville *et al.*, 2015). This is a tool of obvious relevance to instruction and school projects, and at the same time it will be consulted in other settings when discussing environmental issues. This feature of providing access points to knowledge that make it possible for us to operate with advanced conceptual resources integrated into a digital tool without understanding them in full, illustrates how such tools function as 'cognitive amplifiers' (Nickerson, 2005). Many other apps (calculators, step counters, navigators, search engines) have such features, where the user is able to manipulate information without fully understanding how the tool operates. This function of providing shortcuts to significant information and knowledge is an interesting challenge to traditional forms of instruction building on disciplinary boundaries and where you start by learning elementary concepts one by one.

What lies ahead?

There are many features of the mobile technologies and their affordances that are relevant to consider (cf. e.g., Gardner and Davis, 2014). For instance, the rich terrain of chat apps, and social media more generally, encourage writing in a manner that is different from the paper and pencil situation where writing for many was something that was done mainly at school or work. With mobility, writing is a daily activity for people that they engage in on the bus to work or during coffee and lunch breaks. So, even though digital communication is multimodal, it has made writing much more frequent.

The developments within mobile technologies are exerting pressure on the educational system (Säljö, 2010). Children grow up in what Jenkins (2009) refers to as participatory cultures where media play a decisive role for learning and identity formation. Digital tools in all their diversity provide access points to information, knowledge and an incredible range of experiences. Children learn to communicate and think in such environments, and they come to school with established media habits shaped by digital tools. Given that schooling is a mechanism for reproducing skills, knowledge and identities that allow people to participate in social lives as active citizens, the impact on children's cognitive and communicative habits cannot be neglected. Schooling has to engage with issues of how all these resources that children already have some familiarity with, should be integrated into the curricular activities that schools are concerned with. Integrating such elements in meaningful ways has to build on the integrity of education as a human practice, and the role schooling should play in fostering democratic citizens with a critical mindset and equipped for an unknown future. We also have to be realistic – much of what children encounter through digital sources is not educationally beneficial (Peluso, 2012). On the contrary, it is trivial and potentially damaging for society as well as for children themselves. Grappling with these matters is also an important task.

Mobile technologies will not improve education in any linear sense, but they will transform what it means to know, learn and remember in society. And schooling has to take this into account. At present we see how schools are torn between two very strong ideological forces: on the one hand, the pressure to 'go digital' and exploit the potentials of these resources; on the other hand, an increasing use of standardized testing where such tools play little or no role. In fact, students are generally not allowed to use the resources they rely on in everyday life when being assessed. Tests where students are allowed to use mobile technologies, apps and the Internet conflict with the dominant interpretation of how knowledge has to be assessed. In the long run, and given how much we know by means of using technologies, this is an unproductive tension that has to be settled before instruction can begin to make productive use of the potentials of apps and mobile technologies.

References

Beach, R. and O'Brien, D. (2015). *Using apps for learning across the curriculum. A literacy-based framework and guide*. New York, NY: Routledge.

Castek, J. and Beach, R. (2013). Using apps to support disciplinary literacy and science learning. *Journal of Adolescent and Adult Literacy, 56*(7), 554–564.

Castells, M. (1996). *The rise of the network society* (Vol 1). Oxford, UK: Blackwell.

Clark, A. (2003). *Natural-born cyborgs: Minds, technologies, and the future of human intelligence.* New York, NY: Oxford University Press.

Cuban, L. (1986). *Teachers and machines: The classroom use of technology since 1920.* New York, NY: Teachers College Press.

Cuban, L. (2001). *Oversold and underused: Computers in the classroom.* Cambridge, MA: Harvard University Press.

Donald, M. (2010). The exographic revolution: Neuropsychological sequelae. In L. Malafouris and C. Renfrew (eds), *The cognitive life of things* (pp. 71–80). Cambridge, England: The McDonald Institute for Archaelogical Research, University of Cambridge.

Eisenstein, E. L. (1997). *The printing press as an agent of change: Communications and cultural transformations in early-modern Europe.* Cambridge, MA: Cambridge University Press.

Fauville, G., Lantz Andersson, A., Mäkitalo, Å., Dupont, S. and Säljö, R. (2015). The carbon footprint as a mediating tool in student online reasoning about climate change. In O. Erstad, S. Jakobsdottir, K. Kumpulainen, Å. Mäkitalo, P. Pruulmann-Vengerfeldt, and K. Schrøder (eds), *Learning across contexts in the knowledge society* (pp. 183–205). London: Sense.

Findahl, O. (2014). *Svenskarna och internet 2014* [The Swedes and the Internet]. Retrieved from: www.soi2014.se/ (accessed 30 May 2016).

Gardner, H. and Davis, K. (2014). *The app generation. How today's youth navigate identity, intimacy, and imagination in a digital world.* London: Yale University Press.

Gibson, J. (1979). *The ecological approach to visual perception.* Boston, MA: Houghton Mifflin.

Giddens, A. (2002). *Runaway world: How globalisation is shaping our lives*. London: Profile Books.

Hutchison, A. and Reinking, D. (2011). Teachers' perceptions of integrating information and communication technologies into literacy instruction: A national survey in the United States. *Reading Research Quarterly, 46*(4), 312–333.

Hutchison, A., Beschorner, B. and Schmidt Crawford, D. (2012). Exploring the use of the iPad for literacy learning. *The Reading Teacher, 66*(1), 15–23.

Jenkins, H. (2009). *Confronting the challenges of participatory culture: Media education for the 21st century*. Cambridge, MA: MIT Press.

Kramer, S. N. (1963). *The Sumerians: Their history, culture, and character*. Chicago, IL: University of Chicago Press.

MacClanahan, B. and Stojke, A. (2013). Mobile devices for struggling readers in the classroom. In E. Ortlieb and E. H. Cheek (eds), *School-based interventions for struggling readers, K-8* (pp. 143–164). Bingley, England: Emerald.

Marshack, A. (1972). *The roots of civilization: The cognitive beginnings of man's first art, symbol, and notation*. New York, NY: McGraw-Hill.

Nickerson, R. S. (2005). Technology and cognition amplification. In R. J. Sternberg and D. D. Preiss (eds), *Intelligence and technology. The impact of tools on the nature and development of human abilities* (pp. 3–27). Mahwah, NJ: Erlbaum.

Papert, S. (1984). Trying to predict the future. *Popular Computing, 3*(13), 30–44.

Papert, S. (1993). *The children's machine: Rethinking school in the age of the computer*. New York, NY: Harvester.

Peluso, D. C. (2012). The fast paced iPad revolution: Can educators stay up to date and relevant about these ubiquitous devices? *British Journal of Educational Technology, 43*(4), 125–127.

Plowman, L., Stephen, C. and McPake, J. (2010). Supporting young children's learning with technology at home and in preschool. *Research Papers in Education, 25*(1), 93–113.

Richarson, U. and Lyytinen, H. (2014). The Graphogame method: The theoretical and methodological background of the technology. *Human Technology, 10*(1), 39–60.

Rogoff, B. (1993). *Guided participation in cultural activity by toddlers and caregivers*. Chicago, IL: University of Chicago Press.

Säljö, R. (2010). Digital tools and challenges to institutional traditions of learning: Technologies, social memory and the performative nature of learning. *Journal of Computer Assisted Learning, 26*(1), 53–64.

Sandvik, M., Smørdal, O. and Østerud, S. (2012). Exploring iPads in practitioners' repertoires for language learning and literacy practices in kindergarten. *Nordic Journal of Digital Literacy, 7*(03), 204–221.

Texier, P. J., Porraz, G., Parkington, J., Rigaud, J. P., Poggenpoel, C., Miller, C., Tribolo, C., Cartwright, C., Coudenneau, A., Klein, R., Steele, T. and Verna, C. (2010). A Howiesons Poort tradition of engraving ostrich eggshell containers dated to 60,000 years ago at Diepkloof Rock Shelter, South Africa. *Proceedings of the National Academy of Sciences of the United States, 107*(14), 1–6.

Thomas, R. (2001). Literacy in ancient Greece: Functional literacy, oral education, and the development of a literate environment. In D. R. Olson and N. Torrance (eds), *The making of literate societies* (pp. 68–81). Oxford, England: Blackwell.

Vygotsky, L. S. (1978). *Mind in society: The development of higher psychological processes*. Cambridge, MA: Harvard University Press.

World Bank (2012). Access to education. A global report. Retrieved from: http://datatopics. worldbank.org/education/wStateEdu/StateEducation.aspx (accessed 30 May 2016).

2

LEARNING FROM APPS IN THE HOME

Parents and play

Jenny Radesky and Barry Zuckerman

DEPARTMENT OF PEDIATRICS, BOSTON MEDICAL CENTER, BOSTON, MASSACHUSETTS, US

As digital play and learning become increasingly prevalent in the homes of families worldwide, the developmental potential and sequelae of such play should be considered – particularly as digital play becomes a preferred recreational activity for many children. We review the evidence and developmental theories regarding learning from play (social, hands-on, creative, and digital), in domains including cognitive, language, literacy, and social–emotional development. This evidence allows us to highlight areas in which the educational potential of digital play supported with apps is greater, and areas where it continues to show deficits (including allowing a social and emotional milieu for play; open-ended and child-led discovery and play; and displacement of other family or solo activities). The described deficits and their underlying theoretical frameworks can be applied to the next generation of digital game design in order to make future digital learning experiences relevant and connectable to children's three-dimensional, social, and emotional worlds.

Keywords: Digital, play, learning, design, cognition, literacy

Introduction

Emerging technologies, including mobile and interactive screen media, are now embedded throughout the daily lives of young children (Pew Internet, 2015a; Wartella, 2013). Rapid increases in emerging technology ownership have been documented in recent years (e.g., Kabali *et al.*, 2015; Rideout, 2011, 2013), with each successive publication proving the prior's estimates to be significantly outdated. The advent of interactive digital media has raised the promise that digital technology might be a more accessible learning resource, particularly for low-income children who experience a disproportionate amount of learning difficulties and have lower access to developmental resources. However, there is little evidence regarding the effectiveness of commercially available digital products to promote learning, and most parents feel they need help weeding through the vast numbers of 'educational' apps to find the best digital content for their children (Rideout, 2014). This excitement about the promise of digital learning tools has been tempered by concerns that excessive digital media use contributes to child development and health problems, which has led the American Academy of Pediatrics to issue screen time limit recommendations (American Academy of Pediatrics, 2013).

In this chapter, we review the evidence of how young children learn both with and without apps in the home (i.e., outside of schools or early education centers). In order to evaluate the potential ability of apps to support or interfere with different domains of child development and learning, we will apply existing evidence where available and draw implications from theory where data are lacking. This information will inform design recommendations for the next generation of educational games and apps and how they might best be used to support young children's learning, with particular emphasis on the need for greater parent involvement in the digital learning experience.

How young children learn: Parents, play, and relevance for app-based learning

All infants are born learners. Experiences in the three-dimensional and social worlds, primarily through interactions and play with their parents and other caregivers, shape children's developing cognition, language, social–emotional development, and school readiness. Solo and social play allow children to create, explore, and master their world; they learn to conquer anxieties, take on new roles, develop new skills, gain confidence, negotiate and share with siblings and peers, advocate for themselves, and plan and execute ideas at their own pace. When children drive the content and structure of their play, they show more exploration and creativity compared with when play is controlled by parents (Ginsburg and associates, 2007).

Cognitive development

Interactions with caregivers are the primary mechanism by which children develop cognitively. Piaget (1972) observed that caregivers are instrumental in helping children build schematic representations of how the world around them works. Building on this, Vygotsky (1978) introduced the idea of the zone of proximal development – the edge of a child's competence in which they need help from an adult (i.e., scaffolding) to gain a new skill or understanding, which they could not have mastered on their own. In other words, an adult who understands what a child can and cannot do is more effective in helping them learn new skills at the leading edge of that child's developmental functioning.

Under age two years, when children are still in Piaget's sensorimotor stage of development, their understanding of two-dimensional screen media is limited. They can imitate actions performed by a person on a screen (Barr *et al.*, 2007) but can solve visual-spatial problems (e.g., find hidden objects, solve puzzles) much better when the problem is presented in three-dimensional real context, rather than video (Dickerson *et al.*, 2013; Schmidt *et al.*, 2007). It is thought that the cognitive load of transferring information from two to three dimensions is too great for children prior to age 30 months, when attentional controls and symbolic thinking are still developing (Courage and Howe, 2010). Preschool-aged children need to interact with actual physical objects to develop the parietal cortex, which controls visual–spatial processing (Verdine *et al.*, 2014) and which contributes to developing skills in math and science as the child gets older. Thus, a primary limitation of apps in early cognitive development is their lack of sensorimotor input, which some developers are addressing through use of manipulatives (e.g., blocks, toys) to use together with the apps.

Another limitation is the limited extent to which scaffolding of child learning can occur through apps. Digital 'scaffolding' (i.e., giving hints or guiding a child to the correct choice) is common in most interactive digital products including many commercially available reading and mathematics practice apps (e.g., Raz-Kids® Reading Program, or the OneBillion Apps reported in Chapter 9), which are programmed to remember the child's skill level over time and slowly increase the level of challenge. However, scaffolding includes not only the content of learning, but supporting the child's reaction to and persistence in learning. Thus, effective adult scaffolding requires reading and responding to how the child processes information, their level of arousal, or their affective reaction to learning challenges. It is an important area of future study whether children with different attentional or affective reactions to cognitive challenge are more or less engaged by digital scaffolds.

Higher-order thinking: The executive functions

Executive functions start to develop about age four years, but are rooted in experiences as early as infancy. Early secure and responsive relationships promote executive functioning through the development of the dorsolateral frontal cortex and its synaptic connections to the deeper subcortical (e.g., amygdala, where emotional information is processed) and cortical areas (e.g., visual–motor and somatosensory cortices). Conversely, early stressful experiences can lead to decreased synaptic density in these areas, with later clinical evidence of executive functioning difficulties. These 'air traffic controllers' of the brain involve paying attention, working memory, cognitive flexibility, inhibitory control, and planning. Strong executive functions predict early math and reading ability independent of intelligence (Blair and Razza, 2007), and are a strong determinant of college graduation rates (McClelland *et al.*, 2013).

Strengthening of executive functions is a promising area of research in children aged six and older, with early evidence showing that intensive computerized working memory training may be effective for children with vulnerabilities such as ADHD (Bigorra *et al.*, 2015) or prematurity (Grunewaldt *et al.*, 2015). However, results are conflicting (Rode *et al.*, 2014) and lack of benefit has been seen in children with autism (deVries *et al.* 2015).There also continues to be concern that children will not generalize digital skills to their everyday environments (Diamond and Lee, 2009) or that the 'closed-loop' of technology-based problem solving (i.e., the finite number of programmed possible solutions of many commercially available apps (Guernsey and Levine, 2015)) encourages less creativity and critical thinking (Greenfield, 2009).

While more creative games are available (e.g., Minecraft), none have been evaluated for their ability to improve cognitive flexibility or problem-solving thus far. In summary, while commercially available apps are often ideal for conveying the 'what' of knowledge i.e., fact-based learning, explaining difficult concepts in visual or interactive ways; or, quite effectively, advertising to children, more research is needed to know whether apps can promote the 'how' of thinking, i.e., analytic thinking, creativity, and executive functioning.

There is also evidence that screen media use itself – depending on the content and pacing of the material – may be associated with executive functioning deficits. For example, Lillard and Peterson (2011) found that preschoolers showed poorer performance on tasks of executive function development immediately after watching a fast-paced sassy cartoon, compared with a slower-paced cartoon of appropriate prosocial content. Other researchers have found executive functioning deficits at school entry in children exposed to excessive media in early childhood (Barr *et al.*, 2010).This relationship has been attributed to both the stimulating and fast-paced content of some children's programming, and to the displacement of other enriching activities, brain 'downtime,' or parenting interactions that support executive function. While these studies examined primarily TV and video as exposures, rather than apps, the same displacement of other activities/interactions can be assumed to apply. In addition, concern has been expressed that in younger children, who have a strong orienting response to novel stimuli, the salient features of interactive media may be more distracting or lead to more rapid attention shifts during play (Rothbart and Posner, 2015). Further study is therefore required to understand the long-term effects of interactive media on child executive functions.

Language and literacy

Infants' brains are wired to learn language emanating from adult speech. By six months of age, infants' brains recognize and learn sounds used in their specific language (Kuhl *et al.*, 1992). By one year of age, infants know which sounds their language uses, which sounds can be combined, and patterns of words in their language (Kuhl *et al.*, 2006).The exposure-dependent nature of language development is most starkly exhibited by the delays in language and speech in children with hearing loss (Tomblin, 2015). However, exposure to fewer words in infancy and early childhood also has detrimental effects. Hart and Risley (1995) showed that low-income children hear approximately 30 million fewer words, less complex speech, and fewer conversational turns from their caregivers by the time they turn three, and that this 'Word Gap' explains much of the disparities in language and literacy between low- and higher-income children. Lower income parents were also less responsive to their children's utterances, which is a crucial determinant of information-processing abilities (Weisleder and Fernald, 2013).

A large body of research has examined whether high-quality educational programming can teach children language and early literacy skills. The results are strongly age-dependent: children under two and a half cannot learn novel words from videos without parents co-viewing and using the same words in everyday interactions (DeLoache *et al.*, 2010; Richert *et al.*, 2010). However, by preschool age, both traditional and interactive educational digital products can teach children language and literacy skills. For example, the Joan Ganz Cooney Center at Sesame Workshop (2010) evaluated two apps based on PBS shows (*Martha Speaks* and *Super Why*), showing an increase in target-specific vocabulary after regular use of the apps, particularly in 3- to 5-year-olds. Similarly, studies show that children learn content knowledge and vocabulary equally from digital books and print books, as long as salient features of the digital books support the learning objectives, rather than distract from them (Bus *et al.*, 2015). Some literacy apps and products can also adapt to the learner's reading level, are engaging, provide immediate feedback, and offer access to a wider library than might be available in print (see Chapter 11 for a research-based literacy app with such features).

However, it is important to understand whether the use of digital books engages children in more solo reading, at the expense of shared reading experiences. The National Research Council deemed shared reading as one of the most important developmental activities for children (Anderson *et al.*, 1985) because it stimulates more verbal and affective interaction than other activities. By using dialogic reading strategies – labeling objects, asking open-ended questions, commenting on the story beyond the actual pictures, and providing joint attention – parents expose children to more sophisticated speech (Senechal *et al.*, 1996), and build knowledge such as phonemic awareness, rhyming, and comprehension (Isbell *et al.*, 2004). Shared book reading also provides an unhurried time for caregivers and children to exchange ideas and emotions, and build attachment.

A handful of studies show fewer parent–child dialogic interactions and lower child comprehension in digital book reading compared with print, particularly if the digital book has enhancements not relevant to the storyline (Bus *et al.*, 2015). Is the digital book becoming another screen, distracting from parent–child verbal and nonverbal interactions, as television (Kirkorian *et al.*, 2009) and parent texting or scrolling on mobile devices (Radesky *et al.*, 2015) have been shown to do? This will largely be dependent on digital book design, and how well the book prompts parental involvement and supports dialogic teaching behaviors.

Social–emotional development

Parents and caregivers play a critical role in their child's developing sense of self, emotional and behavioral regulation, executive functions, and mental health. Bandura (social learning theory), Bowlby (attachment), Thomas and Chess (temperament/goodness-of-fit), Sameroff (transactional model), and infant mental health (Freiberg and Lieberman) have influenced current thinking and research about caregiver influence on social and emotional development. Their theories propose that the child is an agent of their own learning, observing and interacting with the caregiver in a way that shapes the caregiver's responses to them, which in turn affects the child's developmental course. Child characteristics, such as temperament (e.g., surgency, impulse control, mood) and regulatory abilities (e.g., self-soothing, attention/state regulation abilities, sensory threshold), affect the caregiver's perception of the child and parenting behavior. A good fit between child characteristics and parent response promotes development, while poor 'goodness of fit' can lead to stress, poor caregiver–child co-regulation, and insecure attachment (Rettew *et al.*, 2006). These difficulties, in turn, predict poorer child behavioral health outcomes over time (Nicholson *et al.*, 2011).

Play provides a special opportunity for affective exchanges and enriched experiences between parents and children (Ginsburg and associates, 2007). When parents observe play and/or join in, in response to a child's signals, they show an understanding of and communication with their child regarding the child's experiences, thoughts, and frustrations. Whether play is in real life or in a digital world, the same tenets of parent responsiveness and following the child's lead apply. This is much harder to do when both parent and child have their attention focused on a screen, as has been shown in lab-based studies (Kirkorian *et al.*, 2009; Schmidt *et al.*, 2008). However, certain forms of digital play or creation may be excellent at bringing a parent into a child's world; for example, a child taking photos or videos and then showing them to a parent, or audiorecording/ illustrating stories (Kucirkova *et al.*, 2015).

Regarding social skills, evidence shows that quality TV programmes such as *Sesame Street* and *Mister Rogers' Neighborhood* improve children's understanding of concepts such as friendship, feelings, and how to treat other people (Anderson *et al.*, 2001; Fisch and Truglio, 2001). Sesame Workshop and other app developers have incorporated social–emotional curricula into interactive games (for example, *Cookie Monster's Challenge*, which focuses on impulse inhibition, and Daniel Tiger's Grr-ific Feelings app). While these games are promising, they do remove the naturalistic and social components of nondigital play that have long been the basis of learning social–emotional skills. For example, social learning games such as *Simon Says* or *Red light/Green light 1-2-3* could be transformed into app format, but this would remove the challenge of being sensitive to other children's verbal and nonverbal behaviors, as well co-regulating their behavior with others. Digital games and social stories also have a limited number of programmed options, which are likely to constrain social–emotional learning compared with unstructured, imaginative play.

Importance of child characteristics and 'child-media goodness of fit'

Depending on their temperament, self-regulation skills, and learning style, some children need more explicit scaffolding from their parents to promote their social–emotional development. For example, young children with intense reactivity or negative emotionality may need extra help from parents to learn how to stay calm and problem-solve during frustrating experiences. Children who experience difficulty reading others' nonverbal cues may need additional guidance to understand others' thoughts and perspectives, and how to react socially. However, such difficult-to-parent children may receive less of such assistance from caregivers because they are more likely to spend excessive time using screen media (Radesky et al., 2014b). Similarly, low-income preschoolers with behavioral difficulties are more likely to be given a mobile device to keep them calm or to keep peace and quiet in the house (Radesky et al., 2016). Whether children with social–emotional difficulties are more likely to have negative outcomes from excessive technology use – and concomitant decreases in parent–child scaffolding or solo play – needs to be determined.

Importance of socio-ecological context

Positive early relationships are the strongest buffer against the negative developmental effects of early adversity, as they both help teach children new skills, but also how to stay calm and organized enough to apply those skills. Children who receive sensitive responsive care in the first few years of life are more likely to do better educationally and socially (Sroufe, 1988). Chronic stress in early childhood, especially when related to poverty, affects the brain and leads to learning, memory, and attentional problems (Brunson et al., 2003).

However, lower-income families, who are also more likely to experience stress and adversity, use more digital media at home, but have lower access to quality programming, apps, and hardware (Christakis, 2007; Pew Internet, 2015b) compared with their more well-off peers. Lower-income mothers also interact with their children less around media (Mendelsohn et al., 2008), and report not being familiar with quality digital products, strategies to track or limit their children's technology use, or how to balance digital time with other enriching activities (Radesky et al., in press).

How can apps be evaluated and improved?

The low quality of most commercially available 'educational' apps is highlighted in several recent publications (Hirsh-Pasek et al., 2015; Guernsey and Levine, 2015). For example, in the 184 most popular or award-winning apps that Guernsey and Levine (2015) reviewed, the majority demonstrated a 'lack of transparency, over-hyped or unsubstantiated claims, a lack of curriculum guidance or alignment with standards, a paucity of knowledge about how young children learn among deve-lopers, and an incomplete response to children's literacy needs, especially for struggling readers' (p. 52). Most of the apps they reviewed relied on a limited repertoire of academic skills and did not stimulate higher-order thinking or reading. They also noted that only 2 percent of app developers had tested their apps to ensure that children learned from them. Sarah Vaala provides more details on this research in Chapter 4.

In order to create a framework for evaluation of educational apps, Hirsh-Pasek and colleagues (2015) applied the Science of Learning to app content and design. They argue that, in order for apps to be educational, a child needs to be mindfully engaged (i.e., beyond tapping and swiping). In other words, the app needs to offer knowledge or skills beyond the child's current abilities, and challenge the child to master new abilities. Second, the interface design needs to avoid distracting entertaining elements that interfere with learning or focusing on educational content. Third, the content must be meaningful and relate to the child's broader life, thoughts, and activities. Finally, digital media for young children must be designed to encourage interaction and conversation with parents, so that children can share their knowledge with others. Research to empirically test and refine this evaluation framework is ongoing.

Next generation of digital play

Play – whether social or individual, child-driven, or unstructured – promotes creativity, imagination, dexterity, self-reflection, social skills, and physicality. As more child play becomes digitized, it is crucial that researchers, developers, educators, and clinicians think critically about how developmental theory can guide creation of the best products, while protecting the types of social and unstructured experiences needed to promote higher-order cognition, language, social skills, and emotional regulation.

To offer an analogy, this first generation of apps for young children is likely similar to the Model T, compared with what cars have now become. Much work is needed to move from a crude, basic design with a rough ride to a newer design that more effectively accomplishes its purpose. As new teaching tools and interfaces are designed, the following questions should be addressed:

1. How can the use of apps avoid displacing important activities or family connection?
2. How do we help families find the best content to engage their child's zone of proximal development?
3. How can apps be designed to prompt more child-driven exploration in real life?
4. How can we design apps to include meaningful parent or social participation?
5. How can we ensure that low-income families have access and information so that their children won't fall further behind, but instead build knowledge and competency to thrive in the future?

Consistent with a child's zone of proximal development, it is also important that apps and digital media appropriately challenge children's needed areas of learning. This can be done more easily for literacy and academic skills, where concrete aspects of knowledge development proceed in more predictable ways. It will be much more difficult for technology to teach social and emotional skills, which require flexible scaffolding and modeling of self-regulation and problem-solving by parents. However, this is an area of promise. There are several apps that address emotional development through practicing self-regulation skills (e.g., visual timers, *Calm Counter*) but these must be used with the guidance of a parent. Other apps that aim to teach the parent new ways of managing difficult child behavior (e.g., *Zero To Three Let's Play! Daniel Tiger's Neighborhood*) similarly require important parental involvement.

Parent or family-directed digital content might also serve as a tailored and easily accessible source of parenting guidance and ideas for play. For example, a recent randomized controlled study (York and Loeb, 2014) showed that regular text message 'nudges' to low-income mothers were able to increase the frequency of literacy-stimulating activities they took part in with their preschoolers. Mothers in this study reported appreciating this new source of ideas, which they otherwise would not have known about or attempted. Apps and videos can also display visual models that show parents how to promote their child's development, participate in creative play activities that encourage problem-solving, and how to enhance their interaction with their child, such as *Ready Rosie*'s modeling of parent–child reading, or *Tumble Leaf*'s modeling of child imaginative play.

It is crucial that the next generation of commercial apps involve the input of child development experts, so that digital learning tools use approaches to teach children, not only engage their attention (see work by Rvachew, Kucirkova or Hirsh-Pasek). For example, Maryanne Wolf, a leading expert on literacy, is developing new apps geared to develop specific core skills that are necessary for reading – all based on her neurocognitive research – as part of the *Curious Learning* initiative (Wolf *et al.*, 2014). As app developers start seeking out the guidance of developmental experts and researchers, the onus is on the scientific community to have evidence-based frameworks to recommend and help implementation. Then, once the high-quality apps exist, there must be a systematic, easily accessible, and low-cost method for parents to find them, either embedded in app stores or through curation groups such as Common Sense Media, Moms With Apps, or Children's Technology Review.

To counter the new 'digital divide' between high- and low-income families, more low-cost or free apps are needed that include curriculum-based content, scaffolds that encourage family interactions around content, prompts to disengage from digital play, and that generalize their skills in their natural environment. For example, Leap Pad® devices and some *Sesame Street* apps provide feedback to parents via email about the child's gains, provide ideas for how the parent can help apply their child's new knowledge in the real world, and give tips for parent co-use.

There are several outstanding research priorities that will help guide the next generation of app development. Similar to precision medicine (in which individual variability in biomedical characteristics are taken into account), it is important to understand whether certain children are differentially susceptible to the effects of media, good or bad. In other words, it will be important that apps or digital tools teach children the way they learn, are not too distracting for children with lower sensory thresholds, and encourage more self-regulation in children with difficulties in these areas. Collecting longitudinal data on child health and developmental outcomes, particularly in vulnerable populations, will be important, to understand which patterns, content, and context of use are most helpful or harmful.

With such design considerations, the incredible brain plasticity and developmental potential of early childhood can be maximized by well-designed apps. Similar to how the written word stimulated the development of new brain connections for the reading brain (Wolf, 2007), quality apps may stimulate new brain connections that will help solve the next generation of science and technological problems. However, it will be important that the well-established modes of developing higher-order thinking skills, relationships, and social–emotional skills are maintained, so that this generation's learners can successfully innovate and apply their knowledge.

References

American Academy of Pediatrics Council on Communications and Media. (2013). Children, adolescents, and the media. *Pediatrics, 132*(5), 958–961.

Anderson, R.C., Hiebert, E.H., Scott, J.A. and Wilkinson, I.A.G. (1985). *Becoming a Nation of Readers: The report of the Commission on Reading*. Champaign, IL: Center for the Study of Reading, University of Illinois.

Anderson, D.R., Huston, A.C., Schmitt, K.L., Linebarger, D.L. and Wright, J.C. (2001). Early childhood television viewing and adolescent behavior: The re-contact study. *Monographs of the Society for Research in Child Development, 66*(1), 1–147.

Barr, R., Muentener, P. and Garcia, A. (2007). Age-related changes in deferred imitation from television by 6- to 18-month-olds. *Developmental Science, 10*(6), 910–921.

Barr, R., Lauricella, A., Zack, E. and Calvert, S.L. (2010). Infant and early childhood exposure to adult directed and child-directed television programming: Relations with cognitive skills at age four. *Merrill-Palmer Q, 56*(1), 21–48.

Bigorra, A., Garolera, M., Guijarro, S. and Hervas, A. (2015). Long-term far-transfer effects of working memory training in children with ADHD: A randomized controlled trial. *European Child Adolescent Psychiatry*, 1–15.

Blair, C. and Razza, R.P. (2007). Relating effortful control, executive function, and false belief understanding to emerging math and literacy ability in kindergarten. *Child Development, 78*(2), 647–663.

Brunson, K.L., Chen, Y., Avishai-Eliner, S. and Baram, T.Z. (2003). Stress and the developing hippocampus: A double-edged sword? *Mol Neurobiol, 27*(2), 121–136.

Bus, A.G., Takacs, Z.K. and Kegel, C.A. (2015). Affordances and limitations of electronic storybooks for young children's emergent literacy. *Developmental Reviews, 35*, 79–97.

Chiong, C. and Shuler, C. (2010). *Learning: Is there an app for that? Investigations of young children's usage and learning with mobile devices and apps*. New York: The Joan Ganz Cooney Center at Sesame Workshop.

Christakis, D.A. (2007). What to do about the new and growing digital divide? *Archives of Pediatric Adolescent Medicine, 161*(2), 204–205.

Courage, M.L. and Howe, M.L. (2010). To watch or not to watch: Infants and toddlers in a brave new electronic world. *Developmental Review, 30*, 101–115.

de Vries, M., Prins, P.J., Schmand, B.A. and Geurts, H.M. (2015). Working memory and cognitive flexibility-training for children with an autism spectrum disorder: A randomized controlled trial. *Journal of Child Psychology and Psychiatry, 56*(5), 566–576.

DeLoache, J.S., Chiong, C., Sherman, K., Islam, N., Vanderborght, M., Troseth, G.L., Strouse, G.A. and O'Doherty, K. (2010). Do babies learn from baby media? *Psychology Science, 21*(11), 1570–1574.

Diamond, A. and Lee, K. (2009). Interventions shown to aid executive function development in children 4 to 12 years old. *Science, 333*, 959–963.

Dickerson, K., Gerhardstein, P., Zack, E. and Barr, R. (2013). Age-related changes in learning across early childhood: A new imitation task. *Developmental Psychobiology, 55*(7), 719–732.

Fisch, S.M. and Truglio, R.T. (2001). *"G" is for "Growing": Thirty Years of Research on Children and Sesame Street.* Mahwah, NJ: Erlbaum.

Ginsburg, K. and Committee on Communications and the Committee on Psychosocial Aspects of Child and Family Health. (2007). The importance of play in promoting healthy child development and maintaining strong parent-child bonds. *Pediatrics, 119*(1), 182–191.

Greenfield, P. (2009). Technology and informal education: What is taught, what is learned. *Science, 323*(5910), 67–71.

Grunewaldt, K.H., Skranes, J., Brubakk, A.M. and Lähaugen, G.C. (2016). Computerized working memory training has positive long-term effect in very low birthweight preschool children. *Developmental Medicine and Child Neurology, 58*(2), 195–201.

Guernsey, L. and Levine, M.H. (2015). *Tap Click Read: Growing readers in a world of screens.* San Francisco, CA: Jossey-Bass.

Hart, B. and Risley, T. (1995). *Meaningful differences in the everyday experience of young American children.* Baltimore, MD: Paul H. Brookes.

Hirsh-Pasek, K., Zosh, J.M., Golinkoff, R.M., Gray, J.H., Robb, M.B. and Kaufman, J. (2015). Putting education in 'educational' apps: Lessons from the science of learning. *Psychology Science in the Public Interest, 16*, 3–34.

Isbell, R., Sobol, J., Lindauer, L. and Lowrance, A. (2004). The effects of storytelling and story reading on the oral language complexity and story comprehension of young children. *Early Child Education Journal, 32*(3), 157–161.

Kabali, H., Irigoyen, M., Nunez-Davis, R., Budacki, J.G., Mohanty, S.H., Leister, K.P. and Bonner, R.L. (2015). Exposure to and use of mobile devices by young children. *Pediatrics, 136*(6), 1044–1050.

Kirkorian, H.L., Pempek, T.A., Murphy, L.A., Schmidt, M.A. and Anderson, D.R. (2009). The impact of background television on parent–child interaction. *Child Development, 80*, 1350–1359.

Kucirkova, N., Sheehy, K. and Messer, D. (2015). A Vygotskian perspective on parent–child talk during iPad story sharing. *Journal of Research in Reading, 38*(4), 428–441.

Kuhl, P.K., Williams, K.A., Lacerda, F., Stevens, K.N. and Lindblom, B. (1992). Linguistic experience alters phonetic perception in infants by 6 months of age. *Science, 255*(5044), 606–608.

Kuhl, P.K., Stevens, E., Hayashi, A., Deguchi, T., Kiritani, S. and Iverson, P. (2006). Infants show a facilitation effect for native language phonetic perception between 6 and 12 months. *Developmental Science, 9*(2), F13–F21.

Lillard, A.S. and Peterson, J. (2011). The immediate impact of different types of television on young children's executive function. *Pediatrics, 128*(4), 644–649.

McClelland, M.M., Acock, A.C., Piccinin, A., Rhea, S.A. and Stallings, M.C. (2013). Relations between preschool attention span-persistence and age 25 educational outcomes. *Early Childhood Research Quarterly, 28*(2), 314–324.

Mendelsohn, A.L., Berkule, S.B., Tomopoulos, S., Tamis-LeMonda, C.S., Huberman, H.S., Alvir, J. and Dreyer, B.P. (2008). Infant television and video exposure associated with limited parent–child verbal interactions in low socioeconomic status households. *Archives of Pediatric Adolescent Medicine, 162*(5), 411–417.

Nicholson, J.S., Deboeck, P.R., Farris, J.R., Boker, S.M. and Borkowski, J.G. (2011). Maternal depressive symptomatology and child behavior: Transactional relationship with simultaneous bidirectional coupling. *Developmental Psychology, 47*(5), 1312–1323.

Pew Internet Research Center. (2015a). Technology Adoption by Lower Income Populations. Available at: www.pewinternet.org/2013/10/08/technology-adoption-by-lower-income-populations/

Pew Internet Research Center. (2015b). Digital Divide. Available at: www.pewinternet.org/2015/09/22/digital-divides-2015/

Piaget, J. (1972). *The Psychology of Intelligence.* NJ: Littlefield.

Radesky, J.S., Silverstein, M., Zuckerman, B. and Christakis, D.A. (2014b). Infant self-regulation and early childhood media exposure. *Pediatrics, 133*(5), e1172–1178.

Radesky, J.S., Miller, A.L., Rosenblum, K.L., Appugliese, D., Kaciroti, N. and Lumeng, J.C. (2015). Maternal mobile device use during a parent–child interaction task. *Academic Pediatrics, 15*(2), 238–244.

Radesky, J.S., Peacock-Chambers, E., Zuckerman, B. and Silverstein, M. (2016). Use of mobile technology to calm upset children: associations with social-emotional development. *JAMA Pediatrics, 170*(4), 397–399.

Radesky, J.S., Eisenberg, S., Kistin, C.J., Gross, J., Block, G., Zuckerman, B. and Silverstein, M. (in press). Overstimulated consumers or next-generation learners? Parent tensions about child mobile technology use. *Annals of Family Medicine.*

Rettew, D.C., Stanger, C., McKee, L., Doyle, A. and Hudziak, J.J. (2006). Interactions between child and parent temperament and child behavior problems. *Comprehensive Psychiatry, 47*(5), 412–420.

Richert, R.A., Robb, M.B., Fender, J.G. and Wartella, E. (2010). Word learning from baby videos. *Archives of Pediatric Adolescent Medicine, 164*(5), 432–437.

Rideout, V.J. (2011). Zero to Eight: Children's Media Use in America. Available at: www.commonsensemedia.org/research/zero-to-eight-childrens-media-use-in-america

Rideout, V.J. (2013). Zero to Eight: Children's Media Use in America 2013. Available at: www.commonsensemedia.org/research/zero-to-eight-childrens-media-use-in-america-2013

Rideout, V.J. (2014). *Learning at Home: Families' educational media use in America. A report of the Families and Media Project.* New York: The Joan Ganz Cooney Center at Sesame Workshop.

Rode, C., Robson, R., Purviance, A., Geary, D.C. and Mayr, U. (2014). Is working memory training effective? A study in a school setting. *Public Library of Science, 9*(8), e104796.

Rothbart, M.K. and Posner, M.I. (2015). The developing brain in a multitasking world. *Developmental Reviews, 35*, 42–63.

Schmidt, M.E., Crawley-Davis, A. and Anderson, D.R. (2007). Two-year-olds' object retrieval based on television: Testing a perceptual account. *Media Psychology, 9*(2), 389–409.

Schmidt, M.E., Pempek, T.A., Kirkorian, H.L., Lund, A.F. and Anderson, D.R. (2008). The effects of background television on the toy play behavior of very young children. *Child Development, 79*(4), 1137–1151.

Senechal, M., LeFevre, J.A., Hudson, E. and Lawson, E.P. (1996). Knowledge of storybooks as a predictor of young children's vocabulary. *Journal of Educational Psychology, 88*(3), 520–536.

Sroufe, L. A. (1988). The role of infant-caregiver attachment in development. *Clinical implications of attachment*, 18–38.

Tomblin, J.B., Harrison, M., Ambrose, S.E., Walker, E.A., Oleson, J.J. and Moeller, M.P. (2015). Language outcomes in young children with mild to severe hearing loss. *Ear and Hearing Journal, 36*(Suppl 1), 76S–91S.

Verdine, B.N., Golinkoff, R.M., Hirsh-Pasek, K., Newcombe, N.S., Filipowicz, A.T. and Chang, A. (2014). Deconstructing building blocks: Preschoolers' spatial assembly performance relates to early mathematical skills. *Child Development, 85*(3), 1062–1076.

Vygotsky, L.S. (1978). *Mind in Society: The development of higher psychological processes.* Cambridge, MA: Harvard University Press.

Wartella, E. (2013). *Parenting in the Age of Digital Technology.* Chicago, IL: Northwestern University Press.

Weisleder, A. and Fernald, A. (2013). Talking to children matters: Early language experience strengthens processing and builds vocabulary. *Psychology Science, 24*(11), 2143–2152.

Wolf, M. (2007). *Proust and the Squid: The Story and Science of the Reading Brain.* New York, NY: Harper Collins.

Wolf, M., Gottwald, S., Galyean, T., Morris, R. and Brazeal, C. (2014). The reading brain, global literacy, and the eradication of poverty. *Pontifical Academy of Sciences, 125*, 1–22.

York, B.N. and Loeb, S. (2014). *One Step at a Time: The effects of an early literacy text messaging program for parents of preschoolers.* (No. w20659). National Bureau of Economic Research.

3

FIRST PRINCIPLES OF TEACHING READING WITH E-BOOKS IN THE PRIMARY GRADES

Kathleen Roskos

DEPARTMENT OF EDUCATION AND SCHOOL PSYCHOLOGY, JOHN CARROLL UNIVERSITY, OHIO, US

The digital world is changing what it means to be a teacher of reading in an information age. As the reading program shifts from print to digital resources, it makes new demands on what teachers need to know and be able to do, not to mention their habits of mind as educators. Grounded in e-book research and the early reading knowledge base, a four-part instructional framework is proposed followed by a few first principles of primary grade digital teaching as a framework for change. An example is provided of how a foundational framework and first principles can take shape in the changing early childhood classroom.

Keywords: e-book, literacy, digital, transform, interaction, principles

Introduction

First graders—Mason, Mimi and Kieriana—are the EduCreations experts (EduCreations Inc.). They know the app in and out, and are eager to show how they used it to describe what they know about 'the anatomy of a plant,' as Mason puts it. They each open the app on their iPads (expertly)—and each in turn presents a short digital 'story' of plant structure complete with photos, labels, and narration. Mimi says that we can 'make a compliment' about their work, 'just push the record icon here, but don't talk too loud.'

The classroom in a digital world is indeed changing. Sometimes seismic, sometimes subtle, the changes are transforming what it means to be a reader across devices, learning platforms, search engines, and text formats. It is also changing what it means to be a teacher of reading in an information age. As the reading program shifts from print to digital resources, it makes new demands on what teachers need to know and be able to do, not to mention their habits of mind as educators (e.g., persistence).

In this chapter, I lay out a few *first principles* of primary grade digital teaching of reading. These are first principles because they are emergent, bubbling up from a nascent knowledge base on digital reading in early literacy development and education. In describing them, I draw on research and experience—both being good teachers that open our minds to new possibilities. A word about terminology: use of the term e-book in this chapter includes storyapps and bookapps.

Challenges

The electronic book (e-book) is the next iteration of the book as a technology/ tool for purposes of communication. It reflects the fascinating evolution of the book from papyrus scroll to screen page, from paper and ink to pixel. Like all books, the e-book is a book with physical properties that houses and holds content in symbolic form. It has a front, a back, and pages in between. Like all books, it has a message, awaiting the reader to decode, comprehend, and interpret. Like all books, it uses conventions of written language to tell, explain, and inform.

Unlike paper and ink books, however, the electronic book is digital, which means its content is digitized for electronic transport and its images are pixelated for screen display. Digital has advantages over paper and ink: it can bundle and transport narration, music, animation, hotspots, video, and external links into a book. It can, in short, bring a book to life in new, imaginative ways that expand the reading experience. The brilliant technological advance of the book, however, has its promises and pitfalls for the reader and the teacher.

For the reader, the e-book promises more verbal and nonverbal information for integration to aid print and meaning processing. When reading the e-book, *Bats! Furry Fliers of the Night* (Carson, 2012), for example, seven-year-old James can not only read highlighted words about bats, but also simultaneously see images of bats and hear their wings flap as they fly through the starry night. A twinkling prompt (hotspot) allows him to augment what he is reading while reading, showing an animated graphic of the bat's body that enhances the text. According to Pavio's dual-processing theory (1986), this simultaneity of auditory and visual information as James reads supports his comprehension. In short, two channels of input are better than one in the mental work of reading for meaning. And indeed research with both print and electronic books supports this proposition (Sharp *et al.*, 1995). What the e-book promises in the way of more auditory and visual information may be especially beneficial for students who struggle with reading, doing some of the mental work of reading for them.

But there is a catch (of course). These same auditory and visual inputs can distract the reader from the actual work of reading. Multimedia theory (Mayer, 2005) proposes that when incongruent with the story line, enticing inputs can split attention from reading (decoding + comprehension) and focus it elsewhere—on motoric or exploratory play behaviors, for example, that lead to a cursory reading of text. And again, research indicates that this is indeed the case. Lack of simultaneity and coherence in auditory and visual information (extraneous sounds, hotspots, hyperlinks, busy tool bars) in a digital story derails decoding and reading the text for meaning (Bus *et al.*, 2014). These digital pitfalls, unfortunately, can pose a serious problem for readers, especially those who are at risk and susceptible to distractions.

For the teacher, the e-book promises an exciting curriculum resource that engages and motivates students to read. Every teacher can't help but be intrigued. E-books are contained on amazing electronic and mobile devices. They include inviting digital features that enliven reading instruction, such as narration, animation, rich visuals, and dynamic graphics. They can be collected (lots of them) into a single, portable device and readily retrieved at school and home. They can be organized into an online reading program complete with online assessments and data dashboards. The e-book is different, novel, unfamiliar, and refreshingly new.

But teaching reading with e-books can be risky in an age of accountability. Research on the digital teaching of reading is slim, and early descriptive accounts indicate that implementation may not be easy (Herold, 2015). Teachers, for example, report that they lack technology pedagogical knowledge and need more professional development in how to integrate technology into their classrooms (Hutchison and Reinking, 2011). Several studies describe a serious shortage of quality e-books for purposes of reading instruction, and advise caution in using off-the-shelf commercial e-books for this purpose (Bus *et al.*, 2014). Evidence of effective instructional techniques to teach basic reading and digital reading skills is also lacking. A few descriptive accounts highlight techniques specific to teaching reading with digital books. Schugar *et al.* (2013), for example, identify several considerations, such as teaching students how to transfer print reading skills to e-reading tasks. Others describe frameworks and procedures to capitalize on digital features in teaching early literacy skills (e.g., Shared Book Reading, Roskos, 2014; using iPads, Northrop and Killeen, 2013). As yet, however, emergent practices, such as these, have not been rigorously examined as to their effectiveness.

These cautions aside, using e-books and apps to teach reading is still very inviting to teachers, even as they worry about effective implementation to ensure students are progressing and meeting expectations. Teachers are intrigued with e-books, but hesitant—perhaps rightfully so.

Foundations

Still, from both research and practical experience, we are gaining ground in understanding the role of e-books in reading teaching—enough so to envision a foundational instructional framework that integrates e-books into the reading program. Grounded in e-book research, our own investigative work in classrooms (e.g. Roskos *et al.*, 2011) and the knowledge base on early/beginning literacy instruction (NELP, 2008; NRP, 2000), we propose a four-part instructional framework as shown in Figure 3.1. Below I briefly describe each part in turn.

E-book quality

Several studies have examined the internal design features of the e-book as a literacy learning resource for young children (De Jong and Bus, 2003; McKenna and Zucker, 2006; Roskos and Brueck, 2009). Research is mixed on the benefits of animations, hotspots, dictionaries, and highlights as word-level supports for young readers, but clearer with respect to meaning-level supports. In general, a few digital features at the letter or word-level (e.g., highlights, sounds) may aid letter learning and decoding, but too many and overly busy features can interfere with learning alphabet letter names and print-processing (Evans *et al.*, 2009; Zucker *et al.*, 2009). At the meaning level digital features (animation, sound effects, music) congruent with the story line in terms of both content and time appear to bolster comprehension while interactive features (hotspots, games, dictionaries) have been found to be unhelpful (Takacs *et al.*, 2015). In sum, the digital quality of the e-book matters, which has important implications for instructional decision-making (see Chapter 4 for more details on the educational aspects of apps currently available on the market).

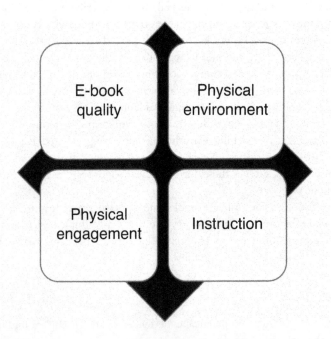

FIGURE 3.1 The four-part instructional framework

Physical environment

The digital classroom is a mobile learning environment where reading occurs across multiple contexts, through social and content interactions, using personal electronic devices. The goal is to weave e-book reading into already well-designed physical learning spaces of the classroom, and not to isolate this way of reading from traditional book reading areas, such as the book corner or library center. As teachers begin to rethink reading teaching using e-books and other apps, reshaping classroom space is a pivotal factor for success. Several design considerations are important (Steelcase Education Solutions, 2014):

- Maintaining space for rich face-to-face interactions in whole and small group learning (e.g., meeting areas);
- Creating flexible learning spaces that support varying activities and modes of learning (e.g., modular activity centers);
- Loosening spatial boundaries between activity areas in classrooms and inside/outside the classroom;
- Designing space to capture and stream information (e.g., a mini-recording studio); and
- Combining high and low tech (e.g., easy access to digital and analog tools, i.e., white boards; writeable walls; etc.).

Physical engagement

Indicators of children's engagement with e-books range from physiological (e.g., eye-tracking) to behavioral (e.g., self-regulation). Visual eye tracking and skin conductance registers, for example, measure visual attention (picture/print) (Evans and St. Aubin, 2010) and arousal levels as indicators of engagement with printed stories (Verhallen *et al.*, 2009). Inhibitory control measures (e.g., *Head-Toes-Knees-Shoulders*, Ponitz *et al.*, 2009) provide behavioral evidence of attention and distractibility. In a study of electronic versus traditional storybooks, Moody *et al.* (2010) described reading engagement as 'children's attentiveness to a storybook and their ability to sustain attention over time' (p. 297) and reported significantly higher levels of child persistence, defined as the ability to complete and maintain participation in shared reading, in e-book over traditional storybook reading conditions. Their results corroborate extant research that shows the benefits of certain digital features (e.g., animations; sound; music) for garnering children's attention in e-book reading. Sumin Zhao and Len Unsworth discuss in this volume (Chapter 7) the novelty of e-books in terms of touch manipulation and the question of how such haptic engagement might encourage readers' increased involvement with the story characters.

More broadly, evidence of children's engagement with e-books includes adult–child motor behaviors *at the screen page*, such as pointing, touching, and gesturing; child attention *to the screen page*, such as staring, watching, and nodding; and children's expressions *about the screen page content*, such as smiling, frowning, puzzling, questioning, and commenting (Roskos *et al.*, 2014). Particularly salient is adult–child shared control of the screen page, which can serve to model and scaffold engagement with the story line, both in terms of print and print/picture match. This is especially important at the outset of instruction to acquaint children with what the screen page has to offer while maintaining a focus on literacy goals.

Instruction

A substantial body of research supports systematic, sequential instruction in basic literacy concepts and skills (Pianta and Hamre, 2009). Structurally, reading research converges on a before-during-after (BDA) framework of instruction where students are primed before reading, guided during reading, and involved in extension activities after reading. Effective instructional techniques, such as graphic organizers, provide teaching protocols and procedures that support effective instruction and boost learning opportunities in a BDA framework. The start point for teaching reading with e-books involves: (1) selecting evidence-based techniques that develop knowledge and skills foundational for reading and writing ability and (2) ensuring fidelity of implementation to achieve learning outcomes. Although as yet few in number, teaching practices specific to e-books should build on and build up the reading pedagogy knowledge base.

First principles

What we know from e-book research and teaching experience, albeit in its infancy, points to several first principles of digital teaching practice. A set of first principles is very important (and needed) to guide the development and implementation of e-books in reading curricula and programs. What follows is a set of principles my colleagues and I have gleaned from our research work and that may prove useful to others when shifting from print to digital reading instruction in primary grade classrooms.

Principle #1: Model digital knowledge, skills and citizenship for students

Crockett *et al.* (2011) propose that *literacy is not enough,* and in their book, titled the same, describe twenty-first-century fluencies for the digital age: problem solving, creativity, analytic thinking, collaboration, communication and ethics, action, and accountability. They argue that we all need twenty-first-century fluencies—and that we must cultivate them within ourselves and as well as within our students.

How does this translate to teaching reading with e-books? In these ways: the effective digital teaching of reading depends on an informed teacher who can model how e-books work on mobile devices, how to organize, manage and use e-books, and how to behave appropriately in an online environment. From the start, teachers need to become thoroughly familiar with the electronic devices they are using for e-book reading—the operating system, settings, Wi-Fi access requirements, IDs, and device management. They need to know how to download and organize a collection of e-books on a device (bookshelf or folder). When using an online reading program, teachers need to be very familiar with the User Guide—how to create student accounts and manage book collections, for example. Before teaching with an e-book, they need to preview and practice the app for its functionality (e.g., read to me, read it myself, auto play), touch skills (e.g., swiping, tapping, double tapping, pinching), and digital features (e.g., music, sound, highlighting, narration, extras). They need to think ahead as to how reading the e-book will address literacy goals. They need to consider appropriate use of device and app to cultivate personal responsibility with digital tools and products. The well-informed teacher is then in a position to regularly model procedural knowledge (the 'how to'), process skills (fluent app use), and responsible e-reading habits for their students.

Principle #2: Choose quality e-books for all learners

Reading e-books can help children learn literacy skills and achieve. E-books can open doors to word learning and comprehension for children who struggle (Bus *et al.*, 2014). The potential of e-books for teaching and learning, however, will not be realized unless they are well chosen.

But what makes for a 'good' e-book—one appropriate for instruction and enjoyable for young children? As yet, standards of e-book product quality have not been established by the book industry, although design guidelines have emerged in key categories (Gonzalez, 2010; Krozser, 2010):

- Multimedia. The multimedia of digital books should enhance the *reading* experience. Audio, video, and image assets should be well integrated with the content and support the construction of meaning. Visuals should incorporate quality images that inform the message.
- Interactivity. The digital medium should be fully utilized to allow readers choice and participation; it should support the flow of text from one screen page to the next. It should allow for augmentations that reach beyond the immediate display of the screen page.
- Usability. The digital book should be easy to navigate and use; it should employ conventions appropriate to books (e.g., a cover page) yet include adaptations best suited to the electronic environment in terms of physical interaction (e.g., touching, orienting to print, scrolling, locating, adjusting, and the like).

Teachers should take advantage of e-book evaluation tools and checklists derived from these categories (e.g., Buckleitner, 2011; Roskos and Brueck, 2009), as well as e-book reviews that are increasingly available online through libraries, professional organizations, and experts to assess e-book quality. In addition, they should be guided by empirical evidence to make selection decisions. At this point, several guidelines should be kept in mind (Takacs, 2015):

- Multimedia elements should illustrate the text as it is being read aloud.
- Animated details should guide attention to visual details that support the story line.
- Interactive features (e.g., hotspots) should be limited during reading and should largely occur at the end of the story line.
- Digital tutors (friendly) during reading may support attention to the story line (Plak *et al.*, 2015).

Principle #3: Establish routines for accessing e-books on digital devices

Every good teacher knows that routines (if not too rigid) can increase instructional time and support a smooth-running classroom. A wealth of information about managing devices and apps in the classroom based on teachers' practical experiences is available online. Teachers should survey this information and collect what may be useful for their own classrooms before *re-inventing the wheel,* thus saving themselves precious planning time. In general, a set of basic routines includes:

- Developing clear procedures for distributing and collecting devices from a storage cart;
- Using a 1:1 device assignment approach so each student has his or her personal device throughout the day and if possible the program year;
- Describing device parts (screen, buttons, headphone jack, volume), management (folders, photos, favorites, energy savers), and e-book tool bars (home, reading options, touch actions, e.g., swipe, tap, pinch, information, extras) using appropriate and accurate digital terminology;
- Posting safe handling rules (e.g., *Stay away from liquids)* and user agreements (e.g., *Only use the app or website assigned by the teacher)*;
- Using hand signals to indicate tech problems during instructional activities.

Principle #4: Adopt and adapt evidence-based instructional techniques for digital reading with e-books

Early literacy teaching enjoys a rich store of evidence-based approaches and techniques. Shared Book Reading in preschool and kindergarten, for example, is a widely recommended approach that when used frequently with effective word- and meaning-level techniques positively impacts literacy development and growth (Zucker *et al.*, 2013). Teachers should apply instructional techniques found to be effective with print books in the teaching of reading with e-books, although some procedural steps may need to be adapted to the screen environment. Read Alouds, for example, can involve joint teacher–student listening, which shifts the teacher role from reader to listener, and thus allows new opportunities to model and scaffold listening comprehension skills. The technique of print referencing (Justice and Ezell, 2004) can capitalize on highlighted words and parts of words to draw children's attention to alphabet letters and sounds. Comprehension skills can be reinforced by digital tutors as students read and re-read e-book stories. In short, what we know about effective early reading instruction can be transferred to instruction with e-books and when properly adapted may even overcome some of the limitations of instruction with conventional books, such as making the book more visible to more children and guiding attention to salient features of print and picture with more 'pointers' (e.g., color).

Principle #5: Link e-books and apps to provide integrated teaching and learning

The call for integrated language arts instruction is not new. That reading, writing, speaking, and listening skills should be developed in concert around compelling themes and topics (e.g., friendship; force and motion) is a disciplinary goal with a long history in the language arts (Farrell, 1991). Teaching the language arts in a digital age, however, is new—very new (and different). Instruction must address not only the integration of language and literacy skills around disciplinary content, but also the integration of technology into learning experiences. This requires linking digital tools and apps together to create learning sequences that afford multiple exposures to content and skills and multiple opportunities to acquire, construct, and transfer learning effectively in new situations. Linking is key! In teaching terms it means connecting a core e-book to related e-books and other apps that extend teacher-led instruction to student-centered studios, hubs, centers, and play areas where students have opportunities to dig into ideas—to explore, rethink, rehearse, and revise their thinking and skills. Digital teaching of the integrated language arts, therefore, is well-planned *and* creative. It is multimodal by design to support a full range of meaning-making modes (oral, written, visual, gestural, tactile, spatial); it sets appropriate expectations to integrate language arts knowledge and skills; it incorporates multimedia to create effective and engaging learning sequences; and it provides for reliable, valid assessments, including self-assessment (Hudson, 2015; Kalantzis and Cope, 2012; Wiggins and McTighe, 2006).

Action

Challenges, foundations, first principles: how do these big ideas take shape in classrooms? There are many wonderful and inspiring examples from classrooms worldwide for sharing, to be sure. In closing I offer one from an urban classroom in the US. Although brief, it hopefully provides a sense of the great shift from print to digital occurring in schools and classrooms.

Second graders file into Mrs Waters' classroom clutching their iPads and ready for reading. They settle in at various café-like spots around the room, open their iPads, and select a title for independent reading from their personal collection. After about 15 minutes, they assemble at tables before an interactive white board and prop-up their iPads. Mrs Waters reminds everyone that they are learning how to read closely to determine what a text says in the informational book *Hibernation* by Tori Kosara (Storia School Edition). Today she models how to use commas as clues to read with proper phrasing, projecting a few screen pages of the story on the smart board; then students practice a few pages with a partner, using their iPads. After the direct lesson, she works with small groups on their iPads to explain how text and illustrations work together to tell key details. She shows them how to *drag and drop a note* on a text page to make a comment. They write a note declaring that the hibernaculum looks crowded with bats! Next she shows them the word search activity on a screen page, and after some prep, tells them to complete it on their own before going to a learning center. A special needs group works with the intervention specialist who helps them practice fluency skills in a related e-book at their instructional level. When not in a small group, students are in the explorer hub—a set of interrelated learning centers that help them to apply and adapt what they are learning to new and different situations. At one center, for example, students are word detectives, exploring content vocabulary in more depth (prepare, shelter, store, substance). Today they use the app, Popplet, to dig into the word *drought,* finding synonyms and photo examples of this weather type. At another a few students are info-trekkers, searching online for more information about hibernation and making notes, which they will share with peers on the hibernation Blogspot. Nearby, two students are in the 'studio,' deeply involved in producing and publishing a narrated photo essay of true hibernators, like the woodchuck, using the app, Write About This.

Some of reading pedagogy in this short vignette is familiar; some is definitely new (e.g., the digital resources). What matters, though, is that the teacher planned a series of integrated digital literacy activities that successively build and strengthen students' literacy knowledge and skills for the future. And that, my friends, is 'lithe and beautiful and immensely generative' teaching (Bruner, 1969, p. 121).

References

Bruner, J.S. (1969). *On Knowing: Essays for the left hand*. Cambridge, MA: Harvard University Press.

Buckleitner, W. (2011, January). The children's ebook revisited. *Children's Technology Review, 19* (130), 6–12. Available at: http://childrenstech.com/

Bus, A.G., Takacs, Z.K. and Kegel, C.A.T. (2014). Affordances and limitations of electronic storybooks for young children's emergent literacy. *Developmental Review.* Doi: 10.1016/j.dr.2014.12.004.

Carson, M.K. (2012). *Bats! Furry fliers of the night*. Bookerella.

Crockett, J., Jukes, I. and Churches, A. (2011). *Literacy is not enough: 21st century fluencies for the digital age*. Thousands Oaks, CA: Corwin.

De Jong, M. and Bus, A. (2003). How well-suited are electronic books to supporting literacy? *Journal of Early Childhood Literacy, 1*(2), 147–164.

Evans, M. and St. Aubin, J. (2010). Instances of attention to print during independent reading of alphabet books by pre-readers. Paper presented at the Seventeenth Annual Conference of the Society for the Scientific Study of Reading, Berlin.

Evans, M.A., St. Aubin, J. and Landry, N. (2009). Letter names and alphabet book reading by senior kindergarteners: An eye movement study. *Child Development, 80*(6), 1824–1841.

Farrell, E.J. (1991). Instructional models for English language arts, K-12. In Flood. J.F., Jensen, J., Lapp, D. and Squire, J.R. (eds) *Handbook of Research on Teaching the English Language Arts* (pp. 63–84). New York: Macmillan.

Gonzalez, G.L. (2010). "E" is for experimentation (not e-Books). *Publishing Perspectives.* Available at: http://publishingperspectives.com/2010/01/"e"-is-for-experiment-not-e-Books/

Herold, B. (2015). Why ed tech is not transforming teaching. *Education Week,* June 11, 2015.

Hudson, T. (2015). *Best Practices for Evaluating Digital Curricula.* Dreambox Learning, Inc.

Hutchison, A. and Reinking, D. (2011). Teachers' Perceptions of integrating Information and Communication Technologies into literacy instruction: A national survey in the U.S. *Reading Research Quarterly, 46*(4), 308–329.

Justice, L.M. and Ezell, H.K. (2004). Print referencing: An emergent literacy enhancement strategy and its clinical application. *Language, Speech and Hearing Services in Schools, 35,* 185–193.

Kalantzis, M. and Cope, B. (2012). *Literacies.* New York: Cambridge University Press. Available at: http://newlearningonline.com/literacies/

Kosara, T. (2012, February). *Hibernation.* New York: Scholastic Paperbacks in the Storia School Collection by Scholastic, Inc.

Krozser, K. (2010, January). Before e-Book experimentation, how about a little back to basics? *Publishing Perspectives.* Available at: http://publishingperspectives.com/2010/01/before-e-Book-experimentation-how-about-a-little-back-to-basics/

Mayer, R.E. (2005). Principles for reducing extraneous processing in multimedia learning: Coherence, signaling, redundancy, spatial contiguity, and temporal contiguity. In R.E. Mayer (ed.), *The Cambridge Handbook of Multimedia Learning* (pp. 183–200). New York: Cambridge University Press.

McKenna, M. and Zucker, T. (2009). Use of electronic storybooks in reading instruction. In A. Bus and S.B. Neuman (eds), *Multimedia and literacy development* (pp. 254–272). New York: Routledge.

Moody, A., Justice, L. and Cabell, S. (2010). Electronic versus traditional storybooks: Relative influence on preschool children's engagement and communication. *Journal of Early Childhood Literacy, 10*(3), 294–313.

National Early Literacy Panel (2008). *A Scientific Synthesis of Early Literacy Development and Implications for Intervention.* Washington, DC: National Institute for Literacy.

National Reading Panel (2000). Teaching children to read: An evidence-based assessment of scientific research literature on reading and its implications for reading instruction. Available at: www.nichd.nih.gov/publications/nrp/report.cfm

Northrop, L. and Killeen, E. (2013). A framework for using iPads to build early literacy skills. *The Reading Teacher, 66*(7), 531–537.

Pavio, A. (1986). *Mental Representations: A dual coding approach.* Oxford, UK: Oxford University Press.

Pianta, R.C. and Hamre, B.K. (2009). Conceptualization, measurement and improvement of classroom processes: Standardized observation can leverage capacity. *Educational Researcher, 38*(2), 109–119.

Plak, R.D., Kegel, C.A.T. and Bus, A.G. (2015). Genetic differential susceptibility in literacy-delayed children: A randomized controlled trial on emergent literacy in kindergarten. *Development and Psychopathology, 27* 69–79. Doi: 10.1017/S0954579414001308.

Ponitz, C.C., McClelland, M.M., Matthews, J.S. and Morrison, F.J. (2009). A structured observation of behavioral self-regulation and its contribution to kindergarten outcomes. *Developmental Psychology, 45*(3), 605–619.

Roskos, K. (2014). The e-book goes to school: Shared book reading 3.0. In S.B. Neuman and L.B. Gambrell (eds), *Quality Reading Instruction in the Age of Common Core Standards* (pp. 190–203). Newark, DR: International Reading Association.

Roskos, K. and Brueck, J. (2009). The eBook as a learning object in an online world. In A. Bus and S.B. Neuman (eds), *Multimedia and Literacy Development* (pp. 77–88). New York: Routledge.

Roskos, K., Burstein, K., You, B.K., Brueck, J. and O'Brien, C. (2011). A formative xtudy of an eBook instructional model in early literacy. *Creative Education 2*(1), 10–17.

Roskos, K., Burstein, K., Shang, Y. and Gray, E. (2014). Young children's engagement with e-books at preschool: Does device matter? *Sage Open.* Doi: 10.1177/2158244013517244.

Schugar, H.R., Smith, C.A. and Schugar, J.T. (2013). Teaching with interactive e-books in grades K-6. *The Reading Teacher, 66*(8), 615–624.

Sharp, D.L., Bransford, J.D., Goldman, S.R., Risko, V.J., Kinzer, C.K. and Vye, N.J. (1995). Dynamic visual support for story comprehension and mental model building by young, at risk children. *Educational Technology Research and Development, 43*(4), 25–42. Doi: 10.1007/bf02300489.

Steelcase Education Solutions (2014). Technology-empowered learning: Six spatial insights. Available at: http://360.steelcase.com

Takacs, Z.K. (2015). *On-screen Children's Stories: The good, the bad and the ugly.* Unpublished doctoral dissertation, Leiden University, the Netherlands.

Takacs, Z.K., Swart, E.K. and Bus, A.G. (2015). Benefits and pitfalls of multimedia and interactive features in technology-enhanced storybooks: A meta-analysis. *Review of Educational Research.* Doi: 10.3102/0034654314566989.

Verhallen, M.J.A.J. and Bus, A.G. (2009). Video storybook reading as a remedy for vocabulary deficits. *Journal for Educational Research Online, 1*(1), 172–196.

Wiggins, G. and McTighe, J. (2006). *Understanding by Design. 2nd Ed.* Upper Saddle River, NJ: Pearson Education, Inc.

Zucker, T., Moody, A. and McKenna, M. (2009). The effects of electronic books on pre-kindergarten-to-grade 5 students' literacy and language outcomes: A research synthesis. *Journal of Educational Computing Research, 40,* 47–87.

Zucker, T.A., Cabell, S.Q., Justice, L.M., Pentimonti, J.M. and Kaderavak, J.N. (2013). The effects of electronic books on pre-kindergarten to grade 5 students' literacy and language outcomes: A research synthesis. *Journal of Educational Computing Research, 40,* 47–87.

Software

EduCreations Interactive Whiteboard v.2.0.11. EduCreations, Inc. Available at: https://itunes.apple.com/us/app/educreations-interactive-whiteboard/id478617061?mt=8

Popplet Lite v. 2.1. Notion. Available at: https://itunes.apple.com/us/app/popplet-lite/id364738549?mt=8

Write About This Free v. 3.9. RSA Group LLC. Available at: https://itunes.apple.com/us/app/write-about-this-free/id601382666?mt=8

PART II

Key app challenges

The second part of the book offers five chapters concerned with the significance of twenty-first-century skills for children's learning with apps. The authors in this section highlight how twenty-first-century skills support a variety of learning outcomes and how they could be incorporated into app-mediated learning and play.

The section begins with a sobering analysis carried out by Sarah Vaala and her team at the Joan Ganz Cooney Center at Sesame Workshop and New America in 2015. Sarah and colleagues undertook a market scan of the top educational apps listed on Apple's App Store, Google Play, and Amazon Marketplace. The aim was to determine the extent to which information was provided that was accurate and helpful for teachers and parents in making discerning decisions about which apps may be most appropriate for developing children's literacy and language skills. Alarmingly, the analysis revealed a minefield of inconsistent and inaccurate information provided by vendors, and major differences in the types of apps available, from store to store. The analysis reiterates earlier messages by the Joan Ganz Cooney Center that the search for quality children's literacy apps presents a confusing and at times confounding landscape for teachers and parents to navigate. Sarah's insightful research highlights major differences in views between 'experts' and app store rankings (represented in 'Top 50' lists) as to what constitutes 'high quality' in language and literacy-focused apps. The chapter is a must read for teachers and parents wanting some down-to-earth, pragmatic advice to help them separate the wheat from the chaff in the app field.

The theme of critical thinking and the need for careful consideration of the place and role of apps in curriculum and learning is continued in Chapter 5, where Nicola Yelland investigates the way teachers in three schools in Victoria (Australia) integrated tablet technologies and apps into their K-8 curriculum. Adopting a framework based on Australia's *Skills for the 21st Century*, Nicola investigated the process by which the teachers assimilated the new technologies into their programmes, specifically evaluating how it supported creativity, critical thinking, collaboration, communication, citizenship, and character education. Detailing a series of interesting case studies, Nicola provides some great examples of how the innovative teachers, working within the constraints of mandated curriculum, were able to seamlessly integrate a range of apps in pursuit of diverse learning goals, adapting their pedagogy and planning to make the best use of affordances the apps offered for developing children's twenty-first-century learning skills. She highlights that the key to the teachers' success in this study was their deep knowledge of curriculum and of the unique ways in which children learn. Being able to identify educationally productive opportunities within the curriculum, and rigorously critique the potential of apps to support these, was crucial to this project's success.

In Chapter 6, Karen Wohlwend and Jennifer Rowsell introduce a framework for evaluating apps for their capacity to support the development of participatory literacy in young children. Given the fundamental changes in the way youngsters use new technologies to build literacy capabilities, the contribution of Karen and Jennifer is particularly timely, as it outlines how learning to read and write can be transitioned from an individual to a collaborative and connected process. The chapter evaluates apps used in three separate studies, each focused on young children's literacy development. The authors provide unique insights into how the different apps and their features provided opportunities for building twenty-first century literacy capabilities, that is, those that arise through interaction and participation. From this analysis, Karen and Jennifer distil an original evaluation rubric or *app mapping tool*. The rubric is built around five participatory literacy principles, which help educators appraise the potential of different apps for participatory literacy development and, perhaps more significantly, highlight the changing nature of literacy learning in the twenty-first century.

Sumin Zhao and Len Unsworth in Chapter 7 delve into the design and content of picture book apps, exploring answers to questions relating to how interactive features embedded within them influence young children's meaning-making. Conceptualising book apps as semiotic artefacts within which different types and forms of resources are combined, Sumin and Len investigate the extent to which some well-regarded picture book apps make use of *intra-* and *extra*-text touch interactives, to assist young readers to make sense of the story and help with textual interpretation. Their analysis reveals some very interesting and mixed results, highlighting the importance of educators and parents undertaking a critical review of the interactive features of apps, and evaluating the extent to which these support learning, before selecting them to use with their children. The chapter delivers a salient reminder that, no matter how well designed apps and their interactives are, learning is a social process and ultimately it is parents and teachers who have the responsibility to help young children make meaning from children's on-screen interactions.

Preparing students for twenty-first-century citizenship and the complex demands of living in rapidly changing environments – and the role technology can play in this process – are the themes of the final chapter in this section. Julie Mueller, Karin Archer, Eileen Wood, and Domenica De Pasquale discuss the importance of merging teachers' and children's agendas when implementing mobile devices in the classroom. Using mixed methods, the researchers videoed the activities and surveyed and interviewed teachers and students in early elementary school classrooms, to determine how they saw the combination of device and app attributes supporting the development of students' self-regulated learning skills. Many of the barriers encountered by the teachers in an elementary school in Southern Ontario Canada ring true for other teachers across the world. While outcomes proved generally favourable and highlighted the flexibility and motivational aspects of the mobile devices, interestingly, both teachers and students were not uncritical of their acceptance of the technology, realising that while it has a place and purpose in learning, it is by no means a 'panacea' or a substitute for poor pedagogy. As the former president of the Canadian Association for Teacher Education, the lead author of the chapter, Professor Julie Mueller, reminds us that while it may be possible for technology to *put the learning in students' hands*, there needs to be careful consideration of the design of learning tasks, and a productive balance must be struck between technology and non-technology-based learning activities. A detailed description of the barriers and possibilities of using mobile devices for student-regulated learning serve as a reference point for other projects focused on innovative pedagogies, twenty-first-century skills and student-centred approaches.

4

READING BETWEEN THE LINES

Market scan and analysis of language- and literacy-focused children's apps

Sarah E. Vaala

JOAN GANZ COONEY CENTER AT SESAME WORKSHOP, NEW YORK, US

This chapter presents findings from a recent scan of the marketplace of language- and literacy-focused apps for young children. The sample was drawn from 'Top 50' educational lists in prominent app stores and from award lists on expert media review sites. Findings indicate that while the market for language- and literacy-focused apps for children is growing, the information provided in app descriptions and apps themselves remains inconsistent. The length of app store descriptions, target age-range guidance, description of purposeful educational design, and adult-directed information within apps, varied widely. Findings also suggest that parents and educators will encounter different apps depending on the sources they use to search for them. The chapter concludes with suggestions for parents and educators to help them locate quality children's apps.

Keywords: Evaluating, selecting, searching, description, quality, parents, content

Introduction

Few would argue with the premise that digital media constitute a critical context of children's development. For example, the average American child between 0 and 8 years of age spends an estimated 3.25 hours per day viewing or interacting with some kind of screen, and an estimated 27 percent of that time is spent with digital devices (Rideout, 2011). Their 4- to 7-year-old Dutch peers use mobile devices, such as smartphones and tablet computers, for approximately 20 minutes per day on average (MijnKindOnline, 2013 as cited in O'Hare, 2014). A 2012 international study of older youth (8 to 18 years) also indicates high rates of mobile device and app use by children in Japan, India, Indonesia, Egypt, and Chile (GSMA, 2013).

Increasingly, mobile technologies are emerging in young children's lives as formal and informal education sources. Children's apps marketed as 'educational' can be found on mobile devices around the world (e.g., GSMA, 2013; O'Hare, 2014; Rideout, 2014). Many parents believe that digital media resources such as apps help children learn content across various educational domains, including language and reading, science, and math (Rideout, 2014).

However, empirical research informing design and use characteristics associated with optimal learning using apps has lagged behind (e.g., Falloon, 2013). Also lacking are regulations for the marketing of apps in app stores, or standards for what information is provided to consumers in pre-purchase descriptions. Following a 2012 market scan and analysis of the children's educational app landscape, authors from the Joan Ganz Cooney Center and New America labeled the children's educational app market as a 'digital wild west' (Guernsey et al., 2012). They found that most literacy-focused apps featured very basic skills, such as alphabet knowledge and phonemic awareness, and that very few offered efficacy metrics to back-up their purported educational value.

Children's language and literacy apps

The extent and nature of children's language- and literacy-focused apps is particularly important to consider, as learning to read and communicate are key developmental tasks during early childhood. The extent of children's emerging literacy skills at the time they begin formal schooling have been linked to longitudinal outcomes, such as their academic achievement in adolescence, above and beyond associations with socio-economic status (Duncan et al., 2007; Farkas and Beron, 2004). Learning to read requires the mastery of a sequence of skills, beginning in infancy as children learn to distinguish the unique phonemes in their parents' native language, and continuing through formal schooling as they build reading comprehension and fluency skills and acquire more advanced vocabulary (Guernsey and Levine, 2015). We have long understood that literacy 'input' can come from many different contexts in children's lives, in addition to formal schooling. Observing or participating in conversations, encountering print in books and out in the world, and observing parents and others interact with print sources, convey information to young children about the nature and value of literacy and oral language, and contribute to their proficiencies as well. Moreover, decades of research into children's learning from television, indicates that children's vocabularies and other literacy skills can be fostered by viewing high-quality educational programs (e.g., Fisch and Truglio, 2000; Wright et al., 2001).

Many parents as well as researchers believe that young children can also learn language- and literacy-related skills from mobile apps, depending on the design and use of those apps (e.g., Falloon, 2013; Flewitt et al., 2014; Rideout, 2014). Parents' trust in apps may be due in part to the fact that many apps carry seductive claims that they are effective language and literacy teaching tools (Guernsey et al., 2012; Shuler, 2012). While researchers and child advocates have called for standards to guide the information provided to consumers of children's apps, particularly those that are marketed as 'educational' (e.g., Shuler, 2012), none have yet been adopted. Rather, it seems that app developers choose the classification of their own apps in stores with very little oversight. In light of the unregulated, uncharted nature of the children's educational app marketplace and the critical role of informal learning tools in children's language and literacy development, a team of researchers from the Joan Ganz Cooney Center and New America endeavored to document aspects of the most highly promoted language and literacy-focused apps for children ages 0–8 years (Guernsey and Levine, 2015; Vaala *et al.*, 2015). This chapter describes important conclusions from that study, and culminates in a list of implications for parents and educators tasked with selecting language- and literacy-focused apps for young children.

Study design

Goals of the study

My team from the Joan Ganz Cooney Center and New America set out in spring 2014 to track trends identified in our earlier app market scans (Guernsey *et al.*, 2012; Shuler, 2012) and dig deeper into the nature of the language and literacy apps currently available to young children. Our primary goals were to gauge the prevalence of language- and literacy-focused apps among popular educational apps, examine the nature of information provided to consumers about the apps, and document various aspects of the apps' content.

More broadly, we wanted to get a sense of the task facing parents and educators searching for quality language- and literacy-focused apps for young children. We wondered: if a parent searched their favorite app store for such products, how many options would they find with minimal searching? What about an educator searching for similar apps at the same time by consulting expert review sites instead? How much information would be provided to such parents and educators before the point of purchase, and what kind of information about the apps' respective educational value would there be to guide their decision-making?

Study methods

To conduct this market scan and content analysis, we first drew a sample of apps from the 'Top Educational' lists in three popular app stores, including the Apple App Store, Google Play, and the Amazon Appstore. To create the sample we collected lists of the 'Top 50' paid and free educational apps in each of the stores on one day a week for 8 weeks, in February and March of 2014. From this pool, we selected the apps that were (1) for children ages 0–8 years old, and (2) claimed to teach language and/or literacy skills. This resulted in a sample of 128 apps (67 free; 61 paid). Next, we collected lists of apps that had won awards in 2013 or 2014 from three expert-review sites: Common Sense Media, Parents' Choice, and

Children's Technology Review. This led to the addition of 55 apps, for a total sample of 183 apps.

Systematic coding of the apps took place in two phases. First, we cataloged aspects of the apps' descriptions across the three app stores. In this step, we recorded characteristics such as the age range of the target audience, specific language and literacy skills taught, and whether app descriptions mentioned underlying educational curricula. In the second phase of coding we downloaded all of the apps and cataloged features within the apps themselves.[1] Examples of this coding include the placement and nature of adult-directed information within the app.[2] In subsequent analyses, we examined distributions of particular aspects of the written app descriptions and app content within the whole sample of apps, and also compared distributions across subsamples of apps (such as those drawn from the 'Top 50 Educational' lists versus apps that had been given awards by expert-review sites; see Vaala et al., 2015). Some of the most intriguing findings are described and discussed below.

Key findings from app scan and content analysis

Availability

At the outset we wondered about the extent of options readily available to parents and educators searching for young children's language and literacy apps. Specifically, how many of the most prominent educational apps promoted by app stores and lauded by expert reviewers are language- and literacy-focused apps for young children (rather than educational apps for older youth and adults, or apps that focus on other skills like math or science)? We assessed the percentage of apps in the 'Top 50 educational' lists in app stores and among expert-awarded apps that claimed to teach language and literacy skills to children 0–8 years. Language/ literacy apps for young children constituted a substantial portion of the most prominently positioned educational apps. In particular, 34 percent of Top 50 paid educational apps, 29 percent of Top 50 free educational apps, and 21 percent of expert-awarded apps met these criteria (and were therefore included in our analysis sample). Thus, parents and educators who are searching for apps for young children that aim to teach language and literacy skills are bound to have a multitude of options from which to choose. What is more, this finding suggests that the rate of language- and literacy-focused apps is on the rise, compared with the market scan conducted by Shuler (2012) several years ago. Using data collected in summer 2011, Shuler found that while 80 percent of the top promoted apps in the iTunes app store were for children or adolescents, only 5 percent of those apps focused on literacy specifically.

Our team also wondered whether the apps that a parent or educator would find among the Top 50 lists promoted in App Stores would be the same apps he or she encountered as expert-awarded apps among review sites. In fact, we found very little overlap: only 11 apps (17 percent of the full sample) were found in the Top

50 educational lists as well as among the expert-awarded apps. In addition, most of the apps in the Top 50 educational lists (71 percent) were found among the 'Top 50' in only one of the three app stores we examined. For example, an app may have been listed in the Top 50 paid educational apps in Apple's app store, but not in Amazon or Google Play. These comparisons suggest that the products that end up in children's hands will vary, based on where a parent or teacher looks for them. It is possible that these samples would overlap to a greater extent if we extended our sampling period. That is, apps that are among the Top 50 educational apps in app stores may win accolades from expert-review sites later on, and vice versa. However, our findings indicate that two people searching at the same time but in different places—namely, different app stores or within expert-review sites—would encounter almost completely different apps.

Adult-directed information: pre-purchase

Amount of information. One of the most compelling conclusions from our findings is that the amount and nature of information provided to parents and educators about individual apps is very inconsistent. This was true of the information provided to them prior to deciding whether to download an app, as well as the adult-directed information displayed within apps themselves. With regards to information presented prior to download, even the sheer length of app descriptions in app stores varied widely. In our sample of apps the length of descriptions varied from 13 to 1,089 words. To put these figures into perspective, there are about 500 words in a typical, single-spaced typed page of text. Thus, parents and educators searching for young children's language- and literacy-focused apps will encounter some options that provide a mere sentence or two describing the content, and others with multiple pages of information on which they could base their decision.

Target user age. The incidence and nature of audience age ranges cited in the descriptions was also variable across apps. Among the 183 apps in our full sample, 71 (39 percent) did not offer any guidance to parents and educators regarding the age or developmental stage of youth for whom the content was best suited. Instead, these app descriptions used terms like 'for kids' or 'children,' without narrowing in on a particular age range for the target audience. In the 112 app descriptions that did give some guidance on an appropriate child-user age range, the majority (82 percent) described age ranges that spanned more than three years (see Figure 4.1). Therefore, in many cases, the same app might end up in the hands of a toddler as well as a third grader. Yet, given their distinct developmental stages, the language and literacy skills these respective children are working to master would be very different. This means that the information provided in app descriptions may lead some parents and educators to download apps with content their children have already mastered, while others end up with apps that are too difficult.

Targeted skills. When reviewing app descriptions in app stores we looked for the particular language and literacy skills that apps purported to teach. In particular, we documented the frequency of skills that are important to emergent readers from

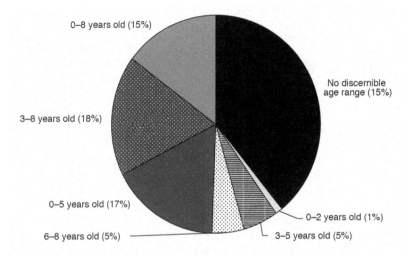

FIGURE 4.1 Child age ranges mentioned in app descriptions

Source: Adapted from Vaala *et al.* (2015)

infancy to age 8. Only 8 of the 23 skills we searched for were found in the descriptions of at least ten apps (5.5 percent of the sample); the remaining 15 strategies were rarely or never encountered in our sample (see the list of these skills in Table 4.1). The most popular skills in our sample of apps are shown in Figure 4.2. To a large extent, these eight skills reflected fairly basic proficiencies that would be appropriate for preschool and kindergarten-age children. For example, many apps focused on alphabet knowledge, phonemic awareness, and sight words. Largely absent were more advanced skills appropriate for an older child, such as grammar or understanding literary forms and genres, as well as more nuanced proficiencies, such as storytelling or self-expression.

Given that the language- and literacy-focused apps for young children that are likely to be most prominent to parents and educators focus on just a limited subset of language and literacy skills, it seems that these tools do not address the full array of proficiencies needed for children to develop into successful readers (Guernsey and Levine, 2015). Parents or educators searching for apps that could aid older elementary school-aged students might end up frustrated at the offerings they encounter in 'Top educational' lists in app stores or via expert-review sites.

Teaching strategies. In addition to the particular skills targeted by the app, we looked for descriptions of *how* those skills were taught. The 22 teaching strategies we watched for were culled from literature regarding how young children learn as well as observations of the kinds of educational activities often found in children's apps. Figure 4.3 shows that nine teaching strategies of the full list of 22 were found in at least ten apps. The nature of the most common teaching strategies was consistent with the disproportionate focus on the preschool- and kindergarten-age range reflected in the targeted skills and age descriptions. That is, the teaching

TABLE 4.1 Language/literacy skills and teaching strategies rarely or never encountered in children's apps

	Number of app descriptions
Language/literacy skill	
Handwriting	9 apps
Storytelling	7 apps
Grammar	6 apps
Bilingual skills (second language learning)	6 apps
Reading fluency	4 apps
Self-expression—written	3 apps
Self-expression—spoken	2 apps
Basic speech production	2 apps
Rhyming	2 apps
Motivation or love of reading	2 apps
Sign language—letters	0 apps
Sign language—words	1 app
Print concepts	1 app
Literary forms/genres	0 apps
General term only (e.g., 'language learning')	4 apps
Teaching strategy	
Defines word or elaborates meaning	8 apps
Asks user-directed questions	6 apps
Suggests external activity to extend learning	6 apps
Includes opportunity for spoken expression	6 apps
Includes opportunity for written expression	5 apps
Includes multiple languages	4 apps
Includes rhyming	4 apps
Includes in-app dictionary	2 apps
Models reading or writing	1 app
Models dialogue	1 app
Includes fill-in-the-blanks activity	1 app
Summarizes narrative content	0 apps
Summarizes concepts	0 apps

strategies mentioned in app descriptions, such as reading onscreen text aloud, tracing, and sounding out words and phonemes, were also geared towards this young age group. More advanced strategies, like including opportunities for written or spoken self-expression, were largely absent (see Table 4.1).

Notably, some teaching strategies shown to be effective in helping preschool and kindergarten children learn language and literacy skills in live settings were also missing from the sample of apps. Particularly troublesome, given the number of apps claiming to teach vocabulary, was the low rate of apps that claimed to define or elaborate on the meanings of words. Other key omitted strategies for this age group include asking the child questions, summarizing narrative and educational content, and modeling reading, writing, and dialogue. It is important to note,

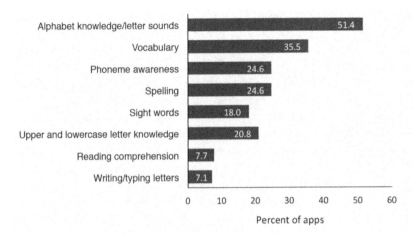

FIGURE 4.2 Language and literacy skills most commonly mentioned in app descriptions

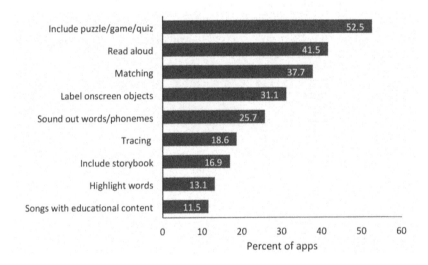

FIGURE 4.3 Teaching strategies most commonly mentioned in app descriptions

however, that some apps may in fact employ these teaching strategies, although they are not explicitly mentioned in the app store descriptions. More in-depth content analyses are needed to examine the distribution and nature of language and literacy skills and teaching strategies actually present in children's apps. What is clear is that parents and educators searching for apps with particular curricular goals or strategies will have more or less luck in locating those apps based on the particular attributes they are looking for. More information about the educational content—both goals and strategies for teaching—would help ensure that caregivers can find appropriate apps for young children.

Benchmarks of educational quality. Our analysis revealed another troubling pattern as well: in many cases, the educational value of apps was not backed up by information regarding what we considered 'benchmarks' of quality educational design. That is, few app descriptions indicated that respective apps had been developed using what we considered purposeful educational design and testing techniques. Namely, it was fairly rare for these descriptions to mention child development, education, or literacy specialists involved in development, underlying educational curricula, or any kind of research testing. We looked for mentions of these elements within app descriptions and on associated app websites because of the precedent set by high-quality educational television programming. Producers of historically high-quality educational television shows for children, such as *Sesame Street*, *Blue's Clues*, *Dora the Explorer*, and others, include child development, education, and content experts in the development of programming, develop a guiding underlying educational curriculum prior to production, and test children's learning and engagement (Anderson, 1998; Anderson *et al.*, 2001; Fisch and Truglio, 2000). As shown in Figure 4.4, we encountered each of these distinct benchmarks in less than 30 percent of apps, while 44 percent contained at least one of the three. Particularly rare was the mention of any app testing. When testing was described, the vast majority of research (91 percent) involved usability and appeal testing only, rather than children's learning from the apps.

Adult-directed information: app content

Location of information. Given that many of the children in the 0–8 age range are not yet able to read independently, adult-directed information within the apps themselves could help parents and teachers explain the mechanics to child-users,

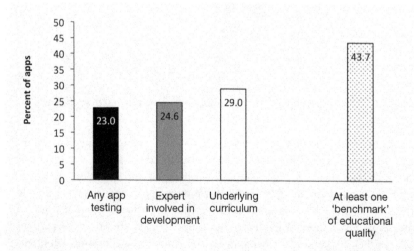

FIGURE 4.4 Incidences of 'benchmarks of educational quality' mentioned in app descriptions

consider ways to enhance the children's learning experience, or troubleshoot problems that might arise during app use. With this in mind, we continued to watch for information available to parents and educators after downloading each app. One promising pattern we discovered was that most apps (79 percent) contained at least some adult-directed information within their actual content. In the majority of cases (76 percent of all apps we studied), this information was presented in a special section oriented towards parents or other adults. In a minority of apps, adult-directed information appeared onscreen right after the app launched (6 percent of apps), or appeared onscreen at various intervals (7 percent).

Types of information. Of greater interest was the nature of information conveyed through adult-directed content. Many of the apps in our sample (40 percent) gave parents and educators information about their basic mechanics (i.e., how to play). Also common were statements or links to apps' privacy or security policies (38 percent of apps). Some of the information we encountered was too diverse to categorize, instead falling into a catch-all category we called 'additional information about the app' (55 percent of apps). For example, some apps gave details about the producers or about the app's characters or plotline. Less frequently encountered was information about child-users' performance (17 percent), the educational content or development of the app (14 percent), tips for enriching use of the app (17 percent), or troubleshooting suggestions (8 percent). Thus, parents and educators are offered different amounts and types of information after they download the apps themselves. Children's experiences may also vary between apps, given that the adults in their lives will be more or less knowledgeable about the educational goals and strategies of various apps, or how to resolve technical problems.

App activities

One fundamental aspect of children's educational apps that has not been well-documented is the nature of activities they actually contain. Our sample of apps excluded any that were *exclusively* e-books; we reasoned that the remaining pool of popular children's language- and literacy-focused apps may vary widely in form or may reflect just a few primary forms of content (e.g., puzzles/games; tracing activities). Moreover, we wondered whether individual apps promoted by app stores and expert-review sites tended to contain a single activity form or several.

As shown in Figure 4.5, we found that the full app sample contained a range of different activities. However, the most commonly encountered activity by far was a game, puzzle, or quiz.[3] We also encountered a number of unique activities that were not common enough to constitute their own categories, and so we created an 'other interactive activity' classification. Such activities were quite common as well, found in 39 percent of all apps. Examples include entertaining, non-goal-directed activities, like dressing up characters, and some educational activities, like creating your own story.

The number of different activities also varied, from just one (32.9 percent) to six or more different kinds of activities (1.8 percent).[4] The average app contained between two to three different activities (mean = 2.36, SD = 1.34).

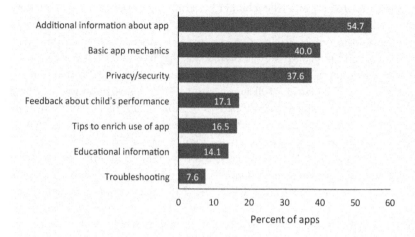

FIGURE 4.5 Nature of adult-directed information within app content

Relating benchmarks to other characteristics

To further investigate the incidence of the 'benchmarks' of educational quality, and to justify that they have import for the nature of app content, we looked for patterns in the prevalence of other app features based on whether or not an app's description mentioned at least one of the benchmarks. The results indicated that incorporating these benchmarks may indeed have important consequences for the information available to parents and educators before downloading an app (i.e., in app descriptions). As shown in Figure 4.6, when at least one of these benchmarks was mentioned in an app's description, that app was somewhat more likely to also mention a specific target age range for child users. More apps with benchmarks than without claimed to target phonemic awareness and sight words, and to use reading aloud and puzzles/games/quizzes as teaching strategies. In addition, descriptions of apps that mentioned at least one benchmark contained about 40 more words on average, compared with apps that did not mention any benchmarks (316 vs. 353 words), and also tended to get slightly higher consumer ratings in app stores (4.15 vs. 3.97 out of 5.0).[5]

There were also several differences in app content based on the presence of one or more benchmarks. When a description cited at least one benchmark, the app was more likely to contain adult-directed information about how to use the app (i.e., mechanics), to give details about the app's educational content, and to provide 'other' additional information about the app (see Figure 4.6). Finally, apps with at least one benchmark mentioned in the description were more likely than other apps to contain tutorials or lessons as activities.

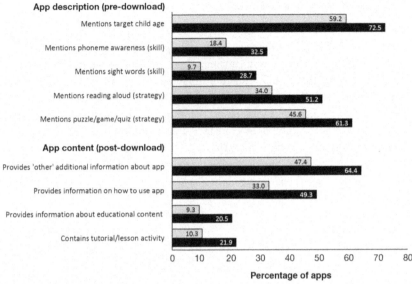

App description (pre-download)

Mentions target child age — 59.2 / 72.5

Mentions phoneme awareness (skill) — 18.4 / 32.5

Mentions sight words (skill) — 9.7 / 28.7

Mentions reading aloud (strategy) — 34.0 / 51.2

Mentions puzzle/game/quiz (strategy) — 45.6 / 61.3

App content (post-download)

Provides 'other' additional information about app — 47.4 / 64.4

Provides information on how to use app — 33.0 / 49.3

Provides information about educational content — 9.3 / 20.5

Contains tutorial/lesson activity — 10.3 / 21.9

Percentage of apps

☐ Has none of the three 'benchmarks' of educational quality
■ Has at least one 'benchmark' of educational quality

Age range $\chi^2(1,183) = 3.49$, $p < .06$; Phoneme $\chi^2(1, 170) = 4.80$, $p < .05$; Sight words $\chi^2(1,170) = 11.05$, $p < .01$; Reading aloud $\chi^2(1,170) = 4.53$, $p < .05$; Puzzle/game/quiz $\chi^2(1, 170) = 4.40$, $p < .05$; Additional information content $\chi^2(1,170) = 4.84$, $p < .05$; How to use content $\chi^2(1,170) = 4.36$, $p < .05$; Educational content $\chi^2(1,170) = 4.36$, $p < .05$; Tutorial/lesson content $\chi^2(1,170) = 4.33$, $p < .05$.

FIGURE 4.6 Differences in app descriptions and app content based on presence of benchmarks of educational quality in app description

Implications for parents and educators

These data suggest a landscape of language- and literacy-focused apps that is growing in size, yet still resembles the 'digital wild west' documented several years ago (Guernsey *et al.*, 2012; Shuler, 2012). While this study did not associate app qualities with actual use or learning outcomes, the patterns of findings indicate that choosing language and literacy apps for young children is a daunting task facing parents and educators. The lack of clear, consistent, and plentiful information about what's in the apps, who they are for, and how they were developed, precludes parents and educators from easily comparing apps and making informed decisions about what products would best fit the needs and interests of children at particular developmental stages. As such, parents and educators should consider incorporating the following suggestions when selecting and using these digital tools with young children.

Consult numerous sources and cross-check information

The apps in our sample had widely varying descriptions in terms of quantity and quality of information. Furthermore, completely different apps were found when searching the 'Top 50' educational lists in app stores, versus scouting expert-review sites. This suggests that parents and educators need to do some extra investigative work when choosing apps, by checking multiple sources for information about a given app. Parents and educators should consult producers' websites as well, as we found these websites sometimes contained information not found in app store descriptions. Beware of review sites that may have conflicts of interest that could bias reviews. Some services charge app producers for reviews or have strong relationships with media producers—these relationships should at least be disclosed clearly (Jussel, 2015).

Looking beyond the 'Top 50' apps is also advised; it is not clear how these lists are created and the apps on these lists seem to be disproportionately geared towards preschool and kindergarten audiences.

Look for signs of educational quality—but keep an open mind

We found that evidence of purposeful educational design, such as child development or education expertise on the development team and an underlying curriculum, was fairly rare within app descriptions. Also rare were mentions of app testing. Yet mentioning at least one of these benchmarks was associated with more and higher-quality adult-directed information, as well as slightly stronger user reviews. Parents and educators scouting for apps should be on the lookout for these benchmarks in app descriptions. A caveat is warranted, however, as it is possible that some producers do incorporate these purposeful design aspects without mentioning them in the app descriptions. Furthermore, it is feasible that many apps are of high quality although they do not incorporate these benchmarks. Scouting for the apps with the benchmarks would be a good place to start, but should not be the only factor to consider when deciding whether to download an app.

Co-use apps with children

Given the lack of plentiful and consistent adult-directed information about apps, parents and educators should strive to frequently co-use the apps they do choose with children. This may be the best way to learn about the educational goals and value of a given app, and to determine whether it is appropriate and engaging for a particular child. Additionally, prior research and theory suggest that jointly engaging in media use with a caregiver can boost children's learning from the experience. Co-use can signal to a child that the app is a learning tool, while also enabling the adult to scaffold the child's use and learning from the app (Takeuchi and Stevens, 2011).

Notes

1. Only 170 apps (of the full sample of 183) were available for download during the second coding phase.
2. For greater detail regarding study methods see Vaala *et al.* (2015). The coding scheme was developed based on earlier research by the Joan Ganz Cooney Center (Shuler, 2012) as well as a prior content analysis of baby DVDs conducted by Vaala and colleagues (Vaala *et al.*, 2010).
3. Unfortunately, it was too difficult to distinguish between these three similar forms of activities reliably. Thus, they were combined in one coding category. For example, at times an educational content quiz came in the form of a puzzle. Or it was difficult to distinguish whether an activity was a game or a quiz.
4. Some apps may have had more than one 'other interactive activity,' but we were unable to tally them given these were coded as one category (i.e., apps were given a '1' for having at least one such activity).
5. Number of words: $t(79) = 1.71, p < .10$; User rating $t(171) = 2.73, p < .05$.

References

Anderson, D.R. (1998). Educational television is not an oxymoron. *Annals of the American Academy of Political and Social Science, 557,* 24–38.

Anderson, D.R., Huston, A.C., Schmitt, K.L., Linebarger, D.L. and Wright, J.C. (2001). Early childhood television viewing and adolescent behavior: The re-contact study. *Monographs of the Society for Research in Child Development, 264*(66), 1.

Duncan, G.J., Dowsett, C.J., Claessens, A., Magnuson, K., Huston, A.C., Klebanov, P., Pagani, L.S., Feinstein, L., Engel, M., Brooks-Gunn, J., Sexton, H., Duckworth, K. and Japel, C. (2007). School readiness and later achievement. *Developmental Psychology, 43*(6), 1428–1446.

Falloon, G. (2013). Young students using iPads: App design and content influences on their learning pathways. *Computers & Education, 68,* 505–521.

Farkas, G. and Beron, K. (2004). The detailed age trajectory of oral vocabulary knowledge: Differences by class and race. *Social Science Research, 33,* 464–497.

Fisch, S.M., and Truglio, R.T. (2000). *G is for Growing: 30 years of research on Sesame Street.* New York: Lea's Communications Series.

Flewitt, R., Messer, D. and Kucirkova, N. (2014). New directions for early literacy in a digital age: The iPad. *Journal of Early Childhood Literacy, 15*(3), 289–310.

GSMA (2013). Children's use of mobile phones: An international comparison 2012. Published online by GSMA and NTT DOCOMO. Available at: www.gsma.com/publicpolicy/wpcontent/uploads/2012/03/GSMA_ChildrensMobilePhones2012 WEB.pdf

Guernsey, L. and Levine, M.H. (2015). *Tap, Click, Read: Growing readers in a world of screens.* San Francisco, CA: Jossey-Bass.

Guernsey, L., Levine, M., Chiong, C. and Severns, M. (2012). *Pioneering Literacy in the Digital Wild West: Empowering parents and educators.* New York, NY: Joan Ganz Cooney Center.

Jussel, A. (2015, August 4). Children's app reviews: Does money talk? [Blog post] ShapingYouth.org. Available at: www.shapingyouth.org/childrens-app-reviews-money-talks/

O'Hare, E. (2014). *Mobile Apps for Children: Criteria and categorization.* Research report for Cinekid.

MijnKindOnline (2013, April). Iene Miene Media, een onderzoek naar het mediagebruik door kleine kinderen, van 0 t/m 7 jaar. Commissioned by Mediawijzer.

Rideout, V.J. (2011). *Zero to Eight: Children's media use in America*. A Common Sense Media Research Study. San Francisco, CA: Common Sense Media.

Rideout, V.J. (2014, January). *Learning at Home: Families' educational media use in America*. A report of the Families and Media Project. New York: Joan Ganz Cooney Center at Sesame Workshop.

Shuler, C. (2012). *iLearn II: An analysis of the education category of the iTunes app store*. New York: Joan Ganz Cooney Center at Sesame Workshop.

Takeuchi, L. and Stevens, R. (2011, December). *The New Coviewing: Designing for learning through joint media engagement*. New York: Joan Ganz Cooney Center at Sesame Workshop.

Vaala, S. E., Linebarger, D. L., Fenstermacher, S. K., Tedone, A., Brey, E., Barr, R. Mosses, A. C. Shwery and Calvert, S. L. (2010). Content analysis of language-promoting teaching strategies used in infant-directed media. *Infant and Child Development, 19*(6), 628–648.

Vaala, S.E., Ly, A., and Levine, M. (2015, December). *Getting a Read on the App Store: A market scan and analysis of children's literacy apps*. New York, NY: Joan Ganz Cooney Center.

Wright, J.C., Huston, A.C., Murphy, K.C., St. Peters, M., Pinon, M., Scantlin, R. and Kotler, J. (2001). The relations of early television viewing to school readiness and vocabulary of children from low-income families: The early window project. *Child Development, 72*(5), 1347–1366.

5

TEACHING AND LEARNING WITH TABLETS

A case study of twenty-first-century skills and new learning

Nicola Yelland

COLLEGE OF EDUCATION, VICTORIA UNIVERSITY, MELBOURNE, AUSTRALIA

The case study presented in this chapter focuses on the twenty-first-century skills of *creativity, critical thinking, collaborations* and *communications* (Partnerships for the 21st century, 2008; Trilling and Fadel, 2009). They are encountered in contexts that require learners to recognise that their futures involve them being effective *citizens* with a good *character*. The examples of new learning documented here illustrate the ways in which the teachers designed learning experiences to encourage the acquisition and use of twenty-first-century skills. They achieved this in collaborative contexts characterised by whole class, small group and individual activities and shared outcomes and strategies with both peers and teachers. The findings from the case study revealed the enthusiasm of the teachers for the use of new technologies in their classroom, and the support of the principals who provided the essential positive leadership that encouraged changes to practice.

Keywords: Citizenship, twenty-first-century, multimodal, creativity, critical, thinking, collaboration

Introduction

Living in the twenty-first-century requires a regular recalibration of skills and knowledge as a result of innovations that seem to constantly appear in our lives (Yelland, 2007). Technology enables and urges us to reconsider the ways in which we engage in everyday activities. There have been calls for a refocusing of curricula away from *content* to the acquisition of *twenty-first-century skills* (e.g. Partnerships for the 21st century, 2008), which have been extended from the original four: *creativity, critical thinking, collaborating* and *communicating* (Trilling and Fadel, 2009), to include *citizenship* and *character education* (Fullan, 2012). Further, it is also recognised that fluency with new technologies will be an essential component of future employ-ment across the range of opportunities (Cuban, 2001).

Fullan (2013) maintained that the process of *disruptive innovation* (Christensen, 1997) with new technologies in education has already begun. As new technologies evolve to become more mobile and flexible to support the acquisition and application of twenty-first-century skills, the need for reconceptualising schooling, teaching and learning has become an imperative for all those interested in making education relevant to future global citizens. In Australia, it began in 2001 with the concept of *new learning* (Australian Council of Deans of Education, 2001) and it has advanced to encapsulate new ways of thinking about diversity and personalising learning, cultivating deep learning and designing learning experiences that are authentic and support knowledge building in globalised contexts (Kalantzis and Cope, 2012). In this context, pedagogies are viewed as knowledge processes (Yelland *et al.*, 2008). This perspective involves designing learning activities that incorporate opportunities for *experiencing* (the known and the new), *conceptualising* (by naming and theorising), *analysing* (functionally and critically) and *applying* (appropriately and creatively) so that learning occurs in contexts where learners are connected to ideas and engaged in action. It resonates with a view of personalising learning that many believe should characterise the schooling experience in the twenty-first-century (e.g. Robinson, 2009; Zhao, 2014).

Fullan (2012, 2013) and Fullan and Langworthy (2014) regarded technology as one of three *big ideas* in education, together with *pedagogy* and *change knowledge*. They contended that it is technology that enables new learning and the use of transformative pedagogies, and that technology incorporates *change knowledge*, since we need to know 'what we should do with all this information to change things, presumably for the better' (Fullan, 2013, p. 1). He suggested four criteria for integrating technology and pedagogy that he argued would result in exciting and innovative learning for all students. They are that the technology needs to be easy to use, available when needed, engaging for both students and teachers and authentic. Fullan (2013) maintained that this alignment is fundamental since 'technology and schooling are operating at cross purposes and have been doing so for some time' (p. 40). Fullan and Langworthy's (2014) *new pedagogies for deep learning* incorporate giving students voice in their learning via project-based inquiries, includes direct instruction where appropriate, and involves teachers and students in planning learning experiences that are both face to face and digitally mediated, thus creating blended learning contexts. Deep learning is aligned with the full range of twenty-first-century skills and takes place in the context of curriculum frameworks that support their acquisition, use and application in authentic contexts.

This type of new learning (Kalantzis and Cope, 2012) can only occur when sustained by effective leaders who support the change process. Effective leaders also provide the enablers, which not only includes the provision of new technologies but also other infrastructure components, policy and professional learning opportunities to support a radical new approach to teaching and learning in schools. They support the implementation of new ideas and practices and are responsible for confirming that the new practices are having the desired effect. At the core of this process is the desire that learners of the twenty-first-century will be lifelong and life-wide learners. That is, that they will be engaged in learning throughout their life span across diverse educational and community contexts. Schools are just one site in a range of learning environments. Learning partnerships will evolve that support citizens to maintain their learning role beyond schools, and provide contexts for students to not only generate new knowledge, but also communicate it to global audiences.

The role of new technologies in these contemporary views of teaching and learning is thus fundamental. The introduction of the iPhone in 2007 and the iPad in 2010, made a significant impact on the availability, ease of use and relevance of new technologies in educational contexts. They were the first examples of what are now called the 'smart' technologies. Both the phones and the tablets introduced us to new types of portable devices, with techniques that generated new actions and added new words to our vocabulary, like 'swiping'. They also reduced the cost of devices and thereby increased access to new technologies for a broader cohort of the population. The ease with which very young children could 'swipe', select and initiate activity on the iPhone and iPad made them very popular and accessible to a much wider age range of young children. The impact on schooling took a bit longer. At the end of 2012 there was scant research literature on the use and impact of the touch technologies on teaching and learning. Now three years on there are more, which focus on early *literacy* (e.g. Flewitt *et al.*, 2014; Merchant, 2015; Lynch and Redpath, 2014), *pedagogy* (e.g. how teachers might use the iPad in your program, e.g. Yelland, 2015; Yelland and Gilbert 2013a, 2014) and how the devices represent opportunities for *multimodal* learning (Yelland, 2015; Yelland, Diezmann and Butler, 2014; Yelland and Gilbert, 2013b). What is apparent is that the iPad has been a game changer due primarily to its mobility, cost and ease of use. Many primary schools have introduced schemes for families to lease, or own, devices (commonly called bring your own devices or BYOD, see Chapter 14) for their children to use in and out of school. For the first time, schools have been infused with new technologies in large numbers so as to raise the level of potential for them to make a difference to teaching and learning scenarios.

Yet, the research literature reveals that, for example, in schools, print literacies are still privileged while many children experience digital literacies in their world outside of schools (Carrington and Robinson, 2009; Flewitt *et al.*, 2014). Flewitt *et al.* (2014) indicated that teachers have reported that a curriculum in which literacy is primarily paper based combined with a lack of time to explore the impact of new technologies on digital literacy, and low confidence with educational uses of technologies, all contribute to this situation being perpetuated, so that:

> the potential of new technologies for young children's literacy development remains largely untapped in educational settings, with a 'digital divide' such that some children develop considerable digital skills and knowledge by partic-

ipating in supported activities at home, whilst others have little or no opportunity to engage with new media at home and even less so in education.

(p. 3)

It is apparent that research that documents the ways in which these new 'smart' technologies represent contexts for new learning in multiliteracies (New London Group, 1996) and for reconceptualising curriculum and pedagogies to align with twenty-first-century skills and deep learning is important.

I have contended (e.g., Yelland, 2007) that what makes learning different in the twenty-first-century are the many and varied opportunities for multimodal learning. Young children are able to build their understandings about concepts using a variety of diverse materials in different formats. For example, they can play in both a 'real' sandpit and an electronic sandpit on screen. Their experiences with popular culture figures such as *Elmo* (Sesame Street) and *Dora the Explorer,* occur via televisions and other screens, and with three-dimensional dolls, puzzles, books and on stage in theatres. This means that they have opportunities to develop understandings about the characters in myriad contexts from a variety of perspectives, and learn from each one of them. New technologies facilitate the exploration of ideas, creativity and the application of knowledge in new and dynamic ways. They connect students with authentic audiences, which they hitherto had no access to. They facilitate the use of twenty-first-century skills to enable deep learning that will support them long after students leave school.

Research design

The case study presented here was part of a larger research project that took place in three Victorian schools, in three different year levels (*Kindergarten,* 4- to 5-year olds; *Year 2,* 7- to 8-year-olds; *Years 7/8,* 13- to 14-year-olds). The Education Department and Microsoft supported the teachers and students, with the provision of Microsoft's Surface Pro II tablets and professional learning opportunities to encourage them to put the new pedagogies into action to promote deep learning using new technologies.

All the case studies were designed to explore the potential of the new technology and document the innovative ways in which tablet technologies could be integrated into the three levels of schooling. Each case study consists of learning scenarios that exemplify the twenty-first-century skills of *creativity, critical thinking, collaboration* and *communication* in the context of new learning and becoming global citizens. In practice, the skills are not encountered in isolation, but rather they are interrelated and complement each other. However, for the purpose of clarity the findings are organised, presented and discussed next under these headings, and connections and relationships between the skills are noted. The examples have been selected because they illustrate the specific types of skills outlined, for the purpose of discussion.

A goal of the project was to document and consider the ways in which tablet technologies could be incorporated into classrooms to promote twenty-first-century learning. This was achieved via participant observation and interactions with teachers and children in their classrooms. Participant observation can be defined as a method in which 'the researcher is taking part, to some degree, in the activities of the people being observed' (Deacon *et al.*, 1999, p. 251). The aim of participant observation is to gain access to everyday practices, which are difficult to describe or reproduce in group discussion or interview (Mikos, cited in Struppert, 2011). Through participation in the context, the researcher can achieve a better understanding of the practice, roles and cultural patterns of the participants (Mikos, cited in Struppert, 2011). Field notes were made while the teacher and class were being observed and then combined with post-observation reflections of the learning scenarios, when the researcher was interacting with the children. The notes and reflections were combined to create a narrative supported with screenshots and samples of the children's work. Data were analysed by coding the learning scenarios to the twenty-first-century skills as a thematic analysis.

The context

The school is in a large country town in the State of Victoria, Australia. It has specialist facilities that include a gym and music and art rooms and had recently constructed a new building that contained purpose-built classrooms for Years 2 and 3. The school had 585 students. There were 77 children in Year 2 with an average age of 7 years 11 months, and a range from 7 years 2 months to 9 years 2 months. There were five Surface Pro II tablets in each of the three Year 2 classrooms. The availability and portability of the Surface Pros meant that the teachers and students could access the tablets when needed. This meant that they could be used in small group rotations and collaborations, for literacy, numeracy and project-based investigative work. The topic of Living Things was being explored during the case study observation periods. The teachers used an inquiry approach in order to explore the issues inherent to the topic, and this resulted in some exciting and vibrant class time populated by children who thrived on challenges and used the tablets enthusiastically.

Findings

As discussed above, the findings describe learning scenarios that are presented under the twenty-first-century skill headings. They represent exemplars that were observed via the participant observer methodology. It was apparent that many more examples could have been included, but these are presented here as being representative examples of the type of learning that was observed in the classrooms.

Creativity

The creative examples provided here are located in story making (narrative) and art. In the first learning scenario of creative writing, the children were required to create narratives using a randomly chosen character, complication and setting. The children planned their narrative and then completed a first draft by hand, which they read to the teacher. They then typed the final draft using the tablet, via the keyboard. The mobility of the Surface Pro and its ready availability made this a seamless process for both the teacher and learner. Seanna wrote about a Superhero Granny:

> *Superhero granny was zooming through the air. Suddenly she heard a "meow, meow, meow". A kitten is stuck somewhere. "I must find that kitten" she said. She eventually found him.*
>
> *"Oh no. Now I am late for netball".*
>
> *"Wait, netball? I meant to say football. Anyway let's go". She went through her fantastic, golden handbag looking for something.*
>
> *"Ah, I've found it, my purple skateboard. Now let's hurry up!"*
>
> *When she got there the crowd was ROARING! Granny kicked the most ENORMOUS goal. She started to feel sick "I think I'm feeling sick because I'm too hot. I will go home and have a rest then I will feel better".*
>
> *So she went home and had a rest. A few minutes later she felt better. "Hooray. I feel better so now I can go and play football."*
>
> *Seanna*

THE END

In a more extensive example, which took place over a period of a week, the children worked in small groups to create e-books for which they used their own hand-drawn illustrations (some were drawn in an app called *Fresh Paint*), and photographs and graphics derived from the Internet. In their investigations of Living Things they were examining life cycles, and based on the information they collected, designed and produced the e-books in groups of up to four children. The children decided which apps they wanted to use and what to say, and then worked together to summarise what they had learnt about life cycles (Figure 5.1). The range and scope of the books were rich and varied, as were the different approaches in the production of the e-books.

Again, the experiences provided the children with the opportunity to reflect on different modalities that they could engage with for their work, and then select the one that they thought was most appropriate to tell their story. In terms of becoming digitally literate, the use of the tablets enabled them to create texts that were both linguistic and oral in content, and also to mix the two elements in dynamic ways that would not have been possible without the technologies. The design process engaged them in the creative process, as well as requiring them to negotiate with peers in the small group contexts. There was a great deal of talk at the planning phase and throughout the writing phase about what information was to be included, as well as discussions and decisions about the format and presentation of the books.

a)

b)
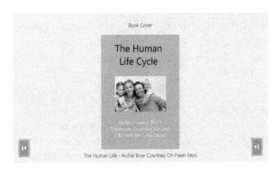

c)

d)

FIGURE 5.1 Year 2 e-books on life cycles (a, b, c, d)

Critical thinking

The Year 2 teachers worked collaboratively to foster the acquisition of literacy and numeracy skills in the context of authentic activity and via investigative explorations that encouraged both creativity and critical thinking. There was an interesting mix of using the Surface Pros, as well as traditional resources (e.g. books, pencils, paints) so that the children could document their thinking for later discussions and reflections on the particular concept under discussion. This was only possible because the tablet was mobile and easy to use. This was evident in many instances, but four examples show how it worked effectively. In the first example the children were using a 100 square and counters to count in threes.

They counted out loud in threes as they placed the counters on the square (Figure 5.2). Then the teacher asked the children what they noticed about the pattern that was created. The children made various responses that the teacher noted. These included:

- They make diagonal lines in a pattern.
- The lines go from short to long and then short again.
- The numbers go 3, 6, 12 this way and 8, 4, 2 that way so that the number is halved each time.

They took a photo of the pattern and two boys imported it into an app called *Explain Everything*, which allowed them to record and summarise their thinking for subsequent discussions.

In the second example, the children built Plasticine boats after listening to Pamela Allen's *Who Sank the Boat?* They then took a photo, and again, using *Explain Everything,* predicted how many paper clips the boat could hold until it sank. They had to record their prediction and then conduct an experiment to test their estimations, to see how close they were. This information was collated in a table and discussions were held to try to figure out reasons why some boats could hold more clips than others. Each group came up with some suggestions and generalisations were made and presented to the whole class.

In the third example, the children were studying push and pull factors and were required to predict how far a toy vehicle could travel when pushed. They used the video facility on the tablet to record their estimates in their small group and then found out who was the closest, as well as discussing the reasons why some pushes were more successful than others.

In the final example the children were studying arrays as an introductory activity to the concept of multiplication (Figure 5.3). They made various arrays and took photos of a range of them. Again they imported the photo into *Explain Everything* and recorded their thinking – bringing it to the surface and saving it for further discussion at a later date when it could then be linked to new learning. These opportunities for enabling discussion were referred to as 'surfacing your thinking' in our interactions.

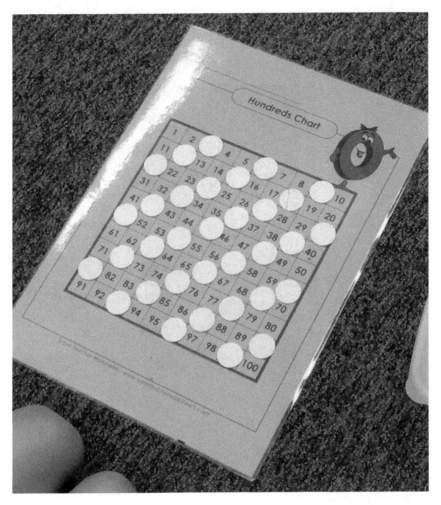

FIGURE 5.2 Counting in threes

In addition, the use of the tablet also enabled the children to engage in 'inking their thinking' where the pen was the primary way in which the students articulated and recorded their deliberations, investigations and findings. Again the results of this work were learning outcomes that not only reflected *what* they had learnt, but also *how* they had achieved it.

As previously stated there was a focus on Living Things (AUSVELS; Science as Human Endeavour) as a topic, but the teachers were flexible and innovative in the range of investigations that could be included under this broad heading. The scope of topics included:

- life cycles;
- living in poverty, use of water and disasters;

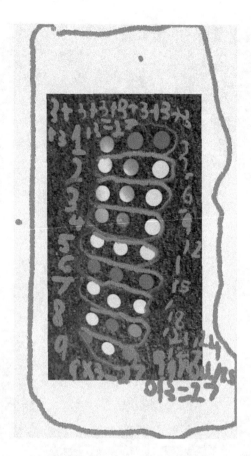

FIGURE 5.3 Mathematical arrays for counting in threes

- recycling and pollution; and
- objects that we use.

The e-books described in the previous section not only encouraged the children to be creative, but also enabled them to embark on investigations that required them to find data and synthesise it effectively for an audience, in a meaningful and appropriate format.

When studying *Building Empathy* the children in one class watched a five-minute video that the teacher had selected from YouTube in a series called *Living on one dollar a day.*[1] Episode 4 was entitled *Disaster Strikes,*[2] and told the story of what happened to a family of farmers in Guatemala when their crop was washed away in a deluge of rain. This acted as a catalyst to introduce other types of natural disasters and there was discussion of an earthquake in Haiti. One of the three activities that the children then embarked on was to use the tablets to find Haiti, locate its neighbours on the map and then search the Internet for information about the earthquake. The children found the maps and Haiti and saved this information to their files. They searched for information about the devastation caused by the earthquake and discussed it in their small groups. They then inserted a screenshot of the map into *Explain Everything* and used the stylus to indicate that an earthquake occurred in Haiti in 2010 (Figure 5.4).

In exploring the topic of recycling, another group of children collated the types of items that they recycle in their family (Figure 5.5). This was followed by a class discussion on what item you recycle most in your family, and selecting the top item. This information was collated in a graph (Figure 5.6) using *Explain Everything*, and each child wrote a sentence about what they observed from the data on the graph. Two boys recorded their observations in the app and then shared it with the group. They noted:

- The top two items that were recycled were bottles and cans (with six people each).
- Four people recycled small packages and three recycled large cardboard boxes.
- Two people recycled water.
- And five indicated that they don't recycle at all (added to this final comment was 'What a pity!')

The graph was not only an example of the use of numbers in a relevant context, but it also provided a context in which the children could use the operations to figure out the solution to addition problems, e.g. 'There are 26 people in our class including our teacher!' and also the difference between numbers, e.g. '12 people recycle bottles and cans, 2 recycle water – so that means 10 more people recycle bottles and cans.'

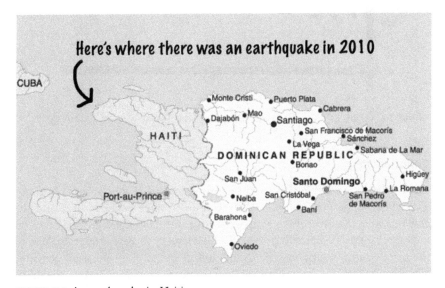

FIGURE 5.4 An earthquake in Haiti

FIGURE 5.5 Things we can do to save our planet (Maisie)

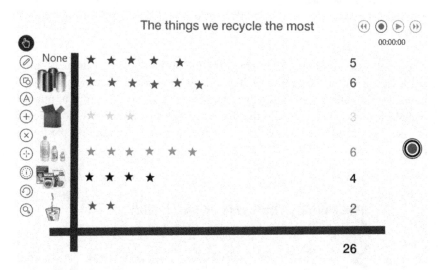

FIGURE 5.6 Graph of the most frequent form of recycling items

Collaboration

The teachers used whole class, small group and individual approaches to learning. The tablets supported teaching and learning in all three contexts. By Year 2 the children were used to collaborating on tasks and the examples provided thus far indicate that they completed these with a high level of success – for example, with the production of collaborative e-books and in the *Explain Everything* activities. The teachers said that they valued the opportunity to provide contexts for building collaborative skills between the children:

the collaborative work on one tablet has been good for lots of reasons ... they've had to learn to share and take turns. On top of that they've actually improved. They've had to learn to take on roles within a group. I've sort of appointed a captain who then made sure that everybody got a turn, so there have been responsibilities that have come out of it as well. (I said to the captain) you're responsible for making sure that everybody in the group gets a turn. And they're quite happy to do that.

(Teacher 2)

This process was facilitated by using the pen, as opposed to typing the detailed information. Creating and placing the text in an appropriate location around a visual stimulus was made easier, and the personal aspect of having the details written by hand made the final product more personal and individualised.

Communication

All three Year 2 teachers indicated that they valued the acquisition of foundational literacy and numeracy skills and encouraged an investigative approach to concepts and topics. As part of this process, time was always made to share information and findings with the whole class, and also at the lower primary assemblies (Years Prep to 3). The children could do this via the whiteboard and projector, and also directly from the tablet for smaller groups. Sharing and communicating findings in these contexts provided valuable opportunities to learn about skills and processes from peers and teachers. It was also evident that the children's knowledge base (e.g., Haiti earthquake) was broadened, with the additional information that had been discovered and recorded in writing by the various members of the class, either individually or in groups. This was summarised by Teacher 2:

We've been using *Explain Everything* ... where the kids have been able to draw on their screen and articulate their thinking verbally, by recording their voice in the program as well ... we share that as a class ... so that's been an interesting exercise...the kids love the pens and being able to write on the screen. That's been good.

Prior to the use of the tablets, all teachers indicated that the children spent part of their 'work' time sharing their strategies as well as the products of their learning experiences. What was different, they said, was that with the tablets, they were able to explain and show the various stages of their thinking with the use of the camera and screen capture facility. This meant that they were able to deconstruct their experience into the component parts as well as present it as a final product. The teachers thought that this was a much deeper level of understanding of the process of learning in the various tasks than they were able to achieve without the technology. In this way, using the technology not only enhanced the final product but also facilitated their reflections on their own learning.

Summary

The examples provided here illustrate the ways in which the use of tablets in this Year 2 classroom afforded the opportunity for the children to gain proficiency in literacy and numeracy in applied contexts, and supported an investigative approach to learning. I have advocated that 'we should not be mapping the use of new technologies onto old curricula, we need to rethink our curriculum and pedagogies in light of the impact that we know that new technologies can have on learning and meaning making in contemporary times' (Yelland, 2007, pp. 1–2). In the 30 years or so since 'microcomputers' were first used in education, we are still only 'tinkering' with curriculum change. Yet, innovative pockets of teachers have been brave enough to explore new ways of working with children in classrooms that incorporate new technologies to challenge traditional notions of teaching and learning. They have achieved this by encouraging greater learner responsibility utilising pedagogies that encourage the use of critical thinking, creativity, collaboration and communicating new knowledge to authentic audiences, both locally and globally. They teach mandated curriculum content using more democratic pedagogies and provide opportunities for children to negotiate their own learning, and with whom they work. They open up possibilities with topics and projects as 'springboards-to-action'. The use of new technologies as part of this process thus becomes natural in terms of the contemporary resources available to them.

In the learning scenarios provided here, the teachers did not just use the tablets as a substitute for paper and pencils or investigations and presentations. They planned as a team, to consider how they might design new learning experiences that would take full advantage of the affordances of the tablets. They did this within the structure of mandated curriculum, and succeeded in demonstrating that their children achieved the required learning outcomes. However, they also went beyond these parameters. They were aware of twenty-first-century learning skills and the idea of deep learning. They deliberately planned to create learning contexts in which the children could experience and practise their use of these skills. Having tablets facilitated this process because it enabled the teachers and children to think of different ways to explore and represent their findings, and share their discoveries. It extended their range of possibilities and encouraged them to reach a consensus about how to proceed with an investigation, and how to present their final product. The learning experiences engaged the children in multimodal learning that incorporated visual with oral, kinaesthetic and aural elements, and thus are much richer than if they were simply completed with pen and paper without any of the other modalities. This is twenty-first-century learning at its most effective.

Notes

1. *Living on one dollar a day* (www.youtube.com/watch?v=Ze72rpWp_Dg)
2. *Disaster Strikes* (www.youtube.com/watch?v=bk9GL1AnMLM)

References

Australian Council of Deans of Education. (2001). *New Learning: A charter for Australian Education*. Available at: www.acde.edu.au

Carrington, V. and Robinson, M. (eds) (2009). *Digital Literacies: Social learning and cultural practices*. Thousand Oaks, CA: SAGE.

Christensen, C. M. (1997). *The Innovator's Dilemma*. Cambridge, MA: Harvard Business School.

Cuban, L. (2001). *Oversold and Underused: Computers in the classroom*. Cambridge, MA: Harvard University Press.

Deacon, D., Pickering, M., Golding, P. and Murdock, G. (1999). *Research Communications: A practical guide to methods in media and cultural analysis*. New York, NY: Oxford University Press.

Flewitt, R., Messer, D. and Kucirkova, N. (2014). New directions for early literacy. *Journal of Early Childhood Literacy*. DOI: 10.1177/1468798414533560.

Fullan, M. (2012). *Great to Excellent: Launching the next stage of Ontario's education agenda*. Toronto: OISE.

Fullan, M. (2013). *Stratosphere: Integrating technology, pedagogy and change knowledge*. Toronto, Canada: Pearson.

Fullan, M. and Langworthy, M. (2014). *A Rich Seam: How new pedagogies find deep learning*. London: Pearson.

Kalantzis, M. and Cope, W. W. (2012). *New Learning: Elements of a science of education* (2nd edn.). Melbourne: Cambridge University Press.

Lynch, J. and Redpath, T. (2014). 'Smart' technologies in early years literacy education: A meta-narrative of paradigmatic tensions in iPad use in an Australian preparatory classroom. *Journal of Early Childhood literacy, 14*(2), 147–174.

Merchant, G. (2015). Keep taking the tablets: iPads, story apps and early literacy. *Australian Journal of Language and Literacy, 38*(1), 3–11.

New London Group. (1996). A pedagogy of multiliteracies. *Harvard Educational Review, 60*(1), 66–92.

Partnerships for the 21st century. (2008). *21st Century Skills, Education and Competitiveness: A resource and policy guide*. Washington, DC: The Partnership for 21st Century Skills.

Robinson, K. (2009). *The element*. New York: Viking.

Struppert, A. (2011). *Developing Intercultural Awareness and Sensitivity through Digital Game Play*. Macquarie University, East Ryde.

Trilling, B. and Fadel, C. (2009). *21st Century Skills: Learning for life in our times*. San Francisco, CA: Jossey-Bass.

Yelland, N. J. (2007). *Shift to the Future: Rethinking learning with new technologies in education*. New York: Routledge.

Yelland, N. J. (2015). Young children as multimodal learners in the Information age. In: M. Renck Jalongo and K. L. Heider (eds), *Young Children and Families in the Information Age: Applications of technology in early childhood*. (pp. 151–163). Dordrecht, Netherlands: Springer.

Yelland, N. J. and Gilbert, C. L. (2014). SmartStart: Creating new contexts for learning in the 21st century. Research report presented to IBM. Available at: www.ipadsforeducation. vic.edu.au/userfiles/files/226543%20Vic%20Uni%20IBM%20Report%20Smart%20 Start%202.pdf

Yelland, N. J. and Gilbert, C. L. (2013a). iPlay, iLearn, iGrow. Research report presented to IBM. Available at: www.ipadsforeducation.vic.edu.au/userfiles/files/IBM%20Report% 20iPlay,%20iLearn%20%26%20iGrow.pdf

Yelland, N. J. and Gilbert, C. L. (2013b). iPossibilities: Tablets in early childhood contexts. *Hong Kong Journal of Early Childhood, 12*(1), 5–14.

Yelland, N. J., Cope, W. and Kalantzis, M. (2008). Learning by design: Creating pedagogical frameworks for knowledge building in the 21st century (Special Invited Issue). *Asia Pacific Journal of Teacher Education, 36*(3), 197–213.

Yelland, N. J., Butler, D. and Diezmann, C. (2014). *Early Mathematical Explorations* (2nd edn.). Melbourne: Cambridge University Press.

Zhao, Y. (2014). *Who's Afraid of the Big Bad Dragon?* San Francisco, CA: Jossey Bass.

6

APP MAPS

Evaluating children's iPad software for twenty-first-century literacy learning

Karen E. Wohlwend and Jennifer Rowsell

SCHOOL OF EDUCATION, INDIANA UNIVERSITY, BLOOMINGTON, INDIANA, US AND FACULTY OF EDUCATION, BROCK UNIVERSITY, CANADA

In this chapter, we introduce a rubric and a map that we developed for comparing early childhood apps on five dimensions of participatory literacies: multiplayer, productive, multimodal, multilinear, and connected. Using exemplar data from our North American classroom studies on children's technology play with iPads, we evaluate and compare four apps to illustrate how the rubric and map can be used to assess each app's potential for developing participatory literacies. A description of each app and an ethnographic data excerpt illustrate how children used each app's features to provide a sampling of the ways that young children actually engaged with the app during classroom play.

Keywords: Participatory literacies, evaluating, multimodal, app mapping, collaboration

Introduction

Three-fourths of U.S. families with young children now have mobile devices such as smartphones or tablets (Rideout, 2013). These accessible digital tools are equipped with touchscreens that respond instantly to a fingertip swipe and are just the right size for young children to handle, carry, and operate. For example, a toddler with a tablet balanced on her lap is learning that the touchscreen is organized by a grid of colorful squarish icons that represent software applications, and importantly with little or no print. Each icon opens an app at the touch of a finger and reading involves more taps … on arrows, 'x', checkmark, trashcan, pencil, plus signs, and so on. These icons are not arranged in the orderly rows of print on a page but are scattered along the top, bottom, or corners of the screen. Touchscreens operate with an expanded set of conventions for interactive modes including finger swipes, icon recognition, and voice controls; in other words 'Concepts Beyond Print' (Wohlwend, 2016). Today's young children are learning printless ways of reading—one finger swipe at a time (Rowsell, 2014). With each tap, our emergent readers are learning interactive and flexible orientations to digital reading: recognizing icons as activators or portals, expecting a finger action to produce a screen change, and persisting when nothing happens, knowing that an area of the screen might contain an invisible icon that may appear when pressed. Furthermore, children understand that screens require new ways of playing, collaborating, and sharing in order to participate in our global digital cultures. Accordingly, in order to be truly educational, the tools we select and provide to children—including apps and tablets—must evolve to recognize all that children already know.

However, the educational apps for the early childhood market tend to rely on an outdated and print-centric model of literacy, apparent in the abundance of apps featuring rote memory tasks such as letter-sound matching or word identification (Shuler, 2012; Vaala, Chapter 4 in this Volume). Knobel and Wilber (2009) identified such an approach as 'Literacy 1.0', a print literacy model that grossly underestimates both the young child's and the technologies' capabilities for meaningful literacy learning, while 'Literacy 2.0' reflects participatory literacies, the new ways we read, write, play, and share ideas using icons, photos, and videos on social media networks. In this chapter, we introduce a way to evaluate the learning potential of apps using a rubric that captures the ways that twenty-first-century learners actually engage in participatory and digital literacies.

Background: New literacies and connected learning

Participatory literacies reflect new ways of thinking about learning to read and write with technology that moves away from the model of an individual reading or typing print on a computer screen (Table 6.1). Instead, participatory literacies reflect the principles of social media like Twitter, YouTube, or Facebook or video games and virtual worlds: global participation, multiplayer collaboration, and distributed knowledge. These principles enable participation in vast digital

TABLE 6.1 Comparing print literacy and participatory literacies

Print literacy	Participatory literacies
Individual reader/writer	Multiple players/designers
Interpreting and crafting	Negotiating and producing
An original and personally meaningful narrative text	Multimodal and mutually engaging interactive contexts
Mediated by peers and teachers in a predictable process	Maintained by groups in fluid multilinear navigation
Located within supportive reading/ writing workshops	Connected to participatory cultures, online networks, and maker playshops

networks through posting, blogging, recording, remixing, uploading, and downloading.

Even very young children play and use participatory literacy practices as they engage the world around them, that is, the literacy practices that have the most relevance for young children today are participatory (Wohlwend, 2010). In this chapter, we examine popular apps designed for young children to compare their usefulness for developing five dimensions of participatory literacies:

1. *Multiplayer or design teams* rather than individual.
2. *Productive*, enabling children to produce their own multimedia rather than simply reading or playing a game someone else has made.
3. *Multimodal* rather than print-centric, using multiple modes (sound, touch, image, music) to manage images, video, or animation.
4. *Multilinear*, using hypertext that allows multiple and dynamic storylines.
5. *Connected*, shared on digital networks.

The three studies

The first study, *Literacy Playshop: Playing with new literacies and popular media in the early childhood classroom* (Wohlwend *et al.*, 2013) is in the fifth year of an ongoing study of teacher-designed early childhood media literacy curriculum funded by the Proffitt Foundation and Indiana University. The studies are conducted at four sites: three multi-age preschool classrooms for 3- to 5-year-old children in university childcare centers (160 children; six teachers) and one kindergarten first-grade multi-age classroom for 5- to 7-year-old children in a public charter school (approximately 150 children; three teachers). Each Literacy Playshop project began with a year of practitioner inquiry sessions to read research on global children's media and critical literacies, to learn filmmaking techniques, and to develop age-appropriate media literacy curriculum. Wohlwend met twice a month with the teaching teams, video-recording the discussions about emerging curriculum for young children that combines collaboration, play, storying, and media production. Researchers visited each classroom two to four times per week during the second half of the year, as teachers implemented their curriculum to video-record classroom play and filmmaking activities and copy children's films and puppet shows. In these Literacy Playshops, children played elaborate stories as they made animation, puppetry, or live-action digital videos with hand-held cameras or tablets. In the following years, Wohlwend and colleagues conducted follow-up research at the sites, visiting at teachers' invitations in subsequent years to document how the teachers revised the Literacy Playshop curriculum over time to better fit their children's interests and school goals. These studies showed that the combination of young children's filmmaking with popular media and digital technologies produces a particularly powerful form of storytelling that sparks invention and collaboration among players. In literacy playshops, even very young children achieved and exceeded academic goals consistent with government accountability standards for literacy, by tapping into individual literacy proficiencies that were grounded in their popular media interests (Wohlwend et al., 2013).

For the second study, a research team (Harwood et al., 2013) conducted a federally funded research study entitled, *Crayons and iPads: Understanding young children's meaning-making processes in learning to be literate,* which focused on observations of the naturalistic experiences within five early years classrooms: two community-based early childhood education not-for-profit programs (for children 3–5 years old), and three full-day kindergarten school-based classrooms. The research team observed, documented, and assessed the ways in which young children constructed meaning within these varied social/cultural settings. Researchers visited each classroom bi-monthly for a seven-month period, observing before and after iPads were introduced into each learning context. The team then recorded 120 hours of classroom interactions, 2,000 photographs, 200 video recordings, and 500 sample artifacts from children. Seven teacher participants and co-researchers were involved in the observation phase of the project. Driven by a desire to capture the impact and social practices that ensued when iPads entered the early years space, the research team focused on children's everyday practices with traditional early years objects and artifacts, such as a sand table, coupled with participatory literacy practices, such as playing a sand table app. The researchers analyzed how the introduction of iPads across these different early years contexts shifted the classroom cultures. Researchers observed if there was a shift in children's interactions, positioning, and practices when iPads entered the classroom space and, if so, how did the culture, social practices, and space shift when they arrived? What was central to the research was capturing a tacit movement between virtual and physical spaces (Burnett, 2015; Burnett et al., 2014) and what these movements implied in terms of redefining or rethinking meaning making in the early years. To do so, the *Crayons and iPads* team documented such aspects of daily classroom life as: classroom cultures; teacher talk; children's meaning-making practices; daily routines; spatial arrangements; and their relationships to pedagogical approaches.

For the third research study, *Tutoring by Design*, Rowsell et al. (in progress) supervised a tutoring program every evening during the school year where teacher education students tutor children, adolescents, and teenagers in the community in literacy skills. One evening a week over nine months, the research team offered iPad tutoring sessions with a focus on participatory literacies pedagogy, featuring multimodal activities; multiplayer practices; and productive work that is multilinear and connected. Focusing on different apps, games, and iBooks (Rowsell, 2014), tutees worked closely with tutors on digital texts that they use significantly outside of school and documented practices, problem-solving, and thinking processes enacted over the course of tutoring sessions. Through fieldnotes, Rowsell's research team noted the particular nature of thinking through iPads, but also visualized the process, as seen in Figure 6.1. Data collection comprised observational fieldnotes taken during tutoring sessions whereby

Rowsell, Colquhoun, and Maues separately sat beside tutors as they worked with tutees over the course of an hour; interviews with tutees after the study; visual footage in the form of photographs and filmed footage; and a research blog to which all of the tutors and researchers contributed.

In Figure 6.1, we have added numbers to differentiate the hour of tutoring in what we think of as multimodal logic or modal learning (Rowsell, 2013), which connects strongly with participatory literacies. Starting in square 1, Peter and Calvin read about how swords are made on a website, then Calvin played with a game app called Minecraft while Peter researched an app called *Mythology* (square 3); then in the next two squares, Calvin and Peter read the Mythology app and concluded the hour in the last box with Calvin and Peter working on a writing piece about Minecraft and mythology..This figure illustrates how *Tutoring by Design* works. Researchers involved in the study focused on visualizing practices and interpreting haptic play to develop a language to describe competencies and thinking processes in participatory literacies. In addition, tutors and researchers contributed to a blog to share and reflect on the project.

Literacy apps and app maps

Our intent in the chapter has been to build on studies of app use by young children (Chiong and Shuler, 2010; Shuler, 2012) to recalibrate app evaluation tools for

An hour of Literacy 2.0 tutoring

FIGURE 6.1 Visualizing thinking with iPads

participatory literacies. In this section, we introduce a rubric and a map for comparing early childhood apps according to five elements of participatory literacies (Table 6.2). In the following sections, we feature four apps used in our classroom studies of early childhood technology to illustrate how the rubric and map can be used to assess the software's potential for participatory literacies. For each app, an app description and an excerpt of classroom play provide a sample of the ways that young children actually engaged with the four educational apps. We analyze these anecdotes according to the rubric and then compare the extent that each app supported key elements of participatory literacies: multimodal, multi-player, productive, multilinear, or connected. (We note here that apps change frequently with increased capabilities and features added or dropped without notice, so that the app maps and rubric scores reflect the data we gathered a year or more prior to publication, at the time each study was conducted.)

TABLE 6.2 Participatory literacies rubric and benchmarks

	High	*Medium*	*Low*
Multiplayer	Accommodates three or more players	Accommodates two players	Accommodates one player
Productive	Enables creative original content additions rather than pre-set components (e.g., make or import own content)	Enables some original content; choices among pre-set images or texts (e.g., range of avatar clothing and features, original story action)	Limited original content, pre-set personalization element (e.g., insert one element to personalize; minimal choices for avatar design)
Multimodal	Enhances meaning through combinations of four or more modes: music, image, sound effects, animation; inspires play with real-world materials	Enables manipulation and combinations of several modes: image, paint, movement (animation), speech, music	Primarily print word-processing tools, supplemented with stamping or basic paint tools
Multilinear	Open-ended storytelling with many tangents (e.g., hypertext, portals as in videogames)	Enables an alternate ending; supports revisions to insert additional events	Enables a single storyline in an unvarying sequence that proceeds from beginning to end
Connected	Saving and facilitated sharing on videosharing sites (e.g., YouTube)	Opportunities to export films for saving and external emailing or posting	Internal network sharing only or proprietary formats that require website registration to view

App examples and literacy anecdotes

Toontastic. To offer an example of how participatory literacies can be enacted in the app *Toontastic*, Rowsell provides excerpts of data from the *Tutoring by Design* study. As discussed earlier, tutees worked with tutors over the course of an hour and focused on apps as the mainstay of the tutoring material. Many of the participants liked *Toontastic* because they could play with movie tropes and the concept of memes (Knobel and Lankshear, 2007). For instance, Alice, seen in Figure 6.2, created a love story about a pirate and a young maiden who fall in love, and then the maiden is kidnapped by an evil green cow who puts her in a dungeon in a castle until her pirate love rescues her.

The format of *Toontastic* is fairly constrained by the story arc that follows consecutively: an introduction, conflict, resolution, and conclusion. Players are expected to stay within this story structure and there are a series of different templates to choose from to construct a given story, or there is the option to create your own story template. In addition, players can add music and animations if desired. What was interesting about different readers was how they strayed from typical storylines and infused their own intertextual elements. For instance, in Alice's short love story, she changed the colour of the evil cow. In the first scene, the cow was brown in line with the template, but in the next three scenes Alice

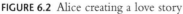

FIGURE 6.2 Alice creating a love story

changed the colour palette and made the cow green and the maiden's dress pink. Furthermore, rather than the pirate being a powerful hero who saves the day, he deferred to the maiden on what to do once he freed her from the castle. Finally, Alice injected bits of popular culture such as the line that she gave the pirate when he confronted the cow: 'Hey cow, say hello to my little friend', which references the iconic line from *Scarface* when Al Pacino faces a group of drug runners with a machine gun and uses this same line. In this way, the productive elements of app play with *Toontastic* emerged from including mimesis or memes into storylines to making the content more edgy, interesting, and connected to other texts.

In Wohlwend's *Literacy Playshop* study, easily recognizable character sets and scenes (e.g., pirates, sharks, and ships; astronauts and spaceships; witches and cauldrons) also inspired memes and facilitated collaboration among players, as players could quickly agree on simple story actions. Children also frequently selected the blank canvas and paint palette to create their own characters and backdrops, although some children became so engrossed in painting they spent far less time on using the character in the animation sequence.

In the *Toontastic* app map (Figure 6.3) below, the highest scores are for multimodal potential and productive capacity as the app enables many ways for players to create original content. Multiplayer play is somewhat enabled as two children can collaborate on a story but too many fingers caused freeze-ups. Most constraining is the connectivity, which (at the time of the study) limited video-sharing to the in-app Toontube network, and the multilinearity of a single, sequential standardized story arc.

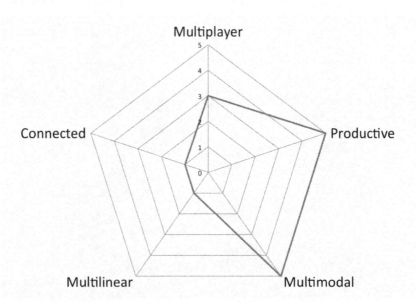

FIGURE 6.3 *Toontastic* app map

Grandma's Kitchen. During Rowsell's *Crayons and iPads* project, researchers documented apps that children played alongside any parallels with similar physical/material worlds, within each context. A popular app was *Grandma's Kitchen*, which is an app where children can cook and bake with an animated grandma character. There were several instances when researchers observed how children moved across a digitized version of cooking and baking practices and emulated these same practices in their kitchen space in the classroom site:

> In the house dramatic play center, four kindergarten-age children were playing a type of cooking game. They found the *Grandma's Kitchen* app (on the tablet) and started playing it too. They were watching the videos in the app and then making the food in their pretend play (that was pictured in the app). For example, the video showed cracking eggs and the children were pretending to break eggs for baking. When the app said, 'give Grandma a kiss', one of the children actually kissed the tablet! As the children played this 'baking game' they drifted back and forth between the app and concrete toys (see Figure 6.4). Children would take information from the app and trial that knowledge with concrete toys. Similarly, play themes that had started within the concrete world (e.g., baking a cake) would be enhanced and extended using the app's content (e.g., using measuring spoons for ingredients). The children then blended this converged experience and knowledge to write a menu with a stylus pen on the tablet. Could the children have achieved their play aims with either the concrete toys or the tablet?

In relation to our rubric and benchmark, children's naturalized movements from *Grandma's Kitchen* had the highest scores for being multilinear and multimodal. Children displayed tremendous flexibility moving across physical and virtual spaces and, equally, they made meaning fluidly and with a fluency of thought and creativity across a variety of modes (virtual and non-virtual modes). Where children showed less potential and productivity in terms of the app was in the area of connectedness—there was very little filming and sharing of events. Rather, children were focused on tasks at-hand and fulfilling a set of practices (Figure 6.5).

PuppetPals. In the *Literacy Playshop* project, researchers documented classroom activity and child-made videos as children used several iPad apps to create animated stories. In the app *PuppetPals* (Polished Play), children could choose characters, and a setting, and then animate a story in real time by manually moving characters onscreen with their fingertips while simultaneously narrating the story (or speaking dialogue), captured by the iPad's internal microphone. Instant playback was crucial in helping preschool children see what was actually onscreen after filming, including the visual, movement, and the audio modes. A few onscreen actions are labeled and require word identification (e.g., the 'back' and 'next' icons for navigating between screens); while some elements use icons (arrows, red button for signaling the beginning and ending of the recording process). Other navigation tools are not labeled at all, but are instead controlled by touch and taps (e.g., tracing

FIGURE 6.4 Photos of parallel play in virtual and physical worlds

around photos to create character cutouts; swiping to scroll through backdrops and characters, dragging and dropping to select characters; pinching and spreading fingers to resize characters and objects; and moving characters to enter, enact, and exit the animation sequence by drag and drop).

In the combined kindergarten/grade one classroom, a group of 6- and 7-year-old children huddled around the iPad at one end of a low table. The girls were dragging characters on and off stage in the PuppetPals app, using the free basic

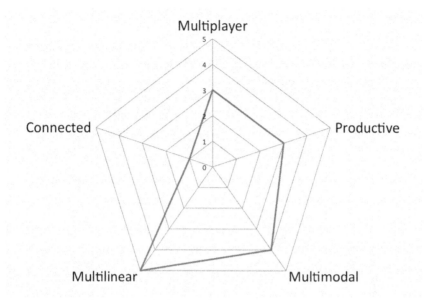

FIGURE 6.5 *Grandma's Kitchen* app map

set of fairy tale characters and castle backdrop. Six hands jockeyed for room on the small rectangular screen, squeezing in to drag, drop, resize, or rotate the cutouts of a princess, knight, dragon, chipmunk, and crow. Suddenly, Allie dragged the princess character rapidly back and forth across the castle, 'Get your booty out of here!' Sierra quickly decided this demand was directed toward her chipmunk character and resized its body, creating a giant chipmunk to challenge the attacking princess. Giggling, the girls begin a fight scene by moving and rotating their characters on and off stage, their moves punctuated by growls and shrieks.

While limiting children's ability to create new plots and original content, the preset cartoon character sets did afford easy recognition of familiar roles and storylines (e.g., princess, dragon, castle), which enhanced multiplayer collaboration as children could quickly join a play scenario in progress. As in Allie and Sierra's play, the app's inclusion of seemingly unrelated characters like the chipmunk and crow opened new possibilities for storylines that the children found humorous and engaging. Additional sets were available for purchase and a 'director's pass' upgrade in the program enabled children to use the iPad camera to import photos and trace a cutout feature that allowed children to create their own puppets or to create custom backdrops. Children spent time gathering toys and classroom materials to take pictures to add to their films. They also took photos of one another to put a friend in the story. Unlike *Toontastic*, there was no paint program to enable modification of the photo or to draw original characters.

The *PuppetPals* app map (Figure 6.6) reflects the high potential for multiplayer collaboration as several children could manipulate characters, which was limited only by the size of the tablet touchscreen, as well as high production capacity for original content that inspired children to photograph classroom toys and import them into their films. Medium levels of connectivity reflect the fact that films could be saved for sharing on external sites. Multimodal manipulation was limited to animation and audio recording as there are no in-app drawing, paint, or music tools. The lowest score is multilinearity: the app's simple design immediately over-writes any unsaved recording; although it does not impose a template for a linear story arc, it also does not enable multiple recordings or revisions.

JibJab Jr. Books. In contrast to the puppetry animation apps, an e-book app had little staying power with children in the *Literacy Playshop* project. They lost interest relatively quickly in the *JibJab Jr. Books* (2011) personalized e-book program in which a child can take a self-portrait with the iPad camera, trace around one's head, and import the cutout to paste it on a cartoon body to create a cartoon chef. In the highly animated musical story book, the child can view the pages as the personalized chef character humorously makes a pizza across the course of the book. Amy, one child who worked with the app on several days, was content to tap on the screen to page through the book, repeatedly showing it to friends at the table. However, her interest faded after two days as the app did not allow her to vary the text content or the sequence of events or to add speech or music. The book could not be shared online and could only be viewed on an iPad with the app.

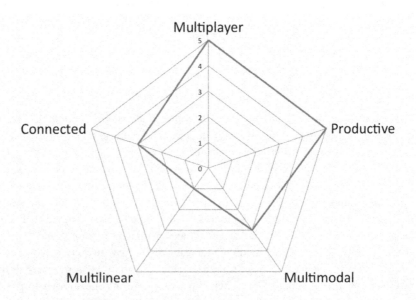

FIGURE 6.6 *PuppetPals* app map

The *JibJab* app map (Figure 6.7) shows an overall low score for digital literacies. The end product of a personalized e-book was quite polished but with little possibility for multiplayer collaboration, original content, multimodal manipulation, storyline flexibility, or sharing among players.

Comparison of apps

A comparison of all four apps reveals that the programs varied widely in their capacity for supporting participatory literacies, but in general, there were lower levels for connectivity and multilinearity, and higher levels for productivity, multiplayer collaboration, and multimodal creativity. Some of the limitations appear technological and related to design features while others appear discursive and related to ideological beliefs about children's abilities or the nature of literacy. For example, low connectivity seems related to safety concerns for limiting children's contact with online others and proprietary interests for generating more users through internal sharing networks. Multilinearity is enabled by more open-ended apps and user interfaces that provide html navigation but are limited by structured story templates or video production that results in a linear film. Productivity appears to be one of the most easily enabled dimensions through a recording option that makes use of the tablet's internal camera and microphone. Higher levels of multimodality require more design features, such as paint or photography programs or pre-loaded libraries of music and sound effect options. Multiplayer collaboration is sometimes limited by the size of the tablet touchscreens or by user interfaces that either limit or become overwhelmed by multiple simultaneous user touches.

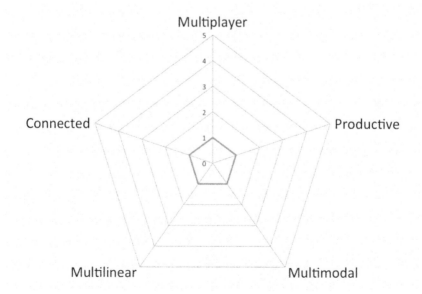

FIGURE 6.7 *JibJab Jr. Books* app map

Discussion: Apps and participatory literacies

Comparing four popular apps makes clear the disparate adoptions of participatory literacies and competencies. There is an open, participatory, and design feel to apps that align with new digital logics. Regarding the logic of participatory literacies, not all apps offered the capacity to make meaning across a variety of modes with peers in an unpredictable, multilinear way, and then to document these practices in some way such as filming a story or remixing familiar and novel characters to create an original film that can be shared with distant others. Instead, apps featured in the chapter exhibited one or two of each benchmarks. There is a skills delivery focus in some apps, or an 'old wine in new bottles' (Lankshear and Knobel, 2003) feel that, in our experience, children see through right away. Given the popularity of the four apps featured in the chapter, it is telling to see whether apps actually align with new ways of thinking and communicating and these comparisons point to larger issues and implications in terms of where we are presently in under-standing and realizing participatory literacies within everyday technologies. In some ways, we are still constrained by what we think of as autonomous views of literacy learning.

There is a grounded mobility from the physical to the virtual across all of the apps that we analyzed. Burnett's research has examined how children move across physical and virtual spaces and manifest immaterial literacies when they do so. Important to the concept of participatory literacies, this productivity and connect-edness between material and virtual worlds invites multimodal sense-making as children use an ensemble of resources through their imaginative engagements. Previous notions of literacy practices in text-oriented paradigms maintain a 'boundedness' to meaning-making. For example, within the *Crayons and iPads* research not only did children play across virtual and physical worlds, but they also would produce texts as a result of this im/material movement and mobility. The research team observed that when children played the *Grandma's Kitchen* app, they

TABLE 6.3 Comparing apps across five dimensions of participatory literacies

Digital storytelling apps	Multiplayer	Productive	Multimodal	Multilinear	Connected
JibJab Personalized e-book	Low	Low	Low	Low	Low
PuppetPals★ Cartoon or photo animation	High	High	Medium	Low	Medium
Toontastic★ Cartoon or photo animation	Medium	High	High	Low	Low
Grandma's Kitchen Producing or making things and interaction with avatars	Medium	Medium	Medium/ High	High	Low

Note: ★Basic levels of the free version of the app limits original content to lowest level; purchase of upgrade required to enable original content would experiment with actions that they completed in the app such as cracking an egg, then they would apply that knowledge to the physical toy egg in the pretend kitchen. Extending this physical play, they would move to a story and drawing centre and sketch out stories from properties within the virtual and physical play— being with Grandma or a family member and baking something. To complete this productive work, they would use a stylus pen on the iPad or crayons and paper. The 'converged' world of the children's play across these contexts offered greater and more dynamic opportunities to combine and develop participatory literacies.

Building on the work of Brian Street and his contention that policy has a tendency to frame literacy as an autonomous skill that we acquire from formalized, school-based approaches to literacy learning and that we cognitively develop and carry with us (Street, 1984), we similarly posit that many commercial apps still work within a print-centric, autonomous model of literacy in a decontextualized approach to learning. That is, such apps need to teach a skill, be used in a solitary way, and follow a linear path. For instance, *Toontastic* does not allow players to stray from conventional storylines and trajectories from an introduction, denouement, conflict, resolution, and conclusion and it is not a format that is conducive to be filmed, converged, and shared with a peer group. Within the set structures of these apps, there is not the openness that allows for problem-solving and experimentation. For example, *JibJab* does not include a multiplayer platform, does not invite productivity and sharing, and there is not much evidence of multimodality. In other words, print-bound apps, although at times engaging, do not invite and foster the kinds of practices and thinking processes participatory literacies make possible.

Our early thinking about a lack of alignment between apps and participatory literacies is that there is a greater need for an ideological approach to app literacies. Applying Street's differentiation between autonomous and ideological models of literacy starts from a belief that knowledge is socially-constructed, and epistemological framings of texts are culturally-mediated. Apps that encourage an autonomous model operate on a dominant assumption: the focus should be on acquiring predominantly language skills through a fun platform that encourages some play, but ultimately with a pedagogic end and played in a solitary way. By contrast, apps that encourage an ideological model provide openness to learner-led design, with potential for multiple players' participation and productive play, where learners can make their own content and use a variety of modes to do so.

References

Burnett, C., Davies, J., Merchant, G. and Rowsell, J. (2014). *New Literacies Around the Globe: Policy and pedagogy*. London: Routledge.

Chiong, C. and Shuler, C. (2010). *Learning: Is there an app for that? Investigations of young children's usage and learning with mobile devices and apps*. New York: The Joan Ganz Cooney Center at Sesame Workshop.

Harwood, D., Rowsell, J., Winters, K.L., Woloshyn, V. and Bajovic, M. (2013). (Grant Amount: $74,968.00). Social Sciences and Humanities Research Council (SSHRC) Insight

Development Grant Award. *Crayons and iPads: Understanding young children's meaning-making processes in learning to be literate.*

Knobel, M. and Lankshear, C. (2007). Online memes, affinities, and cultural production. In M. Knobel and C. Lankshear (eds), *A New Literacies Sampler* (pp. 199–228). New York: Peter Lang.

Knobel, M. and Wilber, D.J. (2009). Let's talk 2.0: Whether it's web 2.0 or literacy 2.0, it's a whole new way of thinking. *Educational Leadership, 66*(6), 20–24.

Lankshear, C. and Knobel, M. (2003). *New Literacies: Changing knowledge and classroom learning.* London: Open University.

Rideout, V.J. (2013). *Zero to Eight: Children's media use in America 2013.* San Francisco, CA: Common Sense Media.

Rowsell, J. (2013). *Working with Multimodality: Rethinking literacy in a digital age.* London: Routledge.

Rowsell, J. (2014). Toward a phenomenology of contemporary reading. *The Australian Journal of Literacy and Language, 37*(2), 117–127.

Rowsell, J., Colquhoun, C. and Maues, F. (in progress). The case of Calvin: Reimaging reading through Minecraft.

Shuler, C. (2012). *iLearn II: An analysis of the education category on Apple's app store.* New York: Joan Ganz Cooney Center.

Street, B. (1984). *Literacy in Theory and Practice.* New York: Cambridge University Press.

Street, B.V. (1995). *Social Literacies: Critical approaches to literacy in development, ethnography, and education.* Harlow: Pearson Education.

Wohlwend, K.E. (2010). A is for avatar: Young children in literacy 2.0 worlds and literacy 1.0 schools. *Language Arts, 88*(2), 144-152.

Wohlwend, K.E., Buchholz, B.A., Wessel-Powell, C., Coggin, L.S. and Husbye, N.E. (2013). *Literacy Playshop: New literacies, popular media, and play in the Early childhood classroom.* New York: Teachers College Press.

Wohlwend, K.E. (2017). Toddlers and touchscreens: Learning "Concepts Beyond Print" with tablet technologies. In R.J. Meyer and K.F. Whitmore (eds), *Reclaiming Early Childhood Literacies: Narratives of hope, power, and vision.* Mahwah, NJ: Lawrence Erlbaum.

7

TOUCH DESIGN AND NARRATIVE INTERPRETATION

A social semiotic approach to picture book apps

Sumin Zhao and Len Unsworth

SCHOOL OF EDUCATION, UNIVERSITY OF TECHNOLOGY, SYDNEY, AUSTRALIA, AND LEARNING
SCIENCES INSTITUTE AUSTRALIA, AUSTRALIAN CATHOLIC UNIVERSITY, SYDNEY, AUSTRALIA

Interactivity is often considered as the defining feature of a book app. However, what constitutes interactivity in the context of apps is not always clear.
We postulate in this chapter a multimodal social semiotic theory of interactivity, which considers interactivity as not simply a function of technology,
but also a resource for meaning-making. We distinguish two basic types of
interactivity—intra-text and extra-text—incorporated in the touch design,
and explore the different functions they perform in a broad range of picture
book apps. In particular, we look at the app version of *The Heart and the Bottle*
in depth, and illustrate how interactive design elements help to create an
interpretative possibility of the story. We suggest that a better understanding
of interactive touch design would promote more effective adult–child
interactions around mobile applications.

Keywords: Interactivity, multimodal, e-book, literacy, semiotic, meaning-
making

Introduction

As a unique aesthetic and literary artefact, picture books have occupied a central
place in contemporary early childhood. They provide, for many young children, the
earliest literacy experience. Joint picture book reading between caregivers and
young children is one of the most effective strategies for fostering emergent
literacy and has profound implications for the long-term literacy development, as
shown by a rich body of research evidence (e.g., Bus *et al.*, 1995; Mol *et al.*, 2008).
The value of picture books for promoting literacy learning has been further
highlighted in the multiliteracies pedagogy movement (e.g., Hassett and Curwood,
2009; Walsh, 2003). As narrative in picture books relies largely on the sophisticated

interplays between verbiage and image (e.g., Lewis, 2001; Nikolajeva and Scott, 2013; Painter *et al.*, 2012), it not only introduces young children to the conventions of print, but also provides them unique opportunities to engage with multiple meaning-making modes such as language and image, resources such as font, colour and layout, and multimodal narrative genres.

As smart phones and tablet computers become increasingly ubiquitous in early childhood, a variety of new forms of 'picture books', such as animated e-books, enhanced e-books, and book applications (or apps) have been made available to young readers. These emerging digital literacy artefacts have brought into question the role of picture books in early literacy. Many advocates consider digital books an improvement on physical picture books, believing that they have the potential to provide new literacy learning opportunities. In their recommendation to teachers, for instance, Hutchison *et al.* (2012, p. 17) suggested that the variety of electronic books available for the iPad provided additional advantages over paper media books, since they afforded students more opportunities to physically interact with and manipulate and transform texts according to their needs and interests.

The sceptics, on the other hand, are concerned that an over-reliance on digital technologies could deprive children of a range of literacy skills that are traditionally developed through engagement with print-based picture books. Enhanced e-books have been reported as being less effective than the print and basic e-book versions in terms of their capacity to support the benefits of co-reading, because they prompted more non-content-related interactions (Chiong *et al.*, 2012; Parish-Morris *et al.*, 2013). In an interview, Mem Fox—a leading Australian picture book author—criticised the mobile app as it 'has no beginning, middle or end, and did not describe forgiveness or courage in adversity' and expressed concern that 'an increasing reliance on technology to teach children how to read could inhibit their empathy and social skills' (Stark, 2013).

The purpose of our chapter is not to take a side in this ongoing debate. Rather, we aim to tackle one of the most basic questions of the debate—how (and if) the picture book app is different from a print book. We believe that a systematic understanding of these emerging digital textual artefacts needs to be developed before we can fully examine the 'losses and gains' (Kress, 2005, p. 6) involved in introducing them into young children's literacy lives. The disciplinary approach we take here is often referred to as (multimodal) social semiotics (Halliday, 1978; Kress, 2009; van Leeuwen, 2005). From this perspective, picture book apps are a semiotic artefact, consisting of various semiotic or meaning-making resources and modes, as well as touch designs. The main task of a social semiotic analysis is to unpack how these various resources have been deployed and how they interact with each other, to make meaning in the narrative context of a picture book.

Between books and apps: Picture book apps as multimedia artefacts

Electronic picture books exist in three typical formats. The first is an e-book, a straightforward digitalisation of the picture book. Some e-books, such as *Mog the*

Forgetful Cat (1970), include read-to-me audios (i.e., the audio recording of an adult reading the book). The second format, which is less common, is an animated or enhanced e-book, in which the original illustrations have been animated. Judith Kerr's 1968 classic, *The Tiger Who Came to Tea,* for example, has been adapted as an animated e-book. Enhanced e-books often contain simple touch functions, such as 'tap to play a video clip'. Picture books can also be turned into a book app—a digital book designed for touch devices, such as tablet computers and smart phones. While e-books and animated e-books are distributed through, and need to be read with, a reading app, e.g., iBook or Kindle, picture book apps are stand-alone mobile applications. Although many picture book apps are the adaptations of existing books, some have been developed independently of a print version (for examples see Sargeant, 2015).

While there are a number of characteristics that distinguish picture book apps from other e-book formats (Kucirkova, 2013), the two focused on here are multimediality and interactivity. To understand the multimedia nature of picture book apps, one useful concept is remediation (Bolter and Grusin, 2000), the idea that digital new media are often fashioned out of older forms of media. Picture book apps are foremost a 'remediation' of the print book. The type of remediation involved typically falls into one of two categories. The first is what Bolter and Grusin describe as 'translucent borrowing', in which the digital medium is presented as a similar, yet 'improved', version of an older medium (2000, p. 46). The second is 'refashion(ing)' in which the digital medium attempts to refashion the older medium/media entirely, while 'still marking the presence of the older media and therefore maintaining a sense of multiplicity or hypermediacy' (2000, p. 46).

When a picture book app is a 'translucent borrowing' of the print book, it maintains the defining features of the print version while incorporating other types of media, such as audio, animation, and interactive games. One such example is *The Wrong Book* app, which is designed as a virtual book with add-on features such as sound effects, motion graphics, and animated characters. When a picture book app 'refashions' the print version, it creates an entirely new (multi)-media experience, while maintaining a sense of reference to the book. *Don't Let the Pigeon Run the App,* for instance, is an app based on Mo Willems' Pigeon series (e.g., *Don't Let the Pigeon Drive the Bus*). While the app maintains the defining features of the books, such as the design style of the characters and narrative pattern, the written words are now delivered through audio by an animated pigeon. Significantly, this transforms the experience from one of 'reading' to one of 'watching'. In this new version, the user is positioned as if they were in 'face-to-face' dialogue with the character, while in the print version the young readers need to infer an imagined dialogue with the pigeon, by decoding the visual and verbal clues within the book.[1]

Regardless of the degree of remediation, a picture book app never fully 'absorbs' the print media. Nevertheless, an important characteristic of a picture book app is that it remains a 'book'. There are many elements in picture book app design that help create a sense of continuity with the print book, even in apps that have been developed without an original book version, such as the *Larry the Lizard series.* One common strategy is to design the interface according to the layout conventions of the print version, rather than adhering to those of screen-based media, such as websites. Many book apps also include a flipped-page design on the bottom right of the screen,[2] which allows the reader to 'turn' the page through a swipe/flip gesture, thus imitating to a degree the experience of physical page-turning. As well as trying to maintain the 'physical' look of the book, many book apps incorporate into their multimedia features the 'discursive norm' (van Leeuwen, 2005) about early literacy and share-book reading practices. For example, one of the common multimedia features in picture book apps is the audio recording function. Parents, teachers, or the children themselves can record their readings of the story, which can be played back at a later time. Though technologically simple, this function promotes app use as a shared and repeatable practice, much like the established early literacy practice of shared picture book reading. In some picture book apps, most notably the *Dr Seuss* series, the readers can tap on individual words that will be then read aloud to them. We suggest this function helps to highlight the decoding and phonic aspect of literacy. More sophisticated use of multimedia features to facilitate forms of early literacy can be found in apps like the *Pigeon*, which incorporates scaffolded learning of story-telling through multimedia interactive elements, where young readers progress from selecting from image options to be incorporated as objects in the story, to the generation of their own choices of objects that they can record, and these are then incorporated into the story.[3]

In summary, picture book apps can be considered as a distinctive category of multimedia artefact. While they tend to incorporate a broader range of media, they nevertheless remain, to varying degrees, faithful to their origins in printed books. The multimedia features of the picture book app often underpin certain notions of literacy and types of literacy practice. While multimediality is an important feature of picture book apps, what ultimately defines the picture book app and distinguishes it from other formats of electronic picture books is its interactivity, a point we shall elaborate on in the following section.

Interactivity in picture book apps: A social semiotic approach to touch design

Interactivity is often considered as the defining feature of a book app. For an app to be approved for distribution by Apple's App Review Board, it needs to have a sufficient level of interactivity (Sargeant, 2015). However, a review of design and education literature suggests that what constitutes interactivity in the context of apps is not always clear. It can refer to several different but related phenomena, which can be collected under the umbrella term 'interaction' (or 'to interact with'). As mobile apps are designed for touch devices, the most salient form of interaction is to physically interact with or touch the screen, e.g. 'they provide further opportunities for students to *physically interact with* and *manipulate* texts' (Hutchison *et al.*, 2012, p. 17, italics added). A second form of interactivity is sometimes discussed as a feature of multimediality, with the latter often presuming the presence of the former, e.g., 'tools that can support highly *interactive, multimedia* experiences' (Chiong *et al.*, 2012, p. 1, italics added). A third type of interactivity concerns personalized content creation, e.g., 'with options for the reader to *further interact* by recording and replaying their own voice with the text' (Hutchison *et al.*, 2012, p. 17, italics added). While the first three types of interactivity focus on the interaction with the apps, the term can also refer to interaction around the apps, including the possibility for children to create their own stories (Kucirkova *et al.*, 2013), and talk generated around the story through the use of an app. This latter type of interaction is where many literacy researchers believe the potential of apps, including picture book apps, for fostering early literacy resides (Krcmar and Cingel, 2014). Shuler (2012, p. 30) has proposed that 'we need better data on how to increase positive interactions between parents and children around touch screen technologies' and Falloon and Khoo (2014) have drawn attention to the potential for teacher intervention in enhancing the nature of interaction among young children around iPad apps. There has been some pioneering research in these areas of interactivity. For example, researchers (Kucirkova *et al.*, 2013; Kucirkova *et al.*, 2014) have shown how parent–child interactions around a self-created story with an iPad app can create opportunities for learning.

Perhaps the most sophisticated and systematic account of interactivity to date is that in Salen and Zimmerman's (2004) seminal work on game design, emphasizing that interactivity is a complex and multifaceted notion that encompasses computing, design, physical, psychological, and cultural dimensions. Our discussion of interactivity, however, is much narrower in scope, focusing exclusively on the *touch design*—the areas (known as hotspots or buttons) in a picture book app that can be activated through multitouch gestures (e.g., tap or swipe) to perform certain functionalities. We postulate that one of the primary functions of interactivity, which is largely missing in the existing accounts, is meaning-making. The meaning-making potential of interactivity is particularly relevant in the context of picture book apps. We will use the two examples of touch design in Figure 7.1 to illustrate our points.

A unit of touch design is made up of three elements: 1) the action—typically a multitouch gesture (e.g., swipe, tap, drag, etc.) or less typically other types of physical action, such as shaking the device; 2) the hotspot or button—the area on the interface that can be activated by gestures; and 3) the outcome or the functionality (such as edit, share, audio recording, etc.), triggered by the action. From a technological perspective, to design interactivity is to translate '*standard gesture*' (an action) into '*functionality*' (an outcome) (Apple Inc., 2015). What mediates between a gesture and its functionality in the interface is a button or a hotspot. While the pairing between action and outcome holds the key to interactivity for a designer (cf. Salen and Zimmerman, 2004), a user/reader experiences various forms of interaction primarily through the hotspots, which need to be represented semiotically in the forms of icon, image or verbiage. Our social semiotic account of touch design and interactivity thus centres on hotspots or buttons.

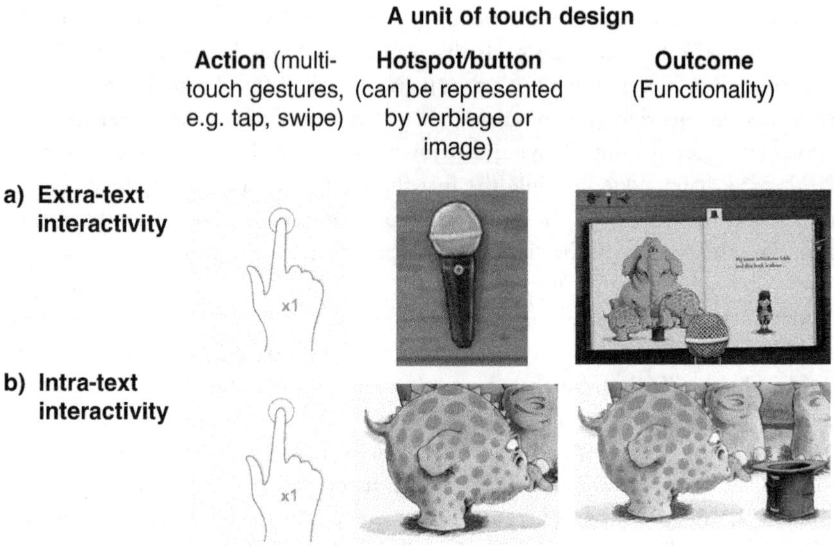

A unit of touch design

Action (multi-touch gestures, e.g. tap, swipe)	Hotspot/button (can be represented by verbiage or image)	Outcome (Functionality)
a) Extra-text interactivity		
b) Intra-text interactivity		

FIGURE 7.1 Touch design: A social semiotic perspective

We distinguish two types of touch design, and each engenders a distinct form of interactivity in picture book apps. In the first type of touch design, as illustrated in Figure 7.1a, the hotspot—the icon of a microphone—'signifies' or 'symbolizes' the functionality—audio recording. When a user/reader taps the microphone, it is likely that they, by decoding the symbolic meaning of the icon, can predict what the outcome of their action will be. Figure 7.1b is an example of the second type of touch design, where the hotspot does not 'signify' or 'symbolize' the outcome. Here, when the reader taps on the monster, the monster will tip the hat and the hat will, as a result, wobble. The image of the monster in this case does not represent either of the outcomes: the tipping or the wobbling. The outcome (tipping and wobbling) needs to be interpreted in context of the narrative (the monster's role in the story). By contrast, in the first type of touch design, the outcome is interpreted solely in relation to the iconic hotspot.

We term the second type of touch design 'intra-text' interactivity, while the first is 'extra-text' interactivity. Intra-text interactivity is of particular interest to us, as it shows that interactivity is not simply a function of technology, but is also a resource for making meaning in the context of picture book apps. When we perform a physical act such as tap or swipe, we perform a semiotic act or an act of meaning-making at the same time. In the following section, we will illustrate our arguments, using the digital book app *The Heart and the Bottle* (Jeffers, 2009) as an example. Specifically, we compare the app version with the print book version, focusing on what narrative elements have been turned into touch design, and what extra functions have been created through touch design.

Touch design and narrative interpretation in **The Heart and the Bottle**

The Heart and Bottle (hereinafter, *H and B*) is a book by award-winning children's picture book author and illustrator, Oliver Jeffers, and was first published in 2009. In December 2010, it was made available as an ISO app. Illustrated in the minimalist mixed-media style Jeffers is noted for, the story centres on a little girl's journey through grief and follows the typical structure of a narrative.[4] In the Orientation stage, we are introduced to an unnamed little girl 'whose head was filled with all the curiosities of the world'. She was close to her grandfather with whom she shared her rich intellectual and emotional life. The Complication stage starts with the little girl finding an empty chair where her grandfather used to sit, symbolising his death. Unsure how to deal with the grief, the girl put her heart in a bottle. The second part of the complication sees the girl as a fully-grown woman with a heart in a bottle hung from her neck, who 'was no longer filled with all the curiosities of the world'. She tried and failed repeatedly to get the heart out of the bottle. Eventually, in the Resolution, the protagonist met another curious little girl who took the heart out for her. The book ends with the Coda, where the woman was able to enjoy a rich inner life again.

In the book, the story is told in a third-person voice and we are not aligned visually or verbally with a particular character's point of the view. Throughout the book, the little girl—the main Participant—is being represented both verbally in the text and visually in the illustration. However, the types of process involving the girl as the Participant are very different in the verbiage and in the image. Verbally, the main process is the Mental Process, which deals with thinking and feeling (e.g. *'She forgot about the stars'. 'Feeling unsure, the girl thought the best thing was to put her heart in a safe place'*). Visually, she is depicted mostly in Action Processes, such as drawing, running, or sawing the bottle. While the narrative is premised on the death of the grandfather, he appears only as a visual Participant, often as the Accompaniment to the little girl's actions. Neither he nor his death is mentioned in the text.

In terms of interpersonal meaning, while the central theme of the story is emotion, there are few explicitly inscribed instances of Affect in the written text. The feelings of the protagonist are largely invoked, for example, *'She forgot about the stars … and stopped taking notice of the sea'*, *'didn't take much notice of anything … other than how heavy and awkward the bottle had become'*. The verbally invoked Affects are enforced through the choice of Ambience—the use of colour to construe emotion. For example, the pages depicting the loving relationship between the girl and her grandfather are filled with vibrant and warm colours. The pages where the girl makes futile attempts to break the bottle are largely blank with little colour, except for a few splashes of red, i.e., the heart. In short, the verbiage and image relation in *H and B* is a complementary one, with each playing a crucial role in creating the narrative and meaning. To reach an interpretation of the story requires a reader to make inferences based on visual clues, verbal tokens, and, more importantly, the complex interactions between the two. For younger readers who are not familiar with the multimodal conventions of picture books, scaffolding support may be necessary for them to form a coherent reading of the narrative and its central theme.

The app adaptation remains largely faithful to the print in terms of the narrative structure, the wording, and illustration. There are two major changes in the app version: 1) layout design—the splitting and merging of the original double page spread into a single screen frame; and 2) the interactive design features. While acknowledging layout as a resource for meaning-making, due to the limitation of this chapter we shall focus exclusively on touch *interactives*.

Touch interactives in the H and B *app*

H and B incorporates both types of touch design and interactivity—extra-text and intra-text. Examples of interactive designs are shown in the following Figure 7.2, which contains two frames, the first depicting the death of the grandfather, and the second showing the change of the protagonist from a curious little girl into an impassive grown-up.

Extra-text *interactives* are typically placed on the margin of a frame. In this frame, there are four hotspots: two are indicated by verbiage—*Menu, Hint,* and two by icons—the *speaker* icon on the top right and the *flipped-page* on the bottom right. Extra-text touch designs have two typical functions in picture book apps. The first is to enable the navigation and use of the app. When a user taps on the Menu button, for example, a thumbnail index of the app frames will appear across the bottom of the screen. The Hint button shows the area a reader can touch (in dotted line) and the type of gesture to activate the functionality of the hotspot (the arrow suggests a drag gesture). The Hint button is a unique design of *H and B* that we would like to highlight, as most picture book apps, and apps designed for young children in general, tend to assume that children possess a complete gesture 'grammar' that they can apply to touch devices. Literature in multigesture design has shown that gesture learning is often required before a user can engage with the system (Kammer *et al.*, 2010). Simply, if a child only has a limited repertoire of multitouch gestures, they will not be able to fully explore the interactive and meaning-making potentials of apps. The second common function of extra-text touch interactive is to facilitate the 'resemiotisation' (Iedema, 2003) of the shared picture book reading practices, a notion we have discussed in the previous section. In Figure 7.2, for instance, when a user taps on the speaker button, a voice will read the text out loud, and when he/she taps on the flipped-page corner hotspot, a page-flipping effect will occur, landing them on the next screen frame.

Intra-text touch *interactives* in picture book apps are often designed using (existing) visual narrative elements, most typically the characters, the background of a page, and various inanimate objects. Figure 7.2b is an example of using the character as a hotspot. When the user drags the little girl towards the top of the screen, she gradually turns into a grown-up and a bottle appears around her neck.

a) Extra-text interactivity (left) and intra-text interactivity and ambience (right)

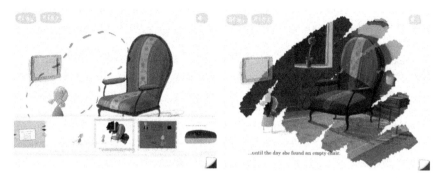

b) Intra-text interactivity and three types of meaning

FIGURE 7.2 Examples of touch design in *The Heart and the Bottle*

Meanwhile, the image in the thought bubble changes from a happy memory of the grandfather to an empty chair. An example of using the background as a hotspot can be found in Figure 7.2a. The whole screen here is a hotspot. If the user performs a swipe gesture across the screen, the Ambience of the image turns gradually from a vibrant warm tone into a muted cold one. Touch designs can also use inanimate objects as hotspots. In *H and B*, the user can frequently interact with the heart and the bottle—the two main symbols of the narrative—and carry out actions that are performed in the story by the girl, such as shaking, hammering, and sawing the bottle.

Meaning-making with touch interactives

When a user interacts with an intra-text interactive design through the physical act of gesturing, he/she also performs an act of meaning-making in the context of the narrative. The touch design in Figure 7.2a, for instance, is a case in which intra-text interactivity activates the interpersonal meaning, that is, 'wiping' colours off the screen in fact signifies the emotional change brought about by the death of the grandfather. In Figure 7.2b, the dragging gesture of the reader facilitates the progression of the narrative. It creates changes to the physical appearance and the inner thoughts of the character (Ideational meaning), marks a shift in mood (Interpersonal meaning), and signals the transition of temporal phases in the narrative (Textual meaning). In the two examples given here, the interactive designs are central to the narrative. Nonetheless, we have observed that many intra-text touch designs in picture book apps are peripheral to the story. One typical example of peripheral interactivity is one in which the user can tap (or tickle) a character and the character will make a sound (e.g., a giggle) or perform an action (e.g., jump). Yet the sound or the action has no relevance to the story, except that it allows the children to 'interact' with the character.

As intra-text touch *interactives* need to be interpreted in the context of the narrative, their designs tend to be unique to each individual picture book app. Our analysis suggests that in *H and B* the majority of the intra-text touch designs are central to the narrative, with a few instances of peripheral interactivity. The most significant touch designs, both in terms of frequency of occurrence and meaning-making potential, are those that use the girl, heart/bottle or background as hotspots. These *interactives* fulfil two main functions in the app version of the story. First, they foreground the narrative perspective of the girl, since readers are literally positioned as the little girl when they perform, via a series of multitouch gestures, actions such as hammering and sawing the bottle. Second, they make explicit and salient the interpersonal dimension of the story, in particular the shifts in emotion, by allowing the user to change the ambience at various points of the story using the swiping gesture. The app version therefore is not simply a multimedia or interactive version of the print. Rather, it constitutes an interpretative possibility (Unsworth, 2014a) of the story, a version of interpretation that creates 'amplified empathy' (Unsworth, 2014b) by aligning us with the emotional life of the little girl.

Implications and recommendations

In this chapter, we argued and demonstrated that interactivity is not simply a function of technology, but also a resource for meaning-making. We hope the following two implications drawn from our analysis will be useful for educators and caregivers exploring picture book apps with children.

Picture book apps can be considered as a version of interpretation of the book. The process of 'touching' and' 'interacting' with various elements in the app is, in a sense, a process of textual interpretation, and could potentially be used for teaching children to make sense of the text, the image and the interactions between the two.

Interactivity is not inherently 'better' or 'distracting'. In choosing book apps for children, it is useful to understand and recognise those that facilitate shared-reading practices, and contain interactive functions that are central to the narrative. With this understanding, adults can draw attention to the interactive elements that are central and discuss and scaffold their meaning-making potential during the shared reading.

Notes

1. The original book series uses a simple story pattern. The main character, the pigeon, bargains for an unreasonable demand he has made, such as to drive the bus or to stay up late, which is then being rejected by someone who is not visually represented in the book. Throughout the book, the pigeon constantly makes utterance such as 'No?', 'No?!' 'What do you say?', which implies the reader is the 'rejecter' here.
2. A similar feature is also presence in the iBook app.
3. In this app, the children are presented with three versions of the pigeon story, referred to as the Egg, the Chick, and Big Pigeon. The Egg contains a story with identical structure to other books in the series, which involves the pigeon demanding to run the app. In the Chick, the children are first asked to make choices from a series of visually represented items on the screen, such as their favourite food, numbers, or stinky things. The choices the children make will then become key elements in the story, e.g. the request the pigeon makes. The Big Pigeon is similar to the Chick, except that the children are no longer being presented with visual choices of story elements. Rather, they have to come up with their own items, and then tap a red button to record them.
4. For the linguistic terminology used in this section please refer to: genre and meta-functions (interpersonal, ideational, and textual) (Martin and Rose, 2008), visual/verbal participants and processes (Kress and van Leeuwen, 1996/2006), ambience (Painter *et al.*, 2012), and appraisal (affect) (Martin and White, 2003).

List of picture books and apps

Jeffers, O. (2009). *The Heart and the Bottle,* London: HarperCollins Children's Books.
Jeffers, O. (2010). *The Heart and the Bottle (ISO App).* Harper Collins. Available at: https://itunes.apple.com/gb/app/heart-bottle-for-ipad/id407795360?mt=8
Kerr, J. (1968). *The Tiger Who Came to Tea.* HarperCollins UK.
Kerr, J. (1970). *Mog the Forgetful Cat.* London: HarperCollins Children's Books.
Willems, M. (2003). *Don't Let the Pigeon Drive the Bus!* Boston, MA: Walker Books.
Willems, M. (2011). *Don't Let the Pigeon Run the App* (ISO App). Disney Publishing Worldwide Applications. Electronic Resource. Available at: https://itunes.apple.com/gb/app/dont-let-pigeon-run-this-app!/id459749670?mt=8

References

Apple Inc. (2015). iOS Human Interface Guidelines. Available at: https://developer.apple.com/library/ios/documentation/UserExperience/Conceptual/MobileHIG/
Bolter, J.D. and Grusin, R.A. (2000). *Remediation: Understanding new media.* Cambridge MA: MIT Press.
Bus, A.G., Van Ijzendoorn, M.H. and Pellegrini, A.D. (1995). Joint book reading makes for success in learning to read: A meta-analysis on intergenerational transmission of literacy. *Review of Educational Research, 65*(1), 1–21.

Chiong, C., Ree, J., Takeuchi, L. and Erickson, I. (2012). *Print Books vs. E-Books: Comparing parent–child co-reading on print, basic, and enhanced e-book platforms*. New York: The Joan Ganz Cooney Center.

Falloon, G. and Khoo, E. (2014). Exploring young students' talk in iPad-supported collaborative learning environments. *Computers and Education, 77*, 13–28.

Halliday, M.A.K. (1978). *Language as Social Semiotic.* London: Arnold.

Hassett, D.D. and Curwood, J.S. (2009). Theories and practices of multimodal education: The instructional dynamics of picture books and primary classrooms. *The Reading Teacher, 63*(4), 270–282.

Hutchison, A., Beschorner, B. and Schmidt Crawford, D. (2012). Exploring the use of the iPad for literacy learning. *The Reading Teacher, 66*(1), 15–23.

Iedema, R. (2003). Multimodality, resemiotization: Extending the analysis of discourse as multi-semiotic practice. *Visual Communication, 2*(1), 29–57.

Kammer, D., Wojdziak, J., Keck, M., Groh, R. and Taranko, S. (2010). *Towards a formalization of multi-touch gestures.* Paper presented at the ACM International Conference on Interactive Tabletops and Surfaces. Saarbrücken, Germany.

Krcmar, M. and Cingel, D.P. (2014). Parent–child joint reading in traditional and electronic formats. *Media Psychology, 17*(3), 262–281.

Kress, G. (2005). Gains and losses: New forms of texts, knowledge, and learning. *Computers and composition, 22*(1), 5-22. Available at: www.sciencedirect.com/science/article/pii/S8755461504000660

Kress, G. (2009). *Multimodality: A social semiotic approach to contemporary communication.* London: Routledge.

Kress, G. and van Leeuwen, T. (1996/2006). *Reading Images: The grammar of visual design.* New York: Routledge.

Kucirkova, N. (2013). Children's interactions with iPad books: Research chapters still to be written. *Frontiers in Psychology, 4*(995). Available at: www.ncbi.nlm.nih.gov/pmc/articles/PMC3871707/

Kucirkova, N., Messer, D., Sheehy, K. and Flewitt, R. (2013). Sharing personalised stories on iPads: A close look at one parent–child interaction. *Literacy, 47*(3), 115–122.

Kucirkova, N., Sheehy, K. and Messer, D. (2014). A Vygotskian perspective on parent–child talk during iPad story sharing. *Journal of Research in Reading, 38*(4), 428–441.

Lewis, D. (2001). *Reading Contemporary Picturebooks: Picturing text.* London: RoutledgeFalmer.

Martin, J.R. and Rose, D. (2008). *Genre Relations: Mapping culture.* London: Equinox.

Martin, J.R. and White, P. (2003). *The language of Evaluation.* London: Palgrave Macmillan.

Mol, S.E., Bus, A.G., de Jong, M.T. and Smeets, D.J. (2008). Added value of dialogic parent–child book readings: A meta-analysis. *Early Education and Development, 19*(1), 7–26.

Nikolajeva, M. and Scott, C. (2013). *How Picturebooks Work* [ebook]. New York: Routledge.

Painter, C., Martin, J.R. and Unsworth, L. (2012). *Reading Visual Narratives.* London: Equinox.

Parish-Morris, J., Mahajan, N., Hirsh Pasek, K., Golinkoff, R.M. and Collins, M.F. (2013). Once upon a time: Parent–child dialogue and storybook reading in the electronic era. *Mind, Brain, and Education, 7*(3), 200–211.

Salen, K., and Zimmerman, E. (2004). *Rules of Play: Game design fundamentals.* Cambridge, MA: MIT Press.

Sargeant, B. (2015). What is an ebook? What is a Book app? And why should we care? An analysis of contemporary digital picture books. *Children's Literature in Education, 46*(4), 454–466.

Shuler, C. (2012). *iLearn II: An analysis of the education category of Apple's app store.* The Joan Ganz Cooney Center at Sesame Workshop.

Stark, J. (2013, November 10). Technology no substitute for reading time: Mem Fox. *Sydney Morning Herald*. Available at: www.smh.com.au/digital-life/digital-life-news/technology-no-substitute-for-reading-time-mem-fox-20131109-2x8dw.html

Unsworth, L. (2014a). Interfacing visual and verbal narrative art in paper and digital media: Recontextualising literature and literacies. *Literacy in the Arts: Retheorising learning and teaching* (pp. 55–76). Switzerland: Springer.

Unsworth, L. (2014b). Point of view in picture books and animated film adaptations: Informing critical multimodal comprehension and composition pedagogy. In E. Djonov and S. Zhao (eds), *Critical Multimodal Studies of Popular Culture* (pp. 202–216). London: Routledge.

van Leeuwen, T. (2005). *Introducing Social Semiotics*. London/New York: Routledge.

Walsh, M. (2003). 'Reading' pictures: what do they reveal? Young children's reading of visual texts. *Reading*, *37*(3), 123–130.

8

PUT THEIR LEARNING IN THEIR HANDS

Apps supporting self-regulated learning

Julie Mueller, Karin Archer, Eileen Wood and Domenica De Pasquale

WILFRID LAURIER UNIVERSITY, WATERLOO, ONTARIO, CANADA

This chapter describes a study of teachers and learners in an elementary school in Southern Ontario implementing iPods and iPads in a pilot study aimed at student engagement and support of twenty-first-century skills. Teacher and student interviews, student surveys, and classroom observations present a picture of self-regulated learning and problem-solving supported by student-centred use of mobile devices, regardless of the application used. It is argued that the impact of mobile technology on young learners in a formal school setting is influenced by the theoretical approach of educators and the context in which the tools are used.

Keywords: Mobile technology, self-regulated learning, pedagogy, iPads, iPods

Introduction

Debate can be heard in parent circles, educational contexts, social media, and general public discussion as to how children should or should not use digital technology; what impact that use has; what types of games or applications should be used or not used; what constitutes 'educational' versus 'entertainment'; and, more recently, the benefits of 'gamification' of learning through mobile technology (PBSKIDS, 2014). Without a doubt, evaluating the impact of mobile technology on young children's learning is a complex endeavour. Before any empirical assessment can be conclusive, the learning outcomes must be defined, that is, what are the desired outcomes of the use of mobile technology, and how is it being used to meet these outcomes? If the outcomes are merely 'keeping children busy', then engagement would be an appropriate measure of success. However, if learning outcomes are connected to twenty-first-century skills, such as creativity, critical thinking, communication, and collaboration, measures of self-regulated learning and problem-solving will be of greater interest. Learning theory that suggests children are active, independent directors of their own learning supports the potential of mobile technology as a twenty-first-century cultural learning tool. A key question then is how early learners and their teachers are using this technology to support learning. This chapter examines this question through an exploration of the implementation and outcomes of using handheld tablet devices (i.e., iPods and iPads) with grade 1 students in an elementary school in Southern Ontario, Canada.

What role does technology play in current learning outcomes?

The Ontario Ministry of Education renewed its vision for 'achieving excellence' in 2014 and included 'expectations for valuable, higher-order skills like critical thinking, communication, innovation, creativity, collaboration and entrepreneurship' (Ontario Ministry of Education, 2014, p. 3). Currently, self-regulation is a key component of student assessments in Ontario elementary schools (Ontario Ministry of Education, 2010). Students must have the knowledge, motivation, and volition to learn. Woolfolk *et al.* (2009) describe the three main steps in the process of self-regulation as analyzing the task, devising a plan and setting goals, and executing the plan to complete the task. Without constant supervision, it is up to learners to employ their own system of incentives in order to remain on task (Bandura, 1991). These self-regulatory skills and metacognitive strategies can be supported and encouraged by emerging mobile technologies. The Ontario government recognizes the role that technology plays in teaching these self-regulatory skills, and has set policy in place to use digital technology across schools in the province at all levels. In the Premier's instructions to the Minster of Education in 2014, the following was included as part of the mandate: 'investing $150 million over three years in technology and learning tools such as new digital tablets, netbooks, cameras, software and professional development for teachers' (Ontario Ministry of Education, 2014, n.p.).

Features of mobile technology such as portability, interactivity, immediate access to information, and easy communication make it a potentially powerful tool for supporting self-regulation. The mobility of the technology allows learning to occur anytime, anywhere, supplementing and reinforcing the learning that occurs inside the classroom (Clough *et al.*, 2008; Looi *et al.*, 2009; Sandberg *et al.*, 2011; Sheng *et al.*, 2010). Mobile technology is capable of scaffolding on an individual basis for a specific subject or task. Communication features of the technology allow for increased opportunities for collaboration (Koszalka and Ntloedibe-Kuswani, 2010; Lieberman *et al.*, 2009; Motiwalla, 2007; Sheng *et al.*, 2010). Mobile devices are interactive and typically enjoyable to use, increasing student engagement and motivation. However, the power of these tools in accessing information as well as communicating with others can be both beneficial as well as problematic. While access to the online world provides students with an endless source of information, it could also serve as a distraction from the teacher or the task at hand (Lui, 2007). Thus, we need to look carefully at the possibilities of mobile technologies when considering their potential to assist in the development of the self-regulated learner.

How do we integrate mobile technology with constructivist pedagogy that supports self-regulated learners?

Education change theorist Michael Fullan in 2013 referred to a *new pedagogy,* suggesting that how we go about teaching needs to change dramatically in response to the integration of digital technology. Fullan refers to three interconnected aspects of change: technology, new pedagogy, and the teacher as a change agent. The catalyst for this change is technology, but success demands more than just getting tablets into the hands of teachers and students. Technology provides the vehicle for teachers to change their instructional delivery methods and have a deeper impact on learning (Mueller and Wood, 2012), but it is no substitute for good pedagogy. Good pedagogy is 'new' in that it is based on a constructivist platform, it is inquiry-based, and fosters deep learning. Learning theory that suggests teachers move from 'sage on the stage' to 'guide on the side' are useful if the learner is indeed recognized as a collaborative partner in charge of their own learning. Hattie's (2012) meta-analysis of the variables that impact effective teaching practice suggests that rather than teachers facilitating learning, they must recognize the need for metacognition, feedback, self-verbalization, goal-setting, and frequent checks on the effects of their teaching. The 'good' pedagogies – or instructional methods based on active learning theories, can utilize digital technologies to support self-regulated learning in even the youngest of learners (Wood *et al.*, 2008).

Changes in emphasis in learning theory or the principles of effective knowledge acquisition and construction need to be shared in relevant, culturally applicable ways. Doing this will create a pedagogical shift that encourages educators to establish routines, develop processes, and choose equipment based on instructional methods that support self-regulated, authentic learning, rather than choosing apps and hardware based on popular marketing (Falloon, 2013b; Falloon, 2015b). The National Educational Technology Standards for Teachers developed in the USA but used in educational systems across the world, demand that as today's teachers plan and design learning environments and experiences supported by technology, they need to 'incorporate digital tools and resources to promote student learning and creativity ... enable all students to pursue their individual curiosities and become active participants in setting their own educational goals, managing their own learning, and assessing their own progress.' (Morphew, 2012, p. 5). This self-regulated learning approach can be scaffolded or hampered by the way that technology is utilized in a classroom or home (Mueller *et al.*, 2011). Any device, game, or app may or may not be used in an 'educational' way. Once we define 'educational', we can examine what tools and approaches are constructive and useful in reaching that end. Achieving this has little to do with the 'tool', but more about how it is used and for what purpose or purposes (Radesky *et al.*, 2015).

A variety of frameworks and graphics have been developed to assist teachers in the integration of mobile technology in their teaching (see also Kathleen Roskos' work in relation to the integration of e-books into classrooms). The emphasis in each of the frameworks is specifically on the intended design of the application in relation to twenty-first-century skills, and is often related to how teachers connect the app to curriculum. Apps can be classified in multiple ways according to categories of use, learning processes, or intended skills.

Sean Junkins (n.d.) freely shares a 'Periodic Table of iPad Apps' on his website (https://sjunkins.files.wordpress.com/2014/06/iste-posters-001.jpg), organizing specific applications by platform (Apple and Google); purpose (creativity, productivity, interacting, and sharing); teacher use; and mathematics.

Andrew Churches (2008) has adapted Bloom's Taxonomy of general thinking skills for the digital age, adding verbs that represent emerging digital tasks, strategies, and learning tools. Based on an app-selection criteria that addresses these thinking skills, Allan Carrington (2015) devised a 'Padagogy Wheel' (Figure 8.2) that incorporates variables that utilize apps from planning to implementation – asking questions about the attributes of learners, variables that motivate them, higher-order learning objectives, and aspects of the technology being integrated. Carrington's visual depiction of pedagogical decisions for app implementation begins at the core of the wheel considering the outcomes of learning and then moves out to cognitive thinking skills, action verbs based on these skills, specific activities that require them, and eventually to individual apps that would support and enhance those activities. For example, the higher-order skill of 'creating' may involve 'producing' done through 'mixing' using the 'iMovie' app.

Each of these graphic-organizers can be useful in a teacher's selection of applications according to their intended use. What should be investigated further is

FIGURE 8.1 Periodic table of iPad apps (Junkins, n.d.)

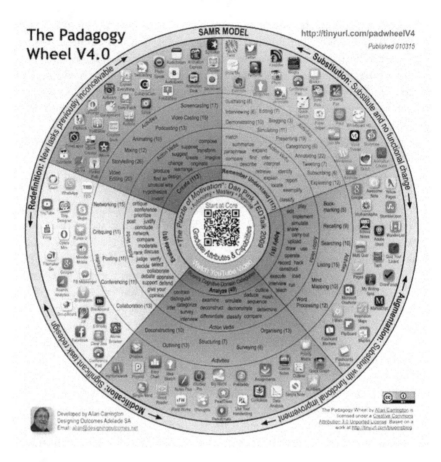

FIGURE 8.2 The padagogy wheel (Carrington, 2015)

students' actual use of apps as learning tools and their integration into the learning environment. What follows is an examination of that integration in the context of an elementary school classroom.

What does learning with apps look like in a student's hands?

Research context. Beyond the theoretical framework of self-regulated learning, the pedagogical strategies, and app classification, a complete picture of children's learning with mobile technology and apps cannot be constructed without consulting and observing children in practice actually using the devices (Falloon, 2013a). A comprehensive mixed methods study was conducted in the field to see what working with apps 'looks like' in the hands of the learners. A progressive schoolboard technology committee in a Southern Ontario city worked collaboratively with researchers to examine the introduction of iPods, iPads, and apps in a public elementary school, working with teachers and children from grades 1 to 6. The school environment included a range of technologies with wireless Internet throughout, an interactive whiteboard, laptop, and sound system with wireless microphones in every classroom, and a computer lab with a class set of Apple computers running both the Windows and Apple operating systems. A mixed suite of the iPods and iPads were used in five classrooms including grades 1, 4, and 6, and two congregated classrooms of students with special education needs. The implementation of the devices was part of a larger pilot project across the urban/rural school district at the beginning of a school board-wide distribution of mobile technology. There were six teacher volunteers who took part in the study presented in this chapter. The key vision of the iPod/iPad introduction for these teachers was to encourage self-regulated learning and higher-order thinking, elevating their use beyond prevailing 'drill and skill' practices.

Research design. In an effort to understand the impact of mobile technology and apps on the internal aspects of self-regulated learning, surveys, interviews, and recorded observations were combined to examine how both the teachers and the young children were using the technology in their classrooms. Researcher observations were conducted in classes, where written field notes and video recordings from a stationary camera on a tripod were made. Students were surveyed at the beginning of the project about their views on using the technology, and their learning preferences.

Results

Older children involved in this study were surveyed in order to obtain measures of student experience with technology and their attitude to learning with apps and tablets, as well as their attitudes towards other learning tools. This was important because a picture of how children in grades 4 to 6 manage apps in their learning can assist teachers in preparing younger children for learning at this later stage. Table 8.1 displays means and standard deviations for all 127 children on their use of computers and mobile technology for a variety of purposes.

Paired sample t-tests indicated that students used computers at home significantly more often to play games than any other use (smallest $t_{(125)} = 5.29, p<.001$). The tests also indicated that students used portable devices at home significantly more often for playing games and listening to music (a few times a week) than connecting with friends, doing schoolwork, or looking up information (smallest $t_{(125)} = 5.08, p<.001$). Overall, the survey results suggest that children use both computers and mobile devices at home more frequently for entertainment than as a learning tool.

Table 8.2 presents the means and standard deviations for students' preferred learning tools. Paired sample t tests related to students' preferences indicated that they believed computers, hand-held technologies, and the teacher's explanation helped them learn significantly better than books or manipulatives (smallest $t_{(125)} = -3.25, p=.001$). Tables 8.1 and 8.2 suggest that although students used technology

TABLE 8.1 Means and standard deviations of student technology use

Purpose	Computer M (SD)	Mobile device M (SD)
Play games	2.84 (0.96)	1.93 (0.97)
Listen to music	2.27 (1.05)	1.99 (1.00)
Connect with friends	1.90 (1.08)	1.32 (0.75)
Do school work	2.18 (0.93)	1.47 (0.85)
Look up information not for school work	2.21 (0.87)	1.46 (0.80)

Note: n=127, 4-point scale from 1=never to 4=more than an hour a day

TABLE 8.2 Means and standard deviations of students' preferred tools for learning

Learning tools	Mean (SD)
Computers	3.26 (0.89)
Teacher talking	3.20 (0.91)
Handheld technology	3.06 (0.89)
Paper worksheets	2.90 (0.84)
Textbooks	2.73 (0.87)
Manipulatives	2.67 (0.99)

Note: n=127, 4-point scale from 1=not at all to 4=a lot

at home for entertainment, students recognized both computers and mobile (hand-held) technology as effective learning tools, in addition to the more traditional role of the teacher as their learning guide.

In addition to quantitative responses to scales measuring preferences, students were asked specifically how the mobile devices 'helped them learn' and also how the tools 'made learning difficult'. The 127 written responses were reviewed and data-driven codes were developed, with over 89 percent agreement between independent raters.

Thematic coding of interviews with a sample of these same students (23 boys and 29 girls) confirmed that the use of the devices had an impact on their learning in three general areas. The areas are presented with students' verbatim responses, which often compared the mobile devices to other learning tools:

1. *Resource tool*: in terms of both positive and negative aspects:
   a. *making it easier to find information*, e.g., 'with a newspaper you have to read right through it, but on the iPod you can just do a search';
   b. *more information being available*, e.g., 'there might be updates on the Internet that are not in a book' and 'we can go on the Internet and get different information from different websites, versus only one type, like with a book or newspaper'; and,
   c. *information not always being easy to find and not necessarily correct*, e.g., 'inform-ation isn't always placed as well as you want it to be.'

TABLE 8.3 General thematic codes in responses to the question of how the mobile devices assist students in learning.

Thematic code	Definition	Example
Activity type	Using apps for specific subject content and skills	'a math app' and 'help with spelling'
Source	Specific sources of information including the application or the Internet	'using the Internet to search things' and 'apps that are educational like Anatomy Lite'
Resource tool	General knowledge-construction capabilities of the tool	'helps me learn about many things I don't know' and 'it helps me because it knows everything I need to know'
Function	Functionality of the device including interactive features, speed, and individual devices for each student	'search when no computer is available' and 'interactive screen to practice things'
Enjoyment	Aspects of the device adding to their enjoyment	'it's more fun to use' and 'it adds fun to learning'

2. *Access and portability*: access was described in terms of information available on the Internet and as use of individual devices in their own hands, wherever they would like to work, e.g., 'we have iPods in case the computers in the class are used up' and 'I can take it back to my desk'.

TABLE 8.4 General thematic codes in responses to the question of how the mobile devices made learning difficult for students.

Thematic code	Definition	Example
Function	Issues with the functionality of the device including small screen, difficulty typing, and breakdown	'it's hard to control' and 'it doesn't always respond to your commands'
Distraction	Distraction from their own device or that of others	'it's hard to concentrate on my work with other apps' and 'all the sounds can be distracting'
Content	Problems with the content available through the device	'it has a lot of information on it, it's hard to pick out the right stuff' and 'the information is confusing to understand'
Nothing	Students specifically stated that there was nothing about the device that made it difficult for them to learn	'nothing'

3. *Engagement:* many students again indicated that the mobile devices 'made learning more fun' and 'it makes you like learning'.
4. *Comparison to other tools:* students most often compared the mobile devices to computers and books, suggesting they were similar to the computer but had easier access, while they were seen as superior to textbooks in terms of amount of information and ease of search, e.g., 'in textbooks you have to read through it versus the iPod where you can just do a search'.

Discussion

The student surveys and interviews indicate that elementary students are examining their learning tools and preferences and are capable of recognizing the potential of these devices to support individualized, self-regulated learning. Mobile technology in the form of apps and tablets facilitates access to information for learning, provides motivation, and ensures the opportunity to rehearse problem-solving strategies involved in the process of turning this information into knowledge, regardless of the apps used and the age of the learner. Additionally, an interview with the grade 1 teacher and analysis of classroom observations of the iPods and iPads in use by the 5- and 6-year-olds provides a more detailed picture of a pedagogical approach that puts even the youngest learners in this school in charge of their own learning. Putting devices in the hands of young learners, and providing scaffolds and opportunities to problem-solve and collaborate, will assist these learners as they develop self-regulation capabilities. In the remainder of the chapter, we discuss the implications of how the pedagogy for younger children needs to be reconceived and developed to support self-regulated learning and twenty-first-century skills from a younger age. We begin with some specific pedagogical knowledge regarding how to address self-regulated learning with mobile technology. We use the example of one teacher with longstanding expertise (21 years in the primary division) to illustrate an experience of implementing mobile technology and apps in the classroom.

Supporting self-regulated learning with mobile technology: A teacher's perspective

Teacher A is an experienced teacher who is comfortable with a variety of forms of technology (including iPads), using them for email, Internet searches, and the creation of student learning resources. She is enthusiastic about using mobile technologies with her 20 grade 1 students in most subject areas (Language Arts, Mathematics, Social Studies, Science and Art). Examples of specific uses of apps in this classroom included interactive books, spelling apps, instructional apps for origami, and drawing apps. She described the three most common or intrusive problems encountered in using mobile technology and apps in the classroom as: downloading apps; time to search for apps; and the screen size of the iPods. Despite these limitations, she sees the mobile devices as 'excellent tools for student learning' and would recommend them to other teachers. Her interview was transcribed, and five key aspects of utilizing mobile devices with young children were extracted:

1. *Learning to use the technology.* Teacher A's approach to learning to use the technology with her students is to 'open the box, put it together, have fun and figure it out!' and 'have students do as much as possible'. 'The bottom line is – you have to play!' She suggests that if the technology is 'accessible to them, they are very quick studies [learn quickly], if you're comfortable letting them have the run of it.' She also learns about using technology from colleagues and through carrying out her own research: 'It's just a time factor in order to learn new technology. I mean you have to do the research, you have to get on it.'

2. *Pedagogical activities.* Teacher A uses apps most frequently in learning centres – with small groups of children using the devices independently for specific tasks that support learning in literacy, numeracy, science, social studies, or art. They rotate through activities with a device and apps on a weekly basis, assisting each other with both the logistics of the technology and the content of the task. For example, children may use the devices to follow step-by-step instructions in an origami activity, working in a small group following whole group instruction on the task with the teacher. She chooses activities that are within her 'comfort zone' as a teacher – 'the listening centre for books, and stories for games and songs'.

3. *Problem-solving using the technology.* Preparation to use the mobile devices as another learning tool is a key consideration for Teacher A. 'It's just a tool, and so like good teachers always do, you have to be prepped for what happens when it's not working. We had names for it when it wasn't working!' Students are expected and taught to problem-solve on their own. 'If they can't problem solve [to get the device working], then they problem solve by doing something else... there are always books at the Smartboard.' 'I'm teaching them all kinds of fun stuff they can do on their own or with me, but they're learning how to use that part of the program so that when they go to use it, even if one of the group of four or five gets it, then they can help the others learn.'

4. *Assessment of and with the technology.* Features of the mobile device itself allow Teacher A to assess what children are doing with the devices, even when she is not able to be directly involved with the students using them. 'We use the camera a lot. The kids take a lot of pictures of what they are doing, and again, I have a quick assessment. If they're working on something I can see who's engaged – not video, but still shot, but I know they're working on it.' Some aspects of the device make it difficult for children to use, but she is 'constantly thinking of grade 1, "how could the students use this"' when she reviews apps. Some tasks are not feasible for these young students as 'not having the fine motor skills for some of the programs – it being a lot of just touch and point!' However, many activities can be done as practice individually – 'kids work on math[ematics] activities because they don't have to do everything on paper'.

5. *Behavioural expectations.* The mobile devices have 'compacted our classrooms, so all of the technology is in one place'. Expectations are set high for students

using the devices. If the teacher is doing something else and what children are doing interferes with another group, they lose the opportunity to use the technology, and 'the children don't usually mess with that. They understand how special it is to have the technology. It is part of them knowing, of teaching them how to be careful.'

Using self-regulated learning with mobile technology: A student's perspective

What does it look like when we actually put the mobile devices into the hands of young learners for the first time in the classroom? The activities can be designed, apps selected, and behavioural expectations set, but what happens when children approach their learning with an iPad or iPod in hand at a young age? Below is an example of a classroom observation of three grade 1 students (two boys; one girl) working at one of five learning centres in a classroom of 19 students. Key aspects of self-regulated learning (knowledge, motivation, volition) can be seen across the 40-minute time period with all three children (see Woolfolk *et al.*, 2009).

The task: Children were seated in a small group at individual desks, each with an iPod on their desk on a small, non-skid mat. Two instructions sheets were given to the group with pictures of an iPod and the app they were to use to write five sentences using their Word Wall words (frequently used words, posted on a bulletin board each week). Observations are described in relation to the key aspects of self-regulated learning:

1. *Knowledge:* Providing an instruction sheet with visual aids ensured all learners had the necessary knowledge to begin the activity. All three students had some knowledge of the apps but relied on each other for support in solving problems, e.g., two children from another group came to help Boy 2 when he asked out loud, 'how to make the "thing" (cursor) go up and down'. He declined their help and tried it on his own. The ability to 'try' things out without risk is a feature of apps that encourages children to attempt things on their own. In this case the young boy was 'thinking out loud' and didn't really require support from others. All three children in the group typed and erased at least once. Boy 1 and Girl 2 tried several different spellings and words. Their attempts were easily corrected or refined with the 'touch of a finger'. Girl 1 learned that if she held her finger down, a letter would repeat. She tried this several times before moving on to finish her sentence. Boy 2 used the Word Wall word 'like' in a sentence – 'Do you like clowns?' When he played it back he answered the question with 'yes'. The app used to write the word in a sentence had become interactive immediately, and provided an 'audience of self'. Only Girl 1 completed all five sentences for the required task, but all three children demonstrated problem-solving and use of some cognitive strategies in attempting to accomplish the task using the app.
2. *Motivation*: In agreement with the student surveys, these children using mobile devices kept their attention on the apps, and not always on the assigned task.

They were motivated to solve problems on their own in an effort to make the device and apps work. Each had their own level of 'script' for utilizing the iPod. Boy 2 shared his thinking out loud, showing the researcher how to unlock the iPod by sliding his finger –'these are so funny, they go back and forth'. Boy 2 left his iPod at one point to explore another group who were making a snack with a blender, but returned when encouraged to do so by the teacher. He appeared to be less motivated to finish the literacy task, and more motivated to be involved in the active cooking activity. Having an audience for sharing appeared to motivate these young children, but the app in use for this activity didn't necessarily provide that. Girl 1 wanted to show the researcher her work upon completion, and smiled when she was given that opportunity. Collaborative apps and networked platforms, such as Edmodo, Twitter, etc., are available for even young children under a teacher's supervision, and can add a social purpose to the type of activity presented here.

3. *Volition*: Having the 'volition' to regulate one's learning is the cognitive process of committing to a decision or course of action. Boy 1 chose to use earphones to avoid distraction from others. This feature of the device assists individual learners in setting a context that works for their learning. Distractions presented by students using other apps did cause interference in this case. Boy 2 chose another app to use, rather than the assigned app for the activity. Girl 1 informed the teacher that he was not following the instructions and he was reminded to open the appropriate app. Limiting apps available on devices may help in directing student activity, but providing choice among several relevant apps can give young learners the opportunity to make choices and build volition for future learning. The instruction sheet provided by the teacher with the picture of the app icon allowed students to easily initiate the app's use. Ensuring students continue to be engaged with the app may require further consideration of motivation and learning outcomes.

Conclusion

Results from this study suggest that the development of self-regulated learning capabilities may indeed be supported by certain affordances of mobile technologies and apps, even when working with young learners. However, to develop self-regulation is a complex process – one that demands high levels of teacher scaffolding, modelling, and, at times, direct intervention in the work practices of young learners. It is unrealistic to expect any form of technology to substitute for 'good' teaching, and while strategies such as allowing young students time to explore and investigate the capabilities of technology are valuable, it is vital that teachers are prepared to step in and assume a more active role to ensure they have the knowledge, skills and capabilities to use devices and apps productively, to build self-regulation competencies.

Regardless of how apps are categorized or selected, teachers support learning by providing opportunities for students to develop metacognitive strategies for problem-solving and troubleshooting when using mobile devices and apps. It is important these processes are modelled and scaffolded by teachers. This Ontario-based experience suggests that even young students are capable of recognizing the potential of mobile technologies and apps to help them learn independently. Teachers have a responsibility to develop a curriculum that allows them to fulfil this potential. Results indicate curriculum designed around thinking skills and self-regulated learning frameworks are a suitable approach. The high level of student engagement witnessed in this study was as much attributable to the design of the learning tasks, as it was to the actual technology.

Teachers addressing implementation of apps with young learners should worry less about the classification of apps into specific areas of learning, and more about the pedagogical approach to using them to support thinking and self-regulation competencies across *all* aspects of students' development (social, affective, and cognitive). The grade 1 teacher in this study recognized the importance of involving her students in learning to use the devices and apps through providing choice and collaborative opportunities to work with apps in small groups, by encouraging and scaffolding children in problem-solving about and with the devices, and by setting high behavioural and work-standard expectations that the children strove to meet. This is, put simply, good teaching. Young children can approach learning using apps and mobile devices in a strategic, self-directed way, with motivation and volition to succeed. However, the technology alone does not guarantee this. Ultimately it is up to teachers to design learning contexts and tasks that set the stage for achieving self-regulated learning goals.

References

Bandura, A. (1991). Social cognitive theory of self-regulation. *Organizational Behavior and Human Decision Processes, 50,* 248–287.

Carrington, A. (2015). *The pedagogy wheel v4.0.* Retrieved from: www.unity.net.au/allans-portfolio/wp/wp-content/uploads/2015/03/Wheel_only_V4_LowRez_650x650.jpg on February 16, 2016.

Churches, A. (2008). *Bloom's Digital Taxonomy.* Retrieved from: http://burtonslifelearning.pbworks.com/f/BloomDigitalTaxonomy2001.pdf on February 16, 2016.

Clough, G., Jones, A.C., McAndrew, P. and Scanlon, E. (2008) Informal learning with PDSs and smartphones. *Journal of Computer Assisted Learning, 24,* 359–371.

Falloon, G. (2013a). What's going on behind the screens? Researching young students' learning pathways using iPads. *Journal of Computer Assisted Learning 30,* 1–19. DOI: 10.1111/jcal.12044.

Falloon, G. (2013b). Young students using iPads: App design and content influences on their learning pathways. *Computers and Education, 68,* 505–521.

Falloon, G. (2015a). Chapter 3: Digital learning objects and the development of students' thinking skills. In N. Wright and D. Forbes, *Digital Smarts: Enhancing learning and teaching.* Hamilton, NZ: Wilf Malcolm Institute of Educational Research.

Falloon, G. (2015b). What's the difference? Learning collaboratively using iPads in conventional classrooms. *Computers and Education 84,* 62–77.

Fullan, M. (2013). *Stratosphere: Integrating technology, pedagogy, and change knowledge.* Toronto: Pearson.

Hattie, J. (2012). *Visible Learning for Teachers.* New York: Routledge.

Junkins, S. (n.d.). The periodic table of iPad apps. Retrieved from: https://sjunkins.files.word press.com/2014/06/iste-posters-001.jpg on June 6, 2016.

Koszalka, T. and Ntloedibe-Kuswani, G.S. (2010). Literature on the safe and disruptive learning potential of mobile technologies. *Distance Education, 31*(2), 139–157.

Lieberman, D.A., Bates, C.H. and So, J. (2009). Young children's learning with digital media. *Computers in the Schools, 26,* 271–283.

Looi, C.-K., Wong, L.-H., So, H.-J., Seow, P., Toh, Y., Chen, W., Zhang, B., Norris, C. and Soloway, E. (2009). Anatomy of a mobilized lesson: Learning my way. *Computers and Education, 53,* 1120–1132.

Lui, C.L. (2007) Teaching in a wireless learning environment: A case study. *Educational Technology and Society, 10*(1), 107–123.

Morphew, V.N. (2012). *A Constructivist Approach to the National Educational Technology Standards for Teachers.* Washington, DC: International Society for Technology in Education (ISTE).

Motiwalla, L.F. (2007). Mobile learning: A framework and evaluation. *Computers and Education, 49,* 581–596.

Mueller, J. and Wood, E. (2012). Patterns of beliefs, attitudes, and characteristics of teachers that influence computer integration. *Education Research International,* Article ID 697357, 13 pages.

Mueller, J., Wood, E., De Pasquale, D. and Archer, K. (2011). Students learning with mobile technologies in and out of the classroom. In A. Mendez-Vilas (ed.), *Education in a Technological World: Communicating current and emerging research and technological efforts.* (pp. 414–420). Formatex Research Center. Retrieved from: www.formatex.info/ict/book/ 414-420.pdf on June 6, 2016.

Ontario Ministry of Education. (2010). *Growing Success: Assessment, evaluation and reporting in Ontario schools* (1st Edition Covering Grades 1 to 12). Toronto, ON: Queen's Printer for Ontario.

Ontario Ministry of Education. (2014). *Achieving Excellence. A renewed vision for education in Ontario.* Toronto: Queen's Printer for Ontario. Retrieved from: www.edu.gov.on.ca/eng/ about/renewedvision.pdf on June 6, 2016.

PBS KIDS. (August 14, 2014). Survey Finds Parents Consider Media and Technology Vital Resources for Elementary School Readiness. Retrieved from: www.pbs.org/about/ blogs/news/pbs-kids-survey-finds-parents-consider-media-and-technology-vital-resources-for-elementary-school-readiness/ on February 16, 2016.

Radesky, J.S., Schumacher, J. and Zuckerman, B. (2015). Mobile and interactive media use by young children: The good, the bad, and the unknown. *Pediatrics, 135(1),* 1–3. DOI: 10.1542/peds.2014–2251.

Sandberg, J., Maris, M. and de Geus, K. (2011). Mobile English learning: An evidence-based study with fifth graders. *Computers and Education, 57,* 1344–1347.

Sheng, H., Siau, K. and Nah, F.F. (2010). Understanding the values of mobile technology in education: A value-focused thinking approach. *The DATA BASE for Advances in Information Systems, 41*(2), 25–44.

Wood, E., Specht, J., Willoughby, T. and Mueller, J. (2008). Integrating computer technology in early childhood environments: Issues raised by early childhood educators. *Alberta Journal of Educational Research, 54*(2), 210–226.

Woolfolk, A.E., Winnie, P.H. and Perry, N.E. (2009). *Educational Psychology,* 4th Canadian Edition. Toronto, ON: Pearson Education Canada.

PART III

Empirical evidence

In Part II, Sarah Vaala and colleagues' analysis of the educational potential of most popular children's apps provided a lucid account of the troublesome relationship between the promises of app designers and the reality of children's learning outcomes. In the opening chapter for this section, Nicola Pitchford and Laura A. Outhwaite present an encouraging study of how a series of interactive educational apps (the onebillion maths apps) enhanced the learning of early mathematical skills in primary school children from Malawi and the UK. In a carefully designed randomised controlled trial, the researchers showed that children growing up in completely different primary education systems can have a similar positive response to apps and, importantly, show similar learning gains. The study not only represents a fascinating cross-cultural study of apps' learning potential, but also alerts us to the importance of the so-far-untapped potential of apps to support the learning of basic skills in any country, regardless of different curricula and instructional possibilities.

This raises the intriguing question of why some apps might lead to increased maths skills and why some are not effective at all. Nigel Calder's chapter provides some answers to this question. Calder summarises extant research in early years and primary maths education supported with apps, which shows children's increased enthusiasm and participation in using maths apps. Such engagement not only has a positive influence on children's attitudes towards mathematics learning, but it can also create a cognitively engaging environment. Well-designed maths apps are a great tool to help build understanding of key counting principles (including approximation of quantities, recognising parts of a whole), for exploring symmetry, and, when used in classrooms for group work, for children to demonstrate and share their thinking process.

In Chapter 11, Kathrin Rees, Susan Rvachew and Aparna Nadig explore the relationship between high-quality apps and learning gains in relation to early literacy. A specific focus is on interactivity and the question of how different forms of interactivity embedded in literacy apps might support or hinder parent–child talk during shared reading. The authors observed 29 parent–child interactions during shared reading with two e-books, each with a different level of interactivity: *Sneak a Snack* (with many hotspots) and *Caillou: What's that funny noise?* (with a modest amount of interactivity and added parent prompts to promote high-quality parent–child talk). Perhaps not surprisingly, the researchers didn't find evidence for the book features alone making a difference to the parent–child talk. Rather, it was the book features, *together with* the idiosyncratic response provided by the child and his/her parent, which appeared to make a significant difference to learning gains. Although interactivity is often considered a static variable which can either undermine or support a child's learning from an e-book (cf. Takacs *et al.*, 2015), Rees and colleagues show that for some parents and children, particular interactive features work well, while for other parents, less well, in terms of the rich dialogue created during shared reading. Notwithstanding this finding, some forms of interactivity (e.g., the parents' prompts enabled by the *Caillou: What's that funny noise?* app), enhance the parent–child dialogue almost universally.

Mifsud and Grech, in Chapter 12, bring our focus back to the classroom and the role of apps in supporting technology-mediated bilingual literacy learning – a current official policy emphasis in Malta given the bilingual situation in Malta (and the government mandate that teaching should happen in English and Maltese). By closely studying the use of bilingual literacy apps in five primary classrooms in Malta over the course of six months, Mifsud and Grech identified three key themes in teachers' accounts, one of which was that the apps made a difference to a child's motivation levels to engage in classroom activities, such as reading and sentence building. As Calder mentions in relation to mathematics apps, increased motivation levels can make a significant difference to learning outcomes. While not formally assessing what these outcomes might be, the authors argue that the possibility of downloading e-books or making audio recordings are especially beneficial features for teaching bilingual literacy. Another beneficial feature, identified in this study, is the possibility to customise literacy-building activities. Teachers were able to individualise writing activities for specific students as well as student groups, supporting collaboration and teamwork. Lastly, Mifsud and Grech outline various strategies the teachers and children applied in their use of tablets to bridge the home–school divide for literacy learning purposes. These included using the tablets to watch teacher-recommended YouTube videos at home, which have significantly enhanced students' motivation for learning. To support future literacy teaching with apps in Malta, there is a clear need for increased professional development in classrooms, not only in relation to teachers' technological competence with the tools, but also their specific deployment in curriculum for literacy learning activities.

In Chapter 13, Elaine Khoo expands our exploration of benefits from the targeted use of apps in her heart-warming account of Max, a young child with cerebal palsy, whose use of an iPad and carefully selected apps has shown substantial benefits not only for Max's learning, but also for his physical coordination and overall development. Elaine's study follows a similar theme to Charles and Louisa's chapter, showcasing how major gains can be achieved when school and home collaborate in a coordinated manner to leverage the maximum learning value from access to mobile devices. Elaine's chapter describes how the combination of device design affordances and very carefully selected apps that demanded specific interaction motions and movements such as sweeping, swiping and stretching, helped improve the dexterity of Max's palsied hand, and at the same time, enhanced his learning engagement and motivation. The study found that the immediacy of feedback and reinforcement provided by the apps were important aspects for supporting Max's learning. When combined with the haptic interface, the interactions were not mediated by peripherals, such as a keyboard or a mouse, and more significant learning interactions were possible. However, as pointed out by Radesky and Zuckerman in Chapter 2, success was strongly linked to high levels of communication and collaboration between home and school, and critical appraisal of apps as being 'fit-for-purpose'. The chapter concludes with a warning that the gains noted in Max's case demanded careful planning and much parental and school engagement, and were not simply the result of having good access to technology.

In Chapter 14, Yanjie Song and Wai Ying Ku from Hong Kong report outcomes from a year-long study exploring a Bring Your Own Device (BYOD) programme supported by a range of carefully selected apps, in elementary school science. This chapter is concerned with illustrating how curriculum design and pedagogy evolved throughout the programme to leverage the full potential of the devices and apps for mastering science knowledge; in particular, for supporting student collaboration and for recording and presenting outcomes from their Biodiversity science inquiry. Song and Ku's account illustrates how the move towards an inquiry-learning approach combined with the capabilities of different apps, each one carefully chosen to support different aspects of the science inquiry, enhanced students' learning independence and motivation, leading to deeper engagement and learning. The chapter documents the importance of integrating changes to teaching pedagogy, curriculum, and learning design with technology use, in the process of bringing about sustainable and effective improvements in students' learning. As argued by Elaine Khoo in Chapter 13, critical to achieving this is a careful selection of apps that are *fit for educational purpose*.

In the final chapter in this section, Jackie Marsh and Dylan Yamada-Rice investigate children's interaction with apps that incorporate elements of augmented reality (AR), to determine the extent to which they are able to promote creativity and play. Drawing on findings from a wide-ranging study involving researchers and children's media industry representatives, Jackie and Dylan evaluated a range of apps containing AR elements against an adaptation of Hughes (2002) Taxonomy of Play and Robson's (2014) Creative Thinking Framework. While all apps proved engaging to the children and promoted play and certain aspects of creativity, the extent to which this was sustained and enhanced children's learning from the interaction, varied greatly. In some cases, AR elements in the apps offered little more than entertainment value, while in others they appeared to be more aligned with supporting educational goals. Continuing the theme of Khoo, and Song and Ku, in the previous chapters in this section, the authors strongly advocate for teachers to carefully consider the selection and use of apps appropriate for their educational purpose and goals. Their analysis is a salient reminder that this technology does not offer a 'one size fits all' solution, but rather its selection and effective use requires critical and discerning evaluation by teachers and parents alike. Given the rising popularity of AR products for young children, collaboration partnerships between educators and designers are crucial, so that the design of AR apps makes them not only attractive, but also creative and educationally valuable.

9

THE USE OF TABLET TECHNOLOGY TO SUPPORT DEVELOPMENT OF EARLY MATHEMATICAL SKILLS

A cross-cultural comparison

Nicola J. Pitchford and Laura A. Outhwaite

SCHOOL OF PSYCHOLOGY, UNIVERSITY OF NOTTINGHAM, NOTTINGHAM, UK

On a global scale, significant inequalities exist in the access to and provision of high-quality education. Some of the most profoundly affected countries that face a crisis in primary education are low- to middle-income countries, especially those in Sub-Saharan Africa. In this chapter we consider how a new series of interactive apps, designed to support the development of early maths skills, can support the learning of primary school children in two radically different educational settings. Children at the start of primary school in Malawi (a low-income country in Sub-Saharan Africa) and the UK (a high-income country in Europe) used the same technology and apps, adapted for their native language, over a short period of time (ranging from six to eight weeks). Despite differences in the educational systems, ages of the children that participated in the studies, and the study designs adopted in each country, learning gains of similar magnitude were found in both countries. Our studies suggest that mobile technologies that use well-designed, curriculum-based, interactive apps can be an effective means of providing the same quality of education to all children around the world.

Keywords: Mathematics, underachievement, cross-cultural, developing, student-centred, interactive

Introduction

It is estimated that 250 million children worldwide do not possess the basic numeracy and literacy skills required to live a healthy and productive life and contribute towards economic growth (UNESCO-GMR, 2013–2014). Many of these children live in low-income, developing countries that require urgent educational reform to address significant disparities in access, quality and equity. Children with learning difficulties, children living in remote locations and girls are particularly vulnerable. Malawi and Uganda are countries that face some of the largest educational challenges globally. Overcrowded classes, limited resources and poorly trained and demoralised teachers, mean that primary education is at crisis point. As a consequence, children make little progress with learning basic skills, often repeat years or withdraw from education early before completing primary school, and become disillusioned with the education system.

Even in developed countries, such as the United Kingdom (UK), many children struggle to learn basic mathematical skills. In the latest Programme for Internal Student Assessment (PISA) of 15-year-olds' maths ability, the UK ranked 26 out of 34 participating countries (OECD, 2012). Further statistics shows that in the UK, by the end of primary school, one in six children do not achieve the government age-expected target levels for numeracy (NIAO, 2013). A 'stubborn-tail of under-achievement' is evident among disproportionate groups of underachieving pupils in the UK (Tymms and Merrell, 2007), particularly those of low socio-economic status (SES) who have been shown to have significantly lower maths ability compared with their peers (Anders et al., 2012; Department for Education [DfE], 2010). It is of no surprise therefore that raising standards in maths education in the UK is a matter of national importance.

To address underachievement in mathematics potential solutions need to engage children from a young age. Early learning experiences are a significant predictor of attainment at the end of primary school (Sylva et al., 2010) and children who develop well throughout the early years exceed UK-expected levels in numeracy and literacy at the end of the first two years of primary education (DfE, 2010). Conversely, children who progress slowly and exhibit low attainment levels in the early years are six times more likely than children who progress at a typical rate to be in the lowest fifth of achievers at the end of the first two years of primary schooling (Department for Children, Schools and Families [DCSF], 2008). It is vital, therefore, that all children develop a strong early foundation in mathematics, particularly those vulnerable to underachievement.

Mobile technologies, such as hand-held tablets, could provide an innovative solution for the learning of basic skills, such as numeracy and literacy, in primary schools across the globe. Hand-held devices, such as Apple iPads, have three novel features that are intrinsic to their potential to offer positive benefits in early education: (i) light-weight mobility; (ii) elimination of dexterity-reliant additional devices (e.g. keyboard and mouse); and (iii) capacity to store multiple child-friendly educational apps (Kucirkova, 2014). Tablet technology with educational apps has the potential to make a positive impact on early primary education through its capacity to deliver child-centred, curriculum-based instruction of a consistent quality to all children, regardless of their ability, location, socio-economic status and gender. Apps that include multiple representations of information, such as pictures, video and animation, varying levels of task difficulty, clear goals and rules, learner control, task feedback and repetition, serve to create an individualised learning environment that places the child in active control of their learning (Falloon, 2013, 2014 Falloon and Khoo, 2014, 2015; Kucirkova *et al.*, 2014).

Educational apps can easily be adapted to different languages and contexts, enabling children in different countries to access the same quality of education. This also allows cross-cultural comparisons to be conducted that assess the effectiveness of tablet interventions in supporting the learning of basic skills in primary school children living in different countries. If learning gains are similar in magnitude (effect size) across countries with radically different educational systems, such as Malawi and the UK, when using the same technology and instructional programme, this will provide evidence for the ubiquity of the effectiveness of the technology in supporting early years education.

In this chapter, we report the first cross-cultural comparison of the use of tablet technology with a series of interactive educational apps to support the learning of early mathematical skills in primary school children living in Malawi and the UK.

onebillion maths apps

The maths apps that we evaluated are developed by onebillion, a UK-based non-profit organisation. The apps are designed to have no learning curve: children can start using them without any training or practice as the apps provide clear instruction through a virtual teacher speaking in the local language. The apps allow each child to progress at their own pace, and guide pupils progressively through a series of age-appropriate, comprehensive activities based on the national curriculum. Text box 9.1 describes the core features of the onebillion apps and the topics covered.

Children interact with the software on an individual basis, with one child working on one Apple iPad connected to a set of headphones (Figure 9.1). The virtual teacher shows the child how to carry out certain activities taught through the apps. For each item in a set of activities the virtual teacher demonstrates the task to the child. This repeated instruction over different items within a particular activity is designed to reinforce the concept being taught. Text box 9.2 gives examples of items from the apps and how the child interacts with the software.

The software provides immediate feedback on every interaction a child makes. Praise is given to pupils for their achievements through positive feedback by providing a bright, high-pitched sound and a large yellow tick when the child makes a correct interaction with the software. Negative feedback is given by a dull, low-pitched sound when a child makes an incorrect interaction with the software. When a child succeeds in completing a series of activity items yellow stars appear on the screen, accompanied with another bright, high-pitched sound. When a child successfully completes an end-of-topic quiz, the virtual teacher congratulates the child and a colourful certificate with their name appears with stars and high-pitched cheering. The certificates can be printed. Materials can be repeated as often as needed, by the child touching the sound symbol in the top right-hand side of the screen (see Text box 9.2), engendering individualised tuition.

This approach ensures that the same quality of maths instruction is given to all pupils in both countries, at a pace that is tailored to their individual needs.

TEXT BOX 9.1 CORE FEATURES OF THE ONEBILLION MATHS APPS

- Four apps based on the national primary curriculum taught in Malawi and the UK
- Delivered to individual children using an Apple iPad Mini connected to a set of headphones
- Teach core mathematical concepts in a progressive order
- Instructions given in the local language (Chichewa in Malawi; English in the UK)
- Guided by a virtual teacher who shows 'how to' over a set of activities
- Drag and drop responses for each activity using tablet touchscreen technology
- Feedback (positive and negative) given on each interaction with the technology
- Required to pass each activity to progress to the next
- Quiz to assess knowledge at end of each set of activities

Topics covered, in order of appearance:

Maths 3–5
- Sorting and matching
- Counting to 3
- Lines and patterns
- Counting 4 to 6
- Where is it? (Covers topics relating to space, e.g. above and below, left and right)
- Counting 7 to 10
- Patterns and shapes
- Numbers 1 to 10
- Comparing
- Add and take away

Maths 4–6
- Shape and position
- Counting to 20
- Sharing
- More counting
- Tell the time
- Add and subtract
- Count in tens and fives
- How tall? How long?
- Count to 100
- 2D shapes
- Number lines
- Fractions

Example 1: Children using the technology in a learning centre in Malawi

Example 2: Child practising patterns and shapes

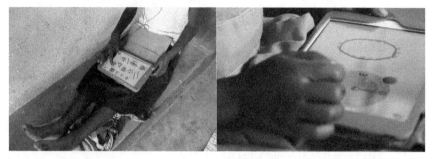

Example 3: Child practising counting objects up to 3

Example 4: Child practising writing numbers 1–10

FIGURE 9.1 Illustrations of children using the tablet technology and interactive apps

Methodology

Two independent studies have been conducted to explore the effectiveness of the onebillion maths apps in supporting the development of early mathematical skills of primary school children residing in Malawi and the UK. Here, we compare results from these two studies to enable cross-cultural comparisons to be drawn. Table 9.1 summarises the methodology employed across studies.

Ethical approval

The Ministry of Education, Science and Technology in Malawi gave ethical approval for the study in Malawi. The School of Psychology, University of Nottingham gave ethical approval for the study in the UK.

Participants

Children in the early years of state primary schooling in Malawi and the UK took part in the studies. The Malawi sample consisted of 283 pupils from Standards 1–3.

TEXT BOX 9.2 EXAMPLES OF ITEMS FROM APPS AND HOW CHILDREN INTERACT WITH THEM

Example I: Counting from 0 to 3 (Maths 3–5)

Virtual teacher: 'Look at the ladybirds on the leaves. Put the numbers in place.' [As the child completes the activity] 'Two ladybirds. No ladybirds zero. Three ladybirds. One ladybird.'

Child: Required to drag and drop the numerals to match the quantities of ladybirds.

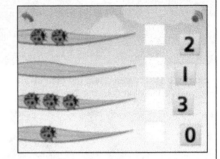

Example II: Numbers 1 to 10 (Maths 3–5)

Virtual teacher: 'There are eight sweets. Add one more.' [After successful first task completion]. 'How many are there now?' [After successful whole task completion] 'Eight add one gives nine.'

Child: Child required to touch the dashed line to add the additional item and then touch the correct number on the number line.

Example III: Numbers 1 to 10 (Maths 3-5)

Virtual teacher: 'Now touch these dots in order. Start with dot one.' [After successful first task completion] 'Colour in your car picture. Use all the colours.' [After successful whole task completion] 'Brilliant, you joined the dots in the right order and coloured in the pictures.'

Child: Required to join the dots together by selecting the numbers in the correct order. Child must then colour the pictures in using the specified number of colours.

TABLE 9.1 Summary of methodology adopted in Malawi and UK studies

Methodology	Malawi	UK
Participants	283 children. Standards 1-3 (6-8 years of age)	61 children. Foundation year (5 years of age)
Design	RCT: between groups (3: Maths Tablet, Non-Maths Tablet, Normal Practice) across time (2: Pre- and Post-test) (★ 2 groups only: Maths Tablet and Normal Practice in Standard 1)	Within-groups (Maths Tablet) across time (2: Pre- and Post-test)
Duration	8 weeks; 30 minutes each day (★15 minutes a day in Standard 1)	6 weeks; 30 minutes each day
Implementation	Class teachers; VSO technical support	Class teachers and teaching assistants
Location	Learning centre: Maths Tablet and Non-Maths Tablet; small group (25 pupils). Usual classroom: Normal Practice; large group (100 pupils)	Quiet area away from usual classroom; small group (10-15 pupils at a time)
Language	Chichewa	English
Assessments	Researcher administered to groups of 50 children with Chichewa translation Tablet based: Maths Concepts, Curriculum Knowledge Paper and pencil based: Generalised Curriculum Knowledge	Researcher administered to groups of 10 children Tablet based: Maths Concepts, Curriculum Knowledge

There were 42 Standard 1 pupils (15 girls and 27 boys) with a mean age of 6 years 10 months, 110 Standard 2 pupils (54 girls and 56 boys) with a mean age of 7 years 7 months, and 131 Standard 3 pupils (70 girls and 61 boys) with a mean age of 8 years 10 months. The UK sample consisted of 61 pupils in Foundation year (26 girls and 35 boys) with a mean age of 5 years 0 months.

Design

Different study designs were employed in Malawi (Pitchford, 2015) and the UK (Outhwaite and Pitchford, in prep). In Malawi, a randomised control trial (RTC) was conducted in an urban primary school in the capital city, Lilongwe. Randomisation was implemented at the pupil level, across gender, within the first three years of primary schooling (Standards 1–3, age 6–8 years). All Standard 2 and 3 pupils registered at the school on the first three days of the 2013–14 school year were randomised to one of three intervention groups: Maths Tablet (intervention group: 38 Standard 2 pupils; 44 Standard 3 pupils), Non-Maths Tablet (placebo group: 35 Standard 2 pupils; 44 Standard 3 pupils), and Normal Practice (control group: 37

Standard 2 pupils; 43 Standard 3 pupils). Due to a relative shortage of children enrolled in Standard 1 at the start of the school year, randomisation was restricted to the Maths Tablet (22 pupils) and Normal Practice (20 pupils) groups only. Both a placebo group (Non-Maths Tablet) and control group (Normal Practice) were incorporated into the RCT design. The Non-Maths Tablet group interacted with a series of educational apps that support musical ability and design skills. These apps place similar demands on manual and attentional processes to the onebillion maths apps. Thus these factors, which might influence learning, were controlled for across the two tablet groups. The Normal Practice control group followed the usual instructional practice that is delivered in primary schools across Malawi. The National Primary Curriculum for maths in Malawi was delivered by the class teacher through the aide of a chalkboard, to a group of children who sat on the floor. Basic numeracy (including mathematics) is taught from Standard 1.

In the UK, a within-groups intervention study was adopted in an urban primary school with two sites in a deprived area in Nottingham. All Foundation year children at each site, for who opt in parental consent was obtained, participated in the study. There was no placebo or control group in the UK study.

Implementation of intervention

In Malawi, class teachers implemented the tablet interventions as part of daily practice for a period of eight weeks. As far as timetabling permitted, the Maths Tablet intervention replaced the usual class-based maths lessons. Children in both the Non-Maths Tablet placebo group and Normal Practice control group received usual instruction in maths through daily class-based lessons. Children in Standards 2 and 3 received the tablet interventions for the equivalent of 30 minutes each day, whereas children in Standard 1 received the tablet intervention for 15 minutes each day. The Voluntary Service Overseas (VSO) in Malawi provided technical support. In the UK, class teachers and teaching assistants implemented the Maths Tablet intervention to all Foundation children at each site for 30 minutes each day over a period of six weeks.

Location of intervention

In Malawi, to limit the possibility of contamination effects across groups within the RCT, a purpose-built classroom ('Learning Centre') was used to administer the tablet-based interventions. The Learning Centre was detached from the main school buildings and accommodated up to 25 children who sat on bamboo mats, individually using tablets connected to headsets. A training session was given to class teachers responsible for administering the tablet-based interventions at the start of the study. They were shown how to use the tablets including turning the tablets on and off, connecting the headsets, storing the headsets, charging and securely storing the tablets, and navigating through the software. Pupils allocated to the Normal Practice control group were given standard maths instruction in their usual classroom setting. This typically involves up to 100 children sat on the floor listening to instruction from the class teacher. Thus, the Non-Maths Tablet placebo group also controlled for differences in the location of interventions.

In the UK, at each site, half of the children in the Foundation class (10–15 pupils at a time) were given the maths apps in a quiet area away from the main class, while the remaining children carried out their usual activities in their classroom. After 30 minutes, the groups swapped over, ensuring that all Foundation children received the maths apps in a quiet area, free from distraction, for 30 minutes each day. As in the Malawi study, class teachers and teaching assistants administering the intervention were shown how to use the technology at the start of the study. This ensured that practice in administering the maths apps was consistent across teachers within each country and between countries.

Assessments

In both Malawi and the UK, children were assessed on two measures of basic mathematical skills at baseline, before the intervention took place (pre-test) and again after the intervention had been completed (post-test). Tablet technology was used to assess mathematical skills of individual children as it enabled performance to be measured objectively, with large groups of children (groups of up to 50 pupils in Malawi and up to 10 pupils in the UK), within a short period of time. English-speaking researchers administered the tablet-based maths assessments in both Malawi and the UK, but in Malawi a class teacher translated the instructions into Chichewa.

Two measures of maths ability were developed specifically for these studies. Maths Concepts consisted of 48 questions assessing a conceptual understanding of mathematics. This test was based on concepts assessed in the Early Grade Mathematic Assessment developed by USAID (EGMA, 2010) and the Numerical Operations subtest of the WIAT-II (Wechsler, 2005). Concepts assessed in this measure included symbolic understanding, numbers in relation to each other, number line understanding, counting, number sense (quantity estimation), simple and complex addition, simple and complex subtraction, and multiplication and division. Curriculum Knowledge consisted of 50 items taken from the activity quizzes in the onebillion maths apps. This measure thus assessed knowledge that is specific to the maths apps. In both measures items of increasing difficulty were presented in a fixed order over successive trials and a discontinue rule was applied so that administration was stopped automatically by the software after a specified number of consecutive fails. This prevented children from becoming disengaged with the assessment process by having to attempt questions that were beyond their ability.

In addition, in Malawi a paper and pencil version of the Curriculum Knowledge measure was given at post-test to assess generalisation of learning to a more conventional context. The Generalised Curriculum Knowledge measure consisted of 50 new items based on those used in the maths apps that the children had not seen before. This was administered to groups of 25 pupils from Standard 2 and 3 in the Learning Centre by a class teacher reading aloud each question in Chichewa.

Results

Learning gains across the intervention period for the Maths Tablet group were calculated in each study. Table 9.2 reports the mean percentage improvement over time and within-group effect size (using Cohen's d, where an effect size of 0.2 is considered small, 0.5 is medium and 0.8 or above is large; Cohen, 1988).

As shown in Table 9.2, in both Malawi and the UK, children receiving intervention with the maths apps made significant improvements in performance on both measures of maths ability over time. Effect sizes were large for all groups except the UK children on the Maths Concepts measure where the effect size was small. This might be expected as the UK children were younger (5 years) than the Malawi children (6-8 years) and they received the maths tablet intervention for a shorter time (six weeks in the UK compared to eight weeks in Malawi).

The RCT design of the Malawi study enabled between-group comparisons to be made. No significant differences were found at pre-test, demonstrating that the groups were matched in maths ability prior to the intervention (Pitchford, 2015). By contrast, at post-test, significant group differences were found for Standard 2 and 3 children, where the Maths Tablet intervention group outperformed the Non-Maths Tablet placebo group and the Normal Practice control group in all but two comparisons. Significant group comparisons are shown in bold in Table 9.3, which reports between-group effect sizes at post-test. As can be seen, medium to large effect sizes were found for all significant group comparisons in Standard 2 and 3. It is worth noting that in Standard 1 the performance at post-test between the Maths Tablet group and the Normal Practice control group did not differ significantly. This might reflect the shorter time Standard 1 children spent using the

TABLE 9.2 Mean improvements in maths ability (% gain) over the intervention period for the Maths Tablet groups in Malawi and the UK. Within-group effect sizes (Cohen's d) reported. For each group, on each measure, significant improvements were made over time (p < .05 at least)

Measure	Malawi			UK	
	Standard	Gain (%)	Effect size	Gain (%)	Effect size
Maths Concepts	1	6.5	0.9	4.6	0.3
	2	12.5	0.9		
	3	9.6	0.8		
Curriculum Knowledge	1	10.6	1.1	21.9	1.0
	2	28.6	1.7		
	3	43.4	2.6		

TABLE 9.3 Between-group effect sizes (Cohen's *d*) across Standards 1-3 in Malawi comparing mean performance at post-test on each measure of maths ability for the Maths Tablet intervention group to the Non-Maths Tablet placebo group and the Normal Practice control group. Significant differences are highlighted in bold (p < .05, at least, bonferroni corrected for multiple comparisons)

Measure	Maths Tablet versus Non-Maths Tablet			Maths Tablet versus Normal Practice		
	Standard			Standard		
	1	*2*	*3*	*1*	*2*	*3*
Maths Concepts	–	0.3	0.0	0.1	**0.6**	0.2
Curriculum Knowledge	–	**0.6**	1.4	0.3	**1.1**	**1.7**
Generalised Curriculum Knowledge	–	**0.7**	**1.9**	–	0.4	**0.8**

maths apps (15 minutes per day) than in Standards 2 and 3 (30 minutes per day). Nevertheless, as shown in Table 9.2, Standard 1 children who used the maths apps made significant learning gains over time whereas their Normal Practice controls did not (p > .05).

Discussion

In this chapter we have compared the effectiveness of a new tablet technology and interactive apps in supporting the development of early maths skills in primary school children living in the Malawi and the UK. Despite major differences in the primary education systems across these two countries, our studies show a similar response to the tablet technology and maths apps by pupils in the early years of primary school. Across time, all children who used the maths apps made significant learning gains, raising both their conceptual understanding of maths and their specific knowledge of maths taught across the curriculum. Furthermore, in Malawi, greater learning gains were found after using the maths apps compared with normal pedagogical practice or using the tablets without the maths software. This illustrates that well-designed, child-centred, curriculum-based software, delivered through hand-held tablets and personal headsets can be an effective means of providing individualised learning in a consistent manner to children living in different countries around the world.

Our studies show that children from developing countries respond just as well as children from developed countries to the onebillion maths apps, as similar effects sizes were found across countries. Over time, children using the onebillion maths apps showed very large effect sizes (ranging from 0.8 to 2.6), despite a short intervention period of just six or eight weeks. These are similar to or greater than the effect sizes shown by other studies with North American or European primary school children that have evaluated different maths software. To date, three studies have been published evaluating maths software that enables within-group effects sizes to be calculated. In these studies, effect sizes range from medium (0.4 for GraphoGame – Exact Numerosity, reported by Räsänen *et al.*, 2009; 0.6 for GameBoy, reported by Shin *et al.*, 2012) to large (0.8 for Comparison Games and 1.2 for Counting Games reported by Praet and Desoete, 2014). Together, these studies suggest that digital educational technologies have the potential to reduce the gap in educational standards around the globe, especially if they are shown to be effective across cultures.

It is likely that the large effects sizes found with the onebillion maths apps arise from specific features incorporated in the onebillion software. In particular, children receive immediate feedback (positive and negative) on each interaction they make with the software, and their knowledge of new concepts is assessed thoroughly by the software through a series of quizzes that require 100 percent success in order to progress to the next set of activities. This engenders retrieval-based learning that has been shown to promote both encoding of new information and the application of knowledge (e.g., Grimaldi and Karpicke, 2014). In Malawi, we showed that learning with the onebillion maths apps generalised to a paper and pencil context, suggesting that children had embedded the knowledge acquired through the apps into their cognitive systems, which allowed them to apply it to a different context (Pitchford, 2015).

We are currently extending our research in collaboration with onebillion and their partners. An integral part of the onebillion maths intervention in developing countries is the use of 'oneclass technology'. This is currently being implemented in Malawi and Uganda. The maths apps are currently used in all oneclass centres and a literacy app aimed at teaching children to read is in development. oneclass technology consists of a dedicated solar-powered classroom (the Learning Centre) that provides a sustainable environment for pupils in remote areas with limited infrastructure and resources, and no access to electricity. Local partner organisations in Malawi (VSO) and Uganda (Haileybury Youth Trust) are responsible for the construction of oneclass centres, using sustainable building materials. Each oneclass is equipped with remote monitoring of individual children's progress through the onebillion apps, data from which are fed back to teachers who are trained to interpret it. This enables teachers to track individual children's progress, assess why they might be struggling to learn, and deliver evidence-based strategies to support each pupil. Another feature of the oneclass technology is a solar-powered projector connected to an Apple TV, which gives teachers an easy means to provide tailored support to small groups of children who are struggling to acquire a particular concept or skill.

The oneclass solution is scalable and involves a considerable transfer of skills to teachers who might not possess knowledge of the curriculum being taught through the apps. The use of tablet technology in the oneclass centres might increase teacher motivation as it supports and enhances their teaching practice. This in turn might improve the level of teacher commitment and engagement in Malawi and Uganda. In addition, the use of tablets to deliver personalised learning might increase children's excitement to learn and improve their behaviour and focus, which in turn could result in a decrease in absenteeism from school and increased levels of self-confidence. We are currently investigating these potential additional benefits of the oneclass technology through further research in Malawi and Uganda. This is important to establish because the oneclass technology and infrastructure has the potential to provide a personalised learning solution for marginalised children worldwide, which could help to reduce the significant inequities in primary education that is currently apparent.

References

Anders, Y., Rossbach, H., Weinert, S., Ebert, S., Kuger, S., Lehrl, S. and von Maurice, J. (2012). Home and preschool learning environments and their relations to the development of early numeracy skills, *Early Childhood Quarterly, 27*, 231–244.

Cohen, J. (1988). *Statistical Power Analysis for the Behavioural Sciences* (2nd ed.). New Jersey, USA: Lawrence Erlbaum Associates.

Department for Children, Schools and Families. (2008). *How Strong is the Relationship between Foundation Stage Profile (2005) and Key Stage 1 (2007)?* DEP2008-1634. Deposited in House of Commons Library.

Department for Education. (2010). *Achievement of Children in the EYFSP.* RR-034. London, UK: DfE.

Early Grade Mathematics Assessment (EGMA): *National Baseline Report 2010.* USAID-funded Malawi Teacher Professional Development Support (MTPDS) Program. Available: http://pdf.usaid.gov/pdf_docs/pnaec139.pdf

Falloon, G. (2013). Young students using iPads: App design and content influences on their learning. *Computers & Education, 68*, 505–521.

Falloon, G. (2014). What's going on behind the screens? Researching young students' learning pathways using iPads. *Journal of Computer Assisted Learning, 30*, 318–366.

Falloon, G. and Khoo, E. (2014b). Exploring young students' talk in iPad-supported collaborative learning environments. *Computers & Education, 77*, 13–28.

Falloon, G. (2015). What's the difference? Learning collaboratively using iPads in conventional classrooms. *Computers & Education, 84*, 62–77.

Grimaldi, P.J. and Karpicke, J.D. (2014). Guided retrieval practice of educational materials using automated scoring. *Journal of Educational Psychology, 106*, 58–68.

Kucirkova, N. (2014). iPads in early education: Separating assumption and evidence. *Frontiers in Psychology, 5*, 715.

Kucirkova, N., Messer, D., Sheehy, K. and Panadero, C. F. (2014). Children's engagement with educational iPad apps: Insights from a Spanish classroom. *Computers & Education, 71*, 175–184.

NIAO. (2013). *Improving Literacy and Numeracy Achievement in Schools.* Retrieved June 9, 2014 from www.niauditoffice.gov.uk/literacy_and_numeracy_2.pdf

OECD (2012). *Programme for Internal Student Assessment (PISA) Results from PISA 2012.* Retrieved January 10, 2015, from www.oecd.org/unitedkingdom/PISA-2012-results-UK.pdf

Outhwaite, L.A. and Pitchford, N.J. (in prep). Effectiveness of a tablet intervention to support the development of early mathematical skills in UK Foundation year children.

Pitchford, N.J. (2015). Development of early mathematical skills with a tablet intervention: A randomized control trial in Malawi. *Frontiers in Psychology, 6*, 485.

Praet, M. and Desoete, A. (2014). Enhancing young children's arithmetic skills through non-intensive, computerised kindergarten interventions: a randomised controlled study. *Teaching and Teacher Education, 39*, 56–65.

Räsänen, P., Salminen, J., Wilson, A.J., Aunio, P. and Dehaene, S. (2009). Computer-assisted intervention for children with low numeracy skills. *Cognitive Development, 24*, 450–472.

Shin, N., Sutherland, L.M., Norris, C.A. and Soloway, E. (2012). Effects of game technology on elementary student learning in mathematics. *British Journal of Educational Technology, 43*, 540–560.

Sylva, K., Melhuish, E., Sammons, P., Siraj-Blatchford, I. and Taggart, B. (eds). (2010). *Early Childhood Matters: Evidence from the effective pre-school and primary education project.* London, UK: Routledge.

Tymms, P. and Merrell, C. (2007). *Standards and Quality in English Primary Schools over time: The national evidence. Evidence to the Primary Review.* Cambridge: Routledge.

UNESCO Education For All Global Monitoring Report 2013/14. *Teaching and Learning: Achieving quality for all.* Available from: http://unesdoc.unesco.org/images/0022/002256/225660e.pdf

Wechsler, D. (2005). *Wechsler Individual Achievement Test 2nd Edition (WIAT II).* London, UK: The Psychological Corp.

10

'MAKES LEARNING EASIER – THEY'RE ACTIVE'

Using apps in early years mathematics

Nigel Calder

UNIVERSITY OF WAIKATO, NEW ZEALAND

This chapter discusses the use of apps in early years mathematics education. It draws together the key threads of research that has been undertaken in learning mathematics through children's tablet apps, and situates this research within a discussion of how apps might be used to support mathematics learning in the early years. It considers the ways in which children's apps could be used effectively to enhance engagement and cognition in mathematics, indicating several key apps and approaches to learning. Both affordances and constraints of using apps for mathematics learning are presented, giving rise to several implications for practice.

Keywords: Mobile technologies, mathematics education, early years, apps, technology

Introduction

We've all seen the video clips: children, as young as two, interacting with iPads, phones, or other mobile technologies in purposeful, meaningful ways. While there is clearly engagement, what is the nature of this engagement and any associated learning? This chapter considers the ways children in the early years might learn when engaging with mathematics through tablet apps, and the pedagogy that might best facilitate learning.

In recent years in educational settings, there has been a proliferation in the availability and usage of mobile technologies (Philip and Garcia, 2015). Their low instrumentation and ease of operation, coupled with the interaction being focused primarily on touch and sight, make them more intuitive than pencil-and-paper technology for young learners. Linked to the increase in mobile technology use is the increased availability of educational apps. However, questions have been raised regarding the appropriateness of the content and pedagogical approaches of teachers using mathematics apps in their classrooms (Larkin, 2013). If apps are an inevitable and relatively enduring element of the evolving digital world, we need to consider the ways they might stimulate children's thinking in a variety of areas, including mathematics, and how teachers might optimise their potential for children's mathematics learning.

Mathematical and logical intelligence are evident in children who are able to recognise and explore patterns, categorise, and work out relationships using objects. It also includes problem-solving and experimenting (Boyes, 2001). In light of the previous chapter reporting some clear learning gains for UK and Malawi children using the onebillion maths apps, this chapter considers how apps more generally might enhance children's mathematics capabilities. The chapter begins by considering the use of iPad apps for learning in general, followed by a brief discussion concerning the nature and place of mathematics in the early years. A section on mathematical apps and discussion of associated pedagogy will consider how children's apps might best be used for mathematics learning. Interwoven through the chapter will be some practical suggestions for learning and teaching practice.

Using iPads and apps in learning mathematics

Transforming the learning experience

Carr (2012) reported that multiple senses are engaged with the use of digital technologies, and that they might reinforce learning and support a variety of learning objectives in mathematics. In particular, the development of number recognition, pre-mathematical skills, and cognitive development have been identified as salient (Howell and MacDonald, 2014). Howell and MacDonald also indicated that social skills and self-esteem were facilitated, and concluded 'that Early Years learners who engage with digital technology achieve better learning outcomes, in particular, literacy and numeracy skills, than peers who do not' (2014, p. 194). Others contend that there is a tendency to over-extend the direct influence that particularly mobile technology has on learning (Philip and Garcia, 2015). As discussed by Pitchford and Outhwaite in this volume (Chapter 9), there is a lot of enthusiasm around mobile technologies supporting basic mathematical skills, with some emerging evidence showing the benefits of well-designed apps for independent mathematical learning. Regardless, there is agreement that the teacher's pedagogical approach and appropriate matching of apps to the learning situation are central in the mathematics learning process (Calder, 2015). Exploring this relationship is the focus of the present chapter.

Teaching and learning mathematics through the use of digital technologies reveal new opportunities for engaging with mathematical concepts and processes. Some mathematics educators contend that digital technologies offer the opportunity to re-envisage aspects of mathematics education, along with alternative ways to facilitate understanding (e.g., Borba and Villarreal, 2005; Calder,

2011). For instance, the visual and dynamic elements of engaging mathematical thinking through digital technologies reposition the types of knowledge and understanding required for learning in mathematics. In a study undertaken by Sinclair and Moss (2012) involving 4- and 5-year-old children using the dynamic geometry software app *Sketchpad* for triangle identification, the children manipulated triangles by moving their vertices. They re-conceptualised their perceptions of triangles and began posing some informal generalisations regarding their properties. Facilitating this type of mathematical thinking would be challenging without the dynamic and visual affordances, and the instant feedback to input, which *Sketchpad* and similar digital technologies offered.

The affordances of digital technologies for mathematics education are well-documented (Sacristan *et al.*, 2010), and learning through apps offers potential advantages that are similar to those identified within other digital technologies. More specifically, apps such as *Multiplier* (Figure 10.1) offer the opportunity to engage dynamically; give instantaneous feedback to input; link various forms of information or data (e.g., numeric, symbolic and visual); and can transform inform-ation or data simultaneously (Calder, 2011).

There are particular attributes and affordances of mobile technologies that support mathematics with young children. Mobile technologies incorporate aural capabilities in the representation of mathematical ideas, while apps such as *Explain Everything* facilitate collaboration and mathematical thinking through students being able to record individual or group presentations of mathematical processes, strategies, and solutions. This video-recording feature of iPads, and the simplicity with which it is enabled, opens up other learning opportunities that would not be

FIGURE 10.1 The visual, numeric and symbolic engagement with the *Multiplier* app

possible with pencil-and-paper approaches. Tablets and iPads also have the capability to manipulate large amounts of 'untidy' data, while simultaneously delivering a visually stimulating environment.

Using apps when collecting and analysing data

The mobile aspect of apps is potentially a powerful enabler for learning, opening up a diverse range of learning situations and allowing the learner to seamlessly transition between them. For example, a child might work on an activity in the classroom, move outside to collect data for the task, work in other spaces (including home) to process and reflect on the data, and then discuss and present their work with other children in their class. Tablets and apps can be brought into the learning situation easily, and be used collaboratively between two or more children (Falloon, 2015), while the apps themselves and the ways that they are used can be changed quickly. Video-recordings using apps *in situ* might be used for data, research or storytelling – all of which might contain mathematical elements. For example, each child or group using an iPad to video-record their personal story of a visit to a farm might edit it using iMovie directly on their device, then sequence the events time wise, facilitating a meaningful measurement task for young children. Counting various animals children see in their recording, and using an app such as *Math Shake* to work out the animal feed and its cost, would also be a suitable early years mathematics task. Mobile technologies and apps enable learners to engage with research and analysis in an ongoing way, within a variety of environments and settings. For example, in statistics, students can collect data directly in the field and do some exploratory data analysis to inform an immediate review of the research question. This mobile characteristic differentiates its use and potential for learning from that of desktop computers. iPads and digital tablets might also be used for more generic processes such as Internet research, preparing reports and presentations and communication (Suhr *et al.*, 2010), all of which are major aspects of statistics education.

Generic features of mobile technologies and apps

Several authors in this book describe the features of mobile technologies and apps that have the potential to enhance learning and I focus specifically on those relevant for learning in mathematics. Hutchison *et al.* (2012) identified that iPads power on and off very quickly, which means that the devices can be easily integrated into learning situations in a spontaneous manner, with minimal disruption. The researchers found that students quickly learnt to navigate the iPad, and when they did encounter problems, they worked collaboratively to resolve them (Figure 10.2). In conjunction with the range of available apps and the ease of access to iPads in the class situation, these aspects suggest that teachers were more likely to use iPads to differentiate the learning for individual students.

FIGURE 10.2 Two students using the *Multiplier* app

Within the appropriate learning environment, apps have the potential to enhance children's attitudes to mathematics and their cognitive engagement. Calder and Campbell (2015) identified the affordances of interactivity and instantaneous feedback provided by apps that foster the learner's willingness to take risks with their learning. Others have reported that the use of mobile devices in the classroom enhanced students' engagement and impacted positively on the classroom environment (Attard, 2015; Suhr *et al.*, 2010). Most apps present the mathematical ideas and processes in a game context, often with extrinsic motivators, such as points, for rewards. A simple games context resonates with elements of play that are intrinsic to learning motivation in the early years.

The integration of the features of tablets, such as video-recording with learning in outdoor settings, offers rich potential for learning in early years mathematics. For example, children photographing five views from a particular point and then others having to identify the point, or using Googlemaps to work out routes and distances between known locations of interest, such as from school to home, would use a similar integrated approach that young children would enjoy, offering rich learning experiences (Calder, 2011). The next section considers the particular features of mobile devices that are particularly suited for effective teaching of early years mathematics.

Haptic and multi-touch affordances

Apps have some particular features that enhance mathematics learning opportunities. While affordances and constraints can be associated with particular digital technologies (Sacristan *et al.*, 2010), there are some that are more generically embedded through a range of settings (Calder, 2011). Allied to the ones outlined in the first section of the chapter, tablets and their apps also offer a multi-touch affordance. The glass display is interacted with through touch, making it more directly responsive to input, and enhancing the relatively high agency of the medium. These haptic actions produce particular effects, that is, the creation and manipulation of mathematical objects are done directly by children touching the screen. There is direct interaction with mathematics phenomena rather than being mediated through a mouse or keyboard, hence making the iPad more suitable for young children than desktop computers (Sinclair and Heyd-Metzuyanim, 2014). Two or more fingers allow gestural expression such as 'pinch' or 'spread' to produce and transform objects (Sinclair and Heyd-Metzuyanim, 2014) giving the potential for cognitive embodiment. This recognises that cognition is related to manifestations of movement, including haptic perception and body language (e.g., Radford, 2014). These gestures may be influential in the development of understanding in geometry and number – two key aspects of early years mathematics. The exploration and understanding of space and movement are central elements of geometry, and hence this would suggest that the movement and spatial aspects of cognitive embodiment would be influential in the facilitation of understanding in geometry.

Early years mathematics learning and apps

Mathematics in the early years is typically centred on the content strands of number, measurement and geometry. For example, the New Zealand early years curriculum, Te Whariki (Ministry of Education, 1996), stipulates a requirement that children develop the ability to use the counting system effectively and engage with mathematical concepts such as numbers, length, weight, volume, shape and pattern in meaningful and purposeful ways. In geometry, Te Whariki recognises the need for 'spatial understandings, including an awareness of how two- and three-dimensional objects can be fitted together and moved in space and ways in which spatial information can be represented, such as in maps, diagrams, photographs, and drawings' (Ministry of Education, 1996, p. 90). Other countries have similar mathematical objectives for the early years. For example, in Canada in Grades K-3, it is expected that children can use symmetry to sort, compare and construct figures (Ng and Sinclair, 2015).

Additionally, play is central in much of the learning in the early years and usually has both cognitive and social dimensions. Children learn through play – by interacting with resources and others, by questioning and hypothesising, by predicting patterns or outcomes, and trying their ideas out (Ministry of Education, 1996). This would include digital play, where apps might facilitate creative and imaginative play, and at the same time develop discrete mathematics skills. App-based games and play-based learning can be mutually supportive of learning mathematics in the early years – they can be 'synchronistic and sympathetic; they support the teaching and learning strategies of the teacher' (Howell and McDonald, 2014, p. 195). Examples of this include apps such as *TouchCounts,* which can be used to facilitate conceptual understanding in particular number concepts and processes, exploration of patterns and the relationships between mathematical concepts (Figure 10.3). Using the counting feature of *TouchCounts* connects the counting of the disks with both symbolic and aural representations, while the ledge enables patterns to be explored. Working in 'operation mode' allows tangible connections between the grouping or separating of objects, and the associated additive processes. There is also scope to use it for problem-solving and experimenting with a range of number properties.

Engagement with mathematics through apps

Much of the literature and discussion regarding the ways iPads and apps might influence the learning experience is centred on the notion of student engagement; of students being actively engrossed and motivated, often by the visual and interactive characteristics of the device and its apps (Carr, 2012; Hill, 2011; Li and Pow, 2011). The inclusion of game-based apps in early years mathematics programmes has likewise enhanced engagement, and is reported to have increased enthusiasm and participation (Attard, 2013). Children enjoy the visual and

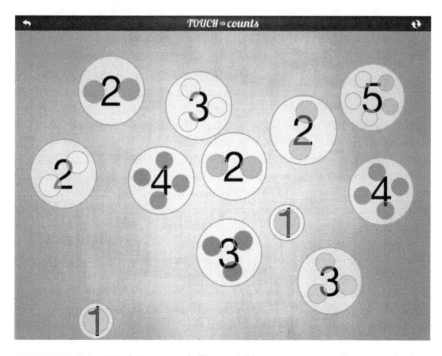

FIGURE 10.3 Using *TouchCounts* to challenge children to group numbers to make fives

interactive features of apps, while the game situation, often with the player placing him or herself in a virtual environment, is perceived as both entertaining and cognitively engaging. Sinclair and Heyd-Metzuyanim (2014) also contend that for many children the iPad becomes an evocative object, one that they relate to on an emotional level.

There are indications that the use of apps might have a positive influence on children's attitudes towards mathematics learning in both pre-school and primary school settings. For example, Willacy (2015) reported attitudinal changes in children attending hospital schools, where much of the learning was undertaken independently in the home. While a positive attitude is a key attribute in the engagement of learners, and the subsequent learning, optimising learning is also contingent on the appropriateness and quality and support of the activity that the learner is being engaged with. While working with 5-year-olds on the *TouchCounts* app, Sinclair and Heyd-Metzuyanim (2014) found that productive mathematical learning occurred when teachers attended to the emotional scaffolding of the child and the cognitive aspects simultaneously. Spencer (2013) also reported positive attitudes and enhanced understanding of numeracy concepts for 5-year-olds when playing game-based apps in their daily mathematics programme. She reported that the app *Know Number Free* supported children to recognise and count numbers, and that apps, with their kinaesthetic features, assist the children to learn. Meanwhile, others have indicated that the use of digital games led to active discussion and inter-student interaction and collaboration (Murray and Olcose, 2011). This collaborative activity is conducive to students' mathematical problem-solving.

Apps and building number sense

Other studies also reported apps supporting mathematical cognitive development. Using mathematical apps with pre-schoolers has highlighted the potential to enhance children's number sense (Spencer, 2013). Spencer's study found evidence that digital play with mathematical apps facilitated improvements with the identification and writing of numbers and the associated quantities, and that the understandings in number were maintained after the specific intervention had finished. Likewise, Baccaglini and Maracci (2015) identified links between using iPad apps and the emergence of number sense in pre-schoolers. They noted that pre-schoolers' understanding of counting principles, approximation of quantities, and subitising and recognising parts of a whole were aspects of number sense that were improved with the use of apps. Attard (2015) also reported increased engagement with mathematics concepts by kindergarten children using apps, with enhanced opportunities for repeated patterning and using mathematical language. She also concluded that 7-year-old students' strategies in subtraction were supported by using *ShowMe* to demonstrate their strategies and communicate thinking.

Greater and more specific use of mathematical language in geometry has also been reported with 5- to 7-year-olds who used *Sketchpad* to explore symmetry and gain understanding of key symmetry properties, such as the image being equidistant from the line of symmetry as the object (Ng and Sinclair, 2015). Interestingly, they suggested that the interplay between different resources and materials, including pencil-and-paper, facilitated functional thinking in geometry. The children explored shapes and their movements on the screen supplemented by pencil and paper activities, the combination of which appeared effective in helping them master the geometry concepts.

Questions of app quality

One element of learning through game-based apps that is often criticised is their tendency to promote repetitive practice of skills (see Guernsey and Levine, 2015 and Vaala in Chapter 4). However, using game-based apps for basic skill development may not be to the detriment of student engagement (Jorgensen and Lowrie, 2012). When mathematics learning is embedded within the apps that the learners engage with on their own terms, they are motivated and the learning doesn't become boring, enabling students to stay on task for significant periods of time (Jorgensen and Lowrie, 2012). Mathematical app games were also reported to evoke student interest with tasks that were otherwise perceived to be repetitive and boring (Carr, 2012).

However, the quality of apps for learning in mathematics is inconsistent. An analysis of mathematics education apps available through Apple's App Store, indicated that relatively few supported mathematical learning with a conceptual understanding focus – most were predominantly drill-and-practice activities (Larkin, 2013). Other research contends that few apps exemplify current best practice in mathematics education (Pelton and Pelton, 2012). While there are some excellent apps that enhance mathematical learning, and there are teachers who have the expertise and motivation to use them appropriately, effective learning is contingent on both of these conditions. Importantly though, drill-and-practice apps can maintain children's interest and be used effectively to develop key early years mathematics skills, such as number recognition. If used effectively with appropriate pedagogy they can also stimulate mathematical thinking (Calder, 2015).

Conclusion

While mobile technologies and apps offer affordances for learning that are evident in some other digital technologies, it is their mobility and the directness of the interaction through touch that differentiates the nature of the mathematical learning from other digital technologies. The direct interaction with the screen enables children to more directly connect their movement to the mathematical property they might be exploring. Being able to shift the site of learning is also conducive to more contextual mathematics learning. This mobility enables greater connection between learning in different contexts and situations. Teachers might integrate the mathematical learning into a range of outdoor settings more seamlessly and with more spontaneity, including linking better with the home environment. In general, apps engage learners through being dynamic and visually interesting. They allow students to explore mathematics concepts in an interactive way. Being able to manipulate objects and explore relationships and patterns through multi-representations of number, reshapes the learning experience and offers potential to enhance mathematical understanding. The particular affordances of the medium offer opportunities to transform the learning experience and influence the mathematical understanding of early years learners.

Within the class environment, mathematics apps also permit flexibility with grouping, foster mathematical language and communication, and can be more spontaneously integrated into classroom programmes. Mathematics apps bring visual, interactive elements to the learning situation, which potentially can support the understanding of geometric properties. The interaction through touch is also appealing and more direct. Using touch to directly interact with the glass display makes them more conducive to learning in the early years. Children can create and manipulate objects dynamically onscreen without this being mediated by a mouse or keyboard. It is a more immediate, explicit interaction. The use of mathematics apps has been shown to enhance mathematical understanding, engagement, cognitive risk-taking and collaboration for early years learners in a range of contexts and situations such as number, geometry, patterning and logical reasoning. Cognitive risk-taking and collaboration are aspects that enhance mathematical problem solving (Calder, 2011).

However, it must be remembered that merely having tablets and apps available, along with the children enjoying them, is not *necessarily* going to facilitate learning. The type of app and the ways they are used are critical for learning to be optimised. Many apps, while perhaps entertaining, don't optimise learning potential. The most effective are those with a creative aspect where the children can create or manipulate within the app or game. However, even the most basic 'consumable' app game can be beneficial, if used purposefully. With appropriate teacher or parent interaction, basic rewards-based games can facilitate the development of particular mathematical skills. Apps can also be used in conjunction with other resources and equipment to make the relationships and connections in mathematics clearer. Importantly, teacher professional learning in using apps effectively in their mathematics programmes needs to be supported. Teachers in the early years need support in the selection of appropriate apps, and guidance or time to best match the apps to the appropriate learning needs and intended objectives.

Overall though, sufficient evidence exists suggesting that the use of apps has a positive influence on the learning of mathematics in the early years. If the app facilitates creative, focused activity or play while being supported by appropriate pedagogy from the teacher, engagement with learning can be optimised and mathematical understandings developed.

References

Attard, C. (2013). Introducing iPads into primary mathematics pedagogies: An exploration of two teachers' experiences. In V. Steine, L. Ball and C. Bardini (eds), *Mathematics Education: Yesterday, today and tomorrow* (Proceedings of the 36th annual conference of the Mathematics Education Research Group of Australasia). Melbourne, VIC: MERGA.

Attard, C. (2015). Introducing iPads into primary mathematics classrooms: Teachers' experiences and pedagogies. In M. Meletiou-Mavrotheris, K. Mavrou and E. Paparistodemou (eds), *Integrating Touch-enabled and Mobile Devices into Contemporary Mathematics Education*. DOI: 10.4018/978-1-4666-8714-1.ch009.

Baccaglini, A. and Maracci, M. (2015). Multi-touch technology and preschoolers' development of number sense. *Digital Experiences in Mathematics Education, 2*. DOI: 10.1007/s40751-015-0002-4.

Borba, M. C. and Villarreal, M. E. (2005). *Humans-with-Media and the Reorganization of Mathematical Thinking: Information and communication technologies, modeling, experimentation and visualisation,* New York, NY: Springer.

Boyes, K. (2001). *Creating an Effective Learning Environment.* Upper Hutt, New Zealand: Spectrum Education Limited.

Calder, N. S. (2011). *Processing Mathematics through Digital Technologies: The primary years.* Rotterdam, the Netherlands: Sense.

Calder, N. (2015). Apps: Appropriate, applicable and appealing? In T. Lowrie and R. Jorgensen (eds). *Digital Games and Mathematics Learning: Potential, promises and pitfalls.* The Netherlands: Springer.

Calder, N. S. and Campbell, A. (2015). "You play on them. They're active." Enhancing the mathematics learning of reluctant teenage students. In M. Marshman, V. Geiger, and A. Bennison (eds), *Mathematics Education in the Margins* (Proceedings of the 38th annual conference of the Mathematics Education Research Group of Australasia), pp. 133–140. Sunshine Coast: MERGA.

Carr, J. (2012). Does math achievement h'APP'en when iPads and game-based learning are incorporated into fifth-grade mathematics instruction? *Journal of Information Technology Education, 11,* 269–286.

Falloon, G. (2015). What's the difference? Learning collaboratively using iPads in conventional classrooms. *Computers & Education, 84,* 62–77.

Guernsey, L. and Levine, M. H. (2015). *Tap, Click, Read: Growing readers in a world of screens.* San Francisco, CA: John Wiley & Sons.

Hill, R. A. (2011). Mobile digital devices. *Teacher Librarian, 39*(1), 22–26.

Howell, J. and McDonald, S. (2014). Digital play: The use of creative technologies in the early years. In Z. Yang (ed.), *Transforming K-12 Classrooms with Digital Technology* (1st ed.). Hershey, PA: Information Science Reference.

Hutchison, A., Beschorner, B. and Schmidt-Crawford, D. (2012). Exploring the use of the iPad for literacy learning. *The Reading Teacher, 66*(1), 15–23.

Jorgensen, R. and Lowrie, T. (2012). Digital Games for Learning Mathematics: Possibilities and Limitations. In J. Dindyal, L. P. Cheng and S. F. Ng (eds), *Mathematics Education: Expanding horizons* (Proceedings of the 35th annual conference of the Mathematics Education Research Group of Australasia). Singapore: MERGA.

Larkin, K. (2013). Maths education: Is there an app for that? In V. Steinle, L. Ball and C. Bardini (eds), *Mathematics Education: Yesterday, today and tomorrow* (Proceedings of the 36th annual conference of the Mathematics Education Research Group of Australasia). Melbourne, VIC: MERGA.

Li, S. C. and Pow, J. C. (2011). Affordance of deep infusion of one-to-one tablet-PCs into and beyond classroom. *International Journal of Instructional Media, 38*(4), 319–326.

Ministry of Education (1996). *Te Whariki.* Wellington: Learning Media.

Murray, O. T. and Olcese, N. R. (2011). Teaching and learning with iPads, ready or not? *TechTrends, 55*(6), 42–48.

Ng, O-L. and Sinclair, N. (2015). Young children reasoning about symmetry in a dynamic geometry environment. *ZDM Mathematics Education, 47*(3). DOI: 10.1007/ s1185 8-014-0660-5.

Pelton, F. L. and Pelton, T. (2012). Sharing strategies with teachers: ipods in math class. In *Society for Information Technology & Teacher Education International Conference,* Vol. 2012, No. 1. (pp. 4363–4366).

Philip, T. M. and Garcia, A. (2015). Schooling mobile phones: Assumptions about proximal benefits, the challenges of shifting meanings, and the politics of teaching. *Educational Policy, 29*(4), 676–707.

Radford, L. (2014). Towards an embodied, cultural, material conception of mathematics cognition. *ZDM, 46*(3), 349–361.

Sacristan, A., Calder, N. S., Rojano, T., Santos, M., Friedlander, A. and Meissner, H. (2010). In C. Hoyles and J-B Lagrange (eds), *Mathematics Education and Technology – Rethinking the terrain* (pp. 179–226). NY: Springer

Sinclair, N. and Heyd-Metzuyanim, E. (2014). Learning number with *TouchCounts:* The role of emotions and the body in mathematical communication. *Technology, Knowledge and Learning, 19,* 81–99.

Sinclair, N. and Moss, J. (2012). The more it changes, the more it becomes the same: The development of routine of shape identification in dynamic geometry environments. *International Journal of Education Research, 51* and *52,* 28–44.

Spencer, P. (2013). iPads: Improving numeracy learning in the early years. In V. Steinle, L. Ball and C. Bardini (eds), *Mathematics Education: Yesterday, today and tomorrow* (Proceedings of the 36th annual conference of the Mathematics Education Research Group of Australasia). Melbourne, VIC: MERGA.

Suhr, K.A., Hernandez, D.A., Grimes, D. and Warschauer, M. (2010). Laptops and fourth-grade literacy: Assisting the jump over the fourth-grade slump. *Journal of Technology, Learning, and Assessment, 9*(5), 1–2.

Willacy, H. (2015). *Exploring the influence of apps for mobile devices on student engagement and differentiated learning in a New Zealand Regional Health School* (Unpublished Master's thesis). University of Waikato, Hamilton, New Zealand.

11

ADULTS AND CHILDREN MAKE MEANING TOGETHER WITH E-BOOKS

Kathrin Rees, Susan Rvachew and Aparna Nadig

SCHOOL OF COMMUNICATION SCIENCES AND DISORDERS, CENTRE FOR RESEARCH IN BRAIN, LANGUAGE AND MUSIC, MCGILL UNIVERSITY, CANADA

In this chapter, we examine how adults in a shared reading context make use of the specific interactive features in three e-books for teaching their pre-schooler about the meaning of text elements. Of particular interest are their attempts to teach children key vocabulary and engage them in inferential talk going beyond concrete story contents. We observed 29 parent–child dyads engaged in shared reading interactions according to a standard protocol that involved a traditional paper book and two different types of e-books. Participants were mothers or fathers reading with their child (aged 3 years 7 months to 5 years 8 months) whose language skills were age-appropriate in a majority language (i.e., either French or English). Four book interactions from two children are presented. It is concluded that interactions with e-books can support co-construction of meaning when the dyad adapts to the interactive features provided. Main strategies of adaptation observed in parents while viewing e-books with their child consisted of verbal nego-tiation of each reader's role as well as the use of parallel talk, which was contingent on the child's activities on the screen. The study calls for a more differentiated look at the interactive features contained in e-books, and how they intersect with parental teaching ability and behavior.

Keywords: Vocabulary, e-book, parental interaction, literacy, language, discourse

Introduction

Shared reading is known to be beneficial for young children: learning about oral and written language is facilitated, as well the development of cognitive concepts regarding story structure. Extensive observational research involving print-based picture books has identified verbal and nonverbal parental behaviors that contribute to this learning (e.g., Haden *et al.*, 1996; Ninio and Bruner, 1978; Snow and Goldfield, 1983). Specific verbal supports include the use of sophisticated language, directly informative talk, and a dialogic reading style (e.g., Hoff, 2010; Martini and Sénéchal, 2012; Weizman and Snow, 2001; Whitehurst *et al.*, 1994). These behaviors, when applied by parents or teachers, have been shown to have a positive effect on young children's language and literacy skills (Bus *et al.*, 1995; Mol *et al.*, 2008).

As mobile media such as smartphones and reading tablets proliferate in the everyday lives of young children (Rideout, 2013), questions arise about the role of e-books in language and literacy learning. E-books break with the traditional book format in several ways. As outlined by Zhao and Unsworth in this volume (Chapter 7) and previously discussed in research, apps' interactive features, multimodal story representation, and customizability enable physical and cognitive engagement by the reader (Kucirkova, 2013). Diversity in the use of these features may have varying effects on shared reading interactions and learning outcomes: the relationship between e-book design and reading outcomes is a recent focus of qualitative and quantitative research (Chiong and DeLoache, 2013; Kucirkova *et al.*, 2013). Direct comparisons of shared reading outcomes in the print versus e-book context yield a common finding: interactive e-book features capture child attention during shared reading, but have a detrimental effect on children's recollection and comprehension of the story content and structure (Parish-Morris *et al.*, 2013). Interactive features distract children from story content, especially when animations are incongruent with the story, and it is clear that parental behavior is also altered during shared reading with e-books. In particular, Parish-Morris *et al.* (2013) saw that parents used more behavior than content-related talk when dyads read enhanced e-books. By contrast, parents used more of the advantageous distancing and story-related utterances in the nonelectronic conditions.

Two systematic reviews focusing on emergent literacy skills as a child outcome have produced ambiguous results regarding the role of the adult as an instructor (Bus *et al.*, 2015; Salmon, 2014). Salmon (2014) suggests that children at risk of learning difficulties in particular will profit from the additional scaffolding of an adult during e-reading. Without contesting the advantage of 'true social contingency' (p. 91), Bus and colleagues (2015) indicate that the inclusion of interactive assistance built into the device, such as a computer tutor modeled on shared reading with an adult, could yield similar beneficial effects for at-risk learners. In addition, Takacs *et al.* (2014) in their meta-analysis of 29 intervention studies concluded that multimedia features can effectively replace adult scaffolding for the teaching of target vocabulary and story comprehension. Given these results, it seems unclear whether in the design of e-books higher emphasis should be placed on interactive features that more effectively replace the adult in the interaction, or more effectively support the adult reader's efforts to scaffold a child's learning. In any case, it is our view that continued research in this area would benefit from a focus on the intersection of specific interactive features of the e-books and specific parental behaviors, as children are learning in the shared reading context. Gross comparisons of 'paper books' versus 'e-books' are likely to be less informative.

The data reported in this chapter originate from a study using a mixed methods approach to explore parent–child interactions during shared reading with paper books and e-books (on an iPad). Previously we have reported quantitative data congruent with the literature showing increases in child engagement and parent behavior-related talk and technology referencing when comparing e-book to paper book reading (Rees *et al.*, 2013). Here we complement these findings with a narrative report of certain observations from our transcripts of reading interactions with two different e-books (their unique feature-profiles are shown in Table 11.1).

Application of a qualitative coding scheme, which links book features to child and adult behaviors, leads us to argue that select interactive features can assist adult readers in their scaffolding efforts when co-reading e-books. In keeping with Marsh's (2005) view that 'digital literacy practices share some of the features of more traditional literacy practices, but there are distinct aspects of text analysis and production using new media' (p. 4), we zoom in on dyads' communicative practices regarding their *meaning-making* about story elements.

Methods

Participants

Participants were parents and their children, recruited from diverse families with respect to language status and education. Immigrant families were recruited from a community home instruction program while other families were recruited from local daycares. All children were prereaders and parents were competent readers in

TABLE 11.1 Feature overview of three books (B1-B3) used in reading protocol B

Book	Story text	Multimedia features				Interactive features		
	Words per page	Animated illustrations	Movie elements	Sound	Music	Hotspots per page	Prompt bar	Living words
B1	2.7	–	–	–	–	–	–	–
B2	33.3	✓	✓	✓	✓	3	–	–
B3	38.5	✓	–	✓	–	3.4	✓	✓

Note: E-books (B2 and B3) were presented on an iPad. ✓ = contains feature; – = does not contain feature. Background music and a recording feature are optional for the iRead With e-book (B3), and were deactivated by us. The classification into multimedia and interactive features follows Takacs *et al.* (2014)

at least their first language, by self-report. Most of the participating children were growing up in households where more than one language was spoken because multilingualism is common in Montreal, although French is the majority language. Overall, 29 reading dyads have been recorded, but two are highlighted in this report because certain events in their transcripts amplified the themes that we raised in the introduction, while being representative of interactions that we observed repeatedly in our recordings. These dyads are described in Table 11.2. One child was read to in his first language (L1), English, while the second child, from an immigrant family, was read to in her second language (L2), French, but both children were typically developing in all respects.

Procedure

All observations were conducted in accordance with the same basic protocol. The week prior to the recording session, the parent was shown the e-books and provided with a brief overview of the features of the digital books that would be used, as part of the informed consent procedure (additional parent questionnaires and child assessments that occurred during this first session will not be reported here). Dyads were video-recorded in a laboratory with two standard digital cameras (Sony Handycam HDR-XR520) from front and rear/side view angles, while sharing three different e-books in fixed order. Parents were instructed to read the e-books like they normally would when they shared books with their child at home. These sessions lasted approximately half an hour.

Reading media

The reading protocol (cf. Table 11.1) began with a wordless picture e-book (B1) *Good Night, Gorilla* (Rathmann, 1994), with only a few speech bubbles repeating the words *Good Night* to accompany the engaging story about zoo animals that would rather sleep with the zookeeper than in their cages. Presented second in the series (B2) was *Sneak a Snack* (Vien, 2013), containing music, spontaneous movie elements, and touch and tilt interactive features on every screen. Several hotspots are highly engaging, although related to the story (e.g., touching distributes jelly

TABLE 11.2 Participant characteristics

Child	Adult						
Identifier	Sex	Age (M/Y)	Language status	Relation to child	Education	Language of readings	Other language in home
D11107	Male	4;8	Typical, L1	Mother	College	English	French
D33101	Female	5;5	Typical, L2	Mother	College	French	Chinese

on bread). The third e-book (B3) was the iRead With app, *Caillou: What's that funny noise?* (Johnson, 2013), featuring *living words* that link animated text with animated illustrations, as well as a *parent prompt bar* that suggests comments or questions congruent with story content in order to promote dialogic exchange by parent and child. Reading media were selected because they were available in English and French and their story content was appropriate for the age range of our participants.

Coding

Front and back views of the video recordings were synchronized on the same screen using Final Cut Pro and then written transcripts were produced using CHAT (Codes for the Human Analysis of Transcripts), the standard transcription tool for the CHILDES (Child Language Data Exchange System) Project to record both verbal and nonverbal aspects of the interaction (see http://childes. psy.cmu.edu). Quantitative analyses of the interactions, including details of adult and child linguistic behavior, will not be described here. Rather, we give a narrative account of how parents of children with typically developing language make use of interactive features provided in e-books, when co-constructing story meaning with their child.

Making meaning in the context of two distinct interactive e-books

A child's oral language abilities at school entry predict later literacy skills (see Lonigan *et al.*, 2008), and this is no less true for L2-learners (see Schmitt, 2008). Vocabulary development forms the foundation for higher-level language comprehension and use in the oral and written domains. In recent years, researchers have shifted from a pure focus on *quantity* to examine the *quality* aspects of child language input as a primary influence on vocabulary development (Huttenlocher *et al.*, 2010, for a discussion). Short- and long-term longitudinal studies call attention to the importance of lexical richness, either in the form of *lexical sophistication* (different rare words) or *lexical diversity* (different word types) in early caregiver speech, for later child vocabulary ability (Hoff and Naigles, 2002; Huttenlocher *et al.*, 2010; Rowe, 2012; Weizman and Snow, 2001).

Lexically rich input supplied by parents also supports the child's ability to engage in *inferencing* during their conversations about stories (Nyhout and O'Neill, 2013; Parish-Morris *et al.*, 2013). Shared storybook reading with preschoolers has been singled out as the context in which some families are especially likely to 'go beyond information that is directly provided in a text to fill in information needed to understand the text or to elaborate on the information given' (Van Kleeck, 2008, p. 628). Children's own use of inferential language seems to reflect their parent's use of it (Morgan and Goldstein, 2004; Van Kleeck *et al.*, 1997), and may support later text-level reading comprehension (Cain *et al.*, 2001; Van Kleeck, 2008).

In the sections to follow, a detailed analysis of examples of shared reading with e-books in a first and second language learning context will be provided. We highlight episodes in which the parent appears to be teaching vocabulary by labeling or defining or otherwise elaborating on word meaning. Alongside, we consider instances where the parent leaves the concrete level and engages in more complex meaning-making through inferential talk, which is thought to promote the child's deep vocabulary knowledge and narrative comprehension (cf. Van Kleeck, 2008).

Case vignettes

D11107 (see Appendix 11.1) engage in a very balanced reading exchange with all e-books. Reading of B2 starts by mother and child looking at the explanations on an introductory technical page about how to find the hidden animations (neither is previously experienced with e-book reading). As soon as the first page of the story opens, the mother reminds her son to not push anything until she tells him to do so. Thus they establish a basic action sequence that consists of the mother reading the complete block of text on a page (on occasion interrupting herself to ask a question), followed by the child interacting with the screen, while the mother follows the child's lead to comment on the results. Box 1 (B2) exemplifies this action pattern for a page that contains a difficult word 'witness'. The mother interrupts her own reading and slips in an elaborative inferencing question to ensure that her son understands this rare word. She subsequently offers him three different verbs that could be used to replace it in this semantic context, which amounts to supplying a word definition. Once she terminates her reading of the text on this page, the child seamlessly moves on to explore the audiovisual animations. From here on, her comments consist of descriptions of the effects the child produces through his touch, using concise vocabulary like 'gurgling', 'floating', or 'sloshing'. Altogether, the mother's main strategy consists of following the child's attention structure, whereby her sophisticated accompanying language aims at mediating and enriching his experience. The section also contains an inferential comment in which the mother uses the mental state verb *think* to remark on a visual animation ('I think it's just the hamster that reacts').

Even though this dyad had successfully established a 'routinized interaction' (Hoff and Naigles, 2002, p. 418) when reading the first e-book, they flexibly adapted their strategies in view of the distinctive features of the second e-book (see Box 1; B3). The iRW e-book offers two opportunities for the child to interact with the screen: first, by touching hotspots in the illustration that are indicated by halos, and second by touching a visually salient *living word* in the text. When touched, living words trigger animations, both in the illustration and around the word itself – a meaningful link is hence established between picture and text (for an example screen see Figure 11.1).

With the second e-book (B3), the mother continues to engage in parallel talk while her son explores the in-picture animations. On page two, a salient animation

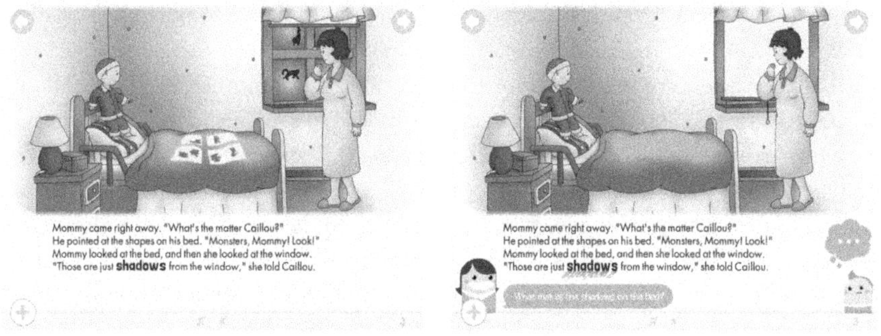

FIGURE 11.1 Example screens from interactive iRead With e-book app

Note: Screen three of the e-book before (left) and after (right) touching the living word 'shadows'. Tapping this word triggers (1) visual and sound effects within the illustration (blind going down and shadows disappearing from blanket), (2) an animation that elaborates the graphics in a meaningful way, (3) a prompt bar providing the parent with suggestions for questions or comments related to the story (in this example a question about causation). Image taken from *What's that funny noise?*, published by Chouette Publishing. All rights reserved. Caillou™ Chouette Publishing (1987) Inc.

causes the shadows to disappear from Caillou's blanket when the blind is lowered. The mother at the outset uses inferencing in the form of a text-to life connection, thus relating the main character's internal state to the child's individual experience in a comparable situation. Both of her inferencing comments feature the adjective *nervous* as an example of emotion state language. Following his initial exploration of the hotspot, the son thereafter repeatedly triggers the animation in a way that is synchronous with the content of his mother's readings (Box 1; B3). These gestures, performed at the correct point in time hence signal story comprehension by the child to the mother. The mother subsequently draws the child's attention to the living word and capitalizes on it by teaching him about basic print concepts, using technical terms like *word* (3x) and *letters* (1x). By the time this dyad has finished reading this one specific screen the child will have been exposed to eight instances of the word 'shadow/shadows'. Although the mother in this example has not provided an explicit conceptual link between light and shadow, she has used the term 'light' in her inferencing comment twice, and through her self-correction made obvious that a 'shadow' is not the same thing as a 'reflection'. The interaction represented in Box 1 (B3) represents an ideal use of the abundant opportunities for word learning offered by the unique features of the interactive e-book, supported by the synchrony in interaction between mother and child. Furthermore, this example attests to the critical influence of coordinated timing of actions to the achievement of a successful joint reading interaction.

In dyad D33101 the child's mother is an immigrant from China who recently entered a home-based preschool education program that provides immigrant parents with tools (books, activity packages) and strategies to support their child's learning in French, the majority language of their new community. The first e-book (see Appendix, 11.2; B2) introduces a dramatic change to the child's relative passivity during reading of the paper book, since the child immediately takes the lead in experimenting with the animations, to which the mother adapts seamlessly by producing parallel talk to comment on the results of her daughter's actions, showing great enjoyment herself in the process. This appears like a very adequate strategy, given the rather high-level, formal style of the story text featuring numerous rare words, which leads to frequent decoding errors by the mother (e.g., Box 2, B2, 'witness', 'être témoin' in the French text). Apart from her difficulties with decoding the written word, it is unclear whether the mother herself possesses a lexical entry for this phonological form; the means to support her own daughter with making meaning in the case of this word might hence be limited. As a logical consequence, she mostly constrains her scaffolding behavior to the use of parallel talk in a describer-style, reiterating the basic vocabulary that she has at her disposal. An example of this is the action verb 'swim' (nager), which she uses three times to describe the animated scene. The mother also employs one inferencing question, suddenly pointing out the wider context (setting) in which this scene takes place (kitchen). This may qualify as a text-based or bridging type of comment, drawing on information that was conveyed in previous parts of the story, and probably used in a strategic way at this point to promote the child's comprehension of the narrative. In sum, the interaction between mother and child definitely benefits from the flexibility of the mother who, for example, never insists on reading all of the text on a page.

Another remarkable change to this dyad's interaction is induced by the second e-book (B3). Though this story contains a similar amount of text (cf. Table 11.1), its language is closer to the colloquial-style language our reader is familiar with. The child continues to be very motivated to explore the touch-animations, often triggering one several times. The mother tolerates these disruptions to her own reading, even when it is unclear whether the child is actively attending to the story, mostly giving nonverbal or very quiet responses.

The sequence (Box 2; B3) starts with a more literal comment from the mother (labeling the object 'shadows'), after which the daughter sets off to explore the touch-animations. Another simple labeling question aims at identifying one of the story's main characters (Caillou's mother). A sudden quality change in the mother's questioning then occurs when she asks the child about the source of the shadows ('It comes from which part?'/'Ça vient de quelle partie?'), thus requiring causal inference. This question is actually prompted by the parent bar, although reworded by her (original prompt: 'What makes the shadows on the bed?'/'D'où viennent les ombres sur le lit?'). Such causal inferencing questions represent the most critical type of inferences essential to story comprehension, due to their hierarchical relation to elements of story grammar (Van Kleeck, 2008).

Towards the end of the sequence both dyad members finally coordinate their activities, when the mother for the first time in the session gets the child to actively produce (repeat) a word. Overall, the child hears the word 'shadows' ten times during this exchange. The appropriate language level of the book for both learners, along with congruent interactive features, facilitated meaning-making for both mother and children as well as synchronization of their activities.

To provide a brief synthesis of the previously discussed examples in the context of making meaning, a differentiated examination approach seems mandatory when evaluating the potential impact of interactivity in e-books. Specific features such as the living words in e-book B3 may be very effective in directing both readers' attention to specific meaning and code-related features of story text, sometimes leading the reading dyad to dwell on a certain word or subject. First, the fact that mothers in dyads D11107 and D33101 frequently repeated the accentuated words in variable syntactic contexts illuminates the data-providing functions of conversation, as discussed by Hoff and Naigles (2002). Being exposed to the same word in large quantities plays to the rapid word learning of preschoolers (and L2-learners in particular), who need to hear words many times and use them to encode new vocabulary (Hoff and Naigles, 2002). Second, both mothers used varied types of inferencing questions and comments, and the mother in D33101 in particular seemed to profit from features such as the parent prompt bar. Future research may clarify whether prompts embedded in e-books, functioning as *scripted questions and comments* (cf. Van Kleeck, 2008), will have differential effects in diverse groups of parents (e.g., parents who are second language learners, parents with reading impairments, parents of children with language impairments). Third, the dyads' ability to use the e-books' interactive features to support meaning-making was facilitated by synchrony in action. The dyads accomplished synchrony via unique strategies, however. The mother in D11107 established a coordinated reading routine through verbal negotiation with her child. The mother in D33101 synchronized her own speech and acts with those of her child, adapting to her child's focus of attention and allowing her child more or less free rein. Thus, our observations are congruent with other research on parent–child interactions; book features and maternal behaviors can interact to promote *synchrony* in action between child, technology, and maternal language input, with subsequent benefits for child learning (e.g., Harris *et al.* 1986; Lindsey *et al.*, 2009).

Conclusion

Taken together, the four vignettes (Appendices 11.1 and 11.2) accentuate the need for viewing shared reading, whether presented in print or electronic format, as a transactional process (Sameroff, 2009). This process is influenced by individual characteristics of the context, the reading partner, the child, and specific book features. To start from the context, we noted a remarkable influence of the conventional book reading script in the e-book context. Given how early on in a child's infancy most dyads begin to coordinate their interactions around physical books (cf. Rossmanith *et al.*, 2014), this is perhaps not very surprising. However, this phenomenon might also be partly reinforced by the comparative research design itself, which is why naturalistic studies assessing families' digital literacy practices in their homes are essential to complement the picture (e.g., Marsh *et al.*, 2015). Apart from this, an important limitation of the reading protocol used in this phase of the study is the lack of control for story content and presentation format, which was addressed in subsequent phases of the research project.

Overall it appears that some parents are able to adapt to interactive e-books with a confined number of hotspots, establishing synchronized interaction and meaning-making through an adjustment in their communicative strategies (e.g., use of parallel talk). Our observations also corroborate the finding from a new study by Parish-Morris and colleagues (2015) that some parents provide rich language in the form of distancing, despite the distractive elements present in interactive e-books. We further found indications that e-books can be designed to promote dialogic reading: features such as living words (e.g., 'shadows' in Boxes 1 and 2; B3) enable parents to teach their child about content and surface characteristics of text in an integrative manner. Other specific interactive features (e.g., parent prompt bar) have the potential to directly influence the level of abstraction present in talk about a story. Future research will have to clarify which groups of readers in particular could benefit from the inclusion of such features, and whether these could in part compensate for the adverse effects of other elements on parent–child dialogue.

Altogether our investigation calls for a more differentiated look at interactive elements and their interplay with the many other features found in e-books. Moreover, our narrative descriptions emphasize the need to take into account individual child and adult learner conditions (their oral language and reading proficiency, respectively), next to a systematic investigation of dyads' previous experience with mobile media (cf. Kucirkova, 2013 and Radesky and Zuckerman, Chapter 2, this volume). This is further underlined by an ensuing component of our study (see Rees, 2015), in which children with typical language (TD-group; $n = 10$) and children with language impairments (LI-group; $n = 10$) demonstrated markedly different patterns of linguistic engagement when reading the same e-book (B3) with a parent. Children in the TD-group participated significantly less in conversation about the story and used language that was syntactically less complex in the e-book condition (B3) in comparison to the traditional book condition (B1). This pattern was only mildly present in the group of children with LI; however, these children's ability to provide verbal responses to their parent's questions appeared compromised in the e-book condition.

Author note

Kathrin Rees, School of Communication Sciences and Disorders, McGill University.
This research is conducted as part of a multistage partnership project titled 'Impact of Digital Tablets on Shared Reading Interactions and Outcomes', funded by a Partnership Development Grant awarded to Susan Rvachew and Aparna Nadig from the Social Science and Humanities Research Council of Canada (SSHRC). We are grateful for the support of our industry partner Tribal Nova (a Houghton Mifflin Harcourt company), two community partners (The Centre for Literacy and HIPPY Montréal), and the Centre for Research in Brain, Language and Music in the conduct of this research. Correspondence should be

addressed to Kathrin Rees, Certified Teacher at Special Education Schools, Baden-Württemberg, Germany (kathrin.rees@mail.mcgill.ca) or to Professor Susan Rvachew, School of Communication Sciences and Disorders, McGill University, Montréal, QC (susan.rvachew@mcgill.ca).

Conflict of interest/declaration of conflicting interests

Susan Rvachew has a financial interest in the iRead With book series as a consequence of her consultations with Tribal Nova on the design of the books during the course of this research program. The partnership between McGill University and Tribal Nova/HMH is governed by a formal agreement that assures McGill's right to publish freely all results of our research involving the iRead With books.

References

Bus, A. G., Van IJzendoorn, M. H. and Pellegrini, A. D. (1995). Joint book reading makes for success in learning to read: A meta-analysis on intergenerational transmission of literacy. *Review of Educational Research, 65*(1), 1–21.

Bus, A. G., Takacs, Z. K. and Kegel, C. A. T. (2015). Affordances and limitations of electronic storybooks for young children's emergent literacy. *Developmental Review, 35*, 79–97. Available at: www. sciencedirect.com/science/article/pii/S0273229714000501 (accessed 12 June 2016).

Cain, K., Oakhill, J.V., Barnes, M. A. and Bryant, P. E. (2001). Comprehension skill, inference-making ability, and their relation to knowledge. *Memory and Cognition, 29*(6), 850–859.

Chiong, C. and DeLoache, Judy S. (2013). Learning the ABCs: What kind of picture books facilitate young children's learning? *Journal of Early Childhood Literacy, 13*, 225–241. doi: 10.1177/1468798411430091

Haden, C. A., Reese, E. and Fivush, R. (1996). Mothers' extratextual comments during storybook reading: Stylistic differences over time and across texts. *Discourse Processes, 21*(2), 135–169.

Harris, M., Jones, D., Brookes, S. and Grant, J. (1986). Relations between the non-verbal context of maternal speech and rate of language development. *British Journal of Developmental Psychology, 4*(3), 261–268. doi: 10.1111/j.2044-835X.1986.tb01017.x

Hoff, E. (2010). Context effects on young children's language use: The influence of conversational setting and partner. *First Language, 30*(3–4), 461–472. doi: 10.1177/0142723710370525

Hoff, E. and Naigles, L. (2002). How children use input to acquire a lexicon. *Child Development, 73*(2), 418–433.

Huttenlocher, J., Waterfall, H., Vasilyeva, M., Vevea, J. and Hedges, L. V. (2010). Sources of variability in children's language growth. *Cognitive Psychology, 61*(4), 343–365. doi: 10.1016/j.cogpsych.2010.08.002

Johnson, M. S. (2013). *Caillou: What's that funny noise?/Quel est ce bruit?* Tribal Nova/HMH (ed.).

Kucirkova, N. (2013). Children's interactions with iPad books: Research chapters still to be written. *Frontiers in Psychology, 4*, 1995. doi: 10.3389/fpsyg.2013.00995

Kucirkova, N., Messer, D., Sheehy, K. and Flewitt, R. (2013). Sharing personalised stories on iPads: A close look at one parent–child interaction. *Literacy, 47*(3), 115–122. doi: 10.1111/lit.12003

Lindsey, E. W., Cremeens, P. R., Colwell, M. J. and Caldera, Y. M. (2009). The structure of parent-child dyadic synchrony in toddlerhood and children's communication competence and self-control. *Social Development, 18*(2), 375–396. doi: 10.1111/j.1467-9507.2008.00489.x

Lonigan, C. J., Shanahan, T. and Cunningham, A. (with the National Early Literacy Panel). (2008). Impact of shared-reading interventions on young children's early literacy skills. *Developing Early Literacy: Report of the National Early Literacy Panel* (pp. 153–171). Washington, DC: National Institute for Literacy.

Marsh, J. (2005). Children of the digital age. In *Popular Culture, New Media and Digital Literacy in Early Childhood* (pp. 1–8). London; New York: RoutledgeFalmer.

Marsh, J., Hannon, P., Lewis, M. and Ritchie, L. (June 18, 2015). Young children's initiation into family literacy practices in the digital age. *Journal of Early Childhood Research*. doi: 10.1177/1476718X15582095

Martini, F. and Sénéchal, M. (2012). Learning literacy skills at home: Parent teaching, expectations, and child interest. *Canadian Journal of Behavioural Science, 44*(3), 210–221. doi: 10.1037/a0026758

Mol, S. E., Bus, A. G., de Jong, M. T. and Smeets, D. J. (2008). Added value of dialogic parent–child book readings: A meta-analysis. *Early Education and Development, 19*(1), 7–26.

Morgan, L. and Goldstein, H. (2004). Teaching mothers of low socioeconomic status to use decontextualized language during storybook reading. *Journal of Early Intervention, 26*(4), 235–252.

Ninio, A. and Bruner, J. (1978). The achievement and antecedents of labelling. *Journal of Child Language, 5*(1), 1–15.

Nyhout, A. and O'Neill, D. K. (2013). Mothers' complex talk when sharing books with their toddlers: Book genre matters. *First Language, 33*(2), 115–131.

Parish-Morris, J., Mahajan, N., Hirsh-Pasek, K., Golinkoff, R. M. and Collins, M. F. (2013). Once upon a time: Parent–child dialogue and storybook reading in the electronic era. *Mind, Brain, and Education, 7*(3), 200–211. doi: 10.1111/mbe.12028

Parish-Morris, J., Hirsh-Pasek, K., Golinkoff, R. M. and Hassinger-Das, B. (2015). *Parent-Preschooler Interaction during Electronic and Traditional Book Reading.* Retrieved from: digitalmediaprojectforchildren.wordpress.com (accessed 16 June 2016).

Rathmann, P. (1994). *Good Night, Gorilla.* London, UK: Penguin Books.

Rees, K. (2015). *Story-Related Discourse by Parent–Child Dyads: A Comparison of Typically Developing Children and Children with Language Impairments Reading Print Books and E-Books.* Retrieved from: https://digitalmediaprojectforchildren.wordpress.com (accessed 16 June 2016).

Rees, K., Tausch, C. and Rvachew, S. (2013). *Who Made The Frog Explode?* Paper presented at the World Social Sciences Forum, Montreal.

Rideout, V. J. (2013). *Zero to Eight: Children's Media Use in America 2013* (pp. 7–38). San Francisco, New York, Washington, Los Angeles: Common Sense Media.

Rossmanith, N., Costall, A., Reichelt, A. F., Lopez, B. and Reddy, V. (2014). Jointly structuring triadic spaces of meaning and action: Book sharing from 3 months on. *Frontiers in Psychology, 5.*

Rowe, M. L. (2012). A longitudinal investigation of the role of quantity and quality of child-directed speech vocabulary development. *Child Development, 83*(5), 1762–1774.

Salmon, L. G. (2014). Factors that affect emergent literacy development when engaging with electronic books. *Early Childhood Education Journal, 42*(2), 85–92. doi: 10.1007/s10643-013-0589-2

Sameroff, A. (2009). *The Transactional Model of Development: How children and contexts shape each other.* Washington, DC: American Psychological Association.

Schmitt, N. (2008). Review article: Instructed second language vocabulary learning. *Language Teaching Research, 12*(3), 329–363.

Snow, C. E. and Goldfield, B. A. (1983). Turn the page please: Situation-specific language acquisition. *Journal of Child Language, 10*(03), 551–569.

Takacs, Z. K., Swart, E. K. and Bus, A. G. (2014). Can the computer replace the adult for storybook reading? A meta-analysis on the effects of multimedia stories as compared to sharing print stories with an adult. *Frontiers in Psychology, 5*(DEC). doi: 10.3389/fpsyg.2014.01366

Van Kleeck, A. (2008). Providing preschool foundations for later reading comprehension: The importance of and ideas for targeting inferencing in storybook-sharing interventions. *Psychology in the Schools, 45*(7), 627–643. doi: 10.1002/pits.20314

Van Kleeck, A., Gillam, R. B., Hamilton, L. and McGrath, C. (1997). The relationship between middle class parents' book-sharing discussion and their preschoolers' abstract language development. *Journal of Speech, Language, and Hearing Research, 40*(6), 1261–1271.

Vien, Isabelle. (2013). *Sneak a Snack/Combine et Tartine*. Brodeur, M. (2013). Sneak a Snack/Combine et Tartine [iPad version]. U.n.I Interactive. Retrieved from https://itunes.apple.com/us/app/sneak-snack-hd-3d-interactive/id657150549?mt=8

Weizman, Z. O. and Snow, C. E. (2001). Lexical input as related to children's vocabulary acquisition: Effects of sophisticated exposure and support for meaning. *Developmental Psychology, 37*(2), 265–279.

Whitehurst, G. J., Epstein, J. N., Angell, A. L., Payne, A. C., Crone, D. A. and Fischel, J. E. (1994). A picture book reading intervention in day care and home for children from low-income families. *Developmental Psychology, 30*, 679–689.

Appendix 11.1

BOX 1. D11107, PROTOCOL B, ORIGINAL LANGUAGE ENGLISH

Book B2
Transcript lines 813–844

M: *What about you Arthur? Did you witness anything?*

M: Do you know what witness means?

C: No.

M: Like did you notice anything, did you see anything, did you hear anything, eh?

C: Ye(a)h.

M: *I was exercising as I usually do, when suddenly I heard a big noise that made the windows tremble. Then, surprisingly I was soaked by milk: it was a real flood, Alex!*

C: [TOUCHES HAMSTER]

M: Like he's gargling, eh?

C: [LEAVES HIS FINGER ON HAMSTER]

M: He's got the hiccups (laughs).

C: [TOUCHES OTHER DETAILS OF THE ILLUSTRATION]

M: I think it's just the hamster that reacts.

C: [PUTS HIS FINGER BACK ON THE HAMSTER AND LETS IT REST THERE]

M: Wanna switch pages?

C: [TILTS IPAD]

M: He's floating all over the place, eh?

M: The milk's sloshing.

C: [TAPS ON ARROW IN BOTTOM RIGHT CORNER]

Book B3
Transcript lines 1167–1205

M: The curtain goes down and it takes the shadow away, didn't it? [POINTS TO CAILLOU'S BLANKET]

C: [TOUCHES BLIND, WHICH MAKES IT GO UP]

M: Eh, like you. When the garage light is on, you get nervous of the shadows in your room.

C: (overlapping speech) No it's (be)cause xxx [TOUCHES BLIND (x3)]

M: Yeah, but you get nervous of the shadow coming from your light and he's got the reflection of the … the shadows from the animals.

M: *Mummy came right away. What's the matter, Caillou? He pointed at the shapes on his bed. Monsters Mummy, look!*

C: [TOUCHES BLIND, WHICH MAKES SHADOWS REAPPEAR]

M: *Mummy looked at the bed, then she looked at the window. Those are just shadows from the window, she told Caillou.*

C: [TOUCHES BLIND, WHICH MAKES IT GO DOWN AND SHADOWS DISAPPEAR]

M: Look, you can click on the word 'shadows'. [POINTS TO LIVING WORD SHADOWS]

C: [TOUCHES LIVING WORD (x2) WHICH MAKES THE BLIND GO UP AND DOWN]

M: Look, do you see how the shadow comes on the word?

M: Look at the word itself when you tou…when you touch it. Watch! See the shadow…

C: Ye(a)h!

M: … of the letters?

M: That's cool, eh?

Appendix 11.2

BOX 2. D33101, PROTOCOL B, ORIGINAL LANGUAGE FRENCH

Book B2
Transcript lines 595–615

M: That's another animals … hamster!

C: [TOUCHES SCREEN AT VARIOUS POINTS]

M: *And you Ar… (Arthur) hamster, what did you witness?* (slow decoding)

C: [CONTINUES TO TOUCH SCREEN UNTIL MILK GETS POURED OUT]

M: Oh! That is all the spilled milk. All the milk in his cage (laughs). She is swim in the milk, right?

C: [REPEATEDLY TOUCHES HAMSTER, WHICH MAKES HIM SPIT OUT LITTLE FOUNTAINS OF MILK]

M: (laughs) He has (x2)… That's in the kitchen or in which corner?

C: [RAISES TABLET]

M: Okay, let's put down.

C: Okay. [CONTINUES TO TOUCH HAMSTER]

M: *I was exer… exercising as I u…usually do, when suddenly I heard a big noise which made the windows tremble. Then, surprisingly I was soaked by milk: it was a (x2) real flood, Alex!* (effortful reading)

M: Oh, she is (x2) swim, right?

C: xxx

M: She is (x2) swim in milk.

C: [PRESSES BOTTOM RIGHT ARROW]

M: Okay, we will change.

Book B3
Transcript lines 859–873

M: This is shadows, look! [POINTS TO WORD OMBRES]

M: There aren't any shadows in (x2) his bed… [POINTS TO ILLUSTRATION]

C: [TOUCHES HOTSPOTS: CAILLOU, BLANKET, MOTHER]

M: When we touch, there are shadows.

M: Who, who is it? [POINTS TO CAILLOU'S MOTHER]

C: [TOUCHES CAILLOU'S MOTHER]

M: It comes from which part?

M: Look! [POINTS TO BLANKET]

C: [TOUCHES CAILLOU]

M: Here, do you see? [POINTS TO WINDOW WITH ANIMAL SHAPES]

C: (nods)

M: *Those are just shadows from the window,* mummy responds.

C: [TOUCHES CAILLOU'S MOTHER]

M: And mummy says: it is not the monsters. [POINTS TO CAILLOU'S MOTHER]

C: [PLAYS WITH CHILD ICON, THEN BLANKET HOTSPOT]

M: That is to touch here? [POINTS TO CHILD ICON]

M: Ah! That is the word 'shadows'! [POINTS TO SHADOWS ON BLANKET, THEN WORD OMBRES]

C: [ATTEMPTS TO TOUCH MORE HOTSPOTS]

M: H., look! [POINTS TO WORD OMBRES]

M: H., look! Repeat after me: shadows. [POINTS TO WORD OMBRES]

C: Shadows. (in a low voice)

M: Louder!

C: Shadows!

M: Shadows! Ye(a)h, shadows.

M: mother. C: child. Italicized font: read text. Normal font: spontaneous speech. [Events described between square brackets]: nonverbal actions. (Parenthetical remarks): descriptive modifiers that pertain to the immediately preceding speech or nonverbal event.

12

LITERACY TEACHING WITH TABLETS IN BILINGUAL PRIMARY CLASSROOMS

The Malta TabLit Study

Charles L. Mifsud and Louisa Grech

CENTRE FOR LITERACY, UNIVERSITY OF MALTA, MALTA

This chapter outlines the ways in which teachers in five primary classrooms in Malta used tablets over the course of six months for the teaching of bilingual literacy. The official policy, as outlined in the National Literacy Strategy for Malta, is of balanced literacy teaching and learning in the two languages of schooling in Malta: Maltese and English. Teachers' planning and preparation, the classroom environment, instruction and pedagogy were documented using a focus group, classroom observations, teacher interviews and reflective diaries and student questionnaires. Findings showed that the teachers integrated the use of tablets in their teaching for a number of creative literacy activities in the two languages, including reading comprehension, and guided and creative writing. The chapter concludes with recommendations for teachers' professional development, including school-based professional and technological support and ways to strengthen school–home links with the use of tablets.

Keywords: Integration, curriculum, literacy, collaboration, differentiation, motivation, engagement

Study background

The National Literacy Strategy for Malta (Ministry for Education and Employment Malta, 2014) outlines the range of skills children need to read and write in Maltese and English, the two languages of schooling in Malta. In order to foster children's bilingualism and biliteracy, they need to be provided with rich learning opportunities in both languages, including access to learning materials in both languages, and engagement in meaningful tasks.

The availability of resources and a sustained focus on the nature and quality of relationships mediating children's experiences around different media and texts are crucial (Green and Hannon, 2007; Neuman and Celano, 2006; Yelland and Masters 2007). As Au and Raphael (2000, p. 170) argue, 'ensuring educational equity involves helping students become literate in all artifacts of literacy, not only those historically used and present in today's society, but those likely to become prominent in the future'. In order to understand the impact of tablets and literacy apps on children's learning in Maltese classrooms, we needed to be aware of the inevitable influence of teachers' practices and attitudes towards the use of technology and, in particular, tablets. Previous research with tablets in classrooms shows that tablets can support teachers to be more flexible and to generate learning materials for students of different abilities and levels, especially with regard to struggling readers (Shuler *et al.*, 2013). They can also allow for increased communication and feedback opportunities between teachers and students (Snell and Snell-Siddle, 2013) and support more autonomous (Wong, 2012) and more personalised learning (Kearney *et al.*, 2012).

Several studies have demonstrated that for technology to have a lasting positive impact, it needs to be integrated into existing classroom practice rather than provided as an 'add-on'. For example, Hutchison *et al.* (2012) showed how one teacher in the US with 23 students in a fourth-grade class was able to meet her curricular print-based literacy goals while simultaneously introducing children to some twenty-first-century skills, such as navigating the different features of a digital text, designing digital learning tools, and communicating with other readers online.

As mentioned by Roskos in Chapter 3, meaningful integration of tablets has the potential to enhance literacy instruction. In our study, we were keen to understand how literacy teachers in Malta integrated tablets into their existing practice. We focused on literacy because of our own expertise in this area, and the official policy emphasis on technology-mediated literacy instruction in Malta. We were also mindful of the emergent evidence concerning the potential of mobile technologies for supporting the teaching and learning of literacy (Plowman and Stephen, 2007; Beschorner and Hutchison, 2013). For example, Flewitt *et al.* (2015) investigated the ways in which iPads might offer new opportunities as well as challenges for teachers in a nursery, a primary school reception class, and a special school in the UK. They found a lot of variability in the ways iPads were used across the three settings, but concluded that well-planned, iPad-based literacy activities can stimulate children's motivation and influence practitioners' perceptions about children's literacy competence.

There needs to be a clear instructional planning framework for teachers to integrate tablets into their teaching. Mishra and Koehler (2006) suggested that the most effective way to integrate technology into classroom instruction is for teachers to simultaneously draw on their technological, pedagogical, and content knowledge (TPACK). This involves an understanding of how technology and content are reciprocally related. However, teachers often have a difficult time using their TPACK in a systematic and useful way (Hutchison *et al.*, 2012).

The research design

Theoretical framework

The primary theoretical referent in our conceptualisation of the study and inter-pretation of findings was Danielson's framework for professional practice (2007). The framework presents a number of components, which have been shown to promote improved student learning. These components are clustered into four domains: 1) planning and preparation; 2) the classroom environment; 3) instruction; and 4) professional responsibilities. Danielson's framework served as a basis for our research question: How are the domains of professional practice influenced by the introduction of tablets in Maltese classrooms for the teaching of literacy?

Study context

Five Grade 3 and Grade 4 (7- to 8-year-olds) classes from four Malta primary schools participated in the study. The teachers and children in these classes were provided with tablets, with a range of devices used across the schools, including Samsung Galaxy Tab 3 and 4, Intel Classmate TL101E1, and LearnPad. In all schools, tablets were provided free by the suppliers, with the view to expanding the programme with the most effective and popular devices later on. All the schools, apart from one of the state schools, allowed children to take them home after the school day. Teachers were free to choose the apps and programs, and were encouraged to share their experiences of using the tablets in regular meetings with other teachers participating in the pilot study. A brief professional development training programme was provided by the e-Learning Department of the Education Ministry in Malta, and involved a number of models for technology-mediated curricula like substitution augmentation modification redefinition (SAMR) and TPACK, including a review of a number of age-appropriate apps. Training in hardware and software solutions was provided by a number of industry partners connected to the project.

Study participants

Five teachers were involved in this study. Two teachers were from one of the state schools, one from another state school and one each from a Church and an Independent school. These teachers were selected because of their specific goal to use the tablets for the teaching and learning of literacy.

Study procedure

An ethnographic approach, where a researcher observed classroom dynamics in their natural settings, was adopted (Gallagher *et al.*, 2015). Permission to conduct the study was granted by the Education Ministry in Malta, and ethical consent was obtained from the University of Malta Research Ethics Committee. A range of language activities in both languages were observed: listening comprehension tasks including listening to recorded readings by the teachers, reading from digital books, reading comprehension, and guided and creative writing activities.

Data collection

At the beginning of the study, a focus group meeting was conducted involving all the participating teachers and a member of their school management team. Initial interviews were conducted with all the teachers. All classroom observations were followed by one-to-one interviews with the classroom teachers. The aim of these interviews was to understand more fully how teachers used the tablets to reach their lesson objectives. A final interview with each participating teacher took place at the end of the study to investigate further the impact the teachers felt that the introduction of tablets had on their pedagogy and literacy teaching, and to what extent they felt this might be sustained beyond the duration of the pilot programme. We also asked the teachers to keep a diary of how they used the tablets, and to record their reflections on the lessons. These were analysed together with the interview data at the end of the study, using thematic analysis. All interviews were audio-recorded and transcribed verbatim by a researcher who is fluent in both Maltese and English. For the purpose of data presentation, we refer to the five teachers participating in the study as: Teachers 1, 2, and 3 from the two state schools, Teacher 4 from the Church school, and Teacher 5 from the Independent school.

Data analysis

The theoretical framework by Danielson (2007) was followed for the data analysis. Coding was related to the four domains and competences presented in this framework. All the raw data from the various sources (focus group, classroom observations, teacher interviews, teacher reflective diaries and student question-naires), were coded thematically by the two authors. Comments were grouped and labelled through analytic-inductive methods with a term that captured the essence of the comments, with preference given to terms used by the participants in the interviews. The authors, who conducted the analysis separately, and a third researcher, who was not directly involved in the study, agreed on the final themes.

Findings

Tablets were used for a wide range of language activities involving reading from e-books, sentence building, listening comprehension, language awareness activities, and guided and creative writing. Teachers used traditional materials, such as handouts, copybooks, and exercise and practice books, in conjunction with the tablets. Before we present the key themes that emerged from the data, we briefly discuss the ways in which the tablets were integrated into literacy teaching in the different classrooms, and for teacher–pupil co-creation of multimedia literacy materials.

The teachers participating in the Malta TabLit Study appreciated the fact that they could use the tablets for both Maltese- and English-language activities. There was some initial concern that the tablets would restrict work in Maltese. However, the teachers were able to make use of a number of tablet-based resources in both languages. By downloading the MultiLing keyboard, the students could write on the tablet using the Maltese font, which was a big advantage in the bilingual classroom. It also provided many opportunities for the students to work together, despite their different language backgrounds. They were also able to create their own materials in both languages using the e-learning platform, Fronter. The teachers pointed out that the tablets helped the students to improve their reading skills in both Maltese and English, as summarised by Teacher 2 from a state school:

> The difference I felt was in reading in both languages, especially in Maltese because 'Postijiet Sbieħ' (Beautiful Places), reader in Maltese. is not easy. Whenever I did it without the use of the tablet, they always got stuck. But since I can put the recording of the book on the tablet and they listen to it, they're becoming more fluent and they have progressed much more.

The children were able to co-create literacy materials with the teachers by using a number of apps. For example, *Storykit* and other apps allowed children to customise images and text, strengthening the connections between different media and the two languages. Teacher 1 from a state school set her class a 'visualisation' task during which the children were asked to read a story from the tablet, to 'imagine' the story, and to draw their ideas from the story in groups, using the app *Story Album*. Each group sent a picture to the teacher via e-mail. Follow-up activities involved predicting the rest of the story, writing the story in their own words, and publishing the final tale in the students' room of their school virtual learning environment. The teacher said that through the use of tablets: 'Learning in both languages has become more interesting and stimulating for the students, that's basically what it's all about'. Teacher 2 from another state school used *Answer Garden* for brainstorming sessions and to increase the students' vocabulary in both languages. The students in the class of Teacher 3 from the same state school got to a stage where they were downloading relevant literacy apps on their own, and sharing them with the teacher and their classmates during the regular class 'Show and Tell' activities.

Another technique adopted for integrating the use of the tablets was for the teachers to set the students a task that involved them searching, reading, and producing their own materials. In the class of Teacher 4 from the Church school, during a creative writing activity, the students were asked to find information about different kinds of dinosaurs on the Internet, and to use the Paint app to draw a picture of a dinosaur. Then they recorded 'describing' words about dinosaurs in a word bank, which was then shared by the teacher on the tablets. Finally, the students were guided to compose and publish a story based on the character they had drawn. In another activity, the students were asked to look for and read online materials about pets, and to shoot a short video of their pet at home. Then they were asked to share this video with the teacher and classmates and to write about their pet. Teacher 5 from the Independent school asked the students to listen to a news report on the interactive whiteboard, which was then discussed in class. She asked the students to browse the Internet on their tablets and to look for a Maltese newspaper of their choice, written in English. The students were asked to look at news reports on this online newspaper and to note the style they were written in. The children showed the reports to each other and also wrote their own news report on the tablet using the Sticky Note application. Some students used the built-in keyboard to type, while others wrote in digital ink with their finger, and this was then transferred automatically to the rest of the document. Our observations show evidence of collaborative writing and problem-solving. The students discussed their reports with the teacher, and corrected and edited the work on their tablets. The final stage of the task was to search for photos related to their report and share these, together with the report, on the school forum, accessible to their friends and parents (Figure 12.1).

Theme 1: Motivation moderating literacy engagement

The first theme that emerged from our thematic analysis was the increased level of motivation that students exhibited towards literacy learning since the introduction of the tablets. All of the teachers described their students as being 'enthusiastic' and that for them, learning has become 'fun'. The students seemed to have become more interested and engaged, especially if they had been less engaged before (due to language or learning difficulties). For these students, the tablets provided an opportunity to showcase their literacy work and share it with others, which had boosted their confidence in their literacy skills. Increasingly students expressed

Step 1: Searching   **Step 2:** Accessing and   **Step 3:** Students writing
the Internet   reading online material   their own material

FIGURE 12.1 Examples of different contexts for tablets' integration into the literacy lessons

more positive comments about the reading lessons and independent reading overall. Teachers too felt more motivated to teach reading, for instance, Teacher 4 told us that she felt that the introduction of the tablets had improved her teaching and made her a 'better teacher'.

All the teachers felt that the tablets made a significant difference to literacy motivation, especially in areas such as reading, creative writing, and sentence building. The teachers maintained that the students seemed more dedicated and eager to learn since the introduction of the tablets. According to Teacher 5, this was mainly due to the tablets' affordances, such as the possibility to download e-books or make audio-recordings:

> Literacy has become more engaging for students in a way that they come and tell me: "Miss, listen to what I have read", "Miss I used Book Creator for this and that". Now to use Book Creator they have to read, they have to write, they have to put things in order, they have to do sequencing. So in this way the tablets have helped because they've engaged students to expand their literacy skills, which previously they did only as part of their homework. I find that really beneficial for students' literacy learning.

Theme 2: Differentiated teaching and learning

The teachers thought it beneficial that many of the e-books their students had access to on the tablets were levelled, and therefore catered for different reading and comprehension levels. Three teachers explained that they were able to create individualised activities for specific students and to send these activities directly to the student's tablets, for example, by creating different levelled quizzes or writing activities.

For example, in a lesson by Teacher 2, photos of animals were downloaded on the students' tablets. The students were divided into three ability groups and set tasks of different levels of difficulty. Group A watched a PowerPoint presentation on farm animals, Group B looked for information on desert animals, and Group C browsed a website called *Camouflage Field Book* that contained information about different environments for animals. The students read and discussed and worked within their group to gather information about different animals, supported by the teacher and support teacher. Each group presented their finished work to the rest of the class using the interactive whiteboard.

Differentiated teaching and learning were particularly salient for children with special educational needs, who seemed to adopt a more positive approach to learning when using the tablets. One teacher mentioned that her student with an autistic spectrum disorder was 'very pleased' to be reading on a tablet. Another teacher observed that her student with attention deficit hyperactivity disorder was 'enthusiastic' about writing on the tablet. The teacher from the independent school said that her student with specific learning difficulties was a more eager participant in literacy activities since the introduction of tablets:

I realised that my special needs student showed more enthusiasm and initiative. He actually wrote his own story without prompting. Usually when given a paper, he was very hesitant and uncooperative. Now by means of the tablet, he worked well and showed pride for managing to do his own work to the best of his ability. That was a very rewarding achievement and experience for him and also for me.

Theme 3: Collaborative learning

The third theme that emerged from the data and teachers' interviews was the belief that the tablet is an effective tool for increasing collaboration and teamwork among students. One example we observed concerned a *Titanic*-themed collaborative literacy session by Teacher 4. This was an English lesson promoting integrated language skills and supported by the LearnPad tablets. After initial brainstorming of what students knew about the *Titanic*, they watched a short documentary about the *Titanic* on their tablets. The class was then divided into small groups of three students. Each group wrote a script of about 60 words about the *Titanic* on the tablet. One of the students read out the script like a newsreader, and another student recorded this on the tablet. The recordings were then viewed and shared with the rest of the class on the interactive whiteboard, with opportunities for peer feedback. The students were extremely excited about this activity, as illustrated in Figure 12.2.

Theme 4: Bridging home and school

The final theme focused on accounts of the teachers about how the tablets continued and reinforced learning happening in the classroom while students were at home. This seemed to be both teacher- and student-mediated. Teacher 1, for

FIGURE 12.2 An example of students (7- to 8-year-olds) working collaboratively when using tablets

example, recorded herself reading a story and sent it to the children so that they could listen to it at home. Students also watched several teacher-recommended YouTube videos at home, enriching their factual knowledge of topics studied in the class. According to Teacher 5, taking the tablets home offered the students the opportunity to access e-books and to continue their independent reading at home: 'There is that excitement of wanting to know what is next in the story, and many do go home and continue reading the set book.'

Teacher 4 highlighted the importance of including parents and caregivers in the process of integrating tablets in teaching and learning: 'I showed the parents how to access the online reading scheme and how to familiarise their children with such a great tool. At this point, the parents were taking notes and seemed eager to try it out at home on their child's tablet.' There was also evidence of parents supporting their children's literacy homework on the tablets: 'I uploaded many useful literacy resources on the Samsung School learning platform for the children to use. I got a lot of positive feedback from the parents as they were able to use these resources to help their children to revise and consolidate on their tablets what was learnt in class.'

Discussion

Technology can increase student engagement and motivation (Chiong et al., 2012), as long as it is used to support effective pedagogy. In the present study, Danielson's Framework for professional practice in teaching provided us with a lens through which to consider effective pedagogy (teaching practice) and look out for examples of effective technology integration. Our findings indicate that, overall, the use of tablets in the five pilot classrooms provided a very positive experience for the teachers and students involved. The teachers designed learning scenarios, activities and assignments which were appropriate to the abilities of their students, making use of the digital resources on the school e-learning platform and on the Internet. They planned for differentiated learning experiences for all children, including children with special educational needs. Classroom assessment of reading and writing was increasingly carried out through the technology. There was a positive attitude from both the teachers and students towards technology use in the classroom. The technology provided opportunities for the students to publish their work online, which could be viewed by other students and parents. There were also increased opportunities for collaborative literacy work among students in the classroom, such as co-creation of multimedia literacy materials. In this way teachers were more likely to tap into children's interests, skills and creativity (Nilsson, 2010). The thematic analysis also revealed that thanks to the tablets, the teachers were able to monitor their students' progress more efficiently and were able to relay this information to parents.

The teachers involved in this project had varied previous experiences with technology. Some of them used technology to a limited extent in their personal lives. However, all the teachers felt they required more professional development about how to integrate the tablets into their teaching and learning. We therefore contend with Hutchison and Woodward (2014) that there is a need for an instructional planning cycle that would guide teachers in using their TPACK. Such a cycle, which could be adopted in schools, is referred to as a 'grounded approach' to technology integration and involves: choosing learning goals, making pedagogical decisions, selecting activity types to combine, selecting assessment strategies, and selecting tools/resources (Harris and Hofer, 2009). The approach is not linear, but recursive, in that decisions and choices, made at each of the five stages of planning, will change as new developments will require adjustments. Reflecting on our findings, this approach could provide a systematic way of integrating technology in an effective manner in everyday literacy teaching and learning across topics, taking into consideration language use, specific learning needs, and expected learning outcomes.

One cannot underestimate the importance of providing teachers with school-based pedagogical and technological support. It was evidently clear that the teachers who received adequate curricular and technological support by IT resource persons in a proactive and timely manner in this study were in a better position to integrate the tablets into their lesson planning and delivery and to meet the challenges that they faced. There should be more opportunities for professional development and for teachers to engage in joint planning and peer teaching.

The students found it relatively easy to access the material introduced at school from their tablets at home. They could easily review work initiated at school, and continue working on it at home. This allowed for increased involvement by parents as they were able to better monitor the work that their children brought from school. We therefore support the current opinion that technology provides a good opportunity to connect school- and home-learning activities (Falloon, 2015; Northrop and Killeen, 2013). However, there needs to be a structured framework for strengthening school–home links and for increased parental involvement through the use of the technology. Parents need to be brought on board as informed partners. Meetings are to be held with parents to inform them about the integration of the technology into their child's learning path, and about the e-learning platform, which allows them access to relevant educational materials. In this way, they can become more active participants in their children's learning journeys.

Conclusion

Carefully planned activities with tablets have the potential to bring about a dramatic and positive change in classrooms. Technology integration decisions are to be incorporated into the ways teachers typically plan for teaching and learning. This development may have a strong impact on the teaching and learning of literacy in our classrooms, including stimulating children's motivation and concentration (Flewitt et al., 2015). The necessary conditions for this to take place seem to be the adequate provision of the required professional education and development of teachers; improved and extended technological and pedagogical support structures in schools; and the design and implementation of a framework for the strengthening of school–home links and increased parental involvement. Effective teaching and technology will continue to evolve as more schools adopt technology-mediated teaching and learning. It is likely that tablets will positively influence this process overall, and in particular literacy teaching in bilingual primary classrooms.

Acknowledgement

We would like to thank the teachers and students who participated in our study.

References

Au, K.H. and Raphael, T.E. (2000). Equity and literacy in the next millennium. *Reading Research Quarterly, 35*(1), 171–188.

Beschorner, B. and Hutchison, A. (2013). iPads as a literacy teaching tool in early childhood. *International Journal of Education in Mathematics, Science and Technology, 1*(1), 16–24.

Chiong, C., Ree, J., Takeuchi, L. and Erickson, I. (2012). *Print Books vs E-books: Comparing parent–child co-reading on print, basic, and enhanced e-book platforms.* New York: The Joan Ganz Cooney Center.

Danielson, C. (2007). *Enhancing Professional Practice: A framework for teaching* (2nd ed.). Alexandria, VA: ASCD.

Falloon, G. (2015). What's the difference? Learning collaboratively using iPads in conventional classrooms. *Computers and Education, 84*, 62–77. doi: 10.1016/ j.compedu.2015. 01.010

Flewitt, R., Messer, D. and Kucirkova, N. (2015). New directions for early literacy in a digital age: The iPad. *Journal of Early Childhood Literacy, 15*(3), 289–310.

Gallagher, T.L., Fisher, D., Lapp, D., Roswell, J., Simpson, A., McQuirter, S.R., Walsh, M., Ciampa, K. and Saudelli, M.G. (2015). International perspectives on literacy learning with iPads. *Journal of Education, 19*(3), 15.

Green, H. and Hannon, C. (2007). *Their Space: Education for a digital generation.* Available at: www.demos.co.uk/files/Their%20space%20-%20web.pdf

Harris, J. and Hofer, M. (2009). Grounded tech integration: An effective approach based on content, pedagogy, and teacher planning. *Learning and Leading with Technology, 37*(2), 22–25.

Hutchison, A. and Woodward, L. (2014). A planning cycle for integrating digital technology into literacy instruction. *The Reading Teacher, 67*(6), 455–464.

Hutchison, A., Bechorner, B. and Schmidt-Crawford, D. (2012). Exploring the use of the iPad for literacy learning. *The Reading Teacher, 66*(1), 9.

Kearney, M., Schuck, S., Burden, K. and Aubusson, P. (2012). Viewing mobile learning from a pedagogical perspective. *Research in Learning Technology, 20*, 14406.

Ministry for Education and Employment Malta. (2014). National Literacy Strategy for All in Malta and Gozo. Available at: http://education.gov.mt/en/Documents/Literacy/ ENGLISH.pdf

Mishra, H.J. and Koehler, M. (2006). Technological pedagogical content knowledge: A framework for teacher knowledge. *Teachers College Record, 108*(6), 1017–1054.

Neuman, S.B. and Celano, D. (2006). The knowledge gap: Implications of leveling the playing field for low-income and middle-income children, *Reading Research Quarterly*, 176–201.

Nilsson, M. (2010). Developing voice in digital storytelling through creativity, narrative and multimodality. *International Journal of Media, Technology and Lifelong Learning*, 6(2), 148–160.

Northrop, L. and Killeen, E. (2013). A framework for using iPads to build early literacy skills. *The Reading Teacher, 66*(7) 531–537.

Plowman, L. and Stephen, C. (2007). Guided interaction in pre-school settings. *Journal of Computer Assisted Learning, 23*(1), 14–21.

Shuler, C., Winters, N. and West, M. (2013). *The future of mobile learning: Implications for policy makers and planners*. Paris: UNESCO.

Snell, S. and Snell-Siddle, C. (2013). Mobile learning: The effects of gender and age on perceptions of the use of mobile tools. Paper presented at The Second International Conference on Informatics Engineering and Information Science, Kuala Lumpur, The Society of Digital Information and Wireless Communications.

Wong, L.H. (2012). A learner-centric view of mobile seamless learning. *British Journal of Educational Technology, 43*(1), 5.

Yelland, N. and Masters, J. (2007). Rethinking scaffolding in the information age. *Computers and Education, 48*(3), 362–382.

13

IPAD-SUPPORTED LEARNING AND DEVELOPMENT FOR A CHILD WITH MILD CEREBRAL PALSY

Elaine Khoo

FACULTY OF EDUCATION, UNIVERSITY OF WAIKATO, NEW ZEALAND

Much has been reported in popular media and educational literature on the relative ease with which children pick up the skills to use iPads. However, iPad use to support students with developmental disability – particularly in the New Zealand educational context – is still in its infancy. This chapter reports on a qualitative case study aimed at understanding the ways in which the iPad can be used to support the learning and development of a student (Max) with mild cerebral palsy, who is currently enrolled in a mainstream primary classroom. Data from interviews and observation with Max and his family highlight how particular affordances and features of applications (apps) were useful for developing the physical functioning of his palsied right hand, and fostering Max's learning. The parents' initiative and home–school connections were also important in determining iPad apps appropriate to Max's needs. Implications for practice are offered for caregivers and educators who work with students who have similar abilities.

Keywords: iPad, disability, children, learning and development, primary school, cerebral palsy

Introduction

Current and emerging research on mobile learning highlights the potential of mobile devices to foster new and different learning and exploration opportunities for children (Clarke and Abbott, 2015; Falloon and Khoo, 2014; Kucirkova *et al.*, 2014a). Despite a growing literature on the impact of adopting iPads across different levels of education, very few studies exists on iPad use to support students with disabilities in the New Zealand context. This chapter reports on a case study exploring the iPad-supported learning and development of a student, Max (pseudonym used), with mild cerebral palsy (CP) (a developmental disability). Max currently attends a normal/mainstream primary school. This study is an extension of an earlier project investigating the educational affordances of the iPad in an early childhood educational (ECE) context from the perspective of teachers, young children and their parents/caregivers (Khoo *et al.*, 2015).

The chapter begins with an overview of relevant studies concerning the educational uses of iPads for students with disabilities, followed by an outline of current New Zealand initiatives for people with disabilities, and details of the study's context and findings. The chapter ends with a discussion of what the findings might mean for current educational practice.

iPads supporting students with disabilities[1]

Mobile and tablet technologies, such as the iPad, have captured the imagination of educators all over the world, fuelling an excitement in the potential of the device to support young children's and students' learning and interests. In the case of students with developmental disabilities and special needs, the iPad offers access to learning opportunities and various information, organisational systems, communication, and emotional supports. Bryant (2012) aptly noted that although technology makes things easier for people without disabilities, particularly makes things *possible* for people with disabilities. The iPad is increasingly recognised as a form of adaptive or assistive technology (Newton and Dell, 2011), a therapeutic and rehabilitation device (Fox, 2011), and as an instructional tool to support the interest and active exploration of students with disabilities (Cumming and Strnadova, 2012).

The iPad's affordances useful for the general population as well as for those with disabilities include its interactive touchscreen, portability, engaging multimodal apps supporting educational and recreational content, longer battery life, and screen size. Students with disabilities readily adopt iPads as they are using the same technology as their peers (Kagohara *et al.*, 2013). iPads are more commonly and socially accepted/-less stigmatising, cost-effective, and affordable, compared with an unknown or awkward/bulky and expensive older forms of assistive technology, such as adjustable keyboards and monitors, speech synthesisers, and so forth (Flewitt *et al.* 2014).

Studies into the kinds of supports iPads provide for students with developmental disabilities are very limited in the New Zealand educational context. Internationally, however, there is emerging evidence that iPad-based interventions can support and enhance a range of curriculum subjects and/or skill deficits/impairments in the classroom, for a broad population of students with disabilities. Strnadova and Cumming's (2013) study across home–school settings revealed a positive teaching and learning experience for students with disabilities and higher engagement in academic tasks. Closer home–school links were also established as a result. Others have observed benefits in the learning of science, spelling, and language (Kagohara *et al.*, 2012; Kucirkova *et al.*, 2014b; Rivera *et al.*, 2014).

Systematic meta-reviews of literature reveal mobile devices to be viable techno-logical aids for teaching and increasing the independence of students with disabilities (Kagohara *et al.*, 2013) and supporting socialisation, communication and recreational activities for individuals with developmental disabilities (including cerebral palsy) (Stephenson and Limbrick, 2013).

Students with disabilities were noted to adopt the iPad quickly and more inde-pendently compared with computer-assisted learning programmes, which required continual adult supervision to ensure successful use (Chmiliar, 2014). The students were motivated and interested to persist with an app-based activity to win or earn points. Indirectly, they practised and refined fine motor skills such as tracing, colouring, and writing to achieve learning or behavioural outcomes, albeit in a multimodal, engaging and entertaining manner (Aronin and Floyd, 2013). Work has also been initiated in areas, such as developing customizable apps for students with impairments to help them learn language, maths, environmental awareness, autonomy and social skills (Fernández-López *et al.*, 2013), and evaluation rubrics have been developed to assess the suitability of educational iPad apps for students with disabilities in schools (Weng and Taber-Doughty, 2015), and in early childhood contexts (More and Travers, 2012).

A New Zealand perspective on the disabled child

In New Zealand, approximately 10 percent of children (90,000) aged up to 15 years live with some sort of disability – learning difficulties, chronic health problems (such as cerebral palsy), psychological disabilities or other physical disabilities (New Zealand Government, 2011). Students with disabilities have the same right to education as other students in New Zealand, as outlined in the Education Act of 1989. There are many more school-aged boys with disabilities than girls, and the majority are enrolled in mainstream primary, intermediate, secondary or composite schools, with 3 percent in special schools. In 2001, the New Zealand Disability Strategy was launched, in part to 'provide the best education for disabled people' (New Zealand Human Rights Commission, 2015, p. 16). Resources required by students with disabilities, such as communication technologies and assistive devices and opportunities for these students to meet peers in other schools, were established. The focus is for educators to understand the learning needs of students with disabilities, improve schools' responsiveness to and accountability for those needs, and promote appropriate, effective and inclusive educational settings (New Zealand Human Rights Commission, 2015). In 2015, the Ministry of Education (MoE) introduced new in-class support funding for students for special education, or those who have high ongoing need to support their learning and achievement (MoE, 2015).

Taken together, current studies evidence the breadth of interest in the iPad's potential to assist students with disabilities to participate more fully in educational environments. This trend, coupled with government interests and initiatives, can facilitate access to more inclusive learning environments.

Research context

Max's background

Seven-year-old Max has mild CP associated with right-side hemiplegia (i.e. paralysis to the right side of the body due to an injury to the left brain hemisphere that controls motor movements). 'Cerebral' refers to the brain while 'palsy' refers to muscle weakness and poor control. CP is a common physical disability in childhood, affecting 2 to 2.5 of every 1,000 children born in the western world. Approximately 7,000 people in New Zealand have some degree of CP (one-third are under 21 years of age) (Cerebral Palsy Society of New Zealand, 2015). A higher percentage of boys than girls tend to be affected. Children with this condition typically experience stiffness and weakness in muscles on the affected side of the body, prefer to use one hand over the other, tend to curl the weaker hand into a fist (claw-like), and have difficulty with movement/walking and balance, as well as fine motor tasks, like writing or using scissors (Children's Hemiplegia and Stroke Association [CHASA], 2015). This condition is lifelong, non-progressive and non-curable. Over time, physical training and therapy can improve physical movements and functioning.

Max was diagnosed at 14 months old when his parents noticed a delay in his physical/motor development. The CP renders the right vertical half of Max's body (arm and leg) weaker than his left, delaying his physical/motor development by two to three years. He experiences a stiffness/muscle tension in his right arm, which causes his right hand to be curled up (claw-like shape). He wears a brace on his right foot to support his walking movements, and he has balance-related issues.

As with most children with hemiplegia in New Zealand, Max attends a traditional school and is integrated into a mainstream classroom. The full primary school (years 1–6) is centrally located in a small town in New Zealand's North Island. Max receives additional learning assistance a few hours each week at school. He also has access to a physiotherapist and occupational therapist. His development is assessed every six months by the physiotherapist who meets with Max's parents and class teacher to create a programme that will meet his needs. At the end of a school year, his teacher for the next school year attends the meetings to be informed of and gather information to support Max's learning needs for the next year. Max does not have any learning difficulty, and is bright and mathematical in his thinking. He has struggled with handwriting using his palsied right hand in the past, and is steadily working on and improving this skill. Max's parents treat him as physically normal as possible, encouraging him to participate in school-based activities and sporting events such as swimming, rugby, and even children's triathlon, to enhance his motor and physical movements.

Data collection

Max first encountered an iPad at the ECE centre he was enrolled in where the initial research project was conducted. He was 4 years old then. Two teachers at the centre who were part of the project brought their personal iPads for the children to explore. The researcher (author of this paper) collaborated with both teachers to understand the impact of adopting the iPad in their practice, and case studied four young children and their families to find out the different ways the iPad supported their developing interests across home–centre contexts (Khoo *et al.*, 2015). Max was one of the children case studied. Max and his family agreed to extend their participation to provide an in-depth interview (audiotaped) and a 1.5-hour observation session (photos, field notes, video recordings) of Max's use of the iPad, at their home.

Analysis of the data

A qualitative interpretive methodology framed the study, as it allowed for careful attention to be paid to the participants' perspectives (Maykut and Morehouse, 1994). Emergent themes from the transcribed interviews and observation data were identified through a process of inductive reasoning (Braun and Clarke, 2006) to highlight the different ways the iPad supported and extended Max's learning and development. In this study, it is recognised that the iPad on its own did not directly cause learning to occur, but it gave rise to the possibility of learning that was essentially situated, spontaneous and personalised, to allow a focus on specific aspects of educational content and/or process engaging to a learner, thus catering to very specific needs of users (Culén and Gasparini, 2011). This study considered the ways Max took up the iPad to serve particular learning and developmental goals that may not have been possible otherwise. Analysis of the data was underpinned by sociocultural theory that directed attention to the interaction between people, the tools they use to achieve particular purposes, and the settings in which the interactions occur (Cole and Engeström, 1993).

Findings

Three themes emerged from the data analysis, and are exemplified through illustrative quotes in the following section. The themes were: the iPad afforded physical flexibility and development; the iPad afforded motivating learning processes and outcomes; and productive iPad use was facilitated when caregivers and teachers are supportive and interested in a student's learning.

The iPad afforded physical flexibility and development

One of the chief reasons for Max obtaining an iPad was to encourage more physical use of his palsied right hand, as he naturally preferred to use his left hand in his daily functioning (see Figure 13.1):

> Max's CP is on his right side so his hand is often like that, like a claw hand, especially when he is tired. We are encouraging him to use that so that he is

aware that he has a right side and a right hand to use. Even if he is like holding his hand with his index finger pointing out, we are happy because he is using his right hand and his right arm (Max's mother).

Max's parents noted his keen interest and engagement with the iPad even when he was younger and at the ECE centre. They thought the device would be beneficial to his developing basic digital skills, which could foster learning through interactive games, and especially for promoting flexibility with his hands:

We've seen how much they [the ECE centre] have used it [the iPad] particularly with Max for his CP. I'm hoping he will get a bit more flexibility with his hands and with his fine motor skills. Because of the CP the muscles aren't growing at the same rate as the tendons and it pulls the arm in. So when he runs he pulls his arm like that [she illustrates], so his tendons are short – they need to be stretched, so that he meets that need. It's worked out really well [with the iPad] (Max's mother).

I think it was actually seeing him on the right hand side, it's that placement of things or touching things carefully [with his right fingers when using the iPad] … because most of it he [Max] gets away with one [the left] hand. We have to keep reminding him to use his right hand. So he's using his left hand and kind of forgets about his right (Max's father).

FIGURE 13.1 The iPad's user-friendly touchscreen

FIGURES 13.2 iPad apps that reinforce the use of two hands are useful to Max. The left and right arrows act as visual and tactile signposts to guide both hands' movements

From a neurological perspective, they highlighted the importance of Max using both his hands to enhance the neurological signals that would stimulate the functioning of the right side of his body:

> The advice from the Child Development Centre (CDC) was to make sure that we stimulate the right side of his body more, getting into the habit of doing that. His brain will then still recognize at some level that he has that right hand. You can improve the nerve signals, the neurological signals over [both hemispheres of the brain], there is some improvement if you can stimulate that side (Max's father).

Along with this aim to enhance flexibility in his hands, the iPad's touchscreen meant Max could intuitively use it with ease compared with a desktop computer. Max's parents valued these affordances for his learning – the smooth surface, effortless tactile input and manipulation (be it swiping or sweeping motions with any finger(s), visually appealing and interactive apps, and speed in accessing an app:

> Easier just to use flat screen … it's just touch slide, moves, condense, enlarge, it's essentially instant access. Compared to the desktop, it's more interactive. The applications designed specifically for the iPad are [visually] bigger, faster, more eye catching, takes less time to download or upload the programmes, no matter wherever you are. It's less complicated … more intuitive for the kids, and it's a lot more fun (Max's mother).

In comparison, a desktop computer was more cumbersome for Max with the indented keys on the keyboard, and having to use individual fingers to type:

> [With the iPad] You don't have that 'down' indentation that you have with the [keyboard] keys, you can tap it or you can use individual fingers or you can use the sweeping motion. On the desktop you have to know 'which F button do I have to push' and then something happens and you might have to shut down and reboot (Max's mother).

Figure 13.3 demonstrates how the iPad's touchscreen affords easy and intuitive manipulation for Max to extend the use of his right hand.

iPad apps designed for players to use both hands were particularly useful for Max. An example of an app Max regularly plays was *Lego Chima Speedorz* (LEGO® Legends of CHIMA: Speedorz™). The app was designed with left and right arrow navigation requiring both hands to play (see Figure 13.4). The fact the game's speed could be moderated and controlled by a player added increasing levels of complexity, appeal and fun. Max's father explained how this was valuable for motivating Max to use both his hands, especially his right one:

FIGURES 13.3 Apps with reward systems such as in Maths Bingo motivates Max's learning

It's useful to have apps that make you use both hands rather than just one or the other. So it forces him [Max] to use his right hand as well because [part of the controls] are on the right hand side. See, it's got arrows one way or the other so you've got to use them both at the same time. And it's a speed thing that he's got to pull down a trigger to make it go faster (Max's father).

Other apps useful in enhancing Max's flexibility in his palsied hand are those involving sweeping motions. The app *Minion Rush* (Despicable Me: Minion Rush) requires a player to collect tokens in the form of bananas throughout the game through swiping and stretching hand movements, which progressively increase in speed. Max's mother saw its value in enforcing physical actions that will extend Max's right hand use. These actions are similar to and complement actions in other activities Max that participates in, such as swimming:

> Minion Rush ... because that's a sweeping action so that's an extension action, and while we try to encourage him to use his right hand, it gives that ... [feel that] extension and that supports what he does in the [swimming] pool – especially with freestyle – trying to get that [big] stretch [when you swim] (Max's mother).

Another app facilitating similar stretching actions was *Angry Birds Star Wars*. Max valued this app to practice the stretching motion for extending his right hand:

> But in the past ... one for games ... I liked the robot one and the Angry Birds Star Wars, because Angry Birds Star Wars you can just stretch your arm back (Max).

The iPad affords motivating learning processes and outcomes

Using the iPad meant that Max could obtain more spontaneous feedback to his input, and in less time than it would otherwise have taken him with other technologies. It was also physically less tedious:

> Time-wise it's pretty much instant [access and output] on an iPad, whereas children with more severe CP, you're not going to get that and the amount of effort it would take for someone with more severe CP than Max, it's incredibly tiring. He gets more tired faster than [other children]. A person with more severe CP is going to [strain] and the effort it would take to type one word ... or even moving the mouse around for this purpose (Max's mother).

iPad apps designed to offer feedback and rewards for correct responses to a learning task were particularly motivating for Max. When learning maths or spelling, Max found apps such as *Monkey Maths*, *Monkey Spelling*, *Splash Maths* and *Maths Bingo* engaged his interest and motivated him to continue to learn in a fun and engaging way (see Figure 13.3).

> At that age you want to keep them interested in learning and do the carrot and stick, rewards. It was Monkey Maths and Monkey Spelling ... Maths Bingo, because you then get to play with the bingo bucks (Max's mother).

She highlighted the touchscreen and instant feedback value of the iPad in facilitating Max's spelling, compared with writing alphabets on paper: 'It's a lot easier for him to learn spelling, he's not having to write it down if he can create the words, you know, do the words on a map [like on *Spellosaur* and *Word Bingo*]' (Max's mother).

Max's father added that apps such as *Paper 53* (a drawing app) were useful to enable Max to design and express his ideas. Max very much enjoyed the freehand construction of his ideas and drawings (see Figure 13.4).

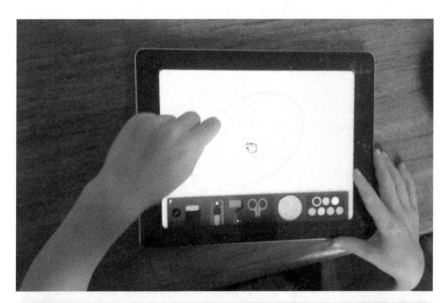

FIGURES 13.4 Max drawing a picture from the cartoon characters 'Tom and Jerry' on *Paper 53*.

Productive iPad use is facilitated when caregivers and teachers are supportive and interested in a student's learning

Max's parents viewed the iPad as part of a growing repertoire of digital tools. They valued Max's learning with and through the iPad as part of the skills expected of the current digital generation, and were supportive of his use:

> ICT is a huge part of the curriculum, even at primary schools. So familiarity with it…so that when they get to school, they are going to have a head start with whatever that they are using, whether it's touchscreen or desktop and a keyboard and a mouse (Max's mother).

When selecting educational iPad apps for Max, Max's father would search for apps of potential interest before downloading them for Max to trial. He used a trial-and-error approach to assess an app's suitability for engaging Max's learning:

> I tend to go onto the App Store and then look through it, do a search on it and I'll just scroll through. Sometimes I'll just scroll through probably a hundred of them just looking [then] open them up, read what they say. There are a few we've downloaded and they weren't suitable and we've just taken them off (Max's father).

Max's father regularly updated their app collection depending on Max's learning and developmental interest. He explained that Max's school has initiated a 'bring your own device' (BYOD) programme. As such, the school has recommended a list of iPad apps to foster learning in different curriculum areas across the school and home contexts. The apps were suitable for all students' learning:

> We've got a list of apps that when they were new entrants [at school] … for Max to use. We've got plenty of apps that they use, they have ones that the school assigns for maths and things. But all the apps are really designed just as an educational tool, not specifically for anyone with CP. Some of these fractions ones [apps that teach about fractions] were recommended by the school (Max's father).

Max's parents cautioned that there was no simple 'one size fits all' solution, and that other parents/caregivers of children with similar abilities would need to trial different strategies to ascertain what works best to support their child:

> I think the big picture is … find out, ask, find out more, and do what works for you … I would read it, I would do the research, and we've done that […] that's not working for us, just because that's what it says [a study has found], it's not a 'one size fits all'. And sometimes professionals in that area aren't necessarily the best people to kind of carry out the recommendations [role]

as such; because while they might be the clinical experts, they're not the 'whole person' experts and they're not – they don't see Max in his home and with us, so just because that's what they say doesn't necessarily mean it's actually going to work for us. So … do the research, talk to people, if that doesn't work, find something else [another solution] (Max's mother).

Max's father further signalled that the way Max used the iPad was but one way forward for him, and that other strategies might exist for those with varying levels of CP severity: 'You almost need to also meet somebody that's got far worse cerebral palsy and see how they use it [the iPad], because this is one very mild end of it, but then the scale goes right through.'

Taken together, these findings portrayed how particular affordances and features of the iPad and apps were useful for engaging and fostering Max's learning, and the ways these intersected with enhancing the physical functioning of his palsied arm. The parents' view of the role of digital technologies and their initiative, coupled with home–school connections, were also important in determining iPad apps appropriate to Max's needs.

Discussion and conclusion

This study adds to current investigations into adopting mobile devices, such as iPads for students with disabilities, to determine ways the devices can support and positively impact upon their learning and development. While the study focuses only on one student with a mild cerebral palsy, the findings are consistent with those of other authors in this volume and researchers who have found the iPad to be appealing to students, and instrumental in supporting and extending their learning and active participation (Chmiliar and Anton, 2015; Kagohara *et al.*, 2013; Rivera *et al.*, 2014).

The iPad's touchscreen in particular has revolutionised the ways students with disabilities can act on, and interact with, learning and entertainment content. In Max's case, the iPad served the dual role of being: 1) a therapeutic tool for reinforcing and extending the physical use of his palsied hand through swiping, sweeping, stretching movements and 2) a learning tool in supporting his literacy and numeracy learning in a fun and interactively engaging manner. Not having to write out letters to spell a word, for example, alleviated the physical exertion he would normally experience, allowing him to concentrate on the spelling/learning task instead.

iPad apps that can support students with disabilities by assisting with their learning and daily functioning are becoming more prevalent and available, and at a low cost. The apps Max used were commonly and economically available to all students in his school to foster the learning of specific content (maths and spelling). They were visually appealing, providing instant feedback in response to input through multimodal means. The fact that he could choose between different apps for different learning (choice of several maths apps) and for recreational purposes (e.g., to personalise drawings) encouraged his participation. Similarly, popular play-based apps that Max used were motivating (e.g., collecting banana tokens or slinging birds) to reinforce and extend the functioning of his palsied hand. Apps designed with features such as double-handed navigation, clear instructional visual–tactile signposts, and a user ability to moderate the pace of a game, were all important to Max's needs. The physical actions these apps fostered (e.g., swiping, stretching) aligned with the recommendations by medical professionals to enhance Max's mobility and flexibility in his right hand, and complemented similar helpful activities across his life (e.g., swimming).

This said, further studies are needed to examine the design of apps appropriate to students with disabilities. Most of the apps that Max used were not research-based. However, an examination of their key characteristics revealed them to be multimodally appealing, and contained engaging content/tasks appropriate to a user's level. They offered control (progressively increasing the speed or difficulty level), clear signposts, spontaneous feedback, and a choice of activities, as well as opportunities for customisation. These should be considered as part of a comprehensive approach to investigating app design, which ought to combine multiple perspectives and disciplines – technical, educational and medical/rehabilitation professionals – if students are to benefit from using apps. Although there are studies that have developed evaluation rubrics to ascertain the suitability of educational apps (Walker, 2011; Weng and Taber-Doughty, 2015), and customisation of apps for individuals with disabilities (Fernández-López *et al.*, 2013), further investigation into how students are using the apps in both formal and informal contexts can provide a richer account to inform future app design.

Further, students with disabilities' learning with and through the iPad can benefit from closer home–school links. As Max's parents highlighted, there was no 'one size fits all' solution for Max. The needs of students with developmental disabilities are different (McNaughton and Light, 2013). In this study, improving physical flexibility in his palsied hand was a key motivation for Max adopting the iPad. For others, it could be a communication, sensory, perceptual or other complex need. The value of an integrated approach involving the student, caregivers and education professionals who are interested in the student's learning and developmental needs, therefore cannot be underestimated. Caregivers and educators should take the initiative to establish closer home–school communication, share ideas and consider the range of apps available and appropriate to select and individualise for a student's needs.

Although the findings from this study will not necessarily be generalisable to a wider population given that the nature of the disability is varied in its diagnoses, severity and presentation within individuals, rich thick descriptions (Lincoln and Guba, 1985) of the setting and data have been provided. These descriptions are intended to contribute nuanced insights into issues and practices relating to iPad-supported learning activities for students with similar conditions. The possibilities offered by current and future mobile devices and tablet technologies are promising and exciting; however, merely having access to a device on its own will not solve the concerns faced by students with disabilities. Access to a device, coupled with careful consideration for the appropriate apps, and tasks designed to suit a student's needs and context, are crucial. Further research investigating the relevant ways mobile devices can be used by students with disabilities is vital if we are to use them as an 'equalising technology' (Chmiliar and Anton, 2015, p.127) to facilitate more equitable participation in learning and development opportunities, given the increasingly important role these devices play in many everyday tasks.

Acknowledgements

The author gratefully acknowledges funding support from the Wilf Malcolm Institute of Educational Research, The University of Waikato, New Zealand. The author is indebted to Max and his family for their participation in this study.

Note

1. In this chapter, the term 'disabilities' is used to encompass cerebral palsy as defined and classified by the Cerebral Palsy Society of New Zealand (2015), New Zealand Government (2011), and New Zealand Human Rights Commission (2015). It is acknowledged that various international literature may have different definitions and conceptions of this term.

References

Aronin, S. and Floyd, K. K. (2013). Using an iPad in inclusive preschool classrooms to intro-duce STEM concepts. *Teaching Exceptional Children*, *45*(4), 34–39.

Braun, V. and Clarke, V. (2006). Using thematic analysis in psychology. *Qualitative Research in Psychology*, *3*(2), 77–101.

Bryant, B. R. (2012). Assistive Technology and support provision for individuals with intellectual and developmental disabilities: Introduction to the topical issue. *Journal of Special Education Technology*, *27*(2), 1–2.

Cerebral Palsy Society of New Zealand (2015). *Cerebral Palsy*. Available at: www.cerebralpalsy.org.nz/Category?Action=ViewandCategory_id=88

CHASA (Children's Hemiplegia and Stroke Association) (2015). *Hemiplegia*. Available at: http://chasa.org/medical/hemiplegia/

Chmiliar, L. (2014). Learning with the iPad in early childhood. In Klaus Miesenberger, Deborah Fels, Dominique Archambault, Petr Penaz, Wolfgang Zagler (eds), Computers Helping People with Special Needs: 14th International Conference, ICCHP 2014 Proceedings, Part 2 (pp. 579–582). Switzerland: Springer.

Chmiliar, L. and Anton, C. (2015). The iPad as a mobile assistive technology device. *Journal of Assistive Technologies*, *9*(3), 127–135. doi: 10.1108/JAT-10-2014-0030

Clarke, L. and Abbott, L. (2015). Young pupils', their teacher's and classroom assistants' experiences of iPads in a Northern Ireland school:'Four and five years old, who would have thought they could do that?' *British Journal of Educational Technology*. doi: 10.1111/bjet.12266

Cole, M. and Engeström, Y. (1993). A cultural-historical approach to distributed cognition. In G. Salomon (ed.), *Distributed Cognitions: Psychological and educational considerations* (pp.1–46). Cambridge: Cambridge University Press.

Culén, A. L. and Gasparini, A. (2011). iPad: A new classroom technology? A report from two pilot studies. *INFuture Proceedings*, 199–208. Retrieved from: http://hnk.ffzg.hr/bibl/InFuture2011/PDF/03%20e-Learning/3-02%20Culen,%20Gasparini,%20iPad%20-%20A%20New%20Classroom%20Technology.pdf

Cumming, T. M. and Strnadova, I. (2012). The iPad as a pedagogical tool in special education: Promises and possibilities. *Special Education Perspectives*, *21*(1), 34–46.

Falloon, G. and Khoo, E. (2014). Exploring young students' talk in iPad-supported collaborative learning environments. *Computers and Education*, 77, 13–28. doi: 10.1016/j.compedu.2014.04.008

Fernández-López, Á., Rodríguez-Fórtiz, M. J., Rodríguez-Almendros, M. L. and Martínez-Segura, M. J. (2013). Mobile learning technology based on iOS devices to support students with special education needs. *Computers and Education*, *61*, 77–90.

Flewitt, R., Kucirkova, N. and Messer, D. (2014). Touching the virtual, touching the real: iPads and enabling literacy for students experiencing disability. *Australian Journal of Language and Literacy*, *37*(2), 107–116.

Fox, Z. (2011, July 26). *4 Ways iPads Are Changing the Lives of People With Disabilities.* Available from http://mashable.com/2011/07/25/ipads-disabilities/

Kagohara, D. M., Sigafoos, J., Achmadi, D., O'Reilly, M. and Lancioni, G. (2012). Teaching children with autism spectrum disorders to check the spelling of words. *Research in Autism Spectrum Disorders*, *6*(1), 304–310.

Kagohara, D., van der Meer, L., Ramdoss, S., O'Reilly, M., Lancioni, G., Davis, T., Rispoli, M., Lang, R., Marschik, P. B., Sutherland, D., Green, V. A. and Sigafoos, S. (2013). Using iPods and iPads in teaching programs for individuals with developmental disabilities: A systematic review. *Research in Developmental Disabilities 34*, 147–156.

Kucirkova, N., Messer, D., Sheehy, K. and Fernández Panadero, C. (2014a). Children's engagement with educational iPad apps: Insights from a Spanish classroom. *Computers and Education*, *71*, 175–184. http://doi.org/10.1016/j.compedu.2013.10.003

Kucirkova, N., Messer, D., Critten, V. and Harwood, J. (2014b). Story-making on the iPad when children have complex needs: two case studies. *Communication Disorders Quarterly*, published online before print, March 6, 2014, doi: 10.1177/1525740114525226

Khoo, E., Merry, R., Nguyen, N. H., Bennett, T. and MacMillan, N. (2015). *iPads and opportunities for teaching and learning for young children (iPads n kids).* Hamilton, New Zealand: Wilf Malcolm Institute of Educational Research.

Lincoln, Y. S. and Guba, E. G. (1985). *Naturalistic Inquiry.* Newbury Park, CA: Sage.

Maykut, P. S. and Morehouse, R. E. (1994). *Beginning Qualitative Research: A philosophic and practical guide.* Philadelphia, PA: Routledge.

McNaughton, D. and Light, J. (2013). The iPad and mobile technology revolution: Benefits and challenges for individuals who require augmentative and alternative communication. *Augmentative and Alternative Communication*, *29*(2), 107–116. doi: 10.3109/07434618.2013.784930

MoE (2015). *In-Class Support Funding for Students with Special Education Needs.* Available at: www.education.govt.nz/school/student-support/special-education/in-class-support-funding-for-students-with-special-education-needs/

More, C. M. and Travers, J. C. (2012). What's app with that? Selecting educational apps for young children with disabilities. *Young Exceptional Children*, *16*(2), 15–32. doi:10.1177/1096250612464763

Newton, D. A. and Dell, A. G. (2011). Mobile devices and students with disabilities: What do best practices tell us? *Journal of Special Education Technology*, *26*(3), 47–49.

New Zealand Government (2011). *Every Child Thrives, Belongs, Achieves. The Green Paper for Vulnerable Children.* Wellington: NZ Government. Available at www.msd.govt.nz

New Zealand Human Rights Commission (2015). *Disabled Children's Right to Education Report*. Wellington: New Zealand. Available at: www.hrc.co.nz/your-rights/people-disabilities/our-work/disabled-childrens-right-education/

Rivera, C. J., Mason, L., Moser, J. and Ahlgrim-Delzell, L. (2014). The effects of an iPad® multimedia shared story intervention on vocabulary acquisition for an english language learner. *Journal of Special Education Technology, 29*(4), 31–48.

Stephenson, J. and Limbrick, L. (2013). A review of the use of touch-screen mobile devices by people with developmental disabilities. *Journal of Autism and Developmental Disorders*, 1–15. http://doi.org/10.1007/s10803-013-1878-8

Strnadova, I. and Cumming, T. M. (2013). iPad integration for students with intellectual disabilities: Increasing access and engagement across settings. Abstracts of the 3rd IASSIDD Asia-Pacific Conference (Tokyo, Japan). *Journal of Policy and Practice in Intellectual Disabilities, 10*, 171. doi:10.1111/jppi.12029

Walker, H. (2011). Evaluating the effectiveness of apps for mobile devices. *Journal of Special Education Technology, 26*(4), 59–63.

Weng, P. L. and Taber-Doughty, T. (2015). Developing an app evaluation rubric for practitioners in special education. *Journal of Special Education Technology, 30*(1), 43–58.

14

ENHANCING SCIENCE LEARNING WITH BYOD (BRING YOUR OWN DEVICE) IN A PRIMARY SCHOOL IN HONG KONG

Yanjie Song and Wai Ying Ku

THE EDUCATION UNIVERSITY OF HONG KONG

This chapter reports on a one-year study investigating how students in a primary school in Hong Kong advanced their content knowledge of science in a seamless inquiry-based learning environment leveraged by BYOD (Bring Your Own Device), taking the topic of 'Flowers and Seeds' in the Biodiversity learning unit as an example. One teacher and 28 Grade 6 students were involved in this study. Qualitative data including pre- and post-domain tests, class observations, student artefacts, online postings, and field notes were collected and analysed to examine students' learning. The findings suggest that effective use of apps, such as Skitch, Edmodo, and Evernote with BYOD using an inquiry-based learning approach, could help younger students advance their knowledge in science, develop personalised learning skills, and gain a better sense of ownership in science learning.

Keywords: Inquiry, pedagogy, seamless, BYOD, science, learning

Introduction

With the advent of the Internet and mobile technologies, learners are provided with more opportunities to learn ubiquitously, in and out of classrooms (Wong and Looi, 2011). However, given the rapid development of technology, there is a gap between research and practice. While past studies have focused on a uniform type of device available to students in seamless learning environments (Song *et al.*, 2012; Zhang *et al.*, 2010), the literature on affordances of multiple device types for learning across different settings is still in its infancy. The potential of personal devices for learning enhancement may remain under-utilised if educators fail to venture into the shifting paradigm in education of today.

Inquiry-based learning is a pedagogy that has been practised in science subjects for decades. Research evidence shows that inquiry-based learning approaches can help students to develop critical thinking skills and achieve intended learning outcomes (Hakkarainen, 2003). However, in the process of inquiry learning, young learners may come across challenges difficult for them to cope with, such as designing appropriate experiments (e.g., what variables to choose, how many variables to change, how to state and test hypotheses), implementing experiments (e.g., make predictions), and interpreting and presenting results (e.g., compare and visualise data, then present these appropriately) (Van Joolingen *et al.*, 2007). The goal of this study was to find out how learners could take advantage of the affordances of mobile devices to support seamless science inquiry learning.

This chapter presents a study on how primary students advanced their knowledge of science using various apps with Bring Your Own Device (BYOD) in a seamless, inquiry-based learning environment. The next section presents literature related to BYOD for seamless learning and inquiry pedagogy, followed by a description of the research design. Then, results are presented and a conclusion is drawn with implications for future research directions.

BYOD (Bring Your Own Device)

Research on teaching and learning leveraged by BYOD Bring Your Own Device (BYOD) has been gaining popularity in recent years (Falloon, 2015; Lai *et al.*, 2013). Alberta Education (2012) defines BYOD as a technology model where students bring a personally owned device to school for the purpose of learning. Having opportunities to personalise their device, students are more likely to access and engage in learning in ways that meet their own needs, using various apps such as Edmodo – a social network platform (Kong and Song, 2015). Allowing students to use their own device has hence become a preferred practice to bridge the gap between home and school learning in many scenarios (Song, 2014). For the purposes of this project, BYOD is defined as the technology model where students bring a personally owned mobile device with various apps and embedded features to use anywhere, anytime, for learning.

Despite existing studies on using BYOD to promote better learning experiences and enhance engagement across time–space boundaries, research on how BYOD works with inquiry-based pedagogy in primary school education, appears scarce. The goal of the present study was to explore how students' advancement of content knowledge might be supported in a BYOD primary school environment. It is likely that students' enthusiasm for using mobile devices in class decreases after a period of time (Kobus *et al.*, 2013), and this suggests that learning cannot be enhanced if teachers solely embed technology into the classroom without pedagogy and content knowledge considerations (Ertmer and Ottenbreit-Leftwich, 2013). In our study, we focused on the potential of inquiry-based learning approaches to improving young learners' science learning leveraged by apps and BYOD.

Inquiry-based pedagogy approach

The concept of inquiry learning stems from Dewey (1916), who believed that education is 'an active constructive process' (p. 46) in which students learn by doing. Inquiry-based pedagogy has been advocated to help learners to construct knowledge and develop higher-order thinking skills (Lakkala *et al.*, 2005; Burden, Chapter 19, this volume). The instructional model of inquiry-based learning consists of probing questions, gathering and analysing data, and constructing evidence-based explanations and arguments via collaborative investigation among learners (Hakkarainen, 2003; Krajcik *et al.*, 2000). Teachers are expected to act as facilitators throughout learners' investigation processes (Hakkarainen, 2003). However, for young learners it is noted that guided inquiry is needed in order to develop content knowledge, inquiry skills, technological proficiency, productivity in collaborative work and reflective ability (Lakkala *et al.*, 2005).

Seamless inquiry-based learning in science

With the proliferation of WiFi networks and increased affordability and choice of portable devices, more and more researchers maintain that mobile devices are already well integrated into students' lives (Falloon, 2015). According to Wong and Looi (2011), '*seamless learning*' refers to 'the seamless integration of the learning experiences across various dimensions including formal and informal learning contexts, individual and social learning, and physical world and cyberspace' (p. 2364). Such a learning environment provides students with opportunities to learn anytime, anywhere without time and place constraints. In this study, *seamless learning* focuses especially on students' learning that spans over school lab, classroom and online settings supported by various apps and BYOD.

To do science inquiry seamlessly, students need to search and share information, collect and create science data, and discuss and coordinate with peers, without time and place constraints. Mobile technologies provide many affordances (i.e., possibilities for action, see Barab and Roth, 2006) to help achieve these goals. The affordances of mobile technologies include tools for multimedia access, multimedia collection, communication, representation, information sharing, knowledge construction, connectivity, reference, and analysis (e.g., Churchill and Churchill, 2008; Song, 2011). Effective use of these affordances in science inquiry in a *seamless learning environment* is conductive to students' knowledge advancement (Kong and Song, 2013).

Research design

Context

This study seeks to answer the question of how students advanced their content knowledge in science inquiry in a seamless learning environment supported by BYOD. The study was situated in a one-year research project titled 'Bring Your

Own Device (BYOD) for seamless science inquiry' and was undertaken in a government-subsidised primary school in Hong Kong. The project took place in a class comprising 28 Grade 6 students (10- to 11-year-olds), and involved five science units with 12 topics. The students were randomly grouped into seven groups of four. 'Flowers and Seeds' was the topic chosen to examine the students' inquiry, and was part of a unit on Biodiversity. Among participating students, 24 brought mobile devices from home, including ten iPads, eleven Android tablets or smartphones, two iPhones, and one iPod. Four students used iPads provided by the school. Students used the devices to take photos, and record videos and audios to fulfil the assignment requirements. They also had access to the Internet with school WiFi, for various other learning purposes.

The teacher had eight years of teaching experience and had taken part in professional development related to using inquiry-based pedagogy to support students' learning, and to provide support with the use of mobile apps. The teacher for the science inquiry project selected three apps, namely Edmodo, Evernote and Skitch. Edmodo is a social learning platform with both web-based and mobile versions. It is a secure microblogging medium that encourages collaborative knowledge construction (Song, 2014). Students could communicate, share information, submit assignments and coordinate learning activities seamlessly across devices. Evernote is a cloud note-taking and archiving application with web, app and desktop clients. Students record their learning process and reflections in the form of text, pictures and audio recordings. Notes are stored on cloud servers and can be accessed anywhere and anytime. The note sharing function on Evernote allows collaboration and exchange of ideas among students. Skitch is an extension of Evernote that allows additional annotation functions, with image and shape editing, and website screenshot captures.

Pedagogical design of students' inquiry into 'Flowers and Seeds'

To support learners in their work, an inquiry learning model based on previous research into inquiry pedagogical design was adopted (Hakkarainen, 2003; Krajcik *et al.*, 2000). The model comprised six elements: (1) 'engage' in question and hypothesis formation; (2) 'explore' the methods and processes of inquiry; (3) 'observe' the phenomena in the experiment; (4) 'explain' the analyses and outcomes of inquiry; (5) 'reflect' on the processes and outcomes of inquiry; and (6) 'share' the findings and reflections. The inquiry-based learning model was implemented in the learning activities for the study of 'Flowers and Seeds' (see Table 14.1). The activities were carried out in four contexts: classroom, home, school lab, and an online learning platform – Edmodo.

Data collection and analysis

Data collection included: (a) pre- and post-tests in biodiversity; (b) student artefacts (postings on Edmodo, postings on Evernote, captured photos, captured recordings,

TABLE 14.1 Seamless inquiry-based learning activities on 'Flower and Seeds'

Activities	Description
Engage (in class)	Students watch a video about how a seed grows in class, then visit the website of 'Discovering Plants in Taiwan' to learn some interesting facts about flowers (http://taiwan-plants.ndap.org.tw)
Explore (at home and on school campus)	Students read online information about plant structures and functions. Then, they explore and take photos of a few types of leaves collected on campus, and find out the scientific names of their findings and upload them to Edmodo
Observe (in school lab)	Students observe and find out the structure of two faba beans and a lily prepared by the teacher, under a magnifying glass. Students are encouraged to make full use of their mobile devices in the observational process
Explain (in school lab)	Students label the parts of seeds and flowers using the mobile app – Skitch, then explain the structures using the voice-recording function on Evernote
Reflect (online)	Students reflect on the guided questions in Evernote, e.g., Q1: What have you discovered from your inquiry process? Q2: How does the structure of seeds affect the process of seed dispersal? (Record your sharing using Evernote)
Share (online and in class)	Students upload their labelled flowers and seeds and reflections on Edmodo for sharing. They also make a presentation in class to share their work

captured videos, worksheets), (c) class observations and field notes. The pre-domain test had two main questions: pre-Question 1 (pre-Q1) *What do you know about flowers and seeds?* and pre-Question 2 (pre-Q2) *Please draw a concept map to show what you know about flowers and seeds.* The post-domain test also had two main questions: post-Question 1 (post-Q1) 'What have you learned most about flowers and seeds?' and post-Question 2 (post-Q2) 'Please draw a concept map to show what you have learned about flowers and seeds.' Concept maps have been widely adopted in science learning as assessment tools to measure students' knowledge development, and to evaluate students' understanding of concept interrelations (Van Zele *et al.*, 2004). Before the project began, the students were instructed that a concept map consists of nodes, lines and line labels, and that students should draw circles for the nodes and arrow lines with labels, to make connections between concepts. The concept maps were drawn on paper-based worksheets.

In order to understand the knowledge advancement made during the science inquiry, a summative approach was used for content analysis, which involved 'counting and comparisons, usually of keywords or content, followed by the interpretation of the underlying context' (Hsieh and Shannon, 2005, p. 1277). The answers and concept maps from the pre- and post-domain tests (pre- and post- Q1 and Q2) were coded and categorised into different types. After that, the numbers in each category were enumerated and explained in context, to develop better understanding of students' knowledge advancement. Lastly, relevant posts that students made on Edmodo and Evernote that related to the development of content knowledge about flowers and seeds were also coded, to examine their learning process and outcomes. For the purpose of triangulation, field notes were used in the data analysis process, whenever necessary.

Results

Twenty-eight pre-domain test sheets and 27 post-domain test sheets were collected. By pairing the pre- and post-domain tests, 25 valid pairs of students' test sheets were obtained. The results of pre- and post-domain tests, each consisting of two questions, are presented below.

Results of pre- and post-Q1

Table 14.2 shows the summarised results of pre-Q1: *What do you know about flowers and seeds?* Seven categories were identified: (a) flowers grow from seeds; (b) there are different types of flowers; (c) flowers attract insects; (d) seeds are found in fruit; (e) the male and female parts of a flower are reproductive organs; (f) seeds can be dispersed in different ways; and (g) others, including individual answers without identical contributions, such as 'water is essential for plant growth'.

The findings show that 31.3 percent of students' answers were focused on 'flowers grow from seeds' and 20.8 percent on 'there are different types of flowers'. The least-reported category was 'seeds can be dispersed in different ways' (6.3 percent). This indicates that the majority of students had prior knowledge that flowers grow from seeds, and there are different types of flowers. However, their reports contained various concepts (e.g., relationships among flowers and seeds, varieties of flowers, etc.). For instance, student 1 reported, 'I knew that seeds come from plants and fruits. Sunflowers face sunlight. Some flowers are poisonous.'

TABLE 14.2 Percentage of each category mentioned by the students in pre-Q1

No.	Categories	n = 48	Percentage of total
(a)	Flowers grow from seeds	15	31.3
(b)	There are different types of flowers	10	20.8
(c)	Flowers attract insects	4	8.3
(d)	Seeds are found in fruit	4	8.3
(e)	The male and female parts of a flower are reproductive organs	4	8.3
(f)	Seeds can be dispersed in different ways	3	6.3
(g)	Others	8	16.7

Table 14.3 shows the summarised results of post-Q1: *What have you learned most about flowers and seeds?* Eight categories were identified: (a) learned more about parts of a flower; (b) learned that pollen is transferred from the anther (male part) to the stigma (female part); (c) learned that flowers can be both male and female; (d) learned more about the relationships among flowers, fruits and seeds; (e) learned that bees and butterflies are pollinators; (f) learned more about the structure of seeds; (g) learned that there are more varieties of flowers; and (h) others, including individual answers without identical contributions, such as 'learned more about the texture and scent of a flower'.

From the students' answers for the post-Q1, it was found that the students' reports were focused more on the topic of parts of a flower, and their description of flowers and seeds was more detailed compared with that in the pre-test. For example, student 1 reported, 'I learned that the male anther of a flower released pollen grains and the female stigma receives the pollen grains during the process of pollination. I also learned that pollen grains are the male gametes. Bees and butterflies are pollinators.'

Results of pre- and post-Q2

Table 14.4 and Table 14.5 show the summarised results of pre-Q2 (*Please draw a concept map to show what you know about flowers and seeds*) and post-Q2 (*Please draw a concept map to show what you have learned about flowers and seeds*). Table 14.4 shows that six categories of related concepts about flowers and seeds were identified: (a) flower parts; (b) requirements for plant growth; (c) seed dispersal; (d) flower reproduction; (e) flower varieties; and (f) seed structure, and the presented concepts in nodes, links and link labels were focused on flower parts (35.1 percent, 36.1 percent, and 37.3 percent, respectively).

TABLE 14.3 Percentage of each category mentioned by the students in post-Q1

No.	Categories	n = 77	Percentage of total
(a)	Learned more about parts of a flower	20	26.0
(b)	Learned that pollen is transferred from the anther (male part) to the stigma (female part)	13	16.9
(c)	Learned that flowers can be both male and female	12	15.6
(d)	Learned more about the relationships among flowers, fruits and seeds	10	13.0
(e)	Learned that bees and butterflies are pollinators	7	9.1
(f)	Learned more about the structure of seeds	6	7.8
(g)	Learned that there are more varieties of flowers	5	6.5
(h)	Others	4	5.2

TABLE 14.4 Pre-Q2 percentage of related concepts in nodes, links and link labels in the map

Related concepts	Nodes		Links		Link labels	
	n = 74	Total (percentage)	n = 72	Total (percentage)	n = 59	Total (percentage)
Flower parts	26	35.1	26	36.1	22	37.3
Requirements for plant growth	16	21.6	16	22.2	14	23.7
Seed dispersal	13	17.6	12	16.7	9	15.3
Flower reproduction	9	12.2	9	12.5	8	13.6
Flower varieties	8	10.8	7	9.7	4	6.8
Seed structure	2	2.7	2	2.8	2	3.4

While Table 14.5 shows that six categories were identified: (a) flower parts; (b) flower reproduction; (c) seed dispersal; (d) seed structure; (e) flower varieties; and (f) others, the presented concepts in nodes, links and link labels were focused mainly on flower parts (40.6 percent, 40.6 percent, and 44.1 percent, respectively). This indicates that before their inquiry into the parts of flowers and seeds, students' knowledge about flowers and seeds tended to be 'common-sense' knowledge. After their inquiry into the parts of flowers and seeds, the students developed more focused and detailed knowledge, indicating deeper understanding of flowers and seeds.

It is noted that the findings of post-Q1 and post-Q2 indicate that after the seamless inquiry into flowers and seeds, students' learning went beyond 'common-sense' knowledge as shown in the findings of pre-Q1 and pre-Q2. Instead, students could concentrate on the problem under investigation and delve into it in depth.

TABLE 14.5 Post-Q2 percentage of related concepts in nodes, links and link labels in the map

Related concepts	Nodes		Links		Link labels	
	n = 138	Total (percentage)	n = 138	Total (percentage)	n = 111	Total (percentage)
Flower parts	56	40.6	56	40.6	49	44.1
Flower reproduction	29	21.0	29	21.0	26	23.4
Seed dispersal	17	12.3	17	12.3	12	10.8
Seed structure	14	10.1	14	10.1	10	9.0
Flower varieties	13	9.4	13	9.4	8	7.2
Others	9	6.5	9	6.5	6	5.4

Using mobile apps in science inquiry

To understand better how knowledge construction is accomplished in seamless, mobile technology-supported inquiry learning, a group was randomly selected and the development of students' artefacts related to flowers and seeds was tracked. The students were encouraged to make use of their personal device to engage in the six inquiry learning activities guided by the seamless inquiry-based learning model. Figure 14.1 shows the inquiry process of the students. The group members carried out the investigation collaboratively. They took pictures of the flower using the camera app on iPad, then labelled parts of the seed (see Figure 14.2) and flower (see Figure 14.3) using the annotation tool Skitch, on their mobile device. They then uploaded their result to the social network platform, Edmodo. The simple annotation tool in Skitch allowed students to show their understanding by labelling the parts of the seed, then share their annotated file on Edmodo as evidence, suggesting that the group members understood the concept of seed and flower structures.

The group members also wrote their reflections on Evernote using their personal device as a tool for knowledge construction. Student 1 reflected:

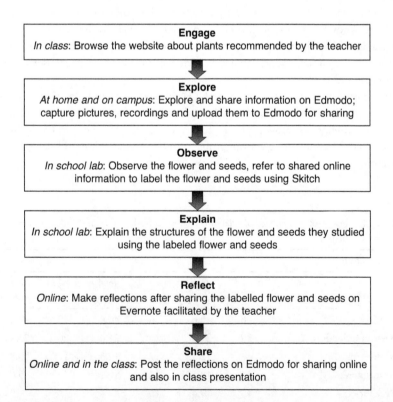

FIGURE 14.1 Group's inquiry learning process

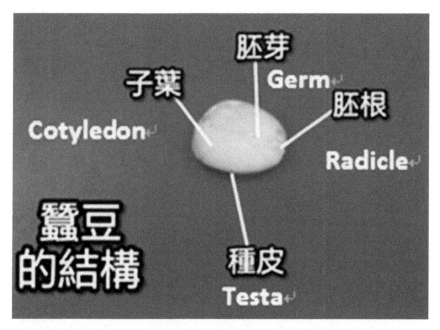

FIGURE 14.2 Group work on the structure of Faba bean

When carrying out the research on flowers, I got to know the parts of the flowers, which I have never heard of, including calyx, petals, stamen and pistil. Also, I discovered that the stamen is not only responsible for producing pollens, but also transferring them to pistil before the insects pollinate. As I investigated the structure of a faba bean, I looked at the cotyledon and the gemma. Faba bean belongs to dicotyledons because the seeds have two cotyledons and it is a flowering plant. The apps on BYOD made it convenient to capture photos for records, and to search for more information online.

While student 1 demonstrated deeper knowledge construction from the inquiry, he also indicated his preference for using apps on his device in the exploratory process. Other student members also reflected their unique experience in the collective learning process. For example, student 2 wrote:

As I learn about the structure of a flower, I feel that it is a very new experience because it is the first time that I touch pollens. Also, I discover a unique scent of faba beans while I study the structure of it. Using BYOD to learn about this topic is very interesting because it involves teamwork and the use of photographs to record the experiment process. I am looking forward to participating in activities of this sort.

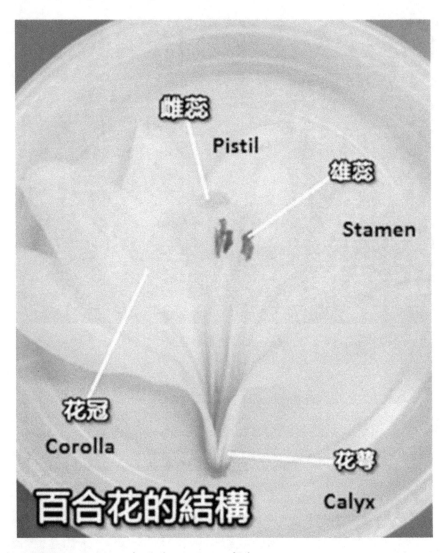

FIGURE 14.3 Group work on the structure of Lily

In addition, the group expressed their positive attitude towards learning with their own device. When they were asked about the opinions of the BYOD project, all students held a positive attitude. One student responded, 'We used Evernote and Skitch when carrying out experiments. They reinforce our learning as we use them for revisions before exams and after lessons.' This suggests that the Evernote and Skitch apps helped students to document their learning process, which was useful for their course review. They also appeared to develop a sense of ownership associated with knowledge construction during the inquiry, through using the apps on BYOD.

Discussion

The study explored students' science knowledge advancement by examining the results of pre- and post-domain tests, the presentation of a group's concept map, and students' reflections posted online. It was found that students' initial understandings and mapped concepts (nodes, links and link labels) and results of the pre-domain test, were predominantly focused on the general knowledge about leaves and flowers. After the inquiry, students' responses to the post-domain test revealed that their understanding had shifted to the parts and reproduction process of flowers and seeds, which indicated a knowledge gain in terms of the plants' structure. In addition, the significant increase of nodes and labels illustrated in the post-domain concept maps reflected students' deeper knowledge on the parts of flowers and seeds. The results suggest that students' learning about flowers and seeds might have been enhanced by the effective use of apps such as Edmodo for sharing online resources searched from the Internet, Skitch for annotating the plants to make their learning visible, and Evernote for reflecting what they had learned. Furthermore, by tracking a group's development of artefacts related to the structures of the faba bean and the lily, it was possible to better understand how the group enhanced their understanding of seeds and flowers in the inquiry process across different learning spaces, using their mobile devices.

The findings show that the integration of apps and BYOD into guided inquiry-based learning might help young learners to advance their content knowledge. The students referred to the shared artefacts on the social network Edmodo, used Evernote, and recorded their observations concerning flowers and seeds at home and school with the support of their mobile devices. The combination of these affordances helped the students gain solid domain knowledge about flowers and seeds, such as the knowledge about the structure and other knowledge of the faba bean, which was beyond 'textbook knowledge'. We observed that during the science inquiry, students maintained a sense of ownership and control over their own learning, which was lacking in prior mobile learning studies where they needed to borrow the devices from school (Corlett et al., 2005).

In addition, the three apps of Skitch, Edmodo and Evernote were used inter-actively in this study by connecting the learning tasks 'seamlessly'. Skitch, an annotation app, was used as a tool to make quick sketches and label the structure of plants as artefacts in the course of the experiment. As Skitch was linked to Evernote – a note-taking app, the artefacts could be directly uploaded to Evernote; then students could write descriptions of the artefacts and take down reflective notes. Thus, it made the artefacts uploading process easier for primary students to achieve without having to save it in the computer first. On the other hand, each note in Evernote had a web-link, which could be embedded in the Edmodo platform. The advantage of it is that students could keep their own 'e-portfolio' in Evernote, and offered them flexibility in choosing the notes they wanted to share. Such functions greatly boosted the flexibility, mobility and interactivity of learning at a relatively inexpensive cost (Wu and Zhang, 2010) and facilitated students' personalised learning by setting their own learning goals, beyond the classroom (e.g., extended school) and following their own learning path (Kearney *et al.*, 2012; Sebba *et al.*, 2007; Song *et al.*, 2012).

In addition, results from the focus group revealed very positive attitudes towards the science inquiry supported by apps and BYOD. Students' comments suggest that the positive attitude was not merely a result of the BYOD's novelty effect (Liu *et al.*, 2009), but was also linked to the authentic seamless inquiry-based learning activities, which encouraged peer learning, and allowed students to put in consistent effort to achieve their intended learning outcomes. The BYOD model was not the sole explanation for assisting students' learning (Ertmer and Ottenbreit-Leftwich, 2013; Kobus *et al.*, 2013). Instead, it was the blend of apps in BYOD and the guided inquiry-based pedagogy that gave momentum to the students' inquiry processes and the fulfilment of their proposed learning goals. Based on our findings, we agree with Ertmer and Ottenbreit-Leftwich (2013) that there is a pressing need that the focus is diverted from technology integration *per se*, to the promotion of technology-enabled learning.

Also, the results suggested that tracing individuals and group inquiry in multiple spaces can make visible the learning process and outcomes (Stahl, 2002). Visible conceptual artefacts such as photos, text, recordings and video clips documented students' learning, and mediated the process progressively. It is interesting to note that students' skills and engagement in science inquiry improved, together with deeper content knowledge construction.

Conclusion

This chapter reported on a study of enhancing students' science learning supported by different apps and BYOD in a seamless inquiry-based learning environment. In this study, the students adopted different apps to help complete the science learning tasks at their own pace and across different spaces, which helped to foster personalised learning and increase independent learning capacities. This is a shift from 'fixed content and fixed timing' of a traditional lesson to 'flexible content and flexible timing' of a mobilised lesson (Looi *et al.*, 2009; Zhang *et al.*, 2010). In addition, by adopting BYOD, students could enjoy the convenience and intimacy of their own mobile devices and the flexible learning activities tailored for their own needs which contributed to a sense of ownership of their own learning. Moreover, in this study, inquiry-based pedagogy in tandem with various apps and the BYOD technological model, appeared to help improve students' learning engagement and knowledge attainment in science.

Acknowledgements

The study was funded by Hong Kong Institute of Education under Small Research Grant (MIT/SRG07/14-15). I thank Mr Cheuk Lun, MA, from Hong Kong Institute of Education Jockey Club Primary School for his collaboration and support to this study.

References

Alberta Education. (2012). Bring your own device: A guide for schools. Available at: https://open.alberta.ca/dataset/5821955f-5809-4768-9fc8-3b81b78257f7/resource/631bf34c-d3e6-4648-ab77-2b36727dca0b/download/5783885-2012-07-Bring-your-own-device-a-guide-for-schools.pdf (retrieved June 25, 2012).

Barab, S. A. and Roth, W.-M. (2006). Curriculum-based ecosystems: Supporting knowing from an ecological perspective. *Educational Researcher, 35*(5), 3–13.

Churchill, D. and Churchill, N. (2008). Educational affordances of PDAs: A study of a teacher's exploration of this technology. *Computers & Education, 50*(4), 1439–1450.

Corlett, D., Sharples, M., Bull, S. and Chan, T. (2005). Evaluation of a mobile learning organiser for university students. *Journal of Computer Assisted Learning, 21*(3), 162–170.

Dewey, J. (1916). *Democracy and Education. An introduction to the philosophy of education* (Reprint 1997), Rockland, NY: Free Press.

Ertmer, P. A. and Ottenbreit-Leftwich, A. (2013). Removing obstacles to the pedagogical changes required by Jonassen's vision of authentic technology-enabled learning. *Computers & Education, 64*(0), 175–182.

Falloon, G. (2015). What's the difference? Learning collaboratively using iPads in conventional classrooms. *Computers & Education, 84*, 62–77.

Hakkarainen, K. (2003). Progressive inquiry in a computer-supported biology class. *Journal of Research in Science Teaching, 40*(10), 1072–1088.

Hsieh, H.-F. and Shannon, S. E. (2005). Three approaches to qualitative content analysis. *Qualitative Health Research, 15*(9), 1277–1288.

Kearney, M., Schuck, S., Burden, K. and Aubusson, P. (2012). Viewing mobile learning from a pedagogical perspective. *Research in Learning Technology, 20*.

Kobus, M. B. W., Rietveld, P. and van Ommeren, J. N. (2013). Ownership versus on-campus use of mobile IT devices by university students. *Computers & Education, 68*(0), 29–41. doi: http://dx.doi.org/10.1016/j.compedu.2013.04.003

Kong, S. C. and Song, Y. (2015). An experience of personalized learning hub initiative embedding BYOD for reflective engagement in higher education. *Computers & Education, 88*, 227–240.

Krajcik, J., Blumenfeld, P., Marx, R. and Soloway, E. (2000). Instructional, curricular, and technological supports for inquiry in science classrooms. In Minstell, J. and Van Zee, E. (eds), *Inquiring into Inquiry Learning and Teaching in Science*. Washington: American Association for the Advancement of Science.

Lai, K. W., Khaddage, F. and Knezek, G. (2013). Blending student technology experiences in formal and informal learning. *Journal of Computer Assisted Learning, 29*(5), 414–425.

Lakkala, M., Lallimo, J. and Hakkarainen, K. (2005). Teachers' pedagogical designs for technology-supported collective inquiry: A national case study. *Computers and Education, 45*(3), 337–356.

Liu, S.-H., Liao, H.-L. and Pratt, J. A. (2009). Impact of media richness and flow on e-learning technology acceptance. *Computers & Education, 52*(3), 599–607.

Looi, C.-K., Wong, L.-H., So, H.-J., Seow, P., Toh, Y., Chen, W. and Soloway, E. (2009). Anatomy of a mobilized lesson: Learning my way. *Computers & Education, 53*(4), 1120–1132.

Sebba, J., Brown, N., Steward, S., Galton, M. and James, M. (2007). *An Investigation of Personalised Learning Approaches used by Schools*. Nottingham: DfES Publications.

Song, Y. (2011). What are the affordances and constraints of handheld devices for learning in higher education. *British Journal of Educational Technology, 42*(6), E163–E166.

Song, Y. (2014). 'Bring Your Own Device (BYOD)' for seamless science inquiry in a primary school. *Computers & Education, 74,* 50–60.

Song, Y., Wong, L.-H. and Looi, C.-K. (2012). Fostering personalized learning in science inquiry supported by mobile technologies. *Educational Technology Research and Development, 60*(4), 679–701.

Stahl, G. (2002). Rediscovering CSCL. In T. Koschmann, R. Hall and N. Miyake (eds), *CSCL 2: Carrying forward the conversation* (pp. 169–181). Hillsdale, NJ: Lawrence Erlbaum.

Van Joolingen, W. R., De Jong, T. and Dimitrakopoulou, A. (2007). Issues in computer supported inquiry learning in science. *Journal of Computer Assisted Learning, 23*(2), 111–119.

Van Zele, E., Lenaerts, J. and Wieme, W. (2004). Improving the usefulness of concept maps as a research tool for science education. *International Journal of Science Education, 26*(9), 1043–1064.

Wong, L.-H. and Looi, C.-K. (2011). What seams do we remove in mobile-assisted seamless learning? A critical review of the literature. *Computers and Education, 57,* 2364–2381.

Wu, J. and Zhang, Y. (2010). Examining potentialities of handheld technology in students' academic attainments. *Educational Media International, 47*(1), 57– 67.

Zhang, B., Chee-Kit, L., Seow, P., Chia, G., Wong, L.-H., Chen, W. and Norris, C. (2010). Deconstructing and reconstructing: Transforming primary science learning via a mobilized curriculum. *Computers & Education, 55*(4), 1504–1523.

15

BRINGING PUDSEY TO LIFE

Young children's use of augmented reality apps

Jackie Marsh and Dylan Yamada-Rice

UNIVERSITY OF SHEFFIELD, SHEFFIELD, UK

This chapter examines young children's use of augmented reality (AR) apps on tablets. Drawing on an Economic and Social Research Council (ESRC)-funded study in the UK, which examined the potential of apps to promote play and creativity, the chapter considers data in which young children used AR apps in a variety of ways. The nature and potential of AR apps for use with young children are reviewed and it is argued that if this technology is to meet its promise, further consideration needs to be given to issues of play and creativity.

Keywords: Augmented reality, creativity, play, thinking, virtual, experiences

Introduction

Virtual and augmented reality

Virtual reality has a long history. At the heart of virtual reality is the concept of fusion. In 1849, the composer Richard Wagner published an essay, 'Outline of the Artwork of the Future', which set out a vision for a synthesis of the arts in which music, poetry and dance co-existed in a single work. Building on Wagner's concept, in 1924 Moholy-Nagy envisaged a 'Theater of Totality', which is:

> A kind of stage activity which will no longer permit the masses to be silent spectators, which will not only excite them inwardly but will let them take hold and participate – actually allow them to fuse with the action on the stage at the peak of cathartic ecstasy.
>
> (Moholy-Nagy, 1924/2010: 281)

Multimedia theorists have identified this tradition as being important in the development of virtual reality (Packer and Jordan, 2002), as the synthesis it envisaged was a precursor to the invention of computer-generated virtual reality in which a simulation of a three-dimensional (3D) image or environment can be interacted with by humans who wear specially designed glasses or headsets that offer a feeling of immersion in the virtual world. In this experience, we see the fusion of action that Moholy-Nagy dreamed of. Augmented reality (AR) is a variation of this phenomenon. AR consists of a blend of the physical world and virtual world. In this blended reality, 3D images or environments are projected onto a physical object, but users are not immersed in the same way as they are with virtual reality experiences.

In the study reported on in this chapter, apps that offered an AR experience for children aged five and under were examined in order to identify how far they fostered play and creativity. Given that such apps are now being used in educational settings, it is important to analyse their potential in order to inform future learning and teaching activities for young children (see Chapter 18).

There have been a number of studies that have considered the potential value that AR might have for children's play and learning. Bai *et al.* (2015) report on a study in which they developed a finger puppet system, FingAR Puppet, which used AR technology to enhance play with the puppets. Fourteen children aged between 4 and 6 years used the system, and their responses were analysed to determine the impact of the activity on children's expression and understanding of emotion, their communication around play, and their divergent thinking. The researchers reported that, based on their analysis, AR technology promoted the expression and understanding of emotion and the verbalisation of pretend play, as the children talked about the transformations of objects. The research team also examined the potential of AR technology for the play of young children with autism (Bai *et al.*, 2013), suggesting that AR can enhance the frequency, duration, and relevance of autistic children's play.

Other studies have also indicated that AR technology can enhance learning and play. Yarosh *et al.* (2008) conducted a study in which they used augmented dress-up clothes and toys to teach American Sign Language to young children. Eight children engaged with the materials and the study found that they were motivating for young children, although system errors meant that the teacher needed to mediate the activities. Hinske *et al.* (2005) developed an Augmented Knights Castle Playset, which linked sound files containing verbal commentaries, sound effects, and information with educational content with specific elements of the playset. One hundred and three primary children aged between 6–10 played with either a non-augmented version of the playset or the AR playset. The research team found that children had very good retention of the vocabulary learned during the play session with the Augmented Knights Castle, even when tested again two months following the study.

AR technology has also been used in science teaching by Kerawalla *et al.* (2006). It was found that AR could be used to help children understand how night and day are created through the interactions of the earth and the sun, but that there were difficulties encountered as a result of the inability of teachers to control elements of the technology. Cascales *et al.* (2013) identified a slight improvement in learning when an experimental group used AR resources when engaging in a topic on animals, as opposed to a control group that used the same resources without the AR element. The two groups of four- and five-year-olds had the same information given to them about a number of animals, but there was a slight increase in the amount of knowledge retained about the animals when the children could examine 3D representations of the animals through the use of AR technology. A number of studies of the use of AR in literacy learning (using books and flashcards) have found the use of AR technology motivates young readers (e.g., Rambli *et al.*, 2013). While these studies offer interesting insights, the methodologies did not involve the use of tablet computers. Arguably, the use of AR technology with tablets provides additional opportunities to blend physical and virtual worlds, because tablets are mobile and use touch-screen technology.

There are, as yet, few studies that examine the use of AR apps on tablets to promote play, creativity and/or learning. Rasalingam *et al.* (2014) report on a study of the *AR Flashcards* app, in which paper-based flashcards containing an animal representing a letter of the alphabet are used in conjunction with a tablet to create 3D images of the animals. The team found that the app was motivating for children, although it was not clear how motivation was measured in this instance. Tomi and Rambli (2013) outline the development of an AR storybook, *The Thirsty Crow*, and report on observations of the responses of visitors to an exhibition in which they had an opportunity to engage with the story. They suggest that AR technology created interest and engagement with the book. While these studies indicate some potential for the use of AR technology in supporting play and learning, neither study employed systematic analysis of children's responses to determine how far the tablet apps fostered motivation, creativity, play or learning. It will be important in the years ahead to develop studies in this area if such apps are to be usefully employed in pre-school settings and schools.

In the study reported on in this chapter, young children's engagement with AR apps on tablets was studied in order to identify how far they fostered play and creativity, given the significance of play and creativity for young children's learning (Vygotsky, 1978). In the next section, the design and execution of the study are outlined.

Research design

The data analysed in this chapter are drawn from a study which was co-constructed between academics, children's media industry representatives and teachers (Marsh *et al.*, 2015). The aims of the study were to examine pre-school children's use of apps on tablets and identify how far apps for pre-school children (aged 0–5), including apps that incorporate AR, promote play and creativity. The objectives of the study were as follows:

1. To collect information about UK pre-school children's access to and use of apps in the home.
2. To identify the most popular apps for pre-school children and develop an understanding of the extent to which these promote play and creativity.
3. To identify the factors that currently inform parents'/caregivers' choices of apps for this age group.
4. To examine the impact of apps (including AR apps) on the play and creativity of pre-school children.
5. To identify the affordances of apps that are particularly successful in promoting young children's play and creativity in order to inform: (i) future app development by the children's media industry and (ii) the future choices of apps for young children by parents/caregivers and early years educators.
6. To increase dialogue and promote knowledge exchange between academics, children's media industry, parents/caregivers and early years educators with regard to pre-school children's use of apps.

In Stage 1 of the study, 2,000 parents of children aged 0–5 who had access to tablets completed an online survey in which their children's use of tablets and apps was explored. Stage 2 consisted of case studies conducted of six families with children aged from birth to 5. This chapter is focused on data drawn from Stage 3 of the study, in which 12 children aged 3–5 who attended Foundation Stage 1 and 2 classes (Nursery and Reception) in Monteney Primary School, located in Sheffield, UK were filmed using the top ten apps identified as favourites in Stage 1 of the survey. In addition, the children were videoed using six AR apps, which were chosen because they were identified as appropriate for the age group. These AR apps were:

*   *AR Flashcards*
*   *Aurasma*
*   *QuivAR (formerly ColAR)*
*   *Mattel Apptivity (Fishing)*
*   *Meet the Animals*
*   *Squigglefish*

Over 20 hours of video from the school observations were analysed, using two separate typologies. Hughes's (2002) taxonomy of play was utilised to identify the types of play in which children engaged as they used the apps. The taxonomy identifies 16 distinct types of play, which are: symbolic; rough and tumble; socio-dramatic; social; creative; communication; dramatic; locomotor; deep; exploratory; fantasy; imaginative; mastery; object; role; and recapitulative. This taxonomy was developed with regard to offline play and so to apply to digital play it was adapted by the team. For example, Hughes (2002) defines 'object play' in relation to play with objects that children see and touch. We adapted this definition to include virtual objects that can be seen on screen, but of course only the virtual representation can be touched and not the object itself. In adapting the definitions in this way, the above types of play could be applied to a virtual environment.

In addition to Hughes' typology (2002), Robson's (2014) 'Analysing Children's Creative Thinking (ACCT) Framework' was used in order to determine the extent to which apps promoted creative thinking (see Appendix 15.1). The ACCT framework enables creative thinking to be identified through observable behaviours and addresses three main areas: exploration, involvement and enjoyment, and persistence. Further, instances of creativity as children engaged with the apps were noted, such as when children created stories or drawings related to the apps.

The study led to a range of findings about children's use of apps on tablets, which are outlined in a series of publications to be found on the project website.[1] In this chapter, the focus is on the children's responses to the AR apps, which are outlined in the next section.

Augmented reality apps: The play–creativity continuum

The AR apps fostered a range of types of play, creativity and creative thinking (see Table 15.1).

All of the apps promoted exploratory play and they certainly led to the range of responses identified in previous studies in which children demonstrated motivation and engagement in the use of AR apps (e.g. Rasalingam *et al.*, 2014; Tomi and Rambli, 2013). For example, the *QuivAR* app caused a ripple of excitement in the Reception class. Following the videoing of children using the *QuivAR* app in which they coloured in pictures of Pudsey, a bear associated with a children's charity in the UK, and created 3D images of the bear using the tablet (see Figure 15.1), it was agreed with the Reception teachers to share the app with the class more generally.

The following extract from fieldnotes captures the children's response:

> Children were able to choose a picture of Pudsey to colour in. They then took turns to use the tablet to create 3D images of Pudsey, which then moved in some way. For example, one picture linked to the tablet represented Pudsey at a disco, dancing to music (including an impressive back flip), whilst another picture linked to an image of the bear playing a guitar, with rock music emanating from the app. The children were entranced, saying such things as, 'He's alive!' It was not possible to manage the activity in a way that enabled one child at a time to interact with the app in isolation. The children clustered around the tablet and at times, the crowd was two or three deep. I sometimes struggled to support children in holding the tablet above their picture, which was placed on the floor for ease of use, as my arms and elbows were jostled by an exhilarated crowd who were trying to get a closer look at Pudsey, brought to life by the app. There was great excitement and the activity had to be extended across the session to enable all the children who wished to participate to do so.
>
> (Fieldnotes, March 2015)

TABLE 15.1 Augmented reality apps, play and creativity

Augmented reality apps	Types of play the app promoted	Types of creativity/creative thinking the app promoted
AR Flashcards	10. Exploratory play 12. Imaginative play	Creative thinking: E1: Exploring E2: Engaging in new activity E3: Knowing what you want to do I1: Trying out ideas I2: Analysing ideas
Aurasma	5. Creative play 10. Exploratory play 12. Imaginative play	Creativity: Drawing Storytelling Creative thinking: E1: Exploring E2: Engaging in new activity E3: Knowing what you want to do P1: Persisting
QuivAR (formerly ColAR)	5. Creative play 10. Exploratory play	Creativity: Colouring pictures Creative thinking: E1: Exploring E2: Engaging in new activity E3: Knowing what you want to do P1: Persisting
Mattel Apptivity (Fishing)	4. Social play 10. Exploratory play 15. Role play 14. Object play	Creative thinking: E1: Exploring E2: Engaging in new activity E3: Knowing what you want to do I3: Speculating I4: Involving others P1: Persisting P3: Completing challenges
Meet the Animals	10. Exploratory play	Creative thinking: E1: Exploring E2: Engaging in new activity E3: Knowing what you want to do I2: Analysing ideas I3: Speculating P1: Persisting
Squigglefish	5. Creative play 10. Exploratory play 12. Imaginative play	Creativity: Drawing Storytelling Creative thinking: E1: Exploring E2: Engaging in new activity E3: Knowing what you want to do I1: Trying out ideas I3: Speculating I4: Involving others P1: Persisting

FIGURE 15.1 Child using the *QuivAR* app

However, the app allowed children to do little more than 'bring Pudsey to life', so to speak. Once the children had enjoyed seeing Pudsey dance and play guitar, they then moved on to other activities. This was also the case with the *AR Flashcards* app, which enabled children to see 3D animals but did not enable them to do very much other than look at the depictions and marvel.

There are some developments in this area that demonstrate promise for the future, however. *Meet the Animals* is a series of books that have apps related to them. Once a tablet is placed over an illustration of an animal in the book, a 3D picture of the animal appears that moves and makes appropriate sounds. A poem about that animal, which appears in print in the book, is retold orally. Children can then also interact with the 3D image to complete jigsaws of the animals. The children in the study enjoyed using this app, although it was questionable the extent to which the ability to complete a jigsaw added to the experience, given that this did not enhance understanding about the animal or its characteristics. It will be important for app producers in the future to move beyond the more presentational features afforded by AR technology, and focus on the aspects of content that promote deep engagement and learning. In the study reported in this chapter, the AR apps that appeared to foster the most extensive periods of engagement were those that promoted the creation of content.

While the apps mentioned to date all supported children's creativity in some way, the apps that were more effective in that regard enabled children to create drawings and artefacts that could be embedded in the app. *Aurasma* is a simple app that enables users to link texts and artefacts to online sites on which videos, podcasts or other creations linked to the physical object can be shared. When the audience points a tablet or smartphone at the original text or object, they can access the related online content. The children at Monteney Primary School found the *Aurasma* app to be motivating and it fostered creativity, in that it enabled children to relate their drawings to an oral retelling of their story, captured on video. The school then created an exhibition of children's written stories that allowed parents to access the video retellings online.[2]

Squigglefish is another app that enables children to create original content. This app enables users to draw sea creatures and then upload them into an aquarium using the camera feature of a tablet, where the sea creatures then float about. Children were keen to draw all kinds of objects to import into the aquarium, not just sea creatures, and the app fostered imaginative play as children created oral narratives about their creations. It would be useful for these kinds of apps to allow children to record such stories directly into the app in the future, which could then enable the production of multimodal stories that could be shared online through the use of videos, as the apps *Puppet Pals* or *Sock Puppets* currently enable users to do.

The final AR app that was analysed as part of this study was the *Mattel Apptivity Fishing Game*. This depicted a pond on the tablet surface, and children played with each other as they attempted to catch fish in the pond to place in their virtual nets. The fish were caught by using physical objects, that is, plastic fishing rods. While the game did support play in that some children took on the role of a fisher as they played, or interacted playfully with their opponent, it did not seem to extend play beyond what might have been observed in watching children play a board game. The app promoted creative thinking, as children had to work out how to catch and retain their fish. It did not, however, foster the kinds of creativity seen with other apps such as *Aurasma* and *Squigglefish,* which enabled children to create original content.

In Figure 15.2, the extent to which each of these apps could be mapped against a play/creativity continuum is outlined. It was found that all apps did foster some level of play and creativity, but this differed in relation to types and extent.

This diagram is not intended to suggest that children should only be introduced to apps that are high in terms of both the types of play and creativity they foster. While *Meet the Animals*, for example, did not promote the range of types of creative thinking as the *Mattel Apptivity Fishing Game* did, it did appear to offer greater depth in terms of its potential for learning, given its aims in introducing children to the features of a wide range of animals. In addition, while *AR Flashcards* offered limited opportunities for interaction, children in general did enjoy using the app and it could offer some children a valuable means of learning phoneme–grapheme correspondence. Ultimately, apps need to be chosen for use in schools in relation to their ability to meet specific needs, which will be different in each case.

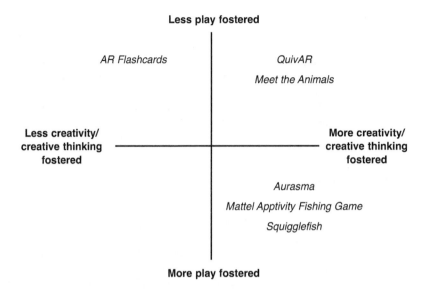

FIGURE 15.2 Apps mapped against the play/creativity continuum

Conclusion

This study found that AR apps had potential to promote a range of types of play and creativity. However, such potential depended on the design of the apps in terms of the way in which they enabled extended use. Simply bringing characters to life, while novel, did not lead to extended play, for example. However, AR apps that enable children to engage in storytelling, narrative comprehension or creative play did demonstrate much potential for their future use in early years settings and schools. AR tablet apps are at an early stage of development, but this area appears to offer important opportunities to promote young children's play and creativity, and future developments in the industry are keenly anticipated.

Notes

1. www.techandplay.org
2. See: http://monteneyelearning.org/staffblogs/monteney/learningjourney/2015/03/21/augmented-reality/

References

Bai, Z., Blackwell, A. F. and Coulouris, G. (2013). Using augmented reality to elicit pretend play for children with autism. *IEEE Transactions on Visualization and Computer Graphics.* Published online ahead of print, DOI 10.1109/TVCG.2014.2385092.

Bai, Z., Blackwell, A. F. and Coulouris, G. (2015). Exploring expressive augmented reality: The FingAR Puppet System for social pretend play. *Proceedings of the ACM CHI*

Conference on Human Factors in Computing Systems (2015). Accessed at: http://dl.acm.org/citation.cfm?id=2702123.2702250

Cascales, A., Laguna, I., Pérez-López, D., Perona, P. and Contero, M. (2013). An experience on natural sciences augmented reality contents for preschoolers. In Shumaker, R. (ed.), *Virtual, Augmented and Mixed Reality Systems and Applications* (pp. 103–112). Berlin, Heidelberg: Springer.

Hinske, S., Lampe, M., Yuill, N., Price, S. and Langheinrich, M. (2010). Let the play set come alive: Supporting playful learning through the digital augmentation of a traditional toy environment. In *Pervasive Computing and Communications Workshops (PERCOM Workshops), 2010 8th IEEE International Conference* (pp. 280–285). IEEE.

Hughes, B. (2002). *A Playworker's Taxonomy of Play Types,* 2nd edn. London: PlayLink.

Kerawalla, L., Luckin, R., Seljeflot, S. and Woolard, A. (2006). "Making it real": Exploring the potential of augmented reality for teaching primary school science. *Virtual Reality, 10*(3), 163–174.

Marsh, J., Plowman, L., Yamada-Rice, D., Bishop, J. C., Lahmar, J., Scott, F., Davenport, A., Davis, S., French, K., Piras, M. and Thornhill, S. (2015). *Exploring Play and Creativity in Pre-Schoolers' Use of Apps: Final Project Report*. Sheffield, UK: University of Sheffield. Accessed at: www.techandplay.org/reports/TAP_Final_Report.pdf

Moholy-Nagy, L. (1924/2010). Theater, Circus, Variety (1924). In M. B. Gale and J. F. Deeney (eds) *The Routledge Drama Anthology and Sourcebook: From Modernism to Contemporary Performance* (pp. 277–285). Abingdon, Oxon: Routledge.

Packer, R. and Jordan, K. (2002). *Multimedia: From Wagner to Virtual Reality*. New York: W.W. Norton & Company.

Rambli, D. R. A., Matcha, W. and Sulaiman, S. (2013). Fun learning with AR Alphabet Book for preschool children. *Procedia Computer Science, 25,* 211–219.

Rasalingam, R-R., Muniandy, B. and Rasalingam, R. R. (2014). Exploring the application of augmented reality technology in early childhood classroom in Malaysia. *Journal of Research & Method in Education, 4*(5), 33–40.

Robson, S. (2014). The Analysing Children's Creative Thinking Framework: Development of an observation-led approach to identifying and analysing young children's creative thinking. *British Educational Research Journal, 40*(1), 121–134.

Tomi, A. B. and Rambli, D. R. A. (2013). An interactive mobile augmented reality magical playbook: Learning number with the Thirsty Crow. *Procedia Computer Science, 25,* 123–130.

Vygotsky, L. (1978). *Mind in Society* (trans. M. Cole). Cambridge, MA: Harvard University Press.

Yarosh, S., Huang, K., Mosher, I. and Topping, M. (2008, April). Playware: Augmenting natural play to teach sign language. In *CHI'08 Extended Abstracts on Human Factors in Computing Systems* (pp. 3249–3254). ACM.

Appendix 15.1 The Analysing Children's Creative Thinking (ACCT) Framework (Robson, 2014)

Category	Operational definition	Example
E: EXPLORATION		
E1: Exploring	Child is keen to explore, and/or shows interest in the potential of a material or activity.	J is trying out buttons on the keyboard, causing a rhythm to play. He plays individual notes with alternate hands, smiling and watching carefully as he makes a note pattern.
E2: Engaging in new activity	Child is interested in becoming involved in an activity and taking an idea forward. The activity could be of his/her own choice or suggested by another child or adult.	A approaches a table covered in paint, where previous children have been working. She picks up a piece of paper from a pile and lays it on the table. Turning it over she spreads the paint that is now printed on it with her fingers.
E3: Knowing what you want to do	Child shows enjoyment or curiosity when choosing to engage in an activity.	K and adult A are standing at the woodwork bench. K has chosen a piece of wood, which he holds. He points to the back of the bench: 'In there.'
I: INVOLVEMENT AND ENJOYMENT		
I1: Trying out ideas	Child shows evidence of novel ways of looking and planning: uses prior knowledge or acquires new knowledge to imagine and/or hypothesise, or to show flexibility and originality in his/her thinking.	A is in the block area. She picks up three semi-circular blocks and lays two of them on the floor to form a circle, which she later calls a 'cheese'. She then puts one foot on each block and 'skates' across the carpet on them.
I2: Analysing ideas	Child shows either verbal or behavioural evidence of weighing up his/her idea, and deciding whether or not to pursue it.	R, N and K are building a tunnel from construction pieces. R watches as N and K build a cuboid, N puts a piece in front of the open end. R: 'No, they won't be able to get out.'

Category	Operational definition	Example
I3: Speculating	Child makes a speculative statement or asks a question of him/herself, or of other children or adults, relating to the activity.	H is outside, looking at herbs in the garden with adult J. H points to a herb and says, 'Yes, but why is this spiky?'
I4: Involving others	Child engages with one or more children or adults to develop an idea or activity: may articulate an idea, seek to persuade others, or show receptivity to the ideas of others.	A, J and C are playing a 'Father Christmas' game in the block area. A: 'I'm Rudolph.' J: 'And he's Rudolph too … . No, he … you can be …' C: (to A) 'You Comet, you be.' A: (to C) 'Why don't you be Comet?' C: 'No, I'm Donner.'

P: PERSISTENCE

Category	Operational definition	Example
P1: Persisting	Child shows resilience, and maintains involvement in an activity in the face of difficulty, challenge or uncertainty. He/she tolerates ambiguity.	In the sandpit E has been filling a large tube with dry sand. He picks up the tube and goes to fill the hopper on a nearby toy lorry, but the sand runs out of the end of the tube. He looks up, smiles, but does not break his concentration, but instead uses his hands to fill the hopper.
P2: Risk taking	Child displays a willingness to take risks, and to learn from mistakes.	M is at the clay. She tries to fill a bottle by inverting it in to a full cup of water, but this causes the water to flow out on to the table. She abandons this and pours water straight from the cup onto the clay.
P3: Completing challenges	Child shows a sense of self-efficacy, self-belief and pleasure in achievement: shows conscious awareness of his/her own thinking.	M has been at the mark-making table, using felt tip pens and paper. He finishes his drawing. M: 'I've finished' (smiling). Adult: Mm. M pats the paper and nods, then picks up the pen and makes a large 'M' in the bottom right corner. 'That's my Muh.' (He continues to write the other letter of his name.) 'I did it, I writ may name myself.'

PART IV

Future avenues

Throughout this book, our contributors have shared their practices and theoretical insights, and explored the question of how the rapid development and proliferation of mobile devices and apps might open up new opportunities for teaching and learning in different ways, across the educational spectrum. In many respects, they have shown that historical structures and traditional forms of education remain largely intact, and highly resistant to any effect from these most recent *technological invaders*. In many Western schools, pedagogical models often fail to capitalise upon technological developments, with outdated assessment systems rewarding students who can regurgitate memorised facts 'transmitted' to them by their teachers. There is no doubt that technology-mediated change comes slowly to education. History is littered with failed attempts to reform the learning process through technology, so why should teachers view this latest 'kid on the block' any differently from those innovations that have come and gone before?

The authors of the first three parts of the book provided snapshots that illustrate how mobile devices and their apps can enhance and extend young children's learning across a wide range of learning goals, needs, activities and contexts. Others provided practical advice and guidance on how parents and teachers might deal with the challenges of identifying suitable apps, and developing new ways of using and managing them for formal and informal learning. Indeed, a common thread among all chapters is that their authors challenge us to 'think different' – as the famous old Apple ad once reminded us – about *how* and *what* we teach our children, and open our minds to the possibilities these new technologies present. In this final section entitled 'Future avenues', the contributors continue this theme by challenging us to look closely at how apps provide opportunities for our children to *learn differently*.

To begin this section, Marilyn Fleer presents a compelling theoretical overview of apps as a means of *digital play*. Using Vygotsky's theory, Fleer makes a case for apps offering a unique opportunity for young children to be scaffolded from an *interpsychological* to an *intrapsychological* worldview, through augmented reality interaction with the characters and situations represented in apps. More specifically, Fleer draws on apps' affordances to challenge us to re-conceptualise *digital play*. App-mediated digital play represents new opportunities for young children to learn about their world, through creating imaginary situations where they can creatively and safely manipulate and change the meaning of objects and actions. Fleer's engagement with Vygotsky's theory also reminds us that we need to reconceptualise the nature of play for the digital age, and that apps can provide uniquely different, but valuable, opportunities for children's digital play.

Garry Falloon's contribution to this section raises important issues about researching young children's interaction with apps, through the use of a unique display data capture system. The system monitored 5- and 6-year olds' learning and thinking processes while they were using the *Pic Collage* app to create a presentation, which they later shared with parents at an information evening. The analysis framework is valuable in its own right and, in this instance, offers insights into how open-format apps can provide fertile learning environments for practising and displaying a wide variety of thinking skills. The data capture system holds a lot of promise for capturing data from children using mobile devices in flexible learning environments, where they are free to move from space to space. While *thinking different* about how to collect data in this study allowed Garry to capture some unique and authentic insights, it also raised an ethical matter concerning the recording of students' private conversations, and the nature of public versus private information in a research activity. There is no doubt that future research in this area requires innovative methods, as well as close scrutiny of the safeguards necessary to ensure privacy and confidentiality for the study participants.

The *think different* theme continues with Natalia Kucirkova's contribution exploring apps as offering *trans-* and *intra*-media learning experiences. Drawing on Siemen's ideas of connectivism, Natalia theorises the potential of apps for affording children new options to learn in different ways. Particular attention is paid to the use of different media forms, children's enhanced agency promoted by the different levels, forms and points of engagement, and the increased opportunities for learning collaboration within and beyond the classroom. As prompted in Marilyn Fleer's chapter, Natalia challenges us to expand our vision of learning, this time by considering how apps enable children to personally connect with different media at different times in different spaces. Far from the 'mono-media' format of traditional learning materials, she highlights how apps facilitate convenient access to diverse learning media. At the same time, she points out how transmedia can be confronting to parents and teachers who struggle with organising and monitoring their children's engagement with individual media. Echoing historical concerns about technology innovations in education, the chapter ends by warning us that no matter how personalised or sophisticated app design and capability becomes, this accounts for little if pedagogical purposes for their use are poorly understood.

Kevin Burden's final chapter raises an intriguing question of how apps' use in classrooms might contribute to develop knowledge communities, where new knowledge-building is seen as a collaborative and constructive process, as opposed to more traditional approaches where the students' focus is on using it to represent or reproduce already known understandings. In this chapter, knowledge community building is conceptualised as being fundamentally different from traditional learning models, which view learning as a passive process happening in certain environments in certain conditions. Kevin argues that the use of mobile technologies and apps offers great potential for supporting flexible and seamless learning in spaces that merge formal and informal environments, facilitating individual and collective knowledge building. Drawing on examples of early years teacher educators, the author provides illustrations to prompt our thinking about how mobile devices and apps offer unique possibilities to help transition learning towards twenty-first-century models based on collaborative, critical and digitally networked knowledge construction. However, on a cautionary note, Kevin warns us that achieving this goal is not easy, and is one that requires educators to fundamentally rethink their role, and how learning tasks are designed and assessed.

The last chapter in this section by Karen Daniels, offers a detailed account of how ethnographic methods can enrich our understanding of children's communication and collaborative engagement in the classroom. Dr Daniels observed 28 children in an early years setting and analysed their talk, hand movements ("focusing on deictic and control movements") and facial expressions while the children were engaged with apps of different designs and content. She found that even when the children used closed or linear apps, they were able to have playful, creative and collaborative experiences that lifted the apps' affordances to another level, perhaps a level not originally anticipated by the designers or teachers. The chapter illustrates how children's playfulness and innovation can come through in the classroom with apps of varied designs and quality. Overall, Karen's chapter illustrates the range of methods applied to the study of children's iPad interactions in school contexts, something we aimed to showcase in this volume.

All together, the five chapters highlight two key issues in relation to this new technological 'kid on the block'. First, in evaluating the efficacy of apps, we need to reflect on their unique features, which may give rise to potentially different learning situations from those observed with previous technologies. Here, some authors point out the affordability of mobiles and apps going some way to responding to the perennial concerns around learner access; while others suggest technical and convenience advantages, such as embedded internet connectivity, compactedness, and portability of the device. Focused on more local features, the possibilities for personalisation and customisation of the devices are further important factors, notably for transmedia and augmented and virtual reality.

Second, we ought not to lose sight of the fact that access and technical features are small parts of a complex equation that will ultimately determine whether or not mobile devices and apps follow the far well-trodden path of their predecessors into a technological abyss. Many teachers across the world are exploring different ways of designing new curriculum to better incorporate the dynamic, personalised, and contextualised ways of learning promoted by iPads, tablets and apps. Government authorities that are investing considerable sums to redevelop teaching spaces and curricula to support the new ways of teaching and learning often support this. The exemplary work of some of these teachers has been shared in this book and illustrates how mobile technologies, when deployed appropriately, can enhance the learning of a diverse range of students. In addition to these two key points, the final section offers some broader theoretical reflections on the implications and significance of such innovative practices, as well as research documenting and evaluating them.

It is our hope that this book alerts readers to the potential of apps for enhancing children's learning and creative opportunities for play, but at the same time, encourages them to be critical in their appraisal of the technology, ensuring that any use is carefully targeted and well-matched to learning or developmental outcomes. We believe that mobiles and apps offer a unique opportunity to develop models more suited for supporting children's skills and capabilities aligned with the needs of living in the twenty-first century. However, it is up to us, educators and parents, to use these resources effectively and to ensure that mobiles and apps are not relegated to the technological scrap-heap, as so many technological 'good ideas' and innovations have been before it.

In closing, we wish to thank all of the book contributors for their insights and ideas. Collectively, they point to the importance of socio-cultural sensitivity, and the need for methodologically and theoretically diverse approaches in orchestrating and evaluating children's learning with apps. This kind of sensitivity is, we believe, important, in an area where a potentially rich innovation runs the risk of being reduced to a technocentric strategy.

16

DIGITAL PLAY

Conceptualising the relation between real, augmented, and virtual realities

Marilyn Fleer

MONASH UNIVERSITY, AUSTRALIA

With the growing availability and easy use of digital devices, our youngest citizens can now engage in new ways of playing (Burke, 2013) both online and offline (Marsh, 2013). In this context, calls for re-conceptualising what is *digital play* have been noted (Zevenbergen, 2007), but no agreement or common perspective on what constitutes *digital play* has been given. What is evident is a diverse range of descriptions of play within these digital contexts. There is limited theoretical discussion about what might constitute the specific nature of *digital play* (Kucirkova *et al.*, 2014), and, as such, researchers do not always make clear what theoretical assumptions or model of play they are using when reporting findings. In this chapter, a theoretical discussion on what constitutes a cultural–historical conception of *digital play* is presented. Four key concepts from Vygotsky's (1966) original conception of play are used to frame this discussion, where the psychological nature of *digital play* is foregrounded. Together, these four characteristics can guide researchers, educators, and app designers about what are the unique psychological determinants of *digital play*.

Keywords: Learning, digital play, imagination, creativity, scaffolding, self-regulation, pivots

Introduction

As digital devices have become commonplace in our communities, and as their interface has become more intuitive, there have been more opportunities for children aged birth to 5 years to engage in *digital play* (Ernest *et al.*, 2014; O'Hara, 2011; Wohlwend, 2011; Zevenbergen and Logan, 2008). Over this time, a parallel amount of research has also been undertaken (Plowman *et al.*, 2010), which focuses on the value of these technologies (Moore, 2014), the place of home-based technologies (Stephen *et al.*, 2008), the relations between home and school use (Gronn *et al.*, 2014; Marsh, 2003), the nature of children's interactions with these devices (Plowman and Stephen, 2005), and the applications available for preschool children (Kjallander and Moiian, 2014), such as for literacy learning (e.g., Wohlwend, 2011).

We know from this body of research that children's engagement with digital devices can make a positive contribution to children's capacity to imagine (Singer and Singer, 2006). We also know that tangibles are valued, as they afford embodied interaction, tangible manipulation, and physical mediation of digital data (see Abeele *et al.*, 2012). We understand a lot more about how children aged 2 to 12 years interact with gestures and interface design, such as tap, drag-and-drop, slide, pinch, spread, spin/rotate, and flick on touchscreen applications (Aziz, 2013). We also understand more about how mothers and toddlers interact (Kucirkova *et al.*, 2014), and how applications allow for creative expressions (Verenikina and Kervin, 2011) when a variety of modes are available for making new meanings (Kjallander and Moiian, 2014).

The term *digital play* has sought to capture the special way that children interact with digital devices (Zevenbergen, 2007 in Burke, 2013), describes how online and offline play are becoming increasingly intermeshed (Marsh, 2013), and shows a realisation that more needs to be understood about the special ways children are now playing in virtual play worlds (see Burke and Marsh, 2013). The studies reviewed in this chapter include various technologies, including apps and touchscreen devices. All these technologies support *digital play*, which, as Radesky and Zuckerman argue in this volume (Chapter 2), can promote higher-order thinking and socio-emotional skills. However, what has been missing from research and commentary has been a theoretical discussion about what might constitute *digital play* with apps.

To fill this gap, this chapter draws upon Vygotsky's (1966) theory of play to better understand the psychological nature of *digital play* for children from birth to 5 years, with apps and touchscreen devices. The theoretical analysis seeks to support researchers, educators, and, potentially, app designers, about what are the unique psychological determinants of *digital play*. It is in line with the important work of Kucirkova *et al.* (2014) who have also sought to theorise interactions with digital devices and young children, but only in the context of shared story reading. This chapter seeks to go broader by using a cultural–historical analysis of *digital play* with apps and touchscreen devices for very young children.

A cultural–historical reading of *digital play*

Digital play as a term has been used by a range of researchers to capture the ways children interact with digital devices (see Edwards, 2013; Ellis and Blashki, 2007; Johnson and Christie, 2009; Linderoth *et al.*, 2002; Moore, 2014; Thai *et al.*, 2009; Verenikina and Kervin, 2011). Mostly, *digital play* is presented as a description of behaviour, where links may or may not be made to a particular theory of play. For example, Plowman and Stephen (2005) note that children negotiate access and take turns, manage operations, such as deciding where to click, and share enjoyment of the action depicted on the screen, and Ljung-Djärf (2008) refers to positions in play, such as the positioning of owner, participant, and spectator in preschool computer play. Similarly, Kucirkova *et al.* (2014) have shown that interactions between mothers and toddlers are engineered to maximise entry points for toddlers to enter the abstract worlds presented on the iPads, through skilful scaffolding and jointly constructed story worlds where genuine problems need to be solved. These are examples of how behaviours in *digital play* are generally expressed in the literature. Less common has been an examination of the play behaviours in relation to theories of play. For instance, types of behaviours have been noted by Moore (2014) in her detailed study of preschool children using iPads with a range of apps during free play time. Pretense play was one type of play observed. She references this term to mean play situations where imaginary situations are evident. She found that children spent more time purposefully exploring the apps, which she called sampling and experimenting. What she noted was that the students' movement between and across these types of play behaviours 'was fluid and reflexive tracking indicated the changeable nature of such movement' (p. 248).

In this chapter, *digital play* seeks to capture more than behaviours and actions, but rather to theorise psychologically about the nature of children's play with apps and on-screen devices using Vygotsky's (1966) original conception of play (see also, Verenikina and Kervin, 2011). In his conception, play occurs when an imaginary situation is created, and children change the meaning of objects and actions to support the imaginary situation. A cultural–historical conception of *digital play* would feature the imaginary situations that are afforded through the apps, and where children can change the meaning of actions and objects using the digital devices.

The first key idea of Vygotsky's (1966) conception of play focused on how play generates the conditions for a child's development in their *zone of proximal development*. This can be understood when we explore how play creates the zone of proximal development. Vygotsky (1966) argued that very young children were likely to hear and resist family or societal rules. In a contemporary context, we might hear this when told, 'Don't touch grandma's smart phone'. In this example, the device is for the adults only. This is an example of a rule imposed from within the child's social and material world (i.e., real world). In play, there is a different situation. In an imaginary play situation, children explore the rules of society by re-enacting them in their play. Vygotsky (1966) argued that in play, the child creates an imaginary situation in which play supports the child to self-regulate and control their immediate wish. It is through play that not only does the child self-regulate their immediate impulse, but the societal rule being imposed upon the child is more consciously considered when s/he role plays with others the scenario of not touching grandma's smart phone – as we might see when one play partner is being grandma imposing the rule and another play partner is being the child who wants to use the smart phone. According to Vygotsky, the rules and roles of society that are experienced interpsychologically are actively being made conscious in play, thus affording intrapsychological development. Vygotsky (1966) made the point that in play a child is 'a head taller than' him or herself (p. 16). Play creates the zone of proximal development because in *digital play* an abstraction of the child's real world (i.e., interpsychological level) can become consciously understood (i.e., intrapsychological level).

In *digital play*, this means that apps should create the conditions to make conscious (intrapsychological level) to children the rules and roles of society (interpsychological level). During children's *digital play* with the digital device, reality is augmented and children are *digitally positioned* within their zone of proximal development, thus affording a higher level of psychological development. Kucirkova *et al.* (2014) refer to multimodal contexts and interactional patterns where toddlers and their mothers 'leveraged specific app affordances' for collectively developed imaginary stories (p. 12). Verenikina and Kervin (2011) in their study of preschool children's use of software at home noted how children engaged in sustained pretense when the apps allowed the children to change the meaning of the virtual characters. They give the example of children as young as three creating a puppet show, where they design their own characters to tell a story. Their research gives evidence of how *digital play* with some software can create imaginary situations that augment reality through exploring with virtual puppets the rules and roles of society. As such, for something to be considered as *digital play* from a cultural–historical perspective, the app must allow for movement from the inter- to the intrapsychological level of development.

The second key idea of Vygotsky (1966) is related to how a child's attitude in the real situation is different to an imaginary situation. Elkonin (2005), a contemporary of Vygotsky, gives the example of his own children who would not eat their porridge at home, but when he introduced the imaginary situation 'as if' they were at preschool, taking off their coat, singing songs, and eating their snacks, then his children ate their porridge quite happily. Their attitude in play was different to their attitude in real life. The rules in reality are imposed on the child (e.g., you must eat this porridge, or don't touch the smart phone). In play the rules are self-created, albeit taken from reality as play scripts, but nevertheless are re-created in play.

In *digital play* where apps support sustained imaginary play, virtual scenarios can be created. Augmented reality can change the actual real-world situation, affording new opportunities for a play attitude to emerge. Augmented reality changes the nature of the relationship between the real world and an imaginary world. A rather porous relationship between reality, representations of reality, and imaginary play situations are promoted through augmented reality. For instance, Moore (2014), who undertook a study of 4- and 5-year-olds using open-ended symbolic play-related apps in one preschool setting (including their families), examined children's *digital play* choices in the context of everyday play practices in the setting. Over ten weeks she examined how children interacted with the open-ended, symbolic-play-related iPad apps during free play time. She found that although preschool children only engaged with pretense 5 percent of the time with apps on an iPad, they did voice their character 'as if' they were the actual character on their screens. She gives the examples of Vera and Beth:

> Vera briefly voiced dialogue for the characters she added to her screen, before quickly reverting to focus on selecting/adding/arranging props. Beth voiced the singing of 'Happy Birthday' as she created her 'party' scene, pulling together both her real-life tablemate, April, and her 'as if' play frame of a party, as indicated by the gingerbread people, presents, cookies, and balloons.
>
> (Moore, 2014, p. 172)

As these examples show, some apps provide a context where rules are followed, representing a *virtual imaginary situation*. These virtual imaginary situations can provide engaging opportunities for self-regulation in *digital play*. For instance, to win or engage in a game may mean dispensing with one's immediate desire to have something or do something. These virtual worlds create new possibilities for children to negotiate rules between play partners and to self-regulate within the *virtual imaginary play* spaces – affording new forms of development. Erstad and Sefton-Green (2013) note in their expansive review of the literature that digital game researchers and online research show how children and young adults 'inhabit rule-bound virtual worlds', which they argue encourages particular forms of social behaviour that support 'being able to act with others on- and offline' (p. 90). In these contexts they use different digital tools to change their agency or power. This aligns with Vygotsky's idea of the child's attitude in play being different. Erstad and Sefton-Green (2013) argue that in the context of the *net generation* 'interaction with digital technologies has changed fundamentally aspects of how young people create, interact with others and develop themselves' (p. 89). This is becoming increasingly relevant for early childhood, as the apps now available and their interface allow for new forms of augmented play not previously possible for such young children.

The third key idea of Vygotsky's (1966) related to how children change the meaning of objects and actions in their play and this has relevance for examining apps and digital devices. Vygotsky's (1966) theory of play provides a powerful way of conceptualising how young children can, through virtual engagement, think differently about their real, imagined, and virtual worlds. For instance, imaginary play creates new situations for children, as we see when children change the meaning of an object they see, giving it a new sense. Vygotsky (1966) wrote about how children see a stick, but in play children give it a new sense – it can become something else, such as a hobbyhorse. The stick acts as a placeholder for new meaning in the imaginary situation. It can be argued that a digital device too, gives the possibility for creating new meaning in everyday life or in virtual imaginary worlds. Erstad and Sefton-Green (2013) when discussing the work of Sherry Turkle, show how players explore different identities when using virtual avatars. Players literally play with new identities and imagine themselves differently, leading to very different ways of conceptualising human development. Similarly, a digital device can also capture a real-world experience, a moment of play, where the photographs act as a digital placeholder for some important action caught through digital means (Fleer, 2014).Vygotsky (1966) wrote that, 'In play, things lose their external motivating force.The child sees one thing but acts differently in relation to what he [or she] sees' (p. 11). The child no longer uses their perception of the concrete object and what it is, but rather works with the new sense of the object being presented. The 'child begins to act independently of what he [or she] sees' (p. 11). These experiences support children to go beyond their immediate perceptions of things, and to think and act in relation to the new meanings in the imaginary situation. Kucirkova *et al.* (2014) andVerenikina and Kervin (2011) in their research also noted how children change the meaning of objects and actions during *digital play*.

The final key idea of Vygotsky's (1966) conception of play, centred on how play supports children to develop from responding perceptually to thinking abstractly in imaginary situations. A divergence between the visual field and the meaning field takes place. As such, children's actions arise from their thoughts rather than from the objects themselves (Vygotsky, 1966).Vygotsky argued that the object (e.g., stick, video clip on iPad) in the imaginary situation becomes a pivot for severing the meaning (meaning of horse) from the real object (a real horse).Vygotsky (1966) argued that the child begins to act according to abstract ideas rather than by what s/he sees.When children capture a photographic image of something in their real world, or video record the actions that surround them, they not only work with a *digital placeholder* of their real world, but they also can use what they capture as a *digital pivot* for thinking and acting in new ways (Fleer, 2014). Play is the source of the child's development, because it acts as a transition for supporting the severing of the real situation to an imaginary situation. This is important for children's psychological development. Digital images and actions can potentially support children to conceptualise their real-world situation as a virtual situation, affording a psychological transition from real to abstract. *Digital play*, theorised in this way, potentially supports children's conceptual transition through severing a child's reliance on concrete real-world objects, opening up a digital context where digitised images are imbued with new meaning, thus augmenting reality.

The long-standing research of Bretherton (1984) has shown that when children give a new sense to an object, they often use metacommunicative language to signal to their play partners how the objects and play actions are to be understood. Vygotsky (1966) refers to this as an important transitional moment in play. The transition becomes evident when the child uses the stick, and rides around acting as a horse rider, making neighing sounds.The accompanying sounds made during play signal to other play partners the new sense given to the stick/object and the new meaning of the imaginary situation. In this process the child's relationship to the real world changes. In the imaginary situation, new actions are possible. Moore also noted evidence of metacommunicative language (2014). She found that during pretense children readily used action words along with their actions executed on the iPad and, when playing in parallel on different iPads, children regularly looked to other children, making comments that signalled differing types of play interaction. She also stated that when preschool children use apps such as *Puppet Pals* they are able to initiate and develop complex make-believe play where narratives features. The technical dimensions of the apps supports the make-believe play and metacommunicative language. She noted that *Puppet Pals* allows for voice recording, selection of characters, the possibility to generate an individual story, and the retrieval of previous images and sounds. Wohlwend and Kargin (2013) have also noted how the play spaces are negotiated in both online and offline actions and social relations – but different ways of negotiating were noted. In using Club Penguin (Disney), they found that children regularly navigated virtual spaces by finding a common server, that they worked together to teach each other in the same play space, and they negotiated through gestures and actions the relational spaces between avatar penguins.

Johnson and Christie (2009) note that digital toys afford many new possibilities for children's play. They argue that digital toys can have a positive effect on what they termed traditional forms of play. As such, it can be argued that apps have the possibility to change the nature of imaginary play. Therefore the virtual world that is created by the child is filled with meaning, but through *digital play* children can create new meaning in these virtual worlds using images as placeholders and pivots as they do in real-world enacted play, as a new form of an *imaginary virtual situation*. The relations between the real world, the imaginary situation, and the virtual world together support moments of transition that capture the uniqueness of *digital play*. This relation is shown in Figure 16.1 below.

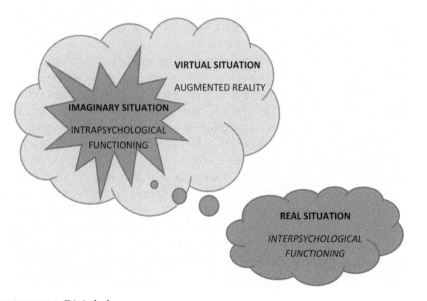

FIGURE 16.1 Digital play

Moore (2014) cites the work of O'Mara and Laidlaw (2011), who described how positioning an iPad within a Toca Tea Party (which included stuffed toys and a physical tea-set), led to a seamless transition between digital and physical forms of play where 'The boundaries between "physical" and "virtual" blur, with all play objects – the iPad, stuffed toys, plastic tea-set – crossing into the realm of imagination and the narrative structures of dramatic playing inside a virtual world' (p. 150). In these moments of play where the imaginary situation is simultaneously virtual and real, children can be both inside and outside of the imaginary situation, acting with real objects and virtual contexts, because both are in the same imaginary situation. These moments of transition can be theorized as *digital play*, because the imaginary play is being augmented digitally, as the objects and actions are given new meaning for a new purpose.

Apps, as described here, appear to create the conditions for thinking in new ways about the real and imagined world, such as when children use open-ended apps that afford 'non-literality', as we see when children use icons and other symbols to represent the 'not-present' (Moore, 2014). Rather than using liquid paint, glue, or wet water, Moore (2014) argues that children are simply using pixelated images, lights, and colours 'as if' they are real. A new type of imaginary situation is being created in these digital contexts.

Some researchers have noted being in and out of real and imaginary situations as key for developing the play itself, but also for psychologically developing children. For instance, it has been argued by Kravtsov and Kravtsova (2010) that moving in and out of imaginary situations supports children to think consciously about their real world. In *digital play*, where children use devices to capture aspects of their real world, they too have opportunities to move in and out of reality. Through augmented forms of reality, children have the possibility to simultaneously see the real form and work with the digital form. How children play with the digital placeholders of their world of course will vary. The educative or playful conditions that families or early childhood educators create for using digital devices, as discussed above, continues to be documented in recent research.

The actions possible in *digital play* are predicated on the app/software affordances (Moore, 2014), the children's skill levels in the games, the available resources to help children, and children's own interests in engaging in *digital play*. As noted by Verenikina and Kervin (2011), not all apps allow for *digital play*. They suggest that if children are to have the opportunity to engage with 'digitally mediated imaginative play with the iPad', then it is important to select 'digital applications, which provide the pre-schoolers with the opportunity of active and sustained engagement in imaginative play' (p. 17). Play, including digital, non-digital, or some other hybrid form, has created new conditions for children's development (Kucirkova *et al.*, 2014). If *digital play* is increasingly becoming the norm for many young children, then it becomes increasingly important to examine how this type of play actually develops children (Verenikina and Kervin, 2011).

Conclusion

It has been shown in this chapter that a cultural–historical conception of play provides a new way of thinking about children's *digital play*. The general literature shows that digital technologies, through their easy-to-use interfaces, support the positioning of children as active agents in *digital play* (Davidson, 2010; McPake *et al.*, 2010; Moore, 2014; Takeuchi, 2012; Wang and Ching, 2003), allow children to follow their interests and develop their play (Genishi, 1989; Genishi and Strand, 1990; McPake *et al.*, 2010; Stephen *et al.*, 2008; Takeuchi, 2012; Verenikina and Kervin, 2011), and show how software and devices afford a diversity of *digital play* actions (Marsh, 2010; O'Mara and Laidlaw, 2011; Verenikina *et al.*, 2010). Although these studies give insights into the context of *digital play*, they do not in themselves provide a theoretical account of the nature of *digital play*, play development, or how *digital play* acts as a source of child development – as is the cornerstone of Vygotsky's (1966) theory of play. This chapter begins to address this gap through a theoretical discussion of the psychological dimensions of *digital play,* thus giving a more nuanced understanding of the nature of what is *digital play* in the early childhood years. The four key characteristics of *digital play* that were theorised in this chapter, foreground how apps and touchscreen devices should:

- Create the conditions with the support of a digital device to make conscious to children the rules and roles of society where a child can play above their actual level of development, and into their potential level of development (that which is in the process of developing).
- Allow children to act 'as if' they are something else in an imaginary situation, to have a new attitude towards the rules and roles of society (the themes of play connect with children's experiences), and for the play to be easily sustained and collectively developed so that children can self-regulate their actions through the play.
- Afford opportunities for children to conceptualise and think differently about their real, imagined, and virtual worlds through being able to act differently to what they see, by capturing and changing the meaning of objects and actions in their play, as we might see when children take on new identities online.
- Support children's development through providing transitions from real to abstract representations by allowing children to create digital placeholders that they can use as digital pivots to think and act in new ways.

When brought together, these four characteristics of *digital play* can guide researchers, educators, and app designers to create the conditions that support, rather than reduce, opportunities for children's development.

References

Abeele, V.V., Zaman, B. and De Grooff, D. (2012). User experience laddering with preschoolers: Unveiling attributes and benefits of cuddly toy interfaces. *Personal and Ubiquitous Computing, 16*(4), 451–465. doi 10.1007/s00779-011-0408-y

Aziz, N.A.A. (2013). Children's interaction with tablet applications: Gestures and interface design. *International Journal of Computer and Information Technology, 2*(3), 447–450.

Bretherton, I. (1984). Representing the social world in symbolic play: Reality and fantasy. In: I. Bretherton (ed.), *Symbolic Play: The development of social understanding* (pp. 3–41). Orlando, US: Academic Press, Inc.

Burke, A. (2013). Stardolls and the virtual playground. How identity construction works in the new digital frontier. In: A. Burke and J. Marsh (eds), *Children's Virtual Play Worlds: Culture, learning, and participation* (pp. 38–58). New York, NY: Peter Lang.

Burke, A. and Marsh, J. (eds) (2013). *Children's Virtual Play Worlds: Culture, learning, and participation.* New York, NY: Peter Lang.

Davidson, C. (2010). 'Click on the big red car': The social accomplishment of playing a wiggles computer game. *Convergence: The International Journal of Research into New Media Technologies, 16*(4), 375–394.

Edwards, S. (2013). Digital play in the early years: A contextual response to the problem of integrating technologies and play-based pedagogies in the early childhood curriculum. *European Early Childhood Education Research Journal, 21*(2), 199–212.

Elkonin, D.B. (2005). On the historical origin of role play. *Journal of Russian and East European Psychology, 43*(1), 49–89.

Ellis, K. and Blashki, K. (2007). The digital playground: Kindergarten children learning sign language through multimedia. *Association for the Advancement of Computers in Education Journal, 15*(3), 225–253.

Ernest, J.M., Causey, C., Newton, A.B., Sharkins, K., Summerlin, J. and Albaiz, N. (2014). Extending the global dialogue about media, technology, screen time, and young children. *Childhood Education, 90*(3), 182–191. doi: 10.1080/00094056.2014.910046

Erstad, O. and Sefton-Green, J. (2013). Digital disconnect? The 'digital learner' and the school. In: O. Erstad and J. Sefton-Green (eds), *Identity, Community, and Learning Lives in the Digital Age* (pp. 87–104). Cambridge: Cambridge University Press.

Fleer, M. (2014). *Theorising Play in the Early Years.* New York, NY: Cambridge University Press.

Genishi, C. (1989). Research Currents: What Maisie knew. *Language Arts, 66*(8), 872–882.

Genishi, C. and Strand, E. (1990). Contextualizing Logo: Lessons from a 5-year-old. *Theory into Practice, 29*(4), 264–269.

Gronn, D., Scott, A., Edwards, S. and Henderson, M. (2014). 'Technological me': Young children's use of technology across their home and school contexts. *Technology, Pedagogy and Education, 23*(4), 439–454. doi: 10.1080/1475939X.2013.813406

Johnson, J.E. and Christie, J.F. (2009). Play and digital media. *Computers in the Schools, 26*(4), 284–289. doi: 10.1080/07380560903360202

Kjallander, S. and Moiian, F. (2014). Digital tablets and applications in preschool – Preschoolers' creative transformation of digital design. *Designs for Learning, 7*(1), 10–33.

Kravtsov, G.G. and Kravtsova, E.E. (2010). Play in L.S. Vygotsky's nonclassical psychology. *Journal of Russian and Easter European Psychology, 48*(4), 25–41.

Kucirkova, N., Sheehy, K. and Messer, D. (2014). A Vygotskian perspective on parent–child talk during iPad story sharing. *Journal of Research in Reading, 38*(4), 428–441

Linderoth, J., Lantz-Andersson, A. and Linderstrom, A. (2002). Electronic exaggerations and virtual worries: Mapping research of computer games relevant to the understanding of children's game play. *Contemporary Issues in Early Childhood, 3*(2), 226–250.

Ljung-Djärf, A. (2008). The owner, the participant, and the spectator: Positions and positioning in peer activity around the computer in pre-school. *Early Years: An International Research Journal, 28*(1), 61–72.

Marsh, J. (2003). One-way traffic? Connections between literacy practices at home and in the nursery. *British Educational Research Journal, 29*(3), 369–382.

Marsh, J. (2010). Young children's play in online virtual worlds. *Journal of Early Childhood Research, 8*(1), 23–39. doi: 10.1177/1476718X09345406

Marsh, J. (2013). Breaking the ice: Play, friendships and online identities in young children's use of virtual worlds. In A. Burke and J. Marsh (eds), *Children's Virtual Play Worlds: Culture, learning, and participation* (pp. 59–78). New York, NY: Peter Lang.

McPake, J., Plowman, L. and Stephen, C. (2010). Digitally divided? An ecological investigation of young children learning to use ICT. *Early Childhood Development and Care.* Retrieved from: http://strathprints.strath.ac.uk/13319/

Moore, H.L.C. (2014). *Young Children's Play Using Digital Touch-screen Tablets* (unpublished PhD thesis). The University of Texas, Austin, USA.

O'Hara, M. (2011). Young children's ICT experiences in the home: Some parental perspectives. *Journal of Early Childhood Research, 9*(3), 220–231.

O'Mara, J. and Laidlaw, L. (2011). Living in the iWorld: Two literacy researchers reflect on the changing texts and literacy practices of childhood. *English Teaching: Practice and Critique, 10*(4), 149–159.

Plowman, L. and Stephen, C. (2005). Children, play, and computers in pre-school education. *British Journal of Educational Technology, 36*(2), 145–157.

Plowman, L., Stephen, C. and McPake, J. (2010). *Growing Up with Technology: Young children learning in a digital world.* London: Routledge.

Singer, D. and Singer, J. (2006). Fantasy and imagination. In D. Fromberg and D. Bergen (eds), *Play from Birth to Twelve: Contexts, perspectives, and meanings* (2nd ed.) (pp. 371–378). New York, NY: Routledge.

Stephen, C., McPake, J., Plowman, L. and Berch-Heyman, S. (2008). Learning from the children: Exploring children's encounters with ICT at home. *Journal of Early Childhood Research, 6*(2), 99–117.

Takeuchi, L. (2012). Kids closer up: Playing, learning, and growing with digital media. *International Journal of Learning and Media, 3*(2), 37–59.

Thai, A.M, Lowenstein, D., Ching, D. and Rejeski, D. (2009). *Game Changer: Investing in digital play to advance children's learning and health.* New York, NY: Joan Ganz Cooney Center. Retrieved from: www.joanganzcooneycenter.org/pdf/GameChanger FINAL.pdf

Verenikina, I. and Kervin, L. (2011). iPads, digital play, and pre-schoolers. *He Kupu: The Word, 2*(5), 4–19. Retrieved from: www.hekupu.ac.nz/index.php?type=journalandissue=15 andjournal=262

Verenikina, I., Herrington, J., Peterson, R. and Mantei, J. (2010). Computers and play in early childhood: Affordances and limitations. *Journal of Interactive Learning Research, 21*(1), 139–159.

Vygotsky, L.S. (1966). Play and its role in the mental development of the child. *Voprosy Psikhologii, 12*(6), 62–76.

Wang, X.C. and Ching, C.C. (2003). Social construction of computer experience in a first-grade classroom: Social processes and mediating artifacts. *Early Education and Development, 14*(3), 335–362.

Wohlwend, K.E. (2011). *Playing their Way into Literacies: Reading, writing, and belonging in the early childhood classroom.* New York, NY: Teachers College Press.

Wohlwend, K.E. and Kargin, T. (2013). *"Cause I know how to get friends–plus they like my dancing" (L)earning the nexus of practice in Club Penguin.* In A. Burke and J. Marsh (eds),

Children's Virtual Play Worlds: Culture, learning, and participation (pp. 79–98). New York, NY: Peter Lang.

Zevenbergen, R. (2007). Digital natives come to preschool: Implications for early childhood practice. *Contemporary Issues in Early Childhood*, *8*(1), 19–29.

Zevenbergen, R. and Logan, H. (2008). Computer use in preschool children: Rethinking practice as digital natives come to preschool. *Australian Journal of Early Childhood*, *33*(1), 2–44.

17

IPADS, APPS AND STUDENT THINKING SKILL DEVELOPMENT

Garry Falloon

TE HONONGA SCHOOL OF CURRICULUM AND PEDAGOGY, TE KURA TOI TANGATA FACULTY OF
EDUCATION, THE UNIVERSITY OF WAIKATO, NEW ZEALAND

In recent years, handheld digital devices such as iPads have become commonplace in many schools in New Zealand. Paralleling this has been discussion about how ubiquitous access to information via these devices provides an ideal opportunity to support the development of critical, evaluative, and reflective thinking skills. This chapter details a study that probed the nature of young students' thinking while using iPads and a content-builder app during a literacy learning task. Using a display recording tool, data were captured of students' physical and oral interactions, which were then analysed using a 'thinking types' framework developed from Anderson and Krathwohl's (2001) revision of Bloom's Taxonomy (cognitive domain). Findings identify the effect of a range of learning 'resources' and environmental variables on how well the students are able to apply different thinking types to the content-building task. They also challenge historical notions of thinking skills existing hierarchically, but rather being exercised as 'fit for purpose' according to the needs of a task. The importance of task knowledge and clear evaluation criteria for encouraging analysis, evaluation, and reflection is identified, and discussion of how devices such as iPads may help facilitate this is provided. Several implications are presented for teachers considering using iPads and apps in this way.

Keywords: Thinking types, collaboration, fit-for-purpose, knowledge, evaluation, framework

Introduction

A persistent problem haunting the integration of digital technology in schools has been difficulties providing visible evidence of its effect on student learning. While some studies have probed tentative links between technology use and student achievement (e.g., Alsafran and Brown, 2012; Liao, 2007), or have documented perceived benefits in niche contexts, such as special education (e.g., Desai *et al.*, 2014; Lin and Nzai, 2014; Mozaffar, 2012; Khoo in Chapter 13, this volume), few studies have attempted to explore, in depth, underlying thinking, and learning processes students engage in while working with digital devices. Developing such knowledge is crucial, given the avalanche of new devices such as iPads and apps presently being consumed seemingly uncritically by schools, and wider rhetoric surrounding the need for students to develop critical, evaluative, analytical, and reflective thinking skills aligned with so-called 'twenty-first-century learning', discussed in detail in Part II. In this chapter, I introduce work being carried out in New Zealand to learn more about the thinking processes of young children using apps for learning in conventional classrooms. It builds on my earlier work exploring app design and use in collaborative learning environments (Falloon, 2013a, 2013b, 2013c, 2015).

Developing and evaluating thinking skills

Developing complex thinking skills is a common theme in literature relating to twenty-first-century learning (Koenig, 2011), and is reflected in curriculum documents worldwide (e.g., Australian Curriculum, Assessment and Reporting Authority, 2010; Department for Children, Education, Lifelong Learning and Skills, 2008; Department for Education and Skills, 2004; Ministry of Education, 2007). Complex thinking skills are viewed by some researchers and education organisations (e.g., Binkley *et al.*, 2012; Gilbert, 2005; OECD, 2013) as essential for equipping future citizens to productively engage in rapidly changing work and social environments. While some evidence exists that thinking skills can develop over time as a result of cumulative experience and informal teaching (Case, 1992), others point to formal education as having a pivotal role in fostering these skills, particularly in early learning (Beyer, 2008).

Past studies have indicated that structured teaching interventions targeted at thinking operations can improve thinking proficiency (Hembree, 1992; Pressley and Harris, 2001). Recent studies have indicated that technology can play an important role in developing student thinking, through activities such as game authorship (Yang and Chang, 2013), simulations, and virtual worlds (Segal, 2006; Yeh, 2004), online collaborative projects (Brindley *et al.*, 2009), and when used within inquiry-based learning (Buckner and Kim, 2014). Some schools have mandated students purchase digital devices such as iPads, positioning them as essential devices for 'twenty-first-century learning' (Crombie, 2014).

Paralleling the increased focus on developing thinking skills has been a proliferation in thinking skills frameworks and taxonomies. These include the revision of Bloom's Taxonomy of Educational Objectives – cognitive domain (Anderson and Krathwohl, 2001), the Structure of Observed Learning Outcomes (SOLO) Taxonomy (Biggs and Collis, 1982), The 'Big 6' Inquiry Framework (Eisenberg and

Berkowitz, 1990), and Marzano's 'New Taxonomy of Educational Objectives' (Marzano, 2000). These frameworks are pragmatic attempts to define different types of thinking for instructional purposes, and interpret them into a 'teacher-friendly' format able to be used for planning and assessment.

Moseley et al.'s (2005) review of 35 Thinking Skill frameworks suggests most bear resemblance to Bloom's original work through their recognition of critical, evaluative, analytical, and reflective thinking (metacognitive) and foundation skills, such as information gathering, comprehension, and factual recall (cognitive). They also noted many frameworks made distinctions between basic and higher-order thinking through tiered hierarchies, describing a prerequisite relationship between lower- and higher-order processing. Others preferred to make 'qualitative distinctions between different types of thinking' (Moseley et al., 2005, p. 372), placing less emphasis on hierarchy and more on the use of skills as 'fit for purpose'. Regardless, the desirability of students practising and building higher-order – or *productive* (Moseley et al., 2005) and *meaningful* (Mayer, 2002) thinking skills – is a common theme in literature.

Digital technology and the development of thinking skills

Several studies suggest benefits from using technology to help build students' thinking skills (e.g., Daud and Husin, 2004; Hopson et al., 2002; Walters and Fehring, 2009; Yelland and Masters, 2005). Presently, attention is turning to the formation of learning environments where the focus is moved from devices towards environments 'that foster within students the disposition for critical thinking' (Hopson et al., 2002, p. 110). This transition aligns with movement towards more student-centred learning, where knowledge is collaboratively developed and supported by an array of technology tools. A number of studies indicate the efficacy of this approach in different contexts at all levels of education (e.g., Hopson et al., 2002; Sela, 2013; Yelland and Masters, 2005; Zurita and Nussbaum, 2004).

This process has gained momentum recently with the advent of affordable tablet technologies such as the iPad. Some New Zealand schools are mandating their purchase, or adopting Bring Your Own Device (BYOD) policies (Stavert, 2013; Song and Ku [Chapter 14]). In New Zealand, these policies have supported schools' moves towards creating 'Modern Learning Environments' (MLEs) (Ministry of Education, 2014), where both physical learning spaces and technical infrastructure are being reconceptualised to be more flexible and supportive of different curriculum designs incorporating digital technologies. Paralleling these developments, teachers are reviewing their pedagogy to align with student-focused inquiry, thinking skills, or project-based learning models. Ubiquitous access to digital tools such as iPads supports this process, helping teachers implement curriculum that builds student thinking capability, enabling 'innovative and imaginative teaching practices to better meet the needs of all students' (Ministry of Education, 2014, p. 1). This chapter reports findings from a study located within such an environment. It explores the types of thinking young students engage in when using iPad apps collaboratively for language learning. Data were gathered using a unique recording system that captured the iPads' display and audio, while students were using the app *Pic Collage* (see https://itunes.apple.com/app/id448639966) to create a presentation for their parents about what one of the principles (cogs) in their school's virtues framework meant to them as a learner (Figure 17.1).

FIGURE 17.1 The school's virtues *COGs* framework

Research context and data method

iPad display and audio data were recorded from 19 five- and six-year-olds attending a 400-student primary (elementary) school in a small provincial town in New Zealand. Their experienced teacher held lead teacher responsibility for eLearning in the school. Over 12 hours of display and audio data were recorded during four sessions over a two-week period in mid 2014. Using the recorder meant a large volume of data could be collected over a short period of time, while students were free to work where they pleased (Figure 17.2). The method also

FIGURE 17.2 Students worked in various locations

produced very authentic data free from possible 'observer effect', such as might be the case if observational or external video methods were used. Data were immediately able to be analysed against the 'thinking types' framework, using Studiocode video coding software (see www.studiocodegroup.com).

Data were collected and analysed responding to the question: How were different types of thinking exercised by young students when authoring content using the app, *Pic Collage*?

The app and the task

Pic Collage is a content-builder app for collating video, images, text, and stickers (small cartoon-like images) into a presentation format. It also includes decorative options such as borders, different fonts and styles, inset or tiled images, and coloured and patterned backgrounds. The students used the app to present their thoughts on one of the school's virtues (cogs), using the following criteria as a guide:

1. It has four pictures and sentences that tell what the cog means to them.
2. It has 'fat' sentences (longer, more detailed).
3. Pictures and sentences are easy to see and read.

These criteria had been developed with the students, and careful explanation of what they meant had taken place. Students were also reminded of them before each session.

The 'thinking types' framework

An analysis framework was developed from Anderson and Krathwohl's (2001) revision of Bloom's Taxonomy (cognitive domain), with categories being context-ualised to suit the focus of this study (Table 17.1). The author and a research assistant developed the category descriptors following a preliminary review of data. The original taxonomy categories that represented levels of thinking as a 'cumulative hierarchical framework' (Krathwohl, 2002, p. 218) have been re-labelled as *Thinking Types*. This responded to data suggesting the exercise of different types of thinking was more deliberate and interactive than hierarchical in nature, being drawn upon by students when required to achieve a desired outcome. Anderson and Krathwohl's reconceptualisation of the original taxonomy's cog-nitive process dimension – specifically, the 'higher-order thinking' categories being redefined as verbs – supported this decision.

Data coding

Separate data files were imported into Studiocode analysis software. Studiocode logs events in video data onto a timeline that can then be replayed individually or

TABLE 17.1 The *ThinkingTypes* framework

Thinking type	Data source	Descriptor
Remembering	Oral from display capture	Verbal evidence of thinking indicating recall of facts and/or processes/procedures.
Understanding	Oral from display capture	Verbal evidence of thinking focused on clarifying or comprehending task demands (what do we need to do? what are the criteria? what do they mean?) and/or processes and procedures (how do we do it?).
Applying	Visual and/or oral from display capture	Recall and use of content-related facts and concept knowledge for building/editing content. Recall and use of technical or procedure knowledge for building/editing content.
Analysing	Visual and/or oral from display capture	Analysis and reflection on operational and technical procedures used for building/editing content (i.e., can we improve how we did this?) Analysis and reflection on content quality (i.e., can we improve our content? How can we improve it?)
Evaluating	Visual and/or oral from display capture	Justification, defence and critique of content (what's been created) and/or features of content (e.g., fonts, colours, layouts, images, backgrounds) and/or reviewing how content meets criteria. Evaluating/critiquing procedures used for building or editing content.
Creating	Visual and/or oral from display capture	Final content assembled and/or edited using appropriate thinking types and resources.

collectively and, if desired, analysed quantitatively. Clicking on a particular code (top right in Figure 17.3) activates and deactivates an event aligned with the code, which forms a code 'block' as illustrated in the timeline (bottom of Figure 17.3).

In total, 36 separate files were generated over the two-week period and collated into bundles – one belonging to each pair. Six randomly selected files were analysed separately by the researcher and assistant to refine descriptors for the thinking types framework. This resulted in substantial refinement of the category descriptors. The assistant then re-coded the six sample files and coded the remaining 30 files using the modified framework. Separate timelines were generated for each file.

Rater agreement

While the assistant was completing coding, the researcher coded a random sample comprising six 'clean' files. These were compared with the same files coded by the assistant, using Kappa inter-rater agreement. It was necessary to restrict the comparison due to the considerable volume of qualifying instances across the nine

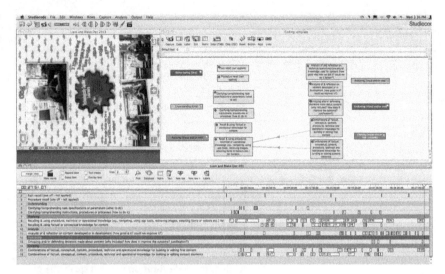

FIGURE 17.3 A typical Studiocode coding setup

descriptor codes. It was decided to 'semi-randomly' select a maximum of 50 instances from each file, but care was taken to select at least some instances aligned with each code. A total of 300 instances were compared, and results are summarised in Table 17.2.

Results

Table 17.3 contains data samples that were coded under each category of the analysis framework; however, due to word constraints, it is not possible to include multiple samples. Additionally, there was also overlap in the use of some thinking types. For example, when building content, students integrally applied previously learnt facts, concepts, and procedures. That is, to build content they drew upon *fact*, *concept*, and *procedure* knowledge, *applying* it to the building task (*creating*). On other occasions, students verbalised facts or procedures that may or may not have related to the task, and were not operationalised. Sample data should therefore be seen as *generally illustrative* of a type of thinking, rather than exclusively belonging to a single thinking type.

TABLE 17.2 Inter-rater agreement

Observed agreements	Chance agreement	Standard error	Confidence interval (CI: 95%)	Kappa (k)	Agreement strength
253	160.9	0.045	0.574–0.750	0.662	Good

Note. Agreement strength rating is according to Landis and Koch's (1977) often-cited scale for rater agreement

Discussion

The most commonly occurring type of thinking was coded as Applying: procedure/technical, with an average time per coded event of just over 13 minutes. Typically this involved students operating the iPad and/or the app, and was associated with using editing tools, text builders, or image capture tools, selecting fonts and backgrounds, and managing or printing files. Of this, recall and use of facts and concepts concurrent with applying technical and procedure knowledge for content building (creating), comprised 9 minutes 18 seconds. Frequently this process required students to draw upon existing fact and/or concept knowledge. Instances of fact recall not linked to Applying were quite rare, with an average time per coded event of just over 1 minute. These were usually 'one-off' statements either not related to the task, or were not used for creating content, for example 'if you want to take a picture ... you press this...' (student R, replying to student T's question about using the iPad's camera, even though this was not used in their outcome).

Initial attempts to separately code data as *either* Remembering (fact recall) *or* Applying (using facts or concepts) proved problematic, as most were linked. A noticeable pattern across the timelines was a blocking or alignment of data coded as Applying *and* Creating. This reflected the close relationship between the two thinking types, which led to modification of the coding template by the addition of a joint activation link between the two categories (see Figure 17.3). There were some instances, however, where data coded as Creating did not involve the use of content-related fact or concept knowledge. Typically, these were procedure or 'technically heavy' activities, where students used app tools to edit content or revise (usually) its appearance. These instances also applied to assembling content, where technical knowledge, such as resizing and moving content, changing fonts, colours, backgrounds and headers was commonly used. Significant time was spent on such activities, with some pairs struggling to efficiently manage the number of choices available to them. The transcript of students O and Z in Table 17.3 illustrates this during their debate over choice of background colour. This process was time-consuming (over 3 minutes), with the eventual outcome being based on personal preference rather than task criteria.

Analysis indicated students spent limited time analysing, reflecting on, and evaluating content they produced, or how they went about producing it (average 2 minutes 45 seconds per coded event). Although quite young, it was pertinent to note that a few students did enter an improvement/refinement 'loop' (Figure 17.4) where they reflected on content, usually evaluating it against criteria or their level of satisfaction with it. A characteristic of these students was that they were unafraid to challenge their workmate, expecting them to justify choices and defend decisions. When reflective and evaluative thinking was applied, it often stimulated improvement in the quality of content or better alignment with criteria. Some students completed two and on one occasion, three refinement cycles, each time improving their work against the criteria. The app's scaffolding tools (word picker, spelling/grammar/ capitalisation checker, etc.) and easy-edit capabilities (changing words, punctuation/ capitals, layouts, colours, fonts, etc.) assisted these students, as they were able to make changes without disruption, untidiness, or the discouragement of starting again from scratch. Data from students L and B and O and Z in Table 17.3 (write 'fat' sentences and poster clarity, respectively) demonstrate this. Figure 17.4 illustrates the relationship between the thinking types and the knowledge, skill, and strategy resources students brought to, and/or utilised during, the task.

Task knowledge and peer and teacher scaffolding were valuable resources used effectively by some students. Task knowledge related to students' understanding of what they were required to do, and how their efforts would be evaluated (i.e., criteria). Understanding criteria was particularly important for those few who displayed reflective and evaluative thinking, as they acted like 'beacons' that guided their review and improvement of content. Data also illustrated the powerful effect of teacher, and to a lesser extent peer, scaffolding. Student thinking benefited from strategic teacher intervention that challenged their decisions, or prompted them to review work against the criteria. The right end of the timeline in Figure 17.3 illustrates this, where there is a noticeable clustering of thinking coded as Analysis.

TABLE 17.3 Sample data coded by *Thinking Types*

	Description	*Recorded dialogue*
Remembering		
Factual recall Verbal evidence of thinking indicating *recall of facts* and/or *processes/procedures*.	Students L and B are creating a text label showing their understanding of the virtues cog, being a 'good *(school name)* learner'.	'...don't forget you have to put a big *(capital)* letter at the beginning... and you need to put a full stop after there *(after 'good' in sentence)* (L)...I know... you don't need to tell me... I've done it anyway... see... *(referring to sentence)*... I've done it right... (B) But sometimes you don't... !' (L)
Understanding		
Clarifying or comprehending task demands and/or processes/procedures. Verbal evidence of thinking focused on clarifying or comprehending *task demands* (what do we need to do? what are the criteria? what do they mean?) and/or *processes and procedures* (how do we do it?).	Students L and B are discussing the need to write full sentences about what each cog means to them to be a *(school name)* learner, and share work with the teacher.	'We need to have some more words... the teacher said we have to use fat sentences... (L) I know! (B)...She said to show her when we've done one... (L) OK... what can we put here? (B) No... we have to show her first! (L) We'll just do this one then we'll show her... is that alright? (B) Write something about Thinking... "Effective Thinkers"' (L).

TABLE 17.3 Continued

Remembering	Description	Recorded dialogue
Applying		
Technical or procedure knowledge. Recall and use of *technical or procedure knowledge* for building or editing content.	Students M and F are creating text for the 'Make a Difference' cog. Student M has made several attempts to spell 'helping' but is having difficulty adding the suffix 'ing'.	'help... ing... (*types 'nig... then deletes*)... (*to self*) 'eng'... help... eng... (M) (*types 'eng', pauses, then deletes*) It's good you don't have to rub stuff out, eh? (F) ...It's simple 'cos (*sic*) you just have to do a backspace if you make a mistake... help... i-n-g... (*sounds letters while typing 'ing'*) That's better... 'ing'... help-ing! (*M continues and types 'others' to finish sentence*). Now that's a good sentence, isn't it F? (M) You need to put it (*text box*) away from the pictures... (F) (*M drags text box to left of cog*). There... now we need our last picture'... (M).
Analysing		
Content quality Analysis and reflection on *content quality*.	Students A and H-M have decided a large image of (*student name*) should go in the background. They selected the image and have inserted it.	'I was going to get you out of the background... (H-M)... What... how? (A)...I wish I had my whole body in there... and my bow... (A) Do it again... you've cut some of your knee off... we can get it better... (H-M) (*A re-enters photo editor*) Now this time don't chop your leg! (*laughing*) (H-M) I'll try not to!' (*giggles*) (A).
Evaluating		
Evaluating how content meets criteria Reviewing how content meets *task requirements* (criteria).	Students O and Z are discussing the colour and pattern of their background. They were evaluating how well it met the task criteria.	'I don't like it... (*pause*)... It doesn't look good with our pictures... it's too dark... remember... we have to have a background that makes our pictures look clear (*criteria*) (*Z re-selects a bright blue*) What about blue? (Z) That looks awesome (O)... But it makes the yellow look funny.... (*pause*) maybe we should try red (Z) (*selects burgundy*) That looks good... nice and clear'... (O).
Creating		
Creating content. Content is assembled and/or edited using appropriate thinking types and resources.	Students A and H-M are assembling their content into a draft layout.	'We've got five pictures... I think that's one too many... (*criteria*) (A) I think we should put the cog in the middle and the other pictures round (*sic*) the outside... and some are too small (H-M)... (*A selects bottom left image and resizes it*) How does that look? Do you think it's big enough? (A) You need to be able to fit the other pictures on too... and don't forget we have to write some sentences'... (H-M).

For the 5 minutes from 19.35 to 24.30 (approx.) the teacher was present with this pair (L and B), challenging them to reflect on how their work met the criteria. Each block in the Analysis row (content) during this period is a student response to teacher challenges. What is interesting is that after the teacher left (at about 24.30), analysis continued as the students debated what they needed to do, before finally agreeing on changes (at about 27.00). Similar data linked to teacher intervention were recorded for other pairs, indicating the important role the teacher has to play in these environments.

Acting in a similar but less powerful way was peer feedback. Although relatively infrequent, questioning and critical interaction between students at times stimulated reflection on content or procedures, sometimes contributing to revision and improvement. This can be seen in L and B's timeline (Figure 17.3) between the 6 and 18 minute marks. Display data indicated benefits from students possessing sound task and criteria understanding, and a solid knowledge base across multiple types (concept, fact, procedure) that they could apply to making improvements.

Students' work and thinking types

Figure 17.4 illustrates the contribution of student learning 'resources' and the interaction of different thinking types, during the content-building process. However, not all resources made equal contributions – nor did all pairs possess the same level or complexity of resources to begin with. Regardless, available resources strongly

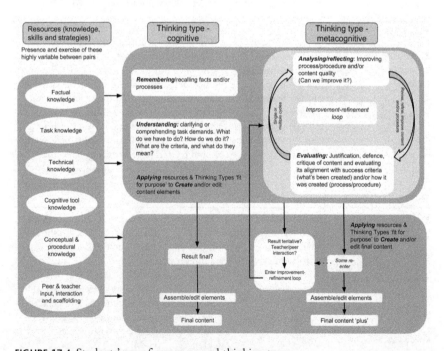

FIGURE 17.4 Students' use of resources and thinking types

influenced student performance and greatly affected the use of different thinking types and consequently students' options and decisions, ultimately impacting upon the outcome. Frequent spikes were noted in technical/procedure application, but interrogation of these revealed many were appearance enhancement and not concept or knowledge focused. Although all students displayed technical and procedure competence, in the absence of sufficient fact or concept knowledge, and a clear understanding of the task and its success criteria, there was a tendency to divert its application to peripheral, aesthetic-related activity.

Thinking types tended to be applied according to the purpose and need at the time (i.e., fit for purpose). At its most basic, this involved students blending resources of variable complexity and quality with appropriate thinking types, to author or edit content for their collage. Generally, this was a straightforward process – they clarified what they needed to do, and applied appropriate resources and thinking types to get it done as quickly as possible. While occasionally analytical, reflective, and evaluative thinking was used, almost exclusively this was applied to aesthetically change content, rather than improve the quality of textual or knowledge components. Personal preference rather than evaluation against criteria was the basis upon which most pairs made these decisions.

Three pairs, O and Z, L and B, and M and F were notable exceptions to this. Verbatim excerpts from data for two of these in Table 17.3 demonstrate reflection on criteria as motivation for changing textual components (L and B's reference to 'fat' sentences), while O and Z's comment suggests critique of background colour choice, based on the appearance criterion. Other triggers of analysis or reflective or evaluative thinking included teacher or peer interaction and feedback. Teacher questioning was the most powerful of these, challenging students to reflect on what they had produced and probing opportunities to improve. This occurred less frequently between students, generally relying on one student possessing knowledge that initiated discussion on how to solve a problem or change content. However, such discussions did not necessarily improve their work or better align it with criteria. Examples were recorded of students entering this loop, reflecting on and evaluating content, then making no changes, or making changes based on personal preference, not task criteria. The shaded square at the top right of Figure 17.4 denotes the cyclic nature of this improvement–refinement loop. Student entry to this was generally predicated on whether they viewed, or were prompted to view, their output as final or tentative.

Conclusion and implications for practice

Acknowledging the limitations of this study, findings do provide tentative insights into the thinking processes of young students using content-builder apps, and flag considerations for teachers intending to use them in their classrooms. First, well-understood task criteria and prompting students to reflect and act on these, appears essential for promoting reflective and evaluative thinking. Demonstrating how criteria manifest in a quality outcome could be advantageous for young children, as their capacity to abstractly conceptualise these may be limited. To be sustainable, teachers should work hard to help students internalise dispositions towards reflective and evaluative thinking, so that they become an automated part of their work process.

Second, care needs to be taken not to automatically equate students' use of technical and procedure knowledge, with developing conceptual knowledge. In a busy classroom it is easy to interpret app engagement as knowledge engagement, but this may not necessarily be the case. Managing options and choices within apps to keep the focus on intended knowledge goals is an important skill for students to learn. Related to this, it would be beneficial to teach students about the range of scaffolding tools many apps provide, and how they can use them efficiently to improve the quality and accuracy of their work. In this study, very few students used these tools to make corrections or improvements. This appeared to be because they were unaware of what the tools did, or how to use them (one student commented that a red line beneath a word indicated it was a 'cool word'). This also applies to potentially useful device features such as the iPad's text-to-speech function, which can help students understand difficult-to-read text.

Consistent with other studies exploring apps in learning (e.g., Getting and Swainey, 2012; Kucirkova *et al.*, 2014; Miller *et al.*, 2013) these students were very motivated, displaying high levels of on-task behaviour. Additionally, ample evidence existed that appropriately designed learning tasks using content-builder apps *can* provide young students with fertile environments within which to exercise a range of thinking types, drawing on these non-hierarchically on a 'fit-for-purpose' basis. Consistent with Krathwohl's (2002) earlier conclusions, in this study task design was critical to building thinking capability. Learning designs of an inquiry, scenario, problem, or project-based nature, or rich tasks requiring students to collate and synthesise information to construct and present knowledge, appear well suited to content builder app use.

Finally, information collected by the display recorder could be valuable to teachers for assessment, reporting, or planning purposes, as it provides visible evidence of students' learning and progress while using technology. While not suggesting busy teachers have the time to analyse hours of display data, researchers using this system in classrooms could provide teachers with useful clips revealing insights into their students' learning and work processes. Such information could be incorporated into students' electronic portfolios, or used for planning or other reporting purposes. It could also be used to identify ways apps can support specific teaching strategies, thereby improving their learning effectiveness. In this study, information was used by teachers to help refine task criteria, and improve how this was communicated to students before and during each session.

Future work using the data recording system is planned for different levels of the school (8- to 11-year-olds), to learn more about the thinking types and strategies older children apply when collaborating on computational and programming tasks. This initial study has revealed the complexity of this process, but many more are needed across different contexts and cultural settings to test its findings.

Acknowledgement

The author gratefully acknowledges the funding support of the Teaching and Learning Research Initiative (TLRI) for undertaking this study.

References

Alsafran, E. and Brown, D. (2012). The relationship between classroom computer technology and students' academic achievement. *Research in Higher Education, 15*, 1–19.

Anderson, L.W. and Krathwohl, D.R. (eds) (2001). *A Taxonomy for Learning, Teaching and Assessing: A revision of Bloom's Taxonomy of Educational Objectives.* Upper Saddle River, NJ: Pearson Higher Education.

Australian Curriculum, Assessment and Reporting Authority. (2010). *Critical and Creative Thinking.* Retrieved from: www.australiancurriculum.edu.au/GeneralCapabilities/critical-and-creative-thinking/introduction/introduction

Beyer, B. (2008). What research tells us about teaching thinking skills. *The Social Studies, 99*(5), 223–232.

Biggs, J. and Collis, K. (1982). *Evaluating the Quality of Learning: The SOLO taxonomy.* New York: Academic Press.

Binkley, M., Erstad, O., Herman, J., Raizen, S., Ripley, M., Miller-Ricci, M. and Rumble, M. (2012). Defining twenty-first century skills. In P. Griffin, B. McGaw and E. Care (eds), *Assessment and Teaching of 21st Century Skills.* Dordrecht, Netherlands: Springer Science + Business Media.

Brindley, J., Walti, C. and Blaschke, L. (2009). Creating effective collaborative learning groups in an online environment. *The International Review of Research in Open and Distance Learning, 10*(3), 1–23.

Buckner, E. and Kim, P. (2014). Integrating technology and pedagogy for inquiry-based learning: The Stanford Mobile Inquiry-based Learning Environment (SMILE). *Prospects, 44*, 99–118.

Case, R. (1992). *The Mind's Staircase.* Hillsdale, NJ: Erlbaum.

Crombie, N. (2014, 18 March). iPads open students' eyes to learning. The Wairarapa Times Age. Retrieved from: www.nzherald.co.nz/wairarapa-times-age/news/article.cfm?c_id=1503414andobjectid=11220852

Daud, N. and Husin, Z. (2004). Developing critical thinking skills in computer-aided extended reading classes. *British Journal of Educational Technology, 35*(4), 477–487.

Department for Children, Education, Lifelong Learning and Skills. (2008). *Skills Framework for 3–19 year olds in Wales.* Curriculum and Assessment Division. Retrieved from: www.pgfl.org.uk/schools/pbf/PembrokeDock/about/Website%20Documents/Maths%20scheme%20of%20work/Skills%20Framework%20%202008.pdf

Department for Education and Skills. (2004). *The National Curriculum: Handbook for secondary Teachers in England.* Qualifications and Curriculum Authority. Retrieved from: http://webarchive.nationalarchives.gov.uk/20130401151715/www.education.gov.uk/publications/eOrderingDownload/QCA-04-1374.pdf

Desai, T., Chow, K., Mumford, L., Hotze, F. and Chau, T. (2014). Implementing an iPad-based alternative communication device for a student with cerebral palsy and autism in the classroom via an access technology delivery protocol. *Computers and Education, 79*, 148–158.

Eisenberg, M and Berkowitz, R. (1990). *Information Problem-solving: The Big Six approach to library and information skills instruction.* Norwood, NJ: Ablex Publishing.

Falloon, G.W. (2013a). Young students using iPads: App design and content influences of their learning pathways. *Computers and Education, 68*, 505–521.

Falloon, G.W. (2013b). What's going on behind the screens? Researching young students' learning pathways using iPads. *Journal of Computer-Assisted Learning, 30*(4), 318–336.

Falloon, G.W. (2013c). Creating content: Building literacy skills in year 1 students using open format apps. *Computers in New Zealand Schools, 25*(1–3), 76–95.

Falloon, G.W. (2015). What's the difference? Learning collaboratively using iPads in conventional classrooms. *Computers and Education, 84*, 62–77.

Getting, S. and Swainey, K. (2012). First graders with iPads? *Learning and Leading with Technology*. August 2012. Retrieved from: http://files.eric.ed.gov/fulltext/EJ991227.pdf

Gilbert, J. (2005). *Catching the Knowledge Wave? The knowledge society and the future of education.* Wellington, New Zealand: NZCER Press.

Hembree, R. (1992). Experiments and relational studies in problem solving: A meta-analysis. *Journal for Research in Mathematics Education, 23*(3), 242–273.

Hopson, M., Simms, R.L. and Knezek, G. (2002). Using a technology-enriched environment to improve higher-order thinking skills. *Journal of Research on Technology in Education, 34*(2), 109–119.

Koenig, J. (2011). *Assessing 21st Century Skills: Summary of a workshop.* National Research Council of the National Academies. Retrieved from: www.sri.com/sites/default/files/publications/imports/21st_century_skills.pdf

Krathwohl, D.R. (2002). A revision of Bloom's Taxonomy: An overview. *Theory into Practice, 41*(4), 212–218.

Kucirkova, N., Messer, D., Sheehy, K. and Panadero, C. (2014). Children's engagement with educational iPad apps: Insights from a Spanish classroom. *Computers and Education, 71*, 175–184.

Landis, J.R. and Koch, G.G. (1977). The Measurement of Observer Agreement for Categorical Data. *Biometrics, 33*(1), 159–174.

Liao, Y.C. (2007). Effects of computer-assisted instruction on students' achievement in Taiwan: A meta-analysis. *Computers and Education, 48*(2), 216–233.

Lin, L. and Nzai, V. (2014). Using iPad apps to enhance literacy skills of English language learners with special needs. *International Journal of Languages and Literatures, 2*(1), 21–29.

Marzano, R.J. (2000). *Designing a New Taxonomy of Educational Objectives.* Thousand Oaks, CA: Corwin Press.

Mayer, R. (2002). Rote versus meaningful learning. *Theory into Practice, 41*(4), 226–232.

Miller, B.T., Krockover, G.H. and Doughty, T. (2013). Using iPads to teach science to students with a moderate to severe intellectual disability: A pilot study. *Journal of Research in Science Teaching, 50*(8), 887–911.

Ministry of Education. (2007). *The New Zealand Curriculum.* Wellington, New Zealand: Learning Media Ltd.

Ministry of Education. (2014). *Modern Learning Environments. Shaping education.* Retrieved from: www.shapingeducation.govt.nz

Moseley, D., Elliot, J., Gregson, M. and Higgins, S. (2005). Thinking skills frameworks for use in education and training. *British Educational Research Journal, 31*(3), 81–104.

Mozaffar, S. (2012). *iPad for Autism: How can the iPad serve as a teaching tool for students on the Autism Spectrum?* Retrieved from: www.academia.edu/7344762/I_Pad_for_Autism_Sheena_Mozaffar

OECD. (2013). *The Skills Needed for the 21st Century.* OECD Skills Outlook 2013, OECD Publishing. Retrieved from: http://dx.doi.org/10.1787/9789264204256-en

Pressley, M. and Harris, K. (2001). Teaching cognitive strategies for reading, writing and problem-solving. In A. Costa (ed.), *Developing Minds: A resource book for teaching thinking* (pp. 266–270). Alexandria, VA: Association for Supervision and Curriculum Development.

Segal, D. (2006). Using computer simulations to teach and assess critical thinking skills in health-related programs. In C. Crawford, R. Carlsen, K. McFerrin, J. Price, R. Weber and D. Willis (eds), *Proceedings of Society for Information Technology and Teacher Education International Conference 2006* (pp. 1402–1403). Chesapeake, VA: AACE.

Sela, O. (2013). Old concepts, new tools: An action research project on computer-supported collaborative learning in teacher education. *MERLOT Journal of Online Learning and Teaching, 9*(3), 418–430.

Stavert, B. (2013). *Bring Your Own Device (BYOD) in Schools: A literature review*. Department of Education and Communities. Sydney, NSW: Creative Commons. Retrieved from: www.det.nsw.edu.au/policies/technology/computers/mobile-device/BYOD_2013_Literature_Review.pdf

Walters, M. and Fehring, H. (2009). An investigation of the incorporation of information and communication technology and thinking skills with year 1 and 2 students. *Australian Journal of Language and Literacy, 32*(3), 258–272.

Yang, Ya-Ting and Chang, C.H. (2013). Empowering students through digital game authorship: Enhancing concentration, critical thinking, and academic achievement. *Computers and Education, 68*, 334–344.

Yeh, C.Y. (2004). Nurturing reflective teaching during critical-thinking instruction in a computer simulation program. *Computers and Education, 42*, 181–194.

Yelland, N. and Masters, J. (2005). Rethinking scaffolding in the information age. *Computers and Education, 48*, 362–382.

Zurita, G. and Nussbaum, M. (2004). Computer supported collaborative learning using wirelessly interconnected handheld computers. *Computers and Education, 42*, 289–314.

18

TRANS- AND INTRA-APPS

Innovating the app market and use

Natalia Kucirkova

MANCHESTER METROPOLITAN UNIVERSITY, MANCHESTER, UNITED KINGDOM

This chapter focuses on cross- or inter-media experiences facilitated by children's apps and the ways in which the so-called 'transmedia apps' could enrich children's learning experiences. Against the backdrop of some worrying commercialisation and personalisation trends, some exciting possibilities with virtual and augmented reality apps are provided. Suggestions for future design of transmedia are outlined with concrete examples and current evidence.

Keywords: Transmedia, in-app purchases, augmented reality, virtual reality, future models, legislation.

Introduction

Children's apps are software programs designed to facilitate a range of experiences, ranging from simple phonics activities to more complex open-ended creative art activities. The current iOS app market contains more than 80,000 apps offered in the educational category, with new apps added on an everyday basis. The big volume of apps makes it hard for parents and teachers to navigate the market and choose the right app for their child (Chiong and Shuler, 2010) and for app designers to identify and maintain their position in the market (Khaddage *et al.*, 2014). In this chapter, I argue that trans- and intra- apps, which bring several app experiences together in a variety of combinations, could provide a new basis for conceptualising and innovating the children's app market.

As the prefix 'trans' indicates, transmedia refers to cross- or inter-media experiences which extend a given story or narrative across various types of media. In their report 'T is for Transmedia', Herr-Stephenson *et al.* (2013) define transmedia as 'any combination of relationships that might exist between the various texts (analogue or digital) that constitute a contemporary entertainment media experience' (p. 2). A typical example would be the Harry Potter franchise, which includes a series of Harry Potter apps for fans to download in addition to reading the Harry Potter books (or listening to the audio-books), watching the films, playing with the toys, computer games, or Lego construction kits. An intra-app, on the other hand, is an app which aggregates various experiences within one software program, offering a seamless and integrated experience. A basic example of an intra-media app experience is an in-app purchase, which wraps an app with several layers of engagement, gradually available to the user.

In this chapter, I use the concept of transmedia and examples of intra-app experiences to examine the present and possible future app models and their potential for children's learning. The trans- and intra-media models are useful concepts because they consider not only what is currently available, but also what lies behind many emerging practices of app engagement and the larger landscape of children's software programs.

I provide some guiding points for future research seeking to develop a better understanding of apps' potential to nurture cross-media and richer learning experiences and outline ways which may be used for identifying pedagogically sound use of intra- and inter-media apps in the classroom and at home. I argue that intra- and inter-media apps can endow children's experiences with a new layer of meaning and offer children further entry points into the rich worlds that surround stories. Moreover, balanced trans- and intra-media app experiences can provide a useful spur to necessary innovation in the currently saturated app market. However, for transmedia apps to reach their potential, careful attention needs to be paid to their commercialisation purposes, data use, and personalisation policies. Young children are largely unaware of the commercial intent of the apps they engage with (see www.commercialfreechildhood.org/) and it is important that app designers, researchers, parents, and teachers (i.e. adults who influence children's choices of apps) are fully aware of the potential benefits as well as pitfalls of trans- and intra-media apps. As such, the chapter might be a useful reference for several stakeholders who are looking for an innovative edge with children's apps.

Theoretical framework

As Säljö explains in Chapter 1, key learning theories (such as behaviourist theory or cognitive theory of learning) do not include technologies in their core conceptualisations. This is understandable given that these theories were developed at a time when technologies were not central to a child's learning experience. With the advent of new digital tools, however, several new formulations of learning (see Verhagen, 2006) have emerged, which specifically address the learning opportunities with technologies.

A useful framework for understanding how inter- and intra-app experiences may contribute to children's learning is connectivism, which is characterised by eight key principles:

- Learning and knowledge rests in diversity of opinions;
- Learning is a process of connecting specialised nodes or information sources;
- Learning may reside in non-human appliances;
- Capacity to know more is more critical than what is currently known;
- Nurturing and maintaining connections is needed to facilitate continual learning;
- Ability to see connections between fields, ideas, and concepts is a core skill;
- Currency (accurate, up-to-date knowledge) is the intent of all connectivist learning activities; and
- Decision-making is itself a learning process. Choosing what to learn and the meaning of incoming information is seen through the lens of a shifting reality. While there is a right answer now, it may be wrong tomorrow due to alterations in the information climate affecting the decision.

(Siemens, 2014, p. 4)

As the name reveals, 'connection' is a key concept in the framework, which is identified and explored as the basis of all learning. Although not a learning theory in and of its own right (Kop and Hill, 2008), connectivism provides some useful concepts in relation to the four key principles of twenty-first-century learning: autonomy, connectedness, diversity, and openness (Tschofen and Mackness, 2012). Unlike other new forms of learning such as Massive Open Online Courses, most apps are designed to foster a remarkably old-fashioned way of learning: the learning experience is limited to the app and often closed to wider engagement (users need to exit the app to connect to wider social networks); emphasis is placed on individual learning and there is little diversity in the app production and content of children's apps (see Garofoli, 2014). What would happen if apps were designed according to the theoretical principle of connectivity? I consider a few key potential learning benefits.

Learning benefits of intra- and inter-media apps

Multiple intelligences. In a paper co-produced by the USC Annenberg Innovation Lab and the Joan Ganz Cooney Center, Herr-Stephenson *et al.* (2013) provide a guidebook to transmedia in the lives of children age 5–11 and outline its applications to storytelling, play, and learning. The key concept the authors present as relevant for learning is that transmedia supports the expression of multiple literacies and intelligences: 'Transmedia engages multiple literacies, including textual, visual, and media literacies, as well as multiple intelligences' (Herr-Stephenson *et al.*, 2013, p. 2). Multiple intelligences is a psychological theory about the mind, originally developed by Gardner (2011), which identified seven distinct intelligences: linguistic, logical–mathematical, musical, body-kinesthetic, spatial, interpersonal, and intrapersonal. Just how exactly could transmedia experiences support multiple intelligences is not yet known, but we could hypothesise that the possibility to engage with texts and narratives in various modes (textual, visual, audio, interactive) allows students to use multiple intelligences. For instance, the Frozen story is available to children as a film (which children can just sit and watch), as a picturebook (which children can enjoy looking at and emerging readers can explore the simple sentences), and as an interactive story app, with which children can create their own snow globes and re-create scenes from the film with frosty drawing tools. As such, the app can provide different entry points to the story world of Frozen, focusing on different elements of the story, different points in the plot timeline, or engage children in the story from different perspectives. Children can respond by producing their own drawings and simple games. While a single app is unlikely to provide opportunities for all the different kinds of intelligences, cross-media apps provide more opportunities through multiple channels of engagement. These are more aligned with the multiple intelligences than static print-based materials, which often privilege the linguistic expression of knowledge over the visceral (physical) and material (see Bourdieu, 1989; Foucault, 1982; Latour, 1987, and Wohlwend and Rowsell, Chapter 6, this volume).

Agency. Transmedia has been proposed to attribute a unique potential to innovate children's engagement with texts and create a symbiosis between agentic involvement and cross-media activity (Jenkins, 2001; 2003). Children's agentic involvement is an important concept in the twenty-first-century: as Kress (2005) reminds us, with new media, children are not only represented but also interactive participants in a narrative. While with static print books readers were positioned as represented characters with pre-determined characteristics, with apps and other digital tools, children can interact with the characters in the book or game; they can customise the narrative or personalise the story characters/avatars. This gives children a sense of agency, achievement and ownership of the story which is important for readers' motivation and pleasure of reading (cf. Appleyard, 1990; Rothbauer, 2004).

Importantly, the emphasis in transmedia experiences is on enriching and enhancing a given story/narrative, and avoiding replication. This means that a good transmedia experience provides users with various depictions and various media treatments of the same content. The focus on the narrative means that the centre of experience is the story rather than the format in which it is delivered. The transmedia theory thus aligns with the contemporary perceptions of platform-agnostic media engagement: children's engagement with stories in any format (digital, print, interactive, or static), is part of the twenty-first-century landscape (Kucirkova, 2014a). For instance, with various apps based around the Cinderella story, children can make the story characters move, choose the colours of Cinderella's dress, record their own voices to tell the story, and share it remotely with their friends. This is different from the previous engagement possibilities with a Cinderella book or film. Each medium adds a different layer to the story and user experience, which is an attractive concept in an era characterised by a multitude of reading devices (e.g., Kobo, Kindle, Nook, iPads).

Collaboration. Yelland in Chapter 5 outlines the importance of collaboration for children's development of twenty-first-century skills. In theory, and emerging evidence supports this assumption, intra- and inter-media experiences support connections among stories and other readers, which, in turn, supports collaboration and creation of new content (see Herr-Stephenson *et al.*, 2013). A frequently cited example of educational transmedia is the digital novel called *Inanimate Alice*. Fleming (2013) outlines how *Inanimate Alice* supports collaboration in classrooms, with readers positioned as direct participants who co-construct the story in multiple ways (including games, puzzles, new stories, story reviews). The novel is highly interactive, enabling readers to take the story to another level, with several supporting mechanisms along the way (e.g., the possibility to remake photostory pages, screenshots, and scripts). Teachers can further encourage co-creation of the story with several worksheet assets, music tracks, and the comic book art provided by the *Inanimate Alice* producers (Fleming, 2013). Based on her experience of using *Inanimate Alice* in classrooms and in libraries as a school librarian, Fleming (2013) argues that the highly collaborative nature of *Inanimate Alice* activities can foster children's empathy, and if implemented well, it can, together with other transmedia learning, connect 'learners around the globe, and therefore leveraging the power of the collective' (p. 377).

Developmental appropriateness of trans- and intra-media

However, transmedia may not work for all children – there are important individual differences in children's responses to apps (see Radesky and Zuckerman, Chapter 2). As Pietschmann *et al.* (2014) argue, children, especially younger children, who do not have the adequate cognitive, emotional, and moral capacity, may not derive the benefits propagated by transmedia enthusiasts. By drawing on developmental theories by Piaget (1953) and Perner (1993), Pietschmann *et al.* (2014) point out that for young children (under the age of 2), connected story experiences don't make much sense as young children can only process some basic features of the content such as colours, shapes, and sounds, but cannot follow complex and connected narratives. Indeed, the fact that children acquire abilities sequentially is also recognised in the current guidance around the use of digital media with young children, which recommends that for children under the age of 2, the use of 2D screens should be limited as they are unlikely to benefit from the content portrayed in this format (APA, 2015).

Thus far, the evidence on developmental appropriateness of children's apps, including intra- and inter-media apps, is mixed, with no longitudinal data on key developmental milestones and learning abilities. What remains as a fact is that intra- and inter-media apps are an attractive concept for app producers, as they both represent an opportunity to expand the audience and market, and thus create more opportunity for increased profit (Sharp, 2014).

How do intra- and inter-media apps fit the current app business models?

The commercial side of intra- and inter-apps

Inter-media apps. A typical model of intra-apps for large entertainment sources is to produce an app as an add-on to an existing suite of products. For smaller app publishers, the process is often reversed, with the production of an app first, followed by a suite of related products. For example, the award-winning app producer Toca Boca™ started with apps and as the success of the company grew, added to their list of products t-shirts, toys, and socks featuring characters from their apps.

Producing transmedia apps is an attractive option for app producers as it represents an opportunity for diversifying their product portfolio and income streams. It is well-known that developing an app is a costly endeavour, with an app's production costs amounting to about $10,000–70,000. Yet, the revenue generated through app purchase is low: an average app costs around $3, which means that app producers need to rely on large number of downloads to cover their costs of production. This makes it difficult for small app producers to survive in the app market. The other difficulty is that the app market is currently over-saturated with children's educational apps, with more than 80,000 (as of 2015) marketed as educational for young children. Children's app producers are therefore looking for a more sustainable and sound business model.

App producers with a suite of apps (particularly those who produce storyapps with a sequel of titles) often operate on the subscription model, charging the customer a regular, recurring fee to use an app. Many parents like this model for children's storyapps as it means that they get new titles on a regular basis, without the need to look for them in the app store. In addition to subscription models, the so-called 'app bundles' have become available since the launch of iOS8. App bundles enable app developers to sell several applications together, at a discounted rate. This model works well for larger app developers who can bundle various apps and thus increase their marketing strategy.

Intra-media apps. Intra-media apps are still relatively new, but several examples exist for connecting apps within each other rather than across media (or apps). App meshing is a process whereby app producers embed hyperlinks into an app or digital book. For example, at the end of the *What is That?* ibook, there is a hyperlink to the Our Story app, which encourages users to create their own digital book, after they have read the *What is That?* story. Such app meshing can be a viable option for app producers seeking to build partnerships with other app companies and thus increase their customer base and connect users' experiences via distinct apps.

Another intra-media option is in-app purchasing. In-app purchases are features within apps, which can be unlocked if the user pays a fee. For instance, with a free children's app, users can remove ads with an in-app purchase or they can buy additional content, 'skip a level to in-game currency that can be used to outfit a character, speed things up, or decorate a room' (www.commonsensemedia.org/

blog/8-ways-to-save-and-spend-on-free-apps). Such an opt-in purchasing process is a popular model with adult digital games but its use with children's apps has come under a lot of criticism.

In the early days of children's apps, there was no legislation and little awareness of the various, often hidden, possibilities of in-app purchases. It was not long until several cases appeared in the newspapers of parents shocked they discovered their child had spent hundreds of dollars for additional features within downloaded apps. Both Apple and Google have profited by marketing free or low-cost apps to children and permitting them to easily purchase in-app features, without incorporating reasonable controls (e.g., the entry of a password, locking the phone etc.). Many parents took legal action against the app producers and thus far Apple has had to refund £32.5m and Google £11.6m to settle formal complaints over unauthorised in-app purchases by children. Despite these legal settlements, in-app purchasing is still available for several children's apps and its availability depends on the country's legislation. In the UK, the Office of Fair Trading has issued guidelines in 2014 that state that app publishers need to provide up-front information about the costs and only accept payment if the account holder provides informed consent. In other countries, for example, Canada, no formal legislation exists, although several guidelines have been issued, including the 'Ethical Framework and Best Practice Review of the children's digital industry in Ontario' by Kids Media Centre, Canada.

One should bear in mind that app developers have little say in how in-app purchases are handled, Apple and Google control 'the customer relationship when in-app purchases are made' (www.informationweek.com/mobile/5-tips-for-building-subscription-based-mobile-apps/d/d-id/1111625?). In-app purchases are thus an example of how intra-media apps can be connected to a double concern of security and commercial exploitation.

Concerns around intra- and inter-media apps

When app producers adopt personalised transmedia as a business model for children's apps, they need to be very careful about secure management of children's personal data and transparent pricing models. Several personalisation techniques exist to connect intra- and inter-media apps, with 31 percent of retailers and brands stating personalisation as one of the top three priorities for 2015. This means that if apps become regular parts of children's media experiences, they become another aspect of the user's data trail that can provide business opportunities. Given that intra- and inter-media apps can engage children at various ages and via various means, retailers can get data on young children's *patterns* of engagement (not just one single activity), which means that developers and network producers can easily build a complex picture of children's needs and preferences. That is sure to sound the alarm bells in any parent and has been criticised for contributing to the increased commercialisation of childhood (see www.commercialfreechildhood.org/).

An update to the Children's Online Privacy Protection Act of 1998 in July 2013, requires all US operators of mobile apps 'to provide notice and obtain parent's consent before collecting personal information from children under the age of 13' (http://thedma.org/wp-content/uploads/COPPA-rule-sept2013.pdf). Similar laws are in place in other Western countries, but adults should bear in mind that not all providers comply with the law and some are still knowingly collecting data from children including their names and e-mail addresses.

The difficulty of intra- and inter-media apps is that they are caught between two worlds: that of sound learning models accompanied by almost philosophical academic rhetoric, and that of a tool to structure a business model. What are the possibilities of intra- and inter-media apps for educational purposes?

Intra- and inter-media apps in education

Fleming (2013, p. 371) asserts that: 'Although transmedia can claim considerable success in the entertainment world, as well as in aspects of business generally, it can be argued that the real roots of transmedia in fact lie in education, as teachers have long sought out diverse resources and strategies to reach and engage their students'. The current educational app market is dominated by apps produced for single and linear experiences (see Wohlwend and Rowsell, Chapter 6, this volume). Teachers often engage with their students in experiences where a narrative is depicted in a variety of resources and artefacts (e.g. books, toys, cartoons, films, and/or games) and carries links to several interconnected curriculum subjects. Apps could be part of such connections and this section outlines the main ways of effectively integrating intra- and inter-media apps into the classroom.

App smashing

Creative teachers are often the best innovators and there are many *online reports, blogs,* and *forums of anecdotal evidence* that show how teachers have engaged in app 'smashing'. App smashing is 'the process of using multiple apps to create projects or complete tasks' (www. k12technology.weebly.com/app-smashing.html) or in other words, using siloed, independent apps in groups. Teachers can group apps by creating app folders on students' devices or using a group of apps for a specific activity. Teachers can also 'smash' a writing app with another app for video recording to extend a text-production activity. This allows children to explore various literacy options and express their ideas in various ways and produce a richer final product.

When looking for more seamless and sophisticated app smashing, mobile device management companies, such as AirWatch™, provide solutions (e.g. the 'Teacher Tools', www.air-watch.com/industries/teacher-tools/) with which teachers can populate specific iPads with specific content. For instance, teachers can select a group of tablets for which they push apps related to literacy skills and add to these a bank of other online resources, including a selection of pictures, pdf files, or website links. As such, apps become part of a digital customised classroom environment, enriching students' learning journeys.

The practice of app smashing or app linking is a recommended technique for teachers implementing apps and digital books in their classrooms. Based on extensive observations of classroom use of iPads, Roskos (see this volume) developed guidance for teachers to use digital books, part of which is the recommendation to combine apps to increase a child's educational experience. The framework contains the following recommendations: (1) Know your device; (2) Know your ebook; (3) Establish routines; (4) *Link apps together* (emphasis added by author) and (5) Be persistent.

As more and more public schools are using tablets and iPads, more and more possibilities for collective app smashing emerge. However, to be able to effectively combine apps, teachers need to have a good knowledge of what apps to choose in the first place. With 10,000s apps advertised as educational, it takes time and considerable effort to find the right app. What strategies can teachers use to streamline the app search process?

Choosing educational apps for the classroom

There are two main search strategies for educational apps. Teachers can either become active in the search process and search for apps in the iTunes store (for iOS-based devices such as iPads, iPhones, and the iPod Touch) or Google Play and Android devices. Alternatively, they can search for apps directly with Google search: with app indexing introduced in May 2015, teachers can search for an app and install it to their device straight away (https://developers.google.com/app-indexing/).

The second strategy is to choose an app reviewed by other users or expert groups. There are several third-party review sites, for example, Common Sense Media Graphite (www.graphite.org/) and Children's Technology Review (www.childrenstech.com) are great sites for teachers who are looking for apps and tips for how to implement them in the classroom. Also, teachers with apps (www.teacherswithapps.com) provide periodically updated tips for the best apps in the classroom.

To be able to apply other users' reviews, or expert reviews to their own context, teachers need some strategies to sort the array. Working with several groups of UK teachers had led me to the formulation (Kucirkova, 2014b) of some rules of thumb in helping teachers decide which apps to use:

- The app needs to be aligned with the specific activity, skill, or experience you aim to foster.
- The app needs to enrich the activity you have in mind.
- Open-ended apps offer more opportunities for children's own creativity and exploration than template-based ones.
- Apps which support shared engagement with others can foster social skills.

- Discuss your choices with other parents, teachers, and the children themselves.
- Consider the added value of the app's use for the offline version of the same activity.

App smashing can ensure that children's experiences are less dictated by commercial interests and more by what their educators (teachers and parents) perceive as important for their development. Teachers' direct involvement in facilitating intra- and inter-app experiences illustrates a possible future direction for children's apps.

Future models of apps

Most children's apps operate as a single-app model, offering intense but short forms of engagement. Such a linear process of engagement has been criticised for negatively impacting young children's mentality, building false expectations around life experiences, and risk-taking (Gardner and Davis, 2013). Increasingly, however, new, brain-inspired models of computing use software, functioning of which is not linear but parallel and often serendipitous. It is foreseeable that the app design will move towards this direction, offering users a sustained, more complex experience, inspired by brain-computing models. What could future app models look like?

Augmented reality apps. Augmented reality is 'a type of virtual reality that aims to duplicate the world's environment in a computer' (www.webopedia.com). Augmented reality apps allow children to engage with a digital activity by overlaying that experience on a real object. For example with the Zoo Burst™ app, children can experience their story as it 'jumps out' of the paper and interact with it. With Smart Car™ from Thames and Kosmos, digital content can be unlocked using physical toys (the toy car comes with augmented reality code cards, which create a virtual city on the tablet screen). Such augmented reality apps can bridge traditional and digital experiences in an unprecedented way, offering children immersive experiences.

The combination of 3D printing with apps is another way to enhance children's experience. At the moment, this is happening through third-party providers, for example, Crayon Creatures™ can turn children's drawings into sculptures by printing the drawings with 3D printing technology. The current process involves the adult sending the artwork to the printers and Crayon Creatures shipping the final artefact back. It is possible, however, that home-based 3D printing connected to apps will become more available and affordable in the future, including for the children's market (see the Printeer™ iPad app kick-starter project).

So that these connections are meaningful and engaging for young children it is likely that the future of apps will see increased use of personalised recommendation systems.

Apps with increased personalisation. Personalised recommendation systems are systems that can predict content a user might be interested in, by drawing on information on the user's past history of engagement and on the user's past activity, stored under the user's profile. Recommendation systems can be helpful for offering additional options for intra- and inter-media apps (especially if users have insufficient knowledge and experience to know which other app might be of interest to them) and they can also simplify the search process for apps of similar content (see Shinde and Kulkarni, 2011). As the recommendation systems become more robust and able to provide content-based, collaborative, and hybrid recommendations (De Campos *et al.*, 2010), the Internet is becoming 'more seamless, more pervasive, personal and even predictive' (Goodwin, 2014, online). It is possible that the strategies currently available for app smashing and meshing will be endowed with intelligent recommendation systems in the future, so that children's learning experiences are more personal and more relevant to their individual profiles.

Imagine, for example, that a user downloads an app for simple literacy skills (e.g. the ABC Spy). After the user has played with the app, s/he would get a personalised recommendation for another app, based on their level of engagement with the previous app. The TinkRbook™ developed at MiT can track the length and length of users' engagement on the back end. The future may see more apps with embedded tracking software (see Falloon, Chapter 17, this volume) that would tailor the content to individual users, pushing personalised recommendations for apps, all within a unified intra-media app package.

In all these developments, it is important to remember that as technology gets more sophisticated, the human interaction around technology needs to be further developed too. As numerous technology evaluation projects remind us (e.g., Slavin *et al.*, 2009; Torgerson *et al.*, 2004), it is the pedagogy contextualising the use of technologies (whether these are tablets, laptops, or interactive whiteboards in the classroom), rather than the device *per se*, which makes a difference to children's learning. It follows that personalised recommendation systems supporting future intra- and inter-media projects need to be informed by the needs and preferences not only of automatically generated data but also of active input by the users. Parents and teachers know the children's needs and preferences best, and their efforts to personalise their children's education need to be accompanied by more capacity-building and training programmes (see Archer *et al.*, 2014 for a similar argument in relation to the well-trained and supported teacher programmes with ICT).

It is also likely that in the future, there will be more programmes personalised according to children's own choices, with more embedded possibilities for children to inform products and activities designed for them. For instance, in addition to textual input, voice-recognition software programs embedded in children's toys (eg Hello Barbie, see www.theregister.co.uk/2015/02/19/hello_barbie/) are likely to break through further on the global market.

Virtual reality apps for children. Marsh and Yamada-Rice explained the difference between virtual and augmented reality in Chapter 15 when describing in detail children's interactions with augmented reality apps. At the time of writing this chapter, virtual reality software is only emerging on the market, with a focus on digital games and improved communication options for adults and teenagers rather than young children. Some pioneering work in this area has been undertaken by groups of technology enthusiasts who aim to bring fun experiences to hospitalised children (e.g. the Osmos Academy in Canada), or teachers who used virtual reality software to connect informal and formal learning experiences in schools (e.g. enabling children a virtual tour of a museum from the classroom). While the development of enriching and educational narratives specifically designed for virtual learning environments will take a few more years, it is clear that virtual reality apps will become part of the transmedia landscape, taking children to literally new dimensions.

To ensure that future developments in this area proceed in an ethical and integral way, it is essential for technology to transparently model and demonstrate how personalisation systems work and how children's data are used to provide a more effective user's experience. Importantly, it is essential that in all these efforts, intra- and inter-media experiences are provided in conjunction with offline experiences, mediated by adults, children's peers, and community partners.

References

American Academy of Pediatrics (APA). (2015). Media and children. Elk Grove Village, IL: American Academy of Pediatrics. Retrieved from www.aap.org/en-us/advocacy-and-policy/aap-health-initiatives/pages/media-and-children.aspx

Appleyard, J. A. (1990). *Becoming a Reader: The experience of fiction from childhood to adulthood.* Cambridge: Cambridge University Press.

Archer, K., Savage, R., Sanghera-Sidhu, S., Wood, E., Gottardo, A. and Chen, V. (2014). Examining the effectiveness of technology use in classrooms: A tertiary meta-analysis. *Computers & Education, 78,* 140–149.

Bourdieu, P. (1977). *Outline of a Theory of Practice* (Vol. 16). Cambridge: Cambridge University Press.

Chiong, C. and Shuler, C. (2010). Learning: Is there an app for that? In *Investigations of Young Children's Usage and Learning with Mobile Devices and Apps.* New York: The Joan Ganz Cooney Center at Sesame Workshop.

De Campos, L. M., Fernández-Luna, J. M., Huete, J. F. and Rueda-Morales, M. A. (2010). Combining content-based and collaborative recommendations: A hybrid approach based on Bayesian networks. *International Journal of Approximate Reasoning, 51*(7), 785–799.

Fleming, L. (2013). Expanding learning opportunities with transmedia practices: *Inanimate Alice* as an exemplar. *Journal of Media Literacy Education, 5*(2), 3.

Foucault, M. (1982). *The Archaeology of Knowledge and the Discourse on Language.* London: Psychology Press. Originally published in 1969 by Paris: Éditions Gallimard.

Gardner, H. (2011). *Frames of Mind: The theory of multiple intelligences.* New York: Basic Books. Republished from original publication in 1983 by NY Basics.

Garofoli, S. (2014). *Low-income teens design apps that reflect their neighborhoods,* SF Gate. Available from www.sfgate.com/politics/joegarofoli/article/Low-income-teens-design-apps-that-reflect-their-5332775.php

Goodwin, T. (2014). Seven shifts that will change marketing in 2015 and beyond, *The Guardian,* originally published: www.linkedin.com/pulse/20141119102703-6433797-6-trends-for-2017-and-beyond. Available from: www.theguardian.com/media-network/2014/nov/20/digital-marketing-trends-2015

Herr-Stephenson, B., Alper, M., Reilly, E. and Jenkins, H. (2013). T is for transmedia: Learning through transmedia play. Los Angeles and New York: USC Annenberg Innovation Lab and The Joan Ganz Cooney Center at Sesame Workshop. Retrieved April (Vol. 10, p. 2015).

Jenkins, H. (2001). Convergence? I diverge. *Technology Review, 104*(5), 93.

Jenkins, H. (2003). Transmedia storytelling, *Technology Review*. Boston, MA: MIT Press.

Kearney, M., Burden, K. and Rai, T. (2015). Investigating teachers' adoption of signature mobile pedagogies. *Computers & Education, 80*, 48–57.

Khaddage, F., Lattemann, C. and Acosta-Díaz, R. (2014, March). Mobile gamification in education engage, educate and entertain via gamified mobile apps. In *Society for Information Technology & Teacher Education International Conference* (Vol. 2014, No. 1, pp. 1654–1660).

Kop, R. and Hill, A. (2008). Connectivism: Learning theory of the future or vestige of the past? *The International Review of Research in Open and Distributed Learning, 9*(3), 1–13.

Kress, G. (2005). *Before Writing: Rethinking the paths to literacy*. London: Routledge.

Kucirkova, N. (2014a). Kindle vs books? Children just don't see it that way, *The Conversation*. Available from: https://theconversation.com/kindle-vs-books-children-just-dont-see-it-that-way-25725

Kucirkova, N. (2014b). How to choose the best educational app for your child, *The Conversation*. Available from: https://theconversation.com/how-to-choose-the-best-educational-app-for-your-child-28170

Latour, B. (1987). *Science in Action: How to follow scientists and engineers through society*. Cambridge, MA: Harvard University Press.

Perner, J. (1993). *Understanding the Representational Mind*. Cambridge, MA: MIT Press.

Piaget, J. (1953). *The Origins of Intelligence in Children*. London: Routledge.

Pietschmann, D., Voelkel, S. and Ohler, P. (2014). Limitations of transmedia storytelling for children: A cognitive developmental analysis. *International Journal of Communication, 8*, 2259–2282.

Rothbauer, P. M (2004). People aren't afraid any more but it's hard to find books': Reading practices that inform personal and social identities of self-identified lesbian and queer young women. *Canadian Journal of Information and Library Science, 28*(3), 89–112.

Sharp, E. (2014). *Once Upon A Time: A Transmedia Story Blog*. Available at: https://erynsharp.wordpress.com/2014/04/16/once-upon-a-time-a-transmedia-story/

Shinde, S. K. and Kulkarni, U.V. (2011). Hybrid personalized recommender system using fast k-medoids clustering algorithm. *Journal of Advances in Information Technology, 2*(3), 152–158.

Siemens, G. (2014). *Connectivism: A learning theory for the digital age*. Available from: http://er.dut.ac.za/handle/123456789/69

Slavin, R. E., Lake, C., Chambers, B., Cheung, A. and Davis, S. (2009). Effective reading programs for the elementary grades: A best-evidence synthesis. *Review of Educational Research, 4*, 1391–1466.

Torgerson, C., Zhu, D., Andrews, R., Beverton, S., Burn, A., Leach, J. and Snowling, M. (2004). A systematic review and meta-analysis of the effectiveness of ICT on literacy learning in English. *The Impact of ICT on Literacy Education*, 5–16.

Tschofen, C. and Mackness, J. (2012). Connectivism and dimensions of individual experience. *The International Review of Research in Open and Distributed Learning, 13*(1), 124–143.

Verhagen, P. (2006). *Connectivism: A new learning theory?* Available from: www.4shared.com/office/ddZv-naA/Connectivism_a_new_learning_th.html

19

A MODEL OF MOBILE KNOWLEDGE-BUILDING WITH APPS FOR PRE-SERVICE TEACHER EDUCATION

Kevin Burden

THE UNIVERSITY OF HULL, UK

Knowledge-building is a well-established theoretical approach to learning that privileges creation over consumption. The development of digital and mobile technologies empowers learners with considerable agency to capture and construct meaning in a multimodal manner that fulfils many of the principles behind knowledge-building. However, this is not yet a widely recognised or used pedagogical strategy in schools and especially in teacher education, where pre-service teachers are seldom provided with opportunities to create original knowledge, building upon the work of previous cohorts, or to share and receive critical feedback from the wider public. This chapter explores how early years pre-service teachers might use mobile technologies and apps, like Book Creator and Puppet Pals, to enact meaningful knowledge-building strategies. It concludes with a summary of implications for teacher educators preparing pre-service teachers.

Keywords: Knowledge-building, knowledge-consumption, collaboration, early years, cognition, constructivism

Introduction

Mobile learning represents a paradigm shift that promises to transform the fixed and bounded certainties of traditional schooling with affordances that support more authentic, ubiquitous, and personalised ways of learning that 'tethered technologies' struggle to match (Kearney *et al.*, 2012; Traxler, 2009). And yet, the underlying structures, cultures, and practices of formal education have remained relatively impervious to the changes that proponents of mobile technologies imagine (Kearney *et al.*, 2015; Lindsay, 2015; Royle *et al.*, 2014). This is particularly evident in teacher education where the introduction of mobile learning has challenged, but not fundamentally changed, the core practices that underpin the preparation and development of new teachers (Baran, 2014; Burden, 2016; Royle *et al.*, 2014).

This chapter explores how the use of mobile technologies and apps supports knowledge-building and how this, in turn, challenges traditional models of early years pre-service teacher education. This amounts to a shift that privileges genuine knowledge creation rather than knowledge-consumption. It draws upon the examples of early years teachers using tablet devices and apps in schools and discusses the implications of these developments for teacher educators and their trainee students. In so doing, this chapter seeks to answer the following question: how can teacher educators harness the affordances of mobile technologies and apps to develop genuine knowledge-building communities?

The challenge of twenty-first-century learning

The transition to knowledge-based economies, combined with the complexity associated with the variety of global challenges facing societies – often referred to as 'wicked problems' since they are resistant to simplistic or predefined solutions (Borko *et al.*, 2009; Rittel and Webber, 1973) – have intensified calls from governments and supranational organisations alike, to enhance the knowledge-building capacities of their citizens (UNESCO, 2005; Hong *et al.*, 2010). There is, however, no agreed consensus on what students need to learn in order to function effectively in such a knowledge-based economy, or how they should learn it (So *et al.*, 2010). Twenty-first-century learning skills are promoted in some circles as one solution (see Fullan and Langworthy, 2013; Trilling and Fadel, 2009). This is a global initiative that promotes new skills and competencies associated with knowledge, such as authentic problem-solving. However, it has also been critiqued as a response based on twentieth-century conceptualisations of learning that fail to take full account of the opportunities afforded by the development of flexible, seamless learning spaces that transcend the traditional boundaries between formal and informal education (Royle *et al.*, 2014). These are now made possible by the affordances of ubiquitous technologies such as mobile phones and tablets, along with the seamless learning environments they engender (see Schuck *et al.*, 2016).

From constructivism to knowledge-building

The principle of constructing knowledge is not new, and many of the learning activities and tasks routinely undertaken in schools and colleges today share a common theoretical heritage with constructivism, which posits that learners construct knowledge and personal meaning out of their own experiences (Duffy and Jonassen, 1992). On a practical level, this is often described as 'learning-by-doing', and in many of its pedagogical instantiations it is described as a situated sociocultural activity, in which learners construct meaning as part of a complex ecosystem involving the cultural artefacts of their immediate surroundings, and their social interactions with other members of their group or society (Lave and Wenger, 1991; Wertsch, 1997). Although constructivism is a theoretical model, it has spurned numerous practical pedagogical approaches, including cooperative and collaborative learning, guided inquiry, project-based learning, and the concept of communities of practice (Lave and Wenger, 1991). What distinguishes knowledge-building from these pedagogical activities is the creation of original, progressive public knowledge, with an 'out-in-the-world character' (IKIT, n.d.).

Knowledge-building

Over a period of 25 years Scardamalia and Bereiter (1991; 1996; 2003; 2006) have developed the concept of knowledge-building, which they define as 'the production and continual improvement of ideas of value to a community, through means that increase the likelihood that what the community accomplishes will be greater than the sum of individual contributions' (Scardamalia and Bereiter, 2003, p. 1371). They contend that knowledge-building is distinct from traditional learning, which is focused on enhancing personal knowledge, since knowledge-building is 'a social, idea-centered process aimed at continually improving ideas represented as community knowledge' (Hong *et al.*, 2010, p. 4).

This type of collaborative activity involving both students and their tutors is not typically undertaken in schools or in teacher education, where learning is characterised instead by the accumulation and consumption of what is already known – rather than the construction of new knowledge and exploration of what is unknown (Scardamalia and Bereiter, 2006). Students are rarely afforded the opportunity to explore knowledge as an object in its own right (objectification), or to construct knowledge that is progressive in the sense that it makes an original contribution to the sum of human knowledge, building upon the work of previous students in a manner that is explicit and understood by learners themselves. Critically, a student's engagement with knowledge seldom leads to the synthesis of higher order representations, such as theory building or grand narratives, but instead to the proliferation of individual tasks and assessment artefacts that are not coherently or logically connected. Given these characteristics, schools have been labelled as 'asymptotic', first-order organisations, which impose a glass ceiling on the extent to which students utilise knowledge which sees them accumulate what is already known, but rarely rise above this, to construct original artefacts of understanding (Scardamalia and Bereiter, 2006). With a few exceptions, this is also the case in initial teacher education, where pre-service teachers are rarely engaged in genuine knowledge-building activities.

The role of technology in knowledge-building

Technology has been used in several ways to support knowledge-building, the most prominent being the Knowledge Forum developed in 1995 at the University of

Toronto, which is based on designs by Scardamalia and Bereiter. This is a computer-mediated communication technology (CMC), which supports shared discourse and collaborative knowledge-building using a variety of graphical tools to build higher-order representations and knowledge artefacts. It has been used extensively to support and capture networked social discourse that is central to the process of knowledge-building (Scardamalia and Bereiter, 2006). It provides students with a set of open-ended scaffolded prompts (e.g., 'I need to understand…' 'This theory cannot explain…'), which they post on the system using digital notes that can be modified and extended by their peers and other experts, thus building upon existing knowledge in order to create something original within the context it is exploring. The collaborative nature of the learning design, whereby students co-construct knowledge through communication, interaction, and discourse rather than as a solitary activity, distinguishes knowledge-building from traditional e-learning practices (Chan and Chan, 2011, p. 1446).

Since its introduction in 1995, empirical research has highlighted the benefits of the Knowledge Forum, including cognition gains, quality of collaboration, discourse, and the knowledge-building process itself (Scardamalia and Bereiter, 2006; Zhang *et al.*, 2009) both in Western and other cultural contexts (Chan and Chan, 2011; van Aalst and Chan, 2007). However, the high literacy threshold of the Knowledge Forum is still perceived by some to be a barrier for very young learners or those with reading difficulties (So *et al.*, 2010), and for those without access to suitable computers, meaning it has been almost impossible to use the software in non-formal settings where access to computers is restricted (So *et al.*, 2009).

Knowledge-building and mobile technologies

Until recently, the focus of technology-enhanced knowledge-building has been around fixed desktop computers in bounded classroom spaces (e.g., the Knowledge Forum) and relatively little research has been undertaken to explore how mobile technologies might support more flexible knowledge-building activities, in both formal and informal contexts. Research in games-based learning and situated cognition hints at the potential value of using mobile devices and augmented reality simulations to support students in constructing collaborative narratives as part of an inquiry-based science visit (e.g., see Squire and Klopfer, 2007). Other studies have also demonstrated the value of using mind-mapping software on mobile devices to construct complex ideas collaboratively (Hwang *et al.*, 2010; Hwang *et al.*, 2011), claiming considerable learning gains compared with traditional approaches.

Some of the most significant developments in this field, however, feature the exploration of knowledge-building *in situ*, where classroom teachers and researchers have worked in partnership to develop and evaluate learning trails that encapsulate the various phases of knowledge-building from idea generation to idea compare/contrast (So *et al.*, 2009). In one of these cases, students used a Google Map on their mobile device to locate and post original notes about various historical sites around Singapore. This enabled them and their peers to revisit these sites (both virtually and physically) to co-construct further knowledge and understanding on heritage sites that were previously undocumented. The researchers claim this ability to connect across contexts (both spatial and temporal) encouraged students to engage in greater depths of knowledge-building discourse than might be the case in a formal classroom setting. In a subsequent study, the same authors expanded upon their earlier work to develop situated learning trails in geography and history (So *et al.*, 2012).

Mobile knowledge-building in teacher education

Despite the growing popularity and use of mobile technologies in schools and by students as personal devices, the adoption of the so-called 'post-PC technologies' (Murphy, 2011) in teacher education – such as mobile phones and tablet devices, remains patchy and uneven, regarded by some with suspicion, concern, and even hostility (Royle *et al.*, 2014). Recent research reveals that while there is growing awareness and interest in mobile technologies in teacher education (Baran, 2014), this is mostly from innovators and early adopters and is far from reaching a tipping point whereby the use of these tools is considered an embedded practice (Thomas and O'Bannon, 2013). A recent international survey exploring the pedagogical uses of mobile technologies by teacher educators (Kearney *et al.*, 2015) revealed how most teacher educators used the devices to replicate existing pedagogical patterns. Few had fully grasped the opportunities to empower students with greater autonomy or to engage them in more connected networked activities through their devices (see Kearney *et al.*, 2012; Burden and Kearney, 2016), thereby exploiting many of the opportunities for seamless and unbounded learning that other studies have previously claimed (Toh *et al.*, 2013).

A model for mobile knowledge-building in teacher education

Initial teacher education is a complex activity requiring pre-service teachers to develop a wide variety of different knowledge-bases, skills, and dispositions, but most of these activities focus on the acquisition and application of existing knowledge, not the creation and sharing of new knowledge. The model (Figure 19.1) captures the essential features of the knowledge-building process defined as inputs, processes, and outputs.

The Knowledge Building Continuum (an original framework)

Inputs. These are contextual factors upon which knowledge-building activities are constructed. They foreground the importance of exploiting and progressing the existing knowledge-base, including previous work undertaken by students (1). This is rooted in the tacit knowledge learners bring with them, giving it personal

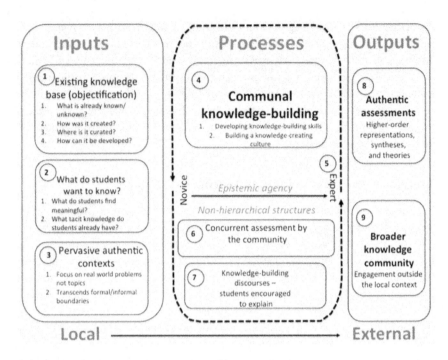

FIGURE 19.1 The Knowledge Building Continuum

Source: Adapted from Scardamalia (2002)

significance and meaning (2). Critically, tasks are set within authentic contexts that focus on genuine real-world problems addressed across both formal and informal settings (3).

Mobile technologies support many of these epistemological contexts. They enable students to spontaneously interrogate the known knowledge-base when confronted by a problem (e.g., watching a YouTube video posted by previous students), independent of spatial or temporal constraints. Through the use of social media and social networking, mobile devices can build a sense of continuity between current and previous cohorts or alumni, enabling progressive knowledge-building to flow. Finally, mobile technologies enable pre-service teachers to experience more authentic and pervasive contexts for knowledge-building since they act as 'boundary crossing objects' (Engeström *et al.*, 1995), supporting 'seamless learning' that pervades both formal and informal contexts.

Processes. Knowledge-building communities nurture highly collegial and egalitarian cultures that support members in developing their own skills and those of the community (4). This culture supports the transformation of novices into experts (5) while also acknowledging the importance of the 'outsider' perspective that novices bring with them. In this sense, construction of knowledge is non-hierarchical and all learners are invested with degrees of epistemic agency (5, 7). Assessment is concurrent, not simply summative (6), and all learners are encouraged to provide critical feedback on the knowledge artefacts whilst under development. This process is aided by dialogic discourse rather than the standard Initiate-Respond-Feedback (IRF) loop (7).

Mobile technologies and apps support these processes by providing the tools to make collaborative knowledge production less complex and therefore more egalitarian; by enabling learners and teachers to cooperate on a more equal basis, given their familiarity and use of social media and mobile technologies in their everyday lives; and by providing mechanisms to support concurrent assessment such as star ratings, recommendations, and favourites (e.g., Facebook). Apps and tools like Showbie also allow for a much richer form of dialogue between learners and teachers, which is dialogic rather than Socratic in nature.

Outputs. Knowledge-building communities aim to construct higher-order outputs that are holistic and authentic, in contrast to the typical assignment instruments used in teacher education that are loosely connected and often artificial. Critically, these outputs make an original contribution to knowledge, albeit at a local level (8). The criteria for originality is described as 'local' because it need only be original in the context of the institution or even the group: e.g., an original approach to teaching a difficult concept in a particular setting. However, for knowledge-building to be effective there must be an overt and well-understood process for learners to engage beyond the local context, in terms of sharing and receiving feedback on the products they have constructed (9).

Both the output artefact and the need to share these more widely with a critical audience can be supported with mobile technologies. Multimodal artefacts constructed with and on a mobile device are cognitively challenging, higher-order representations of knowledge. Given their highly situated affordances, mobile technologies enable pre-service teachers to construct original narratives in highly authentic contexts such as a school placement. In digital format it is more straightforward for students to share these artefacts with a larger audience and in doing so, to receive critical feedback and advice from a worldwide audience (e.g., through a YouTube channel).

The application of mobile knowledge-building in early years settings

For the purposes of this discussion early years is defined as 'the period of life from birth through age 8 years when growth and development is rapid' (Couse and Chen, 2010, p. 75). Although the use of technology by this age group is contentious (cf. Alliance for Childhood, 2010; Cordes and Miller, 2000; NAEYC, 2011), research demonstrates the value of digital technologies, especially for the purposes of motivation and engagement. In recent years, researchers have also focused attention on the use of mobile and touch-sensitive technologies, such as the iPad, in early years settings, although this is not commonly framed around knowledge-building. Nonetheless, mobile phones, tablet devices, and game consoles are an undeniable reality in many early childhood settings and, indeed, many children's homes (Verenikina and Kervin, 2011; Gardner and Davis, 2014). In studying the digital habits of very young learners outside of school, researchers have identified how children use apps and games like Minecraft and Sim City to engage in highly constructivist activities that bear strong resemblance to many of the knowledge-building features identified in this chapter, such as collaboration, task sharing, and mutual support between novices and experts, described here as epistemic agency (see, for example, Verenikina *et al.*, 2010). It is, therefore, increasingly important that pre-service teachers are aware of the cultural contexts and out-of-school digital habitus that many of the young children they will teach in formal school settings experience. The following section explores how knowledge-building can be supported through mobile apps in early years settings and concludes by identifying the implications of this activity for teacher educators and their students.

Knowledge-building apps in early years literacy settings

Traditionally, literacy in schools has been associated with text and the associated skills of reading, writing, listening, and speaking, but the concept of literacy is undergoing something of a transformation as it becomes associated with a much wider repertoire of practices that are multimodal in nature (see Yelland, 2011, p. 10 and Yelland, Chapter 5, this volume). In many respects, this shift from a purely textual definition of literacy also supports many of the principles of knowledge-building, since it draws learners into multimodal forms of meaning-making that young learners can control. This is evident across a range of apps like Book Creator and Puppet Pals that are used widely in early years settings and are designed to support constructivist pedagogies. They enable learners to build their own narratives and storylines by combining text, images, video, sound recordings, and handwriting in a simple interface that is intuitive and easy to learn. This can be undertaken individually, but in many cases it is completed in small groups, enabling young learners to build narratives collaboratively. Sandvik (2009) describes apps like these as multimedia 'scaffolds' for language and literacy learning, since they enable young learners to engage with multimodal texts that invite them to produce meaning for themselves. By contrast, many apps have a behaviourist orientation since they simply feed learners with information, which is the antithesis of knowledge-building.

Book Creator and Puppet Pals apps. Apps like Book Creator and Puppet Pals are widely used worldwide in early years settings, especially in the development of language and literacy skills. Both are intuitive to use with a simple point, click, and drag interface that alleviates many of the fine motor skill difficulties faced by young learners when they construct narratives with traditional media. Book Creator is a story-making app, that enables users to build their own multimodal books and narratives incorporating a wide range of different media (e.g. images, video clips, and sound) captured on the mobile device itself, or imported onto the device from an external source. Books can be of any length and users have the option of including drawings, handwriting, and their own voice (e.g., a narration) directly through the mobile device on which is it constructed, thereby ensuring this can be achieved with a minimal amount of external technical support or guidance. When completed, the books can be exported and shared in various formats that are readable on a wide variety of platforms.

Puppet Pals comes with a selection of pre-populated props, backgrounds, and story characters, although it is essentially content free, like Book Creator, since users are free to design their own narratives and to import their own images and props to construct their own stories. Users construct simple animations and stories by moving the characters and props around and recording these movements to play back as a continuous narrative. Like Book Creator, students can also use the microphone on their mobile device to record their own voice over the animations they have created, thereby constructing a multimodal narrative that can be exported as a short video clip to share with others.

Both apps simplify what would otherwise be a technically complex activity beyond the reach of most students, especially those in early years settings. There is no need for learners to master, or even fully understand, sophisticated or complex software such as video editing, animation, or sound recording, which would pre-viously restrict this kind of multimedia production to students in senior school or post-compulsory education. In this respect, apps like Book Creator and Puppet Pals function as 'cognitive amplifiers' (Nickerson, 2005) that enable even very young learners to access and manipulate knowledge at a level of cognitive sophistication that would not otherwise be possible for this age group. As Säljö points out in Chapter 1 of this book, this challenges traditional conceptualisations of instruction that assume learning is sequential and dependent on understanding the basic building blocks one by one.

Examples of these apps used in early years settings

Although few studies have examined the use of apps, like Book Creator and Puppet Pals, those that have done so reveal how 'cognitive amplifier' apps like these might be used to support knowledge-building approaches to learning in early years settings, and what the implications of these practices might be for pre-service teachers and their teacher educators (but see Chapter 6 in which Wohlwend and Rowsell analyse the twenty-first-century learning possibilities with Puppet Pals).

Inputs/context. It is not always evident from the research literature if, or how, practitioners use these kinds of app to link students with existing knowledge-bases in order to construct progressive knowledge, although one study using Puppet Pals did indicate that the teacher built upon children's existing understanding of fairy-tale folklore as a precursor to the activity (Sandvik *et al.*, 2012). Given the malleable characteristics of digital artefacts, it is feasible for teachers to use the outputs from a previous cohort of early years students (e.g., a digital book or story) as the starting point for new students. These are then challenged to extend the narrative (e.g., add another chapter) or re-work the existing text with additional information and insights, building upon the work of previous students as is the case in projects involving mature students working with these apps (cf. Naylor and Gibbs, 2015).

In effect, these artefacts grow into a living archive that stimulates future projects and inquiries.

Similarly, the use of these apps to construct narratives informed by personal experience, grounds the activity in the tacit knowledge and experiences learners bring with them, thus imbuing it with greater personal meaning and significance. Sandvik *et al.* (2012) refer to these meaning-making processes as 'literacy events' that involve not just texts but pictures, photographs, images, and video. Their significance for the individual learner is likely to be considerable, and this is further reinforced when it is set in an authentic and meaningful context, such as one project that required students to use their device to capture images of litter in the school playground, which then was used to construct an eBook about the local nature of a global problem. Students are able to use this kind of app on a mobile device outside of formal classroom settings to undertake situated knowledge-building, collecting digital artefacts, and commentaries in the field. A study of iPad use in Norway showed how kindergarten students were quite capable in using their iPads in this way to document the events of an excursion that was later used in class as the basis of a Puppet Pals narrative (Sandvik *et al.*, 2012).

Processes. Early years practitioners invariably design activities and experiences for their learners that involve collaboration and sharing, and these are also central features of communal knowledge-building. This is evident in the few research studies that explore the use of apps in early years settings (cf. Sandvik *et al.*, 2012; Flewitt *et al.*, 2014), but even more noticeable is the non-hierarchical organisation of tasks and activities associated with the use of these apps that suggest novices and experts work alongside each other and are both granted considerable epistemic agency in this respect. In the study cited previously, five-year-old children worked in small groups alongside their teacher to co-construct a narrative using the app Puppet Pals, as part of a project to enhance second language competency. More experienced users worked alongside beginners in this activity, but all were allowed equal access to the software, including the teacher. Säljö, Chapter 1 of this volume, describes this kind of interaction as an 'egalitarian interactional structure' that is characteristic of a genuine knowledge-building community.

Outputs. There is little or no explicit reference in these studies to the assessment procedures adopted, or the broader involvement of a public community to provide critical feedback to the creators, which are both essential elements in genuine knowledge-building communities. We might assume, however, that if these tasks are set in an authentic context that addresses real-world problems or issues, there is also likely to be an authentic audience who might provide critical feedback. In effect this is an integrated, authentic assessment procedure for the task, which might conceivably provide an opportunity to share the finished artefact with the public. In the case of the Puppet Pal study, the audience for the play was other young children in the school, who watched the performance projected onto a large screen. However, this could be extended by involving parents/grandparents as 'critical' reviewers, either in the school (e.g., by attending a class display of work) or virtually by means of the mobile device itself that students take home to be watched with their family.

Implications for teacher education

This chapter has identified how the theory of knowledge-building can be transferred into practice using the affordances of mobile technologies and a variety of simple apps to encourage students to develop original narratives and explanations. It has described an original model of knowledge-building using mobile devices that includes inputs, processes, and outputs. Although the practical examples are situated in early years settings, the model also has implications for how teacher educators prepare their students to become teachers. It demonstrates how the use of these apps on mobile devices is relatively simple and intuitive to learn, which suggests this type of pedagogical activity is likely to grow in importance in early years settings.

It is important, therefore, that teacher educators prepare their students to use mobile technologies in ways that support the knowledge-building strategies that have been described in this chapter. This involves role-modelling these practices themselves since this has been shown to be extremely effective in encouraging trainee students to adopt new pedagogical practices (Lunenberg et al., 2007). Teacher educators need to consider how they can ensure their students have opportunities to work with mobile technologies in settings that support knowledge-building activities, rather than simply using mobile devices as transmission tools for information that characterises the use of many apps on these devices. To achieve this, teacher educators may find it useful to audit their current practices with mobile devices using the knowledge-building model described in this paper. This may challenge them to reconsider how they currently approach their practice and in particular, to what extent they provide their students with the preconditions and support necessary to undertake genuine and original knowledge construction. Do they, for example, make explicit the work of previous cohorts of students, offering opportunities for new students to build progressively upon previous experiences? And to what extent are they prepared to work as co-authors with their students, sometimes in positions of expertise but also receptive to learning new ideas themselves as novices? Critically, they need to identify how the completed work of students can be distributed and shared with a larger audience outside of their immediate context, enabling students to receive critical feedback as knowledge-builders from a wider audience. Teacher educators may consider how they could use their existing networks and partnerships to facilitate such feedback, and this in turn would support trainee teachers in gaining a more authentic experience of what it is to be a global teacher in the digital world.

Finally, it would be disingenuous to ignore the issue of assessment since this is such a powerful and dominant driver in teacher education. Knowledge-building is closely aligned with notions of authentic assessment since it is predicated on a number of philosophical principles, such as the need to ensure activities draw upon students' existing real-world interests and backgrounds. Studies that have investigated the application of knowledge-building in teacher education (see Naylor and Gibbs, 2015) have identified the need to recognise and reward the processes as well as the final product, and this needs to be foregrounded by teacher educators if they wish to realise knowledge-building in their practices.

Conclusion

This chapter has outlined a pedagogical model for knowledge-building in initial teacher education that exploits the multimodal affordances of mobile technologies and intuitive apps like Book Creator and Puppet Pals. In reviewing how these apps and those like them are starting to be used in early years settings, it suggests that pre-service early years teachers need to be familiar and confident with the technologies and the philosophy that underpin their use in constructivist practices like this. The adoption of an explicit knowledge-building curriculum in initial teacher education would enhance the ability of pre-service teachers to support these practices, but it is also evident that some significant elements of knowledge-building require more careful consideration if this is not simply to be a replication of existing constructivist classroom activities. In particular, there is a need to give greater consideration to the assessment of the products students produce if they are to be genuinely authentic and therefore meaningful, and this is closely associated with the need to give further thought and consideration to how the final outputs produced through knowledge-building are shared with a genuine audience or public, in such a way to garner realistic and critical feedback that is used to improve future outputs.

Resolving such issues will be a necessary but not sufficient step forwards in shifting the dominant culture and attitudes of teacher educators, who perceive knowledge-building to be cognitively more demanding than learning existing knowledge. As Scardamalia and Bereiter point out:

> Creating new knowledge and learning existing knowledge are not very different as far as psychological processes are concerned. There is no patent reason that schooling cannot have the dynamic character of scientific knowledge-building. If there are insurmountable obstacles, they are more likely to be of a social or attitudinal than of a cognitive kind.
>
> (Scardamalia and Bereiter, 1996 p. 270)

References

Alliance for Childhood. (2010). *Campaign for a Commercial-free Childhood*. Retrieved from:: www.allianceforchildhood.org/

Baran, E. (2014). A review of research on mobile learning in teacher education. *Educational Technology and Society, 17*(4), 17–23.

Borko, H., Whitcomb, J. and Liston, D. (2009). Wicked problems and other thoughts on issues of technology and teacher learning. *Journal of Teacher Education, 60*(1), 3–7.

Burden, K. (2016). Barriers and challenges facing pre-service teachers use of mobile technologies for teaching and learning, *International Journal of Mobile and Blended Learning,* 8(2), 1–22.

Burden, K. and Kearney, M. (2016). Future scenarios for mobile science learning, *Research in Science Education, 46*(2), published online before print.

Chan, C. and Chan, Y. (2011). Students' views of collaboration and online participation in Knowledge Forum. *Computers and Education, 57*(1), 1445–1457. doi:10.1016/j.compedu. 2010.09.003

Cordes, C. and Miller, E. (2000). *Fools' Gold: A critical look at computers in childhood.* College Park, MD: Alliance for Childhood. Retrieved from: http://drupal6.allianceforchildhood. org/fools_gold

Couse, L. and Chen, D. (2010). A tablet computer for young children? Exploring its viability for early childhood education. *Journal of Research on Technology in Education, 43*(1), 75–96, DOI: 10.1080/15391523.2010.10782562

Duffy, T.M. and Jonassen, D. (eds) (1992). *Constructivism and the Technology of Instruction: A conversation.* Hillsdale NJ: Lawrence Erlbaum Associates.

Engeström, Y., Engeström, R. and Kärkkäinen, M. (1995). Polycontextuality and boundary crossing in expert cognition: Learning and problem solving in complex work activities. *Learning and Instruction, 5*(4), 319–336.

Flewitt, R., Messer, D. and Kucirkova, N. (2014). New directions for early literacy in a digital age: The iPad. *Journal of Early Childhood Literacy, 15*(3), 289–310.

Fullan, M. and Langworthy, M. (2013). *Towards a New End: New pedagogies for deep learning.* Washington: Collaborative Impact.

Gardner, H. and Davis, K. (2014). *The App Generation. How today's youth navigate identity, intimacy, and imagination in a digital world.* London: Yale University Press.

Hong, H., Scardamalia, M. and Zhang, J. (2010). Knowledge society network: Toward a dynamic, sustained network for building knowledge. *Canadian Journal of Learning and Technology/La Revue Canadienne De L'Apprentissage Et De La Technologie, 36*(1). Retrieved from: www.cjlt.ca/index.php/cjlt/article/view/579/282

Hwang, G. J., Shi, Y. R. and Chu, H. C. (2010). A concept map approach to developing collaborative Mindtools for context-aware ubiquitous learning. *British Journal of Educational Technology, 42*(5), 778–789.

Hwang, G. J., Chu, H. C., Lin, Y. S. and Tsai, C. C. (2011). A knowledge acquisition approach to developing Mindtools for organizing and sharing differentiating knowledge in a ubiquitous learning environment. *Computers and Education, 57*(1), 1368–1377.

IKIT, Institute for Knowledge Innovation and Technology. Retrived from: http://ikit.org/ kb.html

Kearney, M., Schuck, S., Burden, K. and Aubusson, P. (2012). Viewing mobile learning from a pedagogical perspective. *Research in Learning Technology, 20.*

Lave, J. and Wenger, E. (1991). *Situated Learning: Legitimate peripheral participation.* Cambridge: Cambridge University Press.

Lindsay, L. (2015). Transformation of teacher practice using mobile technology with one-to-one classes: M-learning pedagogical approaches. *British Journal of Educational Technology.* doi: 10.1111/bjet.12265

Lunenberg, M., Korthagen, F. and Swennen, A. (2007). The teacher educator as a role model. *Teaching and Teacher Education, 23*(5), 586–601.

Murphy, G. (2011). Post-PC devices: A summary of early iPad technology adoption in tertiary environments *e-Journal of Business Education and Scholarship of Teaching, 5(*1), 18–32.

NAEYC. (2011). *Technology in Early Childhood Programs Serving Children from Birth through*

Age 8. Draft position statement. Retrieved from: https://larrycuban.files.wordpress.com/2011/11/draft-technology-in-early-childhood-programs-4-29-2011-1.pdf

Naylor, A. and Gibbs, J. (2015). Using iPads as a learning tool in cross-curricular collaborative initial teacher education. *Journal of Education for Teaching, 41*(4), 442–446.

Nickerson, R. S. (2005). Technology and cognition amplification. In R. J. Sternberg and D. D. Preiss (eds), *Intelligence and technology. The impact of tools on the nature and development of human abilities* (pp. 3–27). Mahwah, NJ: Erlbaum.

Royle, K., Stager, S. and Traxler, T. (2014). Teacher development with mobiles: Comparative critical factors. *Prospect, 44*, 29–42.

Rittel, H. and Webber, M. (1973). Dilemmas in a general theory of planning. *Policy Sciences, 4* (2), 155–169.

Sandvik, M. (2009). Digitale læringsressurser – nye tekster, arbeidsmåter og muligheter. I: Østerud, S. (red.): Enter. *Veien mot en IKT-didaktikk.* Gyldendal Akademisk.

Sandvik, M., Smørdal, O. and Østerud, S. (2012). Exploring iPads in practitioners' repertoires for language learning and literacy practices in kindergarten. *Nordic Journal of Digital Literacy, 7*(3), 204–221.

Scardamalia, M. (2002). Collective cognitive responsibility for the advancement of knowledge. In B. Smith (ed.), *Liberal Education in a Knowledge Society* (pp. 67–98). Chicago, IL: Open Court.

Scardamalia, M. and Bereiter, C. (1991). Higher levels of agency for children in knowledge-building: A challenge for the design of new knowledge media. *The Journal of the Learning Sciences, 1*, 37–68.

Scardamalia, M. and Bereiter, C. (1994). Computer support for knowledge-building communities. *The Journal of the Learning Sciences, 3*(3), 265–283.

Scardamalia, M. and Bereiter, C. (1996). Engaging students in a knowledge society. *Educational Leadership, 54* (3), 6–10.

Scardamalia, M. and Bereiter, C. (2003). *Knowledge-building.* In *Encyclopedia of Education* (2nd ed., pp. 1370–1373). New York, NY: Macmillan Reference.

Scardamalia, M. and Bereiter, C. (2006). Knowledge-building: Theory, pedagogy, and technology. In K. Sawyer (ed.), *Cambridge Handbook of the Learning Sciences* (pp. 97–118). New York: Cambridge University Press.

Schuck, S., Kearney, M. and Burden, K. (2016). Exploring mobile learning in the Third Space. *Teaching, Pedagogy and Education, 25*(1), published online before print.

So, H. J., Seow, P. and Looi, C. K. (2009). Location matters: Leveraging knowledge-building with mobile devices and Web 2.0 technology. *Interactive Learning Environments, 17*(4), 367–382.

So, H. J., Seah, L. H. and Toh-Heng, H. L. (2010). Designing collaborative knowledge building environments accessible to all learners: Impacts and design challenges. *Computers & Education, 54*(2), 479–490.

So, H. J., Tan, E. and Tay, J. (2012). Collaborative mobile learning in situ from knowledge-building perspectives. *Asia-Pacific Education Researcher, 21*(1), 51–62.

Squire, K. and Klopfer, E. (2007). Augmented reality simulations on handheld computers. *Journal of the Learning Sciences, 16*(3), 371–413.

Thomas, K. and O'Bannon, B. (2013). Cell phones in the classroom: Preservice teachers' perceptions. *Journal of Digital Learning in Teacher Education, 30*(1), 11–20.

Toh, Y., So, H. J., Seow, P., Chen, W. and Looi, C. K. (2013). Seamless learning in the mobile age: A theoretical and methodological discussion on using cooperative inquiry to study digital kids on-the-move. *Learning, Media and Technology, 38*(3), 301–318.

Traxler, J. (2009). Learning in a mobile age. *International Journal of Mobile and Blended Learning, 1*(1), 1–12.

Trilling, B. and Fadel, C. (2009). *21st century skills: Learning for life in our times.* San Francisco, CA: John Wiley & Sons.

UNESCO. (2005). *Towards Knowledge Societies.* New York: UNESCO Publishing

van Aalst, J. and Chan, C. K. K. (2007). Student-directed assessment of knowledge-building using electronic portfolios in Knowledge Forum. *The Journal of the Learning Sciences, 16,* 175–220.

Verenikina, I., Herrington, J., Peterson, R. and Mantei, J. (2010). Computers and play in early childhood: Affordances and limitations. *Journal of Interactive Learning Research, 21*(1), 139–159.

Verenikina, I. and Kervin, L. (2011). iPads, digital play and pre-schoolers. *He Kupu, 2*(5), 4–19.

Wertsch, J. (1997). 16 Collective memory: Issues from a sociohistorical perspective. Mind, culture, and activity: *Seminal papers from the laboratory of comparative human cognition,* 226.

Yelland, N. (2011). Reconceptualising play and learning in the lives of young children, *Australasian Journal of Early Childhood, 36*(2), 4–12.

Zhang, J., Scardamalia, S., Reeve, R. and Messina, R. (2009). Designs for collective cognitive responsibility in knowledge-building communities, *Journal of the Learning Sciences, 18*(1), 7–44.

20

YOUNG CHILDREN IN AN EDUCATION CONTEXT

Apps, cultural agency and expanding communicative repertoires

Karen Daniels

SHEFFIELD HALLAM UNIVERSITY, UNITED KINGDOM

This chapter examines video recorded interactions of children's engagement with touchscreens in an early education setting. The extracts are taken from an ethnographic research study that explored children's expanding repertoires for meaning making as these emerged throughout their first year of school. The episodes presented in this chapter draw on observations of children's spontaneous interactions with and around two iPad apps. Findings reveal how children's engagement with iPads has the potential to simultaneously confer children's cultural agency and further expand children's repertoires for meaning making. The discussion that follows provides nuanced interpretations of how touchscreens might contribute positively to young children's early learning and play experiences.

Young children's use of technologies at home

Studies carried out in the home clearly illustrate that young children's meaning-making practices are shaped by their access to a range of digital resources. Marsh (2004) and Giddings (2014), for example, show how very young children engage with screens and digital texts in the home with playfulness, agency and creativity. When young children enter educational settings, many bring with them extensive understandings and experience of making meaning using digital tools (Yamada-Rice, 2011; Levy, 2009).

Despite compelling research evidence that touchscreens can support early learning and play, Yelland (2011) reminds us how digital technologies are still not seen by all as providing valuable play opportunities for children. Tensions still exist between some principles and practices of early learning and the use of screens with young children (Lynch and Redpath, 2014). In contrast to this view, Wolfe and Flewitt (2010) demonstrate how access to digital technologies in the home, mediated by adult support, can equip children with metacognitive strategies that enable them to engage with more sophistication with digital (and non-digital) tools in the classroom. The implication of these insights is that some children may be less well-equipped than others to utilise digital tools in meaningful ways. A long-standing concern expressed by educators and researchers is founded on the dissonances that exist between young children's language socialisation in the home and its relationship with success in school (see Heath, 1983). This concern is further complicated when access to meaningful engagement with digital resources is brought to the discussion. Indeed, the ways in which we judge the appropriateness of touchscreens as part of young children's early educational experiences will have a profound impact on the range and type of experiences to which children have access. It is vital, therefore, that early years practitioners recognise and respond to the findings in research into digital technologies (McPake, Ploughman and Stephen, 2012) in order that they can build on children's daily experiences and provide opportunities for children to access digital technologies as part of their early education experiences.

Cultural agency and semiotic resources

In order to provide a theoretical frame for the observations that follow, I will bring together a social semiotic conceptualisation of young children's learning with understandings of young children's cultural agency as described by Corsaro (2005). Elsewhere, I have examined the ways in which young children's peer cultures emerge in their play and learning experiences in school settings (Daniels, 2014; forthcoming). I argue that in order to understand early learning more fully, we need to view children's activity through an expanded lens that takes into account the range of semiotic resources that children use in order to make meaning, express cultural agency and create peer cultures. In this chapter, I apply this framework to explore children's interactions around iPad apps in order to explore how such activity might confer young children's cultural agency and simultaneously expand their semiotic resources for meaning-making.

I draw on naturalistic observations of young children's interactions with and around touchscreens, in order to examine:

- the features of the communication orchestrated during collaborative engagement around touchscreens;
- the ways in which children's agentic use of apps might confer cultural agency; and
- how both of the above might culminate in the expansion of children's communicative repertoires.

In the examples of data provided and the discussion that follows, children are seen as cultural agents who express their agency through their meaning-making activity. The work of Corsaro (2005) demonstrates how children innovatively and creatively participate in society by appropriating information from the adult world to address their own peer concerns. Here, children can be seen to be doing more than merely internalising the adult world, but instead acting upon it and changing it in some way, and, in turn, creating their own peer cultures. When playing, children express cultural agency as they infuse their activity with their experiences of texts, stories, games, popular culture figures and other experiences gained at home and in school. Key to the ensuing exploration in this chapter is that children are cultural agents, which implies acknowledging children's agency in their interactions with iPad apps. In particular, I look closely at the ways in which this agency is expressed, or comes into being, through children's interactions with the iPad apps, in order to explore how these interactions might facilitate children's peer cultures.

Young children's activity is guided predominantly by synaesthetic activities, which draw upon all the senses and use visual, kinaesthetic and gestural modes (Kress, 1997). Playful engagement with the world enables children to draw on social practices, explore the material qualities of images and objects and construct social spaces multimodally, for example, through talk, gaze, gesture and sound (Wohlwend, 2015). Acknowledging a social semiotic perspective on young children's playful interaction with the world provides a lens through which to view their agency, and view this as a process of learning and development. Kress (2010) reminds us that, 'as the child engages with meaning-making engagement with an aspect of the world, their resources for making meaning and therefore, acting in the world, are changed - they are augmented' (p. 175). The collaborative orchestration of communicative practices that take place during this playful activity manifest as an expression of children's cultural agency, and such activity shapes their peer cultures. This lens of interpretation of young children's meaning-making activity is essential to this study, as learning and development are now intimately connected to the types of meaning-making tools available, and a child's increasing mastery of these tools (Kress, 2010).

Gesture, touch and semiotic repertoires

When we consider the multimodal affordances of touchscreens alongside a social semiotic view of play and learning, it is not surprising that such devices are appealing to very young children and can foster positive play, support child development and offer novel ways of interacting (Geist, 2012). Kucirkova et al. (2013, 2014), for example, demonstrate how interactions around a personalised story-sharing app involve the orchestration of gesture, gaze, posture and facial expression. Furthermore, the authors note how the materiality of touchscreens is significant to the interactions that take place around them. Walsh and Simpson (2014) refer to the significant communicative tools of gesture and touch and how these are brought to the fore during touchscreen interactions. Similarly, Merchant (2014) identified the important role of the hands and the body as a group of toddlers and their facilitating practitioner interacted around an iPad app. Merchant (2014) developed a typology of hand and body movements that typically occur in such contexts. These include stabilising movements, where a child uses hands and/or knees to hold/support the iPad, control movements, for example, precision tapping and swiping and deictic movements, which refer to pointing gestures directing attention to the screen.

The study: context of the episodes and data selection

As is recommended practice in the Early Years Foundation Stage (DFE, 2012), the statutory curriculum for children from birth to five in England, the children in this study had access to a range of carefully selected and organised resources that they could use freely for extended periods of time during the school day. There were twenty-eight children aged four and five in the class. The class teacher had selected from a range of available apps and downloaded these onto the three iPads provided by the setting for this classroom. From these apps, the children could select freely. The apps examined in this chapter include Toca Robot Lab by Toca Boca© (see Figure 20.1) and Story Maker by Lego Friends©. Toca Robot Lab enables the children to build a robot and guide the robot through a maze, collecting stars as he or she is propelled along by the game player, towards the shipping unit. Lego Story Maker© allows children to design a multimodal narrative, selecting from a range of character images, accessories and story settings. It has editing and read aloud functions, with the possibility of adding speech and music.

FIGURE 20.1 Building a Robot: Toca Robot Lab by Toca Boca©

Methodology: Data collection, selection and analysis

I collected data by using a small hand-held camera, with the intention to capture both children's facial expressions and actions, and also the screen of the iPad. I followed the children's movements and choices around the classroom, filming their activity. Data selection involved repeated observation of the film clips, followed by the multimodal transcription of short selected episodes of activity. This facilitated close examination of children's communicative practices in individual episodes and across episodes.

Coding of activity in a table format (see Tables 20.1–20.3) enabled the filmed episodes to be transcribed and analysed. Speech was recorded first to give sequence to the episode; haptics and gaze transcribed afterwards. Key activity on the screen of the iPad that followed and prompted children's responses is also transcribed. In order to draw particular attention to the role of haptics in the communicative repertoires, I drew on Merchant's (2014) typology of hand movements, focusing on deictic and control movements. Transcribing in this way facilitated analysis of the orchestration of communicative resources taking place during the interactions. Each table then, is a representation of how activity developed moment-by-moment, in time sequence.

To interpret the tables, one needs to look at the activity, which is recorded chronologically from the top of the table downwards. By looking horizontally, children's simultaneous orchestration of communicative resources can be seen. Looking vertically outlines the sequence of events. In this way, insights into the orchestration of communicative resources prompted by the iPad app and the children's actions can be explored. Each table is preceded by a narrative observation to provide context to the information in the table. This is taken from my observational notes during the fieldwork. Permission from the parents and school was gained to film the children, and negotiated ongoing assent (Flewitt, 2006) was secured from children during the filming episodes.

Findings: Observing play and apps

Episode 1: Louise, Sally, Mazie and Kehinde building a robot

Louise, Sally, Mazie and Kehinde, who regularly play together, are sitting in the carpet area of the classroom during a morning session. Louise is holding the iPad, to her right are Mazie and Sally and to her left is Kehinde. All eyes are on the iPad and Louise holds it with both hands and is resting it on her knees (stabilising movement). The robot is on the screen and currently it has a body and legs. The task now is to complete the robot by sliding the selection panel at the bottom of the screen and to select from an array of possible heads and arms. These require the user to drag and drop (control movement) the chosen limb/body part into position. At this point, the app makes a short and sudden electronic sound 'czzzt' as parts of the robot fix into position.

TABLE 20.1 Building a robot

Speech/gaze	App	Movement: precision tapping/swiping (control)	Movement: deictic/ gestural	Commentary
Mazie: *Oh! Have that one then!* Mazie: *Why don't you have that one… that funny one…?* Children watch silently Kehinde sings: *Know that, know that… I've got the look…* Mazie: *That one! That one!* Sally: *That one!* Girls watch robot Mazie: *Same!* Sally: *Yea!* Girls watch robot, look to each other and smile	Czzzt! Czzzt! Head is 'fixed' into position on screen. Eyes blink intermittently Arm clicks into position: Czzzt! Arm clicks into position: Czzzt! Robot on screen blinks twice: Czzzt!	Touches sliding bar at bottom of page Louise selects head indicated by Mazie, and drags and drops into position Louise: Touches screen and moves selection bar from side-to-side Louise: Selects a rainbow patterned arm and drags and drops it into position Louise: Selects second arm, matching rainbow pattern, and places it on the other side of the robot's body	Mazie points to app Louise: Finger hovers over bar, poised to make a selection Louise: Hand hovers over the robot arm selection bar at the bottom of the screen Sally: Points to robot arm	Louise takes-up Mazie's suggestion of the 'funny' head Blinking of robot draws their silent attention to the app/ mirrored gesture and gaze across group Kehinde's song here seems to be celebrating the robot's appearance – acknowledging Louise's choice Louise responds to Sally and Mazie's suggestion. Sally's pointing prompts Louise's action Again – girls watching the fixing of the robot arm – watching carefully as it moves into position. Mazie acknowledging Louise's choice. Sally agreeing The robot blink is anticipated, and the girls enjoy the event and acknowledge this to each other

In this episode it is clear that the children are confident in their use of control movements for the app's operation – in this case the drag-and-drop function. The theme of building a robot is certainly appealing to the children and it is apparent that they have enjoyed this activity many times before as they anticipate the robot's responses. The children point and gesture while the building of the robot is taking place, offering suggestions and ideas. What stands out in this episode is how Mazie, Kehinde and Sally not only make suggestions, but also acknowledge the actions of Louise as she makes her own decisions. It is clear that although Louise is operating the app, it is by no means a solitary activity. As they enjoy the shared experience of building the robot, the camaraderie between the girls, seemingly prompted by the opportunity to make collaborative choices that incur visual and auditory responses for the iPad, emerges and is sustained. What we also see here then is an example of how the deictic movement of hovering over the app appears to communicate Mazie's choice before she has made it. This appears to fuel anticipation amongst the group, which in turn further prompts engagement with the app. Once the robot is given arms, it blinks twice and comes to life. The anticipated and lived emotional satisfaction of this culminating event begins with a moment of silence and stillness as the children look at the screen, which is reciprocated across the group as the girls look to each other and smile.

Episode 2: Blaise and Harry steer the robot: Toca Robot Lab by Toca Boca©

Blaise and Harry are at a later stage in the Toca Robot Lab game sequence. The aim of the game now is to guide the robot through the maze, taking him to the shipping unit, following the white arrows, and gathering stars along the way. The pair have been playing this game for some time now, sitting in the carpet area side-by-side. Blaise is stabilising the iPad using his knees and at times his left and/or right hands are placed either side of the iPad. In order to keep the robot moving, and to prevent it from falling down deeper into the maze, he is continually swiping it across and up the iPad 'page'.

We can see in this episode how Blaise, confident in the haptic skills needed to operate the app, is exploring the app in a playful way, enjoying 'failing' the mission to watch the robot fall back down into the maze, almost subverting the object of the app. He confidently uses both hands to speed up this part of the game, moving quickly towards the part of the game he is enjoying – the robot's tumble down the maze. He repeatedly draws Harry in to watch this sequence, and appears to link it to his experience of computer games as he is on a 'mission'. Again, although Blaise is carrying out most of the control movements, we can see how he draws Harry into the activity. He links the exaggerated haptic movements to sweep the robot up the screen, to the gesture of throwing his hands up towards his head. Harry watches this merging of control movement and gesture intently. Blaise is keeping Harry involved and Harry is duly entertained.

TABLE 20.2 Steering a robot

Speech/gaze	App	Movement: precision tapping/swiping (control)	Movement: deictic/gestural	Commentary
Blaise: *Watch it! Watch … this!* Harry (looking at screen): *And then he'll be trapped!!* Blaise: *AARRGH!* Harry: *Oh!* Harry: *Ah!* Blaise: *I like that bit!* Harry: *Can I have a go now?* Blaise: *Watch it! Watch it! After I have completed this mission*	Robot moving rapidly vertically up the screen Robot begins to tumble down, deep into the maze	Blaise: Guides the robot from left to right across the screen, swiping with forefinger Blaise drags the robot to the right of the screen, disregarding the white arrows Blaise: Begins to swipe upwards using left and right forefingers alternately Blaise: Positions the robot over a long vertical drop in the maze Blaise: Guides robot back up the maze using left and right hand swiping movements	Harry: Leans in closer to screen. Clasping hands together Blaise: Quickly pulls both hands away from screen, dramatically raising them up above his head. Harry: Leans closer to the screenLooks to Blaise	Harry's body language and gesture signalling his involvement Blaise is subverting the game here Blaise speeding up the movement of the robot Harry: Predicting what might happen Blaise's drama and quick glances to Harry, show how he is checking he has his attention Blaise screams as if he is the falling robot….The quick succession of their exclamations take place as the robot is falling Harry signalling his interest Blaise decides to repeat this sequence. He is speeding up the movement – using both hands. Blaise maintaining Harry's attention… Uses word from gaming experience

Episode 3: Josie and Jane: Let's make a pop group! Story Maker by Lego Friends©

Josie and Jane are sitting in the book area of the classroom on a small bench – an informal place where children frequently share books or just chat. Josie is balancing the iPad on her knee with a classmate sitting either side of her. I recognise Lego Friends Story Maker©. Josie turns the screen to me and uses the arrow icon in the corner of the screen, revealing a page called 'My Book Title'. Jane reaches across, extends her finger and presses the 'person' icon on the screen. A menu array of possible story characters appears at the bottom of the screen. Josie turns the iPad back towards her and settles it onto her knees (stabilising movement). Jane and Josie are negotiating which characters to choose from the slide bar menu. Jane accidently selects the story setting selection menu.

In this third episode, children were developing haptic skills necessary to access the app. They used the drag-and-drop function to select images, and Josie made some attempts to resize and re-align images. The complexity of this app did appear to be beyond the reach of the children, and the activity around it focused on selecting characters and accessories and did not progress beyond this. What appeared

FIGURE 20.2 Making a pop group

TABLE 20.3 Josie makes a pop group

Speech/gaze	App	Movement: precision tapping/swiping (control)	Movement: deictic/gestural	Commentary
Josie: *No!... Persons!* Jane: *Boy... boy... boy* Jane: *My big sister has got that other person. There!* Josie: *Err...* Jane: *Get her a doggie!* Josie: *Need her! She's nice look!* Jane: *She can be a kid!* Josie: *Yes – she's the singer...* Jane: *Get a microphone for her...* Josie: *What about a handbag? No!* Jane: *Get her a doggie!*	Characters re-appear at bottom of page Another character is aligned on screen Five characters now aligned on screen Centre character is now holding a guitar	Josie: Reselects row of people Josie: Selects and aligns another character Josie: Slides row of possible characters from side-to-side with right index finger Josie: Selects and draws a person to array Uses thumb and forefinger to realign and resize characters Josie: Selects, drags and drops a guitar onto middle person in array	Josie pulls her hands away from screen Josie: Re-adjusts iPad on knees (stabilising movement) Josie: Moves hands away from screen – outstretches arms Josie: Moves hands back to iPad and re-stabilises Jane: Points to character on array Josie: Moves Jane's hand away and points back to screen Jane: Points to array at bottom of screen Jane: Points to accessory icon	Josie signalling her exasperation at Jane's intervention – she wants the character choices menu back Josie resisting Jane's attempt to make a choice Jane repeats 'boy' three times to assert her choice Jane drawing on home experiences Josie persuading Jane which characters they need for the pop group Jane has taken up Josie's intentions here... Jane persists with her suggestion

significant were the ways in which the children drew upon the haptic skills they had already mastered, and attributed their own understandings and experiences in order to generate a meaningful shared experience with the app. Josie, for example, drew on her cultural and media experiences of Lego characters and of pop groups and the objects and accessories they may have. By contrast, Jane appears to want to create a family scene, with a 'boy' and a 'doggie'. We can see how Josie draws from her knowledge of pop groups, and selects characters to join the on-screen array.

She knows about what pop bands might need and the accessories a girl band might want to have. She resists Jane's suggestion to add a 'doggie' to the line-up, or to select a 'boy' member of the band. Josie makes direct reference to particular characters in the app. The comment 'My sister has got that one', seems to refer to familiar characters in other *Lego Friends* apps. Josie was clearly the most demonstrative member of the group, and she used her repertoire of communicative resources in order to steer the direction of the play. She appeared to exaggerate the stabilising movements needed to hold the iPad as a way of expressing this. Her stabilising movement moved into the gesture of throwing her hands into the air. Jane intervened and persisted in providing suggestions to shape the direction of the play, and although Josie resisted these, she continued to follow Josie's choices, taking these into account.

Discussion: Apps in the classroom – possible sites for collaborative cultural engagement and expanding communicative repertoires

In this chapter, I explored episodes where children spontaneously and playfully took up touchscreens in order to examine the communicative repertoires that are orchestrated through such activity. What was clear across all three episodes was the way in which children collaboratively brought peer interests and concerns to the app, and the ways in which this shaped the ways the app was used and what the app *became* in the classroom. We have seen how children collaboratively interact around apps and as they do so, the app offers an opportunity for creative engagement as the children learn to control it, explore its possibilities and imbue it with meanings significant to them. In this way, the apps become a site for engagement amongst peers where friendships, relationships and shared interests emerge. These shared interests culminate in the emergence of children's peer cultures for this group, as they bring their experiences, their concerns and their interests to the activity. In turn, they transform such activity into an activity that is relevant and significant to their own lives. Children's desire to build friendships and bring their shared and individual experiences to the episodes drove much of the interaction. Blaise drew on his knowledge and language of gaming to predict what might happen to the robot as he frantically tried to keep it moving. His deliberate 'mistakes', causing the robot crash to the bottom of the maze, and his exaggerated haptic control movements as he rapidly swiped the robot upwards, were with the intention of entertaining his friend, Harry. In Episode 3, Josie, stabilising the iPad, appears to be the dominant decision-maker in this episode. She claims territory, expressing her knowledge and experience from outside school, gained from spending time with her older sister. Apparent in all the episodes is the good humour and the 'togetherness' with which the children created activity meaningful to them as they played with the apps.

The ways in which children collectively transformed the apps through their activity is only part of the story. The iPads and apps prompted the children's interests and a range of semiotic resources, including touch, facial expression, gesture, talk and movement as they played together with and around the iPad. The potential for meaning-making brought to the fore via the use of deictic, control and stabilising movements (Merchant, 2014) and its orchestration with other semiotic resources, such as speech and facial expression, was significant in that it provided children with opportunities to explore and extend their communicative repertoires. When applying Merchant's typology of hand movements to these examples, we can see how the deictic movements that spontaneously arise, often prior to a control movement, are interpreted by the children, and how they become shared anticipated events. In Episode 1, Maizie, Kehinde and Sally quickly anticipated and interpreted the ideas and intentions of others through the gestures that took place, and how these were often prompted or lead into the haptic 'actions' needed to operate the app. Episode 3 illustrates how the very demonstrative Josie used deictic movements and stabilising movements, not only to control the iPad, but also to communicate her dominant role in the group. It is evident how swiftly and seamlessly these young children integrated such movements into their repertoires, blending what they know and what they can already do, with more novel ways of expression brought about by touchscreen interactions.

What was noticeable in this study, was that even when children were presented with apps that were linear or closed, the children often transformed them into experiences with a multiplicity of meanings and choices. This was achieved through children's playfulness and through their fluid management of meaning as it emerged moment-by-moment. At times, this appeared to occur because of the children's lack of knowledge of the 'right way' to operate the app, as in Episode 3. This playfulness and shared management of meaning conferred and secured their peer cultures and provided them with opportunities to collaboratively share and extend their communicative repertoires. Furthermore, this activity reflected and provided children with the opportunity to try out a broader set of meaning-making practices that linked to their shared cultural experiences.

I argue that the possibilities of touchscreen technologies may, as yet, not be altogether realised in many early years classrooms. Apps used in classrooms often have very specific pedagogical goals in mind: for example, to support skills in early literacy and numeracy. If we are to further our understanding of the learning potential of such devices, we may need to look beyond such goals when we observe children's interactions with and around touchscreens.

References

Corsaro, W. (2005). *The Sociology of Childhood*. Thousand Oaks, CA: Pine Forge Press.

DFE. (2012). Statutory Framework for the Early Years Foundation Stage. Available at: http://webarchive.nationalarchives.gov.uk/20130401151715/https://www.education.gov.uk/publications/standard/allpublications/page1/dfe-00023-2012 (accessed 19 July 2016).

Daniels, K. (2014). Cultural agents creating texts: a collaborative space adventure. *Literacy*, 48(2):103–11.

Daniels, K. (forthcoming). Exploring enabling literacy environments: young children's spatial and material encounters in early years classrooms. *English in Education.* Available at: http://onlinelibrary.wiley.com/doi/10.1111/eie.12074/abstract (accessed 19 July 2016).

Flewitt, R. (2005). 'Conducting research with young children: some ethical considerations'. *Early Child Development and Care,* 175(6):553–65.

Geist, E. (2012). 'A qualitative examination of two year-olds interactions with tablet based interactive technology.' *Journal of Instructional Psychology,* 29(1):26–35.

Giddings, S. (2014). *Gameworlds: Virtual Media & Children's Everyday Play.* New York: Bloomsbury.

Heath, S. B. (1983). *Ways With Words: Language, Life and Work in Communities and Classrooms.* New York: Cambridge University Press.

Kress, G (2010). *Multimodality: A social semiotic approach to contemporary communication.* London: Routledge.

Kress, G (1997). *Before Writing: Rethinking the paths to literacy.* New York: Routledge.

Kucirikova, N., Messer, D., Sheehy, K. and Flewitt, R. (2013). Parent–child narrative accompanying a personalized iPad story. *Literacy,* 47(3):115–22.

Kucirkova, N., Sheehy, K. and Messer, D. (2014). A Vygotskian perspective on parent-child talk during iPad story sharing. *Journal of Research in Reading.* Available at: http://online library.wiley.com/doi/10.1111/1467-9817.12030/abstract (accessed 18 July 2016).

Levy, R. (2009). *You Have to Understand Words ... But Not Read Them.* In Young children becoming readers in a digital age. *Journal of Research in Reading,* 32(1):75–91.

Lynch, J. and Redpath, T. (2014). 'Smart' technologies in early years education: A meta-narrative of paradigmatic tensions in iPad use in an Australian preparatory classroom. *Journal of Early Childhood Literacy* 14(2):147–74.

McPake, J., Plowman, L. and Stephen, C. (2012). Pre-school children creating and communicating with digital technologies in the home. *British Journal of Educational Technology* 44(3):421–31.

Marsh, J. (2004). The techno-literacy practices of young children. *Journal of Early Childhood Research* 2(1):51–66.

Merchant, G. (2014). Keep taking the tablets, iPads, story apps and early literacy. *Australian Journal of Language and Literacy* 38(1):3–11.

Walsh, M. and Simpson, A. (2014). Exploring literacies through touch pad technologies: The dynamic materiality of modal interactions. *Australian Journal of Language and Literacy* 37(2):96–105.

Wohlwend, K. (2015). Making, remaking and reimagining the everyday: Play, creativity and popular media. In J. Rowsell and K. Pahl (eds) *Routledge Handbook of Literacy Studies.* London: Routledge.

Wolfe, S. and Flewitt, R. (2010). New technologies, new multimodal literacy practices and young children's metacognitive development. *Cambridge Journal of Education* 40(4):387–99.

Yamada-Rice, D. (2011). New media, evolving multimodal literacy practices and the potential impact of increased use of the visual model in the urban environment on young children's learning. *Literacy* 45(1):32–43.

Yelland, N. (2011). Reconceptualising play and learning in the lives of young children. *Australian Journal of Early Childhood* 36(2):4–12.

INDEX

ABC Spy 262
absenteeism 133
access points 10–11
ACCT (Analysing Children's Creative Thinking) 211
ADHD (attention deficit hyperactivity disorder) 17, 169
adult-directed information 46, 50–2, 54
advertising 8, 17, 260
affordability 176, 194, 221, 237, 261
affordances 6, 9, 11, 40, 70; AR 210; bilingualism 169; BYOD 192–4, 203; cultural agency 282; digital play 226, 230; disabilities 176, 182, 187; empirical evidence 119; future adventures 220–1; mathematics 137, 139–40, 143–4; self-regulation 113; teacher education 265–6, 271, 275–6
agency 140, 220, 227, 255, 270, 272, 274, 280–92
AirWatch 259
Alberta Education 193
Allen, P. 64
alphabet 30, 35, 43, 47, 184, 209
Amazon Appstore 44–5
Amazon Marketplace 39
American Academy of Pediatrics 15
amygdala 16
Anderson, L.W. 235, 240
Android 195

Angry Birds Star Wars 184
animation 28–31, 75, 78–80, 82, 84, 91, 122, 142, 148, 152–4, 273
Answer Garden 160
App Review Board 92
App Store 10, 39, 44–6, 143, 186
Apple 10, 39, 44, 46, 92, 107, 122–4, 132, 219, 258
apps 7–8, 11, 62, 74–9, 81; activities 51; AR 119, 207–18; BYOD 186, 192–206; chat 11; comparison 85–6; cultural agency 280–92; disabilities 175–91; e-books 89; empirical evidence 117–20; evaluation 21; examples 261–2, 266, 273–5; first principles 27, 32–6; future adventures 219–22; home learning 15–26; industry 8, 119, 258; innovation 252–64; instructional uses 9–10; inter-apps 257–9, 261–3; intra-apps 252–64; knowledge-building 265–79; literacy 75–81, 84–7; maps 40, 73–88; market scan 42–55; mathematics 121–33, 135–46; participatory literacies 85–7; self-regulation 102–16; skill development 235–51; sociocultural perspective 3–14; storytelling 10, 47, 75, 92, 138, 215, 254; student thinking 235–51; teacher education 265–79; touch screen design 89–101; trans-apps 252–64

AR (augmented reality) 119, 207–18, 220–1, 223–32, 261–2, 268
AR Flashcards 209–10, 213–14
Archer, K. 41, 102–16, 262
assessment 1, 12, 29, 34–5, 45; app maps 76, 78; bilingualism 171; BYOD 196; disabilities 177–8, 186; e-books 150, 155; empirical evidence 118; future adventures 209, 211; market scan 45; mathematics 122–4, 127, 129–30, 132; self-regulation 102–4, 111; skill development 236–7, 248; teacher education 267, 270–1, 274–6
assistive technology 176–7
attachment theory 19
Attard, C. 142
Au, K.H. 164
audio recording 81, 84–5, 91–4, 118–19, 137–8; AR 214; bilingualism 166–7, 169–71; BYOD 195, 204; digital play 229; e-books 150; future adventures 220; skill development 238–9; teacher education 272–3; trans/intra-apps 255
audits 275
Aurasma 210, 214
Australia 39, 58, 61, 90
autism 17, 169, 208
autonomy 86–7, 164, 254, 269
avatars 227, 229, 255

Baccaglini, A. 142
Bai, Z. 208
Bandura, A. 19
Barab, S.A. 194
Bats! Furry Fliers of the Night 28
before-during-after (BDA) framework 32
behaviourism 4, 272
benchmarks 50, 52–4, 81, 86
Bereiter, C. 267–8, 276
best practice 143, 258
bias 54
Big 6 Inquiry Framework 236
bilingualism 118, 163–74
biology 4–5
blogging 36, 75, 77, 195, 258–9
Blogspots 36
Bloom's Taxonomy 105, 236–7, 240, 255
Blue's Clues 50
Bolter, J.D. 91
Book Creator 169, 272–3, 276

books 3, 5, 9, 60, 62; action 35–6; app maps 76, 84–5; AR 209; bilingualism 166–7, 169, 171; book industry 33; bookapps 28; BYOD 203; challenges 28–9, 35; empirical evidence 117–20; first principles 27–36; foundations 29–32, 35; home learning 19; market scan 43–5; meaning-making 147–62; new learning 64, 70; picture books 89–101; self-regulation 105, 107–8, 110–11; touch screen design 89–101; trans/intra-apps 253–7, 259–60, 262
Bretherton, I. 228
Bryant, B.R. 176
Building Empathy 66
Burden, K. 220–1, 265–79
Burnett, C. 86
Bus, A.G. 148
business models 257–9
buttons *see* hotspots
BYOD (bring your own devices) 59, 119, 186, 192–206, 237

Caillou: What's that funny noise? 118, 151, 153–4
Calder, N. 117–18, 135–46
calendars 5, 8
Calm Counter 22
cameras 8, 69, 75, 83–5, 103, 107, 111, 150, 200, 214, 243, 284
Camouflage Field Book 169
Campbell, A. 139
Canada 41, 103, 258, 263
Canadian Association for Teacher Education 41
caregivers 15, 18–20, 49, 54, 89; AR 210; bilingualism 171; disabilities 176, 179, 186, 188; e-books 89, 98, 151
Carr, J. 136
Carrington, A. 105
cartoons 83–4, 240, 259
Cascales, A. 209
cerebral palsy 175–91
certificates 123
challenges 28–9, 35, 39–41, 61, 70; bilingualism 164, 172; BYOD 193; future adventures 219–20; mathematics 122; skill development 244, 246; teacher education 266, 273, 275
change knowledge 57

character education 58
CHAT (Codes for the Human Analysis of
    Transcripts) 151
checklists 33
Chichewa language 124, 129–30
child development 9–11, 15, 22–3, 50, 54;
    characteristics 20–1; cultural agency
    282; digital play 231; disabilities 182;
    market scan 50, 54; social-emotional
    19–23; thinking 235–51
CHILDES (Child Language Data
    Exchange System) Project 151
Children's Technology Review 45, 260
Chile 42
China 153
Christie, J.F. 229
Churches, A. 105
citizenship 11, 32, 40, 57–60
clay tablets 5
cloud servers 195
Club Penguin 229
cognitive amplifiers 11, 273
cognitivism 4, 15–16
collaboration 4, 10, 40, 57, 60; app maps
    74–5, 80, 83–5; bilingualism 168, 170–1;
    BYOD 194–5, 200; cultural agency
    281–2, 286, 290–1; disabilities 179;
    empirical evidence 117–20; future
    adventures 219–22; mathematics 132,
    137–8, 142; new learning 64, 70;
    self-regulation 102–4, 106, 110, 113–14;
    skill development 236–8, 248; teacher
    education 267–8, 271–2, 274;
    trans/intra-apps 256, 262
Colquhoun, C. 76
Common Sense Media 23, 44, 260
communication 5–6, 9, 11, 19, 28; app
    maps 86; AR 210; bilingualism 164;
    BYOD 194–5; challenges 40; cultural
    agency 280–92; digital play 228;
    disabilities 176–7, 188; e-books 149,
    156; empirical evidence 119; expanding
    repertoires 280–92; first principles 32;
    mathematics 138, 142, 144; new
    learning 57, 59–60, 69–70;
    self-regulation 102–3; teacher education
    268; trans/intra-apps 262
Comparison Games 132
comprehension 18, 28, 30, 33, 35, 43, 148,
    151–4, 166, 169, 215, 225

computer-mediated communication
    (CMC) technology 268
concept maps 196–8, 203
connected learning 74–6, 78, 80–1, 86
connectivism 220, 253–4
connectivity 7–8, 80, 84–5, 194, 221
constructivism 104, 194, 221, 266–7, 272,
    276
Cookie Monster's Challenge 19
Corsaro, W. 281
Counting Games 132
Crayon Creatures 261
Crayons and iPads 76, 81, 86
Creative Thinking Framework 119, 211
creativity 1, 8, 15, 17, 21–2; app maps 81,
    85; AR 207–18; bilingualism 166–7,
    169, 171; challenges 40; cultural agency
    280–1, 290; e-books 32, 35; empirical
    evidence 119; future adventures 220–2;
    mathematics 140, 144; new learning
    57–8, 60–2, 64, 66, 70; self-regulation
    102–5; trans/intra-apps 252, 259–60
critical thinking 39–40, 57, 60, 64–8, 70,
    102–3, 193, 237
Crockett, J. 32
cross-cultural comparisons 121–34
Cuban, L. 6
Cumming, T.M. 176
cuneiform 5
curation groups 22
Curious Learning 22
curricula 7–9, 11, 19–20, 22; app maps 75;
    bilingualism 164–5, 172; challenges
    39–40; cultural agency 276; disabilities
    176, 186; empirical evidence 117–19;
    first principles 29, 32; future adventures
    221; market scan 45, 49–50, 54;
    mathematics 122, 124, 127–9, 131–2,
    140; new learning 57–60, 70;
    self-regulation 105, 114; skill
    development 236–7; teacher education
    276; trans/intra-apps 259

3D printing 261
Daniel Tiger's Grr-ific Feelings 19
Daniel Tiger's Neighborhood 22
Daniels, K. 221, 280–92
Danielson, C. 165–6, 171
De Pasquale, D. 41, 102–16
decoding 28–30, 91–2, 94, 154, 161

deep learning 58, 60, 70, 104
design 1, 4–5, 8, 10, 15, 18, 21, 23, 30–1, 33, 35, 40–1; app maps 75, 84–5; bilingualism 164–5, 171, 173; BYOD 193–5; digital play 224; disabilities 182, 184–6, 188–9; e-books 89–101, 148; empirical evidence 117, 119–20; future adventures 220–1; market scan 43–4, 50, 54; mathematics 123, 127–8, 130–1; new learning 60; self-regulation 104; skill development 236–7, 248; teacher education 268; touch-screens 89–102; trans/intra-apps 252
desktop computers 138, 140, 182, 186, 195, 268
Desoete, A. 132
developers 16, 19, 21–2, 44, 257–8, 260
Dewey, J. 194
digital divide 22, 59
digital technology 5–11, 90, 102–4, 136–7, 143; cultural agency 280; disabilities 187; mathematics 136–7, 143; next generation 22–3; play 15, 21–2, 223–34; skill development 235, 237; sociocultural perspective 3–14; teacher education 271
digital tools 4–7, 10–12, 15, 22–3; app maps 73–4, 77, 81; bilingualism 164, 170–2; BYOD 194, 196, 200, 203; cultural agency 280–2; disabilities 176, 179, 186–7; empirical evidence 117; first principles 35; market scan 39, 42–5; self-regulation 102–11; skill development 237, 243, 248; sociocultural perspective 3–14; teacher education 268–9, 271, 275; trans/intra-apps 253, 255, 259
digital tutors 34–5, 76–7
dimensionality 15–16, 60, 140, 208, 263
disabilities 175–91
distractibility/distractions 28–9, 31, 98, 103, 109, 113, 156
DNA 4
document societies 5
Donald, M. 5
Don't Let the Pigeon Run the App 91–2
Dora the Explorer 50, 60
dorsolateral frontal cortex 16
Dr Seuss 92
dual-processing theory 28

e-books (electronic books) 27–38, 51, 89–101, 147–62; app maps 84; bilingualism 66; empirical evidence 118; enhanced 90–1, 93, 142–4; meaning-making 147, 151–5; new learning 64, 70; self-regulation 105
e-mail (electronic mail) 22, 110, 167, 259
e-portfolios (electronic portfolios) 203, 248
Early Years Foundation Stage 283
ecological context 20
Edmodo 113, 193, 195–7, 200, 203
EduCreations Inc 27
edutainment 8
Egypt 42
Elkonin, D.B. 226
empirical evidence 117–20
EMS (external memory systems) 4
engagement 2–4, 9, 11, 16, 18; app maps 74–5, 78, 83, 86–7; AR 208–13, 215; bilingualism 163, 168–9, 171–2; BYOD 193, 195–6, 200, 204; cultural agency 280–2, 286, 290; digital play 223–4, 226–7, 230; disabilities 176–7, 179–80, 184, 186–8; e-books 90, 96, 148–52, 156; empirical evidence 117–19; first principles 29–32, 35; future adventures 220–1; home learning 21–2; market scan 50, 54; mathematics 122, 129, 132, 135–44; new learning 57–60, 62, 65, 70; physical 31–2; self-regulation 102–3, 110–11, 113–14; skill development 236–7, 248; teacher education 267, 269, 271–2; trans/intra-apps 253–5, 258–62
England 283
English language 118, 124, 127, 129, 150–1, 160, 163, 166–8, 170
entrepreneurship 103
epistemology 87, 270
Erstad, O. 227
Ertmer, P.A. 204
ethics 32, 125, 165–6, 220, 258, 263
Europe 131
evaluation 1, 15, 17–18, 20–1, 31; app maps 73–88; BYOD 196; disabilities 177, 188; e-books 33, 155; future adventures 221–2; mathematics 132; skill development 236–7, 241, 243–5, 247–8; teacher education 268; trans/intra-apps 262

Evernote 195–7, 200, 202–3
evidence-based techniques 22, 32, 34–5, 132, 194
excessive screen time 15, 17, 20
experts/expertise 22, 27, 34, 39, 44; bilingualism 164; disabilities 187; market scan 44–7, 50–1, 54; mathematics 143; self-regulation 110; teacher education 268, 270, 272, 274–5; trans/intra-apps 260
Explain Everything 64, 67–9, 137
explorer hubs 36

Facebook 74, 271
Falloon, G. 93, 220, 235–51, 262
feedback 10, 18, 22, 104, 119; bilingualism 164, 170; disabilities 184, 187–8; mathematics 122–4, 132, 137, 139; skill development 246–7; teacher education 271, 274–6
Final Cut Pro 151
FingAR Puppet 208
Fleer, M. 219–20, 223–34
Fleming, L. 256, 259
Flewitt, R. 59, 164, 274
Fox, M. 90
French language 147, 150–1, 153–4, 161
Fresh Paint 62
Fronter 167
Fullan, M. 58, 104
functionality 7–8, 33, 93–4, 96, 109
future adventures 219–22
future research 2, 155–6, 193, 220, 253

GameBoy 132
games 8–10, 19, 30, 51–2, 74–8, 81; cultural agency 282; disabilities 180; e-books 91; gamification 102; mathematics 132, 139–44; self-regulation 102, 104, 107–8, 111; skill development 227; teacher education 268, 271; trans/intra-apps 253, 255–9, 262
Gardner, H. 254
geography 8, 269
gestures 34, 92–4, 96–8, 140, 153, 224, 229, 282–3, 285–7, 289–91
Giddings, S. 280
globalization 6, 58–60, 70, 74
goals 9, 31–5, 40, 44, 49; app maps 75;

bilingualism 164–5, 172; BYOD 193–4, 204; cultural agency 291; disabilities 179; empirical evidence 120; future 219; market scan 51, 54; mathematics 122; new learning 59–60; self-regulation 103–4, 114; skill development 248
Good Night, Gorilla 150
goodness of fit 19–20, 119
Google 105, 258, 260, 268
Google Maps 139, 268
Google Play 39, 44, 46
grammar 47
Grandma's Kitchen 81, 83, 86–7
GraphoGame-Exact Numerosity 132
Grech, L. 118, 163–74
Grusin, R.A. 91
Guatemala 66
Guernsey, L. 20
guided participation 10
Gutenberg, J. 5

habitus 272
Haileybury Youth Trust 132
Haiti 66–7, 69
hand signals *see* gestures
haptics 31, 77, 119, 139–40, 284, 286, 288–91
Hart, B. 18
Hattie, J. 104
health 15, 19
The Heart and the Bottle 94–5, 97–8
Hello Barbie 262
hemiplegia 178
Herr-Stephenson, B. 252, 254
Heyd-Metzuyanim, E. 142
Hibernation 36
higher-order thinking 16, 21–3, 105, 194, 224, 237, 240, 268, 271
Hinske, S. 208
Hirsh-Pasek, K. 21–2
history 1, 5, 35, 207, 219, 261
Hoff, E. 155
home learning 8–9, 14–26, 104, 107–8, 138–9; bilingualism 168–71; BYOD 193, 195–6, 200, 203; cultural agency 280–2, 289; digital play 223; disabilities 176; e-books 149–50; empirical evidence 118–19; homework 169, 171; mathematics 142, 144; teacher education 272

Hong Kong 119, 192–206
hotspots 28–30, 34, 93–4, 96–8, 118, 150, 152–3, 156, 162
Howell, J. 136
html 85
Hughes, B. 119, 210
Hutchison, A. 90, 138, 164, 172

iBook 76, 91, 257
identity formation 11
ideology 1, 12, 85, 87
iMovie 105, 138
in-app purchases 253, 257–8
Inanimate Alice 256
India 42
Indiana University 75
Indonesia 42
inferencing 151–5
info-trekkers 36
inputs 262, 269–71, 273–5
inquiry-based learning 104, 192–6, 200, 203–5, 236, 268
instruction 2–3, 5–11, 29–35, 58; bilingualism 164–5, 172; BYOD 194, 196; disabilities 176, 188; e-books 148–50; empirical evidence 117; mathematics 122–4, 128–9; self-regulation 103–4, 110–13; skill development 237; teacher education 273
Intel Classmate 165
inter-media apps 252–9, 262–3
interactivity 8–9, 14, 16–19, 30, 33–4, 36; app maps 73–4; BYOD 203; disabilities 176, 180, 182, 187; e-books 36, 89–101, 147–62; empirical evidence 117–19; first principles 36; future adventures 219–20; interactives 40, 96–7; market scan 51; mathematics 118, 123, 131, 139, 141–2, 144; meaning-making 147, 151–6; self-regulation 103, 107, 109–10, 112; trans/intra-apps 255–6, 262; whiteboards 262
interfaces 21, 85, 92–3, 119, 223–4, 227, 231, 272
Internet 4, 6–7, 9, 12, 62, 66; bilingualism 167–8, 171; BYOD 192, 195, 203; future adventures 221; mathematics 138; new learning 66; self-regulation 107–10; trans/intra-apps 262

interpretation 12, 28, 40, 77, 89–101; BYOD 193, 196; cultural agency 282, 284, 291; disabilities 179; mathematics 132; skill development 237, 248
interpsychology 220
intervention specialists 36
intra-apps 252–64
intra-media learning 220, 253
intra-psychology 220, 226
iOS 157, 252, 260
iPad 7, 10, 27, 29, 36; app maps 73–88; bilingualism 164; BYOD 195, 200; cultural agency 281–4, 286, 288–91; digital play 225, 227–30; disabilities 175–91; e-books 90, 93; empirical evidence 118; future adventures 221; mathematics 122–4, 135–43; new learning 59; self-regulation 103, 105–7, 110, 112; student thinking 235–51; teacher education 271, 274; trans/intra-apps 255, 259–61
iPhone 59, 195, 260
iPod 103, 106–10, 112–13, 195, 260
Iraq 5
iRead With 151, 153
IRF (Initiate-Respond-Feedback) loop 271
iTunes 45, 260

Japan 42
Jeffers, O. 94
Jenkins, H. 11
JibJab 84–7
Joan Ganz Cooney Center 18, 39, 43–4
Johnson, J.E. 229
Junkins, S. 105

Kargin, T. 229
Kerawalla, L. 208
Kerr, J. 91
Kervin, L. 226, 228, 230
Khoo, E. 93, 118–20, 175–91
Kids Media Centre 258
kinaesthesia 70, 142, 282
kindergartens 34, 47–8, 54, 60, 75–6, 81–2, 142, 274
Kindle 91, 255
Knobel, M. 74
Know Number Free 142
knowledge communities 221

Knowledge Forum 267–8
knowledge-building 265–79
Kobo 255
Koehler, M. 164
Kosara, T. 36
Krathwohl, D.R. 235–6, 240, 248
Kravtsov, G.G. 230
Kravtsova, E.E. 230
Kress, G. 255, 282
Ku, W.Y. 119, 192–206
Kucirkova, N. 22, 220, 225–6, 228, 252–64, 282

Laidlaw, L. 230
LAN (local area network) 6
language 3, 8, 15, 17–18, 21; app maps 77, 87; bilingualism 163, 166–8, 170, 172; challenges 39; cultural agency 281, 287, 290; digital play 228; disabilities 176–7; e-books 90, 147–56; first principles 28; integrated arts 35; market scan 42–54; mathematics 123–4, 127, 140, 142, 144; self-regulation 110; skill development 238; teacher education 272, 274
Langworthy, M. 58
laptops 7, 262
Larry the Lizard 91
leadership 58–9
learning 3–13; active 135–46; app maps 73–88; at home 14–26; centres 111–12, 125, 127–8, 130, 132; challenges 266; digital technology 6–9; disabilities 175–91; lifelong 59; mathematics 135–46; mobility 7; new 57–72; out-of-school 8–9; outcomes 32, 39, 53, 65, 70, 102–3, 113, 117–18, 136, 148, 172, 193, 204, 236; potential 1–2; science 192–206; self-regulation 102–16; sociocultural perspective 3–13; tablet devices 57–72; theory 19, 103–4, 253; traditional 1–2, 7, 11, 18, 31, 64, 70, 76, 90, 108, 148–9, 156, 166, 178, 204, 208, 219–21, 229, 261, 265–8, 272–3
LearnPad 165, 170
legislation 258
Lego Chima Speedorz 182
Lego Friends 283, 288–90
Levine, M.H. 20
lexical diversity/sophistication 151

Lieberman, D.A. 19
Lillard, A.S. 17
literacy 8–10, 17–18, 21–2, 28–30; app maps 73–88; AR 209; biliteracy 163–74; challenges 39–40; cultural agency 291; disabilities 187; e-books 89–90, 92, 148–9; empirical evidence 118; events 274; first principles 30, 32–6; knowledge-building 268, 272, 274; Literacy 1.0 model 74; Literacy 2.0 model 74; market scan 42–55; mathematics 118, 121–2, 132; new learning 59, 61, 64, 69; self-regulation 111, 113; sociocultural perspective 3–13; tablet computers 163–74; teacher education 268, 272; trans/intra-apps 259, 262
Literacy Playshop 75, 80–1, 84
living words 151–3, 155–6, 161
Ljung-Djärf, A. 225
Looi, C.-K. 194
low-income families 14, 18, 20–2, 121

Malawi 117, 121–5, 127–33
Malta 118, 163–74
Maltese language 118, 163, 165–8
manipulatives 16
Maracci, M. 142
market scan 42–56
marketing 43, 104, 257–8
Marsh, J. 119, 207–18, 262, 280
Martha Speaks 18
Marzano, R.J. 236
Math Shake 138
mathematics 8, 16, 43, 45, 105; active learning 135–46; cross-cultural comparison 121–34; disabilities 177–8, 183–4, 186–7; empirical evidence 117–18; self-regulation 105, 109–11; trans/intra-apps 254
Maths Bingo 183–4
Mattel Apptivity 210, 212, 214–15
Maues, F. 76
meaning-making 30, 33–5, 40, 74, 76; app maps 78, 81, 86; cultural agency 280–2, 289–91; digital play 224; e-books 90, 93–9, 147–57; teacher education 266, 268, 270, 272, 274, 276
Meet the Animals 210, 212–15
mental health 19

Merchant, G. 282, 284, 291
mergers 4
meshing 257, 262
Mesopotamia 5
metacognition 103–4, 114, 237, 281
microblogging 195
microphones 81, 85, 94, 107, 273
Microsoft Surface Pro II tablets 60–2, 64
Mifsud, C.L. 118, 163–74
mind-mapping 268
Minecraft 17, 77, 272
Minion Rush 183–4
Mishra, H.J. 164
Mister Rogers' Neighborhood 19
MLEs (Modern Learning Environments)
   237
mobile devices/mobility 7–12, 14, 18, 20,
   29; app maps 73; application 269,
   271–2; bilingualism 164; BYOD 192–6,
   200, 203–4; challenges 41–3; disabilities
   175–7, 187–9; e-books 90–2, 148, 156;
   empirical evidence 119; first principles
   29, 31–2; future adventures 219–22;
   knowledge-building 265–79;
   mathematics 122, 135–9, 143; new
   learning 57–61, 64; self-regulation
   102–14; teacher education 265–79;
   trans/intra-apps 258–9
Moholy-Nagy, L. 207–8
Monkey Maths 184
Monkey Spelling 184
Moody, A. 31
Moore, H.L.C. 225–8, 230
Moseley, D. 237
Moss, J. 137
motivation 2, 29, 41, 103, 114; AR 208–9,
   211, 214; bilingualism 164, 168–9,
   171–2; digital play 217, 228; disabilities
   177, 179, 182–4, 188; e-books 154;
   empirical evaluation 118–19;
   mathematics 139, 141, 143;
   self-regulation 103, 105, 110, 112–14;
   skill development 247–8; teacher
   education 271; trans/intra-apps 255
Mueller, J. 41, 102–16
multi-touch affordances 139–40
multilinear learning 74–6, 78, 80–1, 84–6
MultiLing keyboards 167
multimedia learning 28, 33–5, 75, 90–3, 98,
   148–9, 167, 171, 194, 208, 272–3

multimodal learning 11, 59–60, 70, 74–8,
   80–1; app maps 84–7; AR 214; cultural
   agency 282–4; digital play 226;
   disabilities 176–7, 187–8; e-books 90,
   96, 148; teacher education 271–3, 276
multiplayer learning 74–6, 78, 80, 83, 85–7
multiple intelligences theory 254–5
Multiplier 137
music 6, 8, 28, 30–1, 33; app maps 75,
   78–9, 84–5; AR 207, 211; cultural
   agency 283; e-books 149–50;
   mathematics 128; new learning 61;
   self-regulation 107; trans/intra-apps
   254, 256
Mythology 77

Nadig, A. 117, 147–62
Naigles, L. 155
narrative interpretation 89–101
National Educational Technology Standards
   for Teachers 104
National Literacy Strategy for Malta 163
National Research Council 18
navigation 4, 8, 11, 33, 39; app maps 81, 85;
   bilingualism 164; digital play 229;
   disabilities 182, 188; e-books 96;
   mathematics 128, 138
Netherlands 42
neuroscience 4
New America 39, 43
New Learning 57–72
New Zealand 140, 175–8, 236–7
New Zealand Disability Strategy 177
non-literality 230
Nook 255
North America 131
Norway 274
numeracy 8, 10, 61, 64, 69–70, 111, 122,
   128, 136, 142, 187, 291

object play 210
Office of Fair Trading 258
O'Mara, J. 230
OneBillion Apps 16, 117, 123–33, 136
oneclass technology 132–3
Ontario Ministry of Education 103
operational skills 9
Ottenbreit-Leftwich, A. 204
Our Story 257
out-of-school learning *see* home learning

Outhwaite, L.A. 117, 121–34, 136
outputs 184, 247, 269, 271, 273–6
outsourcing 4
overcrowding 122

Pacino, A. 80
Padagogy Wheel 105
Paint 167
Paper 53 155
parents 9, 14–26, 39–40, 43–7, 49–54; AR
    210, 214; bilingualism 168, 171–3;
    cultural agency 284; disabilities 176,
    178, 180, 182, 186–8; e-books 92–3,
    148–56; empirical evaluation 118–20;
    future adventures 219–20, 222;
    mathematics 128, 144; self-regulation
    102; skill development 238; teacher
    education 274; trans/intra-apps 252–3,
    257–9, 261–2
Parents' Choice 44
parietal cortex 16
Parish-Morris, J. 148, 156
participatory cultures/literacies 11, 74–9,
    85–7
Pavio, A. 28
PBS 18
PCs (personal computers) 6, 269
PDAs (personal digital assistants) 7
pedagogy 8–10, 29, 32, 36, 89; app maps
    76, 87; bilingualism 164, 166, 171–3;
    BYOD 192–5, 204; challenges 40–1;
    cultural agency 291; empirical evidence
    119; future adventures 219–20;
    mathematics 131, 135–6, 143–4; new
    learning 58–60, 70; self-regulation
    104–6, 110–11, 114; skill development
    237; teacher education 266–7, 269, 272,
    275–6; trans/intra-apps 253, 262
peer cultures 281–2, 290–1
Periodic Table of iPad Apps 105
Perner, J. 256
personalised learning 58, 132, 164, 179,
    188; BYOD 193, 204; cultural agency
    282; future adventures 220–1; teacher
    education 265; trans/intra-apps 253,
    255, 258, 261–3
Peterson, J. 17
phonemes 10, 18, 43, 47–8, 52, 214
Piaget, J. 15, 256
Pic Collage 220, 238, 240

picture books 9, 40, 89–191
Pietschmann, D. 256
PISA (Programme for Internal Student
    Assessment) 122
Pitchford, N. 117, 121–34, 136
play 1–2, 29, 35, 39, 107; AR 208–14;
    cultural agency 280–90; digital 223–34;
    disabilities 182–4, 188; empirical
    evidence 119; future adventures 219–22;
    mathematics 139–40, 142, 144; parents
    14–26
Plowman, L. 225
podcasts 214
Polished Play 81
Popplet 36
popular culture 60, 80, 282
poverty 20
PowerPoint 169
Praet, M. 132
pre-purchase information 46
pre-service teachers 265–79
prematurity 17
preschool learning 7, 10, 16–18, 20, 22; app
    maps 75, 81; AR 209–10; digital play
    224–7, 229–30; e-books 34, 151, 153,
    155; market scan 47–8, 54; mathematics
    142; teacher education 265–79
primary grade teaching 27–38
print referencing 35
print-centricity 74–5, 87
Printeer 261
printing press 4
privacy 51, 220, 259
problem-solving 17, 20, 22, 76, 87, 103,
    110–12, 114, 136, 141–2, 168, 266
processes 267–71, 274–6
productive learning 75–6, 78, 80–1, 85–7,
    105, 113, 121, 142, 179, 186, 194, 236
professional development 29, 103, 118,
    164–5, 171–2, 265–79
Proffitt Foundation 75
profit 256, 258
prompt bars 151, 153, 155–6
proto-literacy 7
Puppet Pals 10, 81–3, 214, 229, 272–4, 276
puzzles 16, 51–2, 60, 256

quality 18–20, 22–3, 29–30, 33–4, 39;
    bilingualism 163; e-books 151, 154;
    empirical evidence 117–18; future

adventures 221; market scan 43–4, 50, 52–4; mathematics 121–4, 142–3; skill development 241, 243, 245, 247–8; teacher education 268

QuivAR 210

quizzes 8, 51–2, 123–4, 129, 132, 169

Radesky, R. 1, 14–26, 119, 156, 224

Raphael, T.E. 164

Räsänen, P. 132

Raz-Kids Reading Program 16

Read Alouds 35

reading 16, 21–3, 40, 73–5, 89; digital play 224; market scan 42–55; programs 27, 29, 33; shared 18, 31, 96, 99, 118, 147–9, 152, 155–6; teacher education 268; teaching principles 27–38; trans/intra-apps 253

Ready Rosie 22

Rees, K. 117–18, 147–62

remediation 91

reviews 33, 40, 44–7, 51, 54; bilingualism 165, 172; BYOD 202; digital play 224, 227; disabilities 177; e-books 92, 148; mathematics 138; self-regulation 108, 111; skill development 237, 240–1, 244–5; teacher education 274, 276; trans/intra-apps 256, 258, 260

Risley, T. 18

Robson, S. 119, 211

Roskos, K. 2, 27–38, 105, 164, 260

Roth, W.-M. 194

routines 34, 76, 104, 155, 260, 266

Rowsell, J. 40, 73–88, 273

Rvachew, S. 22, 117–18, 147–62

safety 34, 85, 220

Salen, K. 93

Säljö, R. 1–13, 273–4

Salmon, L.G. 148

Sameroff, A. 19

SAMR (substitution augmentation modification redefinition) 165

Samsung Galaxy Tab 165, 171

Sandvik, M. 10, 272, 274

scaffolding 10, 15–16, 20, 22, 32, 35; digital play 225; e-books 92, 96, 99, 148; future adventures 220; market scan 54; mathematics 142; self-regulation 103–4, 110, 113; skill development 243–4, 248;

teacher education 268, 272

Scardamalia, M. 268

Scarface 80

Schugar, H.R. 29

science 4, 8, 11, 16, 21; AR 208; BYOD 192–206; disabilities 176; empirical evidence 119; market scan 43, 45; new learning 65; self-regulation 110; teacher education 268

screenshot capture 61, 67

scribal schools 5

scripted comments/questions 155

scrolling 18, 33, 82, 186

seamless learning 1, 40, 62, 138, 144; BYOD 192–6, 199–200, 203–4; cultural agency 291; digital play 221; e-books 152, 154; future adventures 221; teacher education 266, 269–70; trans/intra-apps 253, 259, 262

search engines 11, 27

Second World War 6

security 51

Sefton-Green, J. 227

self-regulated learning 20, 22–3, 31, 41, 102–16, 225, 227, 231

semiotics 40, 89–101, 281–3, 291

sensorimotor stage 16

Sesame Street 19, 22, 50, 60

Sesame Workshop 18–19, 39

Shared Book Reading 29, 34

shared reading 18, 31, 96, 99, 118, 147–9, 152, 155–6

Shin, N. 132

shortcuts 9, 11

Show and Tell 167

ShowMe 142

Shuler, C. 44–5

Siemens, G. 220, 254

Sim City 272

Simpson, A. 282

Sinclair, N. 137, 142

situated learning 269

Sketchpad 137, 142–3

Skills for the 21st Century 39

Skitch 195–6, 200, 202–3

Smart Car 261

smartphones 4, 7, 9–10, 42, 73, 90–1, 135, 148, 195, 214, 225–6

smashing 259–60

Sneak a Snack 118, 150

social learning theory 19
social media 11, 74, 102, 270–1
social networks 193, 200, 203, 254, 270
social skills 19, 21, 90, 136, 177, 260
social-emotional development 19–23
socialisation 5, 177, 281
socio-cultural perspective 3–13
Sock Puppets 214
Socratic method 271
software 6–10, 103, 123, 165; app maps
    73–88; digital play 226, 231;
    mathematics 123, 128–9, 131–2, 137;
    skill development 240; teacher
    education 268, 274; trans/intra-apps
    252–3, 261–3
SOLO (Structure of Observed Learning
    Outcomes) 236
Song, Y. 119, 192–206
sound recording *see* audio recording
special educational needs 10, 36, 107, 164,
    169–71, 175–91, 236
Spellosaur 185
Spencer, P. 142
Squigglefish 210, 212, 214–15
standardised testing 12
Stephen, C. 225
Sticky Note 168
Story Album 167
Story Maker 283, 288–90
Storykit 167
storytelling 10, 47–8, 75, 78, 86, 92, 138,
    212, 215, 254
Street, B. 87
stress 16, 19–20
Strnadova, I. 176
Studiocode 240, 242
subscriptions 257–8
Super Why 18
supported learning 175–91
Sweden 7
symbolic activity 1, 3–5, 8–9, 16, 28; AR
    210; digital play 226, 230; e-books
    94–5, 97; mathematics 123, 129, 137,
    141
synchrony 140, 151, 153, 155–6

tablet computers 7–10, 39, 42, 57–70,
    73–5, 81, 84–5; AR 209–11, 213–15;
    BYOD 195; e-books 148; empirical
    evidence 118; future adventures 222;

literacy 163–74; mathematics 121–30,
    135–44; self-regulation 103–4, 107, 110;
    teacher education 266, 269, 271;
    trans/intra-apps 259–60
tacit knowledge 76, 269, 274
Takacs, Z.K. 148
targeted skills 46–7, 52
Taxonomy of Play 119, 210
Te Whariki 140
teacher education 265–79
Teacher Tools 259
teaching strategies 47–9, 52, 248
teamwork 118, 170, 201
technology 4–12, 14, 17, 20, 22–3; app
    maps 74–5, 78, 85–6; AR 208–9, 213;
    assistive 176–7; bilingualism 164–5,
    171–3; BYOD 192–4, 200, 204;
    challenges 39–41; cultural agency
    280–1; digital play 223–4; disabilities
    168; e-books 88, 90–2, 96; empirical
    evidence 114; first principles 28–9, 31,
    35; future adventures 219–22; invaders
    219; knowledge-building 265, 267–9;
    learning outcomes 102; market scan 43;
    mathematics 121–33, 135–40, 143; new
    learning 57–60, 62, 69–70; oneclass
    132–3; self-regulation 102–6, 107–8,
    110–14; skill development 235–8;
    teacher education 265–71, 275–6;
    technocentrism 222; technophiles 6;
    tethered 265; trans/intra-apps 253,
    259–63
television 4, 6, 18, 43, 50, 60
temperament 19–20
templates 79, 84–5, 243, 260
textbooks 108, 110, 203
texting 18
Thames and Kosmos 261
thinking 4–5, 23, 35, 39, 193–4; app maps
    74, 76–7, 86–7; AR 208, 211–12,
    214–15; different 219–20, 247; digital
    play 219, 224, 228, 230–1; empirical
    evidence 117, 119; higher-order 16–17,
    21–3, 104–5, 184, 194, 214, 224, 226,
    230, 237, 240, 259, 268, 271;
    mathematics 136–7, 142–3; new
    learning 64–7, 69–70; self-regulation
    102–3, 105, 107, 112–14; skill
    development 235–51
Thinking Types 240–1, 244

The Thirsty Crow 209
The Tiger Who Came to Tea 91
TinkRBook 262
Toca Boca 257, 283, 286
Toca Robot Lab 283, 286–7
Toca Tea Party 230
Toontastic 79–80, 83, 86–7
Toontube 80
Top 50 lists 39, 44–7, 54
Toronto University 268
touch-screens 7, 9, 73, 84–5, 93; AR 209;
    cultural agency 280–2, 290–1; design
    89–101; digital play 224, 231; disabilities
    176, 180, 182, 184, 186–7; e-books 161;
    mathematics 124
TouchCounts 141–2
TPACK (technological, pedagogical and
    content knowledge) 164–5, 172
tracking 31, 200, 225, 262
traditional learning 1–2, 4, 7, 11, 18; app
    maps 76; bilingualism 166; BYOD 204;
    digital play 229; disabilities 178;
    e-books 31, 90, 148–9, 156; future
    adventures 219–20; new learning 64, 70;
    self-regulation 108; teacher education
    265–8, 272–3; trans/intra-apps 261
trans-apps 252–64
transactional model 19
transmedia learning 221, 252–9, 263
troubleshooting 51, 114
Tumble Leaf 22
Turkle, S. 227
Tutoring by Design 76–7, 79
twenty-first century skills 7, 32, 39–41,
    57–70, 73–87; bilingualism 164;
    challenges 266; future adventures 221–2;
    self-regulation 102–3, 105, 110; skill
    development 236; teacher education
    266; trans/intra-apps 254–6, 266
Twitter 74, 113

Uganda 122, 132
underachievement 122
United Kingdom (UK) 122–33, 164,
    210–11, 258, 260
United States (US) 15, 35, 42, 104, 129,
    164, 259
Unsworth, L. 31, 40, 89–101, 148
usability 7, 33, 50
USAID 129

user agreements 33
User Guides 33

Vaala, S. 21, 39, 42–56, 117
Verenikina, I. 226, 228, 230
video 16–19, 22, 28, 33, 41; app maps
    74–6, 78, 80–1, 85; AR 210–11, 214;
    bilingualism 168, 171; BYOD 195–6,
    204; challenges 41; digital play 228;
    disabilities 179; e-books 91, 150;
    empirical evidence 118; mathematics
    122, 135, 137–9; new learning 64;
    self-regulation 107, 111; skill
    development 240; teacher education
    270, 272–3; trans/intra-apps 259
virtual reality 4, 207–11, 223–34, 236,
    261–3, 269
vocabulary 10, 18, 36, 43, 48, 59, 148,
    151–2, 154–5, 167
VSO 127–8, 132
Vygotsky, L. 4, 15, 219–20, 224–8, 231

Wagner, R. 207
Walsh, M. 282
What is That? 257
Who Sank the Boat? 64
Wi-Fi 6–7, 33, 107, 194–5
WIAT-II 129
wicked problems 266
Willacy, H. 142
Willems, M. 91
Windows 107
Wohlwend, K. 40, 73–88, 229, 273
Wolf, M. 22
Wolfe, S. 280
Wong, L.-H. 194
Wood, E. 41, 102–16
Woodward, L. 172
Woolfolk, A.E. 103
word banks 168
Word Bingo 185
Word Gap 18
word searches 36
Word Wall 112
worksheets 196, 256
World Wide Web 6
Write About This 36
writing 5, 11, 259, 272
The Wrong Book 91

Yamada-Rice, D. 119, 207–18, 262
Yarosh, S. 208
Yelland, N. 39, 57–72, 256, 272
YouTube 66, 74, 78, 118, 171, 270–1

Zero To Three Let's Play! 22

Zhao, S. 31, 40, 89–102, 148
Zimmerman, E. 93
zone of proximal development 15, 21–2, 225
Zoo Burst 261
Zuckerman, B. 1, 14–26, 119, 224